East-West Relations and the Future of Eastern Europe

East–West Relations and the Future of Eastern Europe

Politics and Economics

Edited by

MORRIS BORNSTEIN
ZVI GITELMAN

and

WILLIAM ZIMMERMAN
The University of Michigan

London
GEORGE ALLEN & UNWIN
Boston   Sydney

GEORGE ALLEN & UNWIN LTD
40 Museum Street, London WC1A 1LU

© Morris Bornstein, Zvi Gitelman and William Zimmerman, 1981

British Library Cataloguing in Publication Data

East–West relations and the future of Eastern Europe.
1. Europe, Eastern – Foreign relations – Europe, Western
I. Bornstein, Morris   II. Gitelman, Zvi
III. Zimmerman, William
327′.0947   D1058

ISBN 0-04-330317-X

Set in 10 on 11 point Times by V & M Graphics Ltd, Aylesbury Bucks
and printed and bound in Great Britain by
William Clowes (Beccles) Limited, Beccles and London

Contents

Preface

Both domestic and foreign policy considerations led Eastern European nations in the 1970s to involve their economies more deeply with the developed capitalist countries of the West, although Eastern Europe remained closely linked politically, economically, and militarily with the USSR. Increasing economic interdependence with the West encompassed trade, technology transfer through industrial cooperation, and credit to finance them. However, the ability of Eastern Europe to develop ties with the West was subsequently curtailed by the sharp increase in world oil prices and the resulting inflation and slowdown in economic growth in industrialized market economies. As a result, policymakers in Eastern Europe have had to reevaluate the possibilities for economic relations both with the West and with the East.

In this book a team of scholars analyzes the interaction of economic and political forces at three interlocking levels – international, regional, and national. Part One examines the evolution of East–West political and economic relations in the 1970s and prospects for the 1980s. Part Two considers the implications of developments in East–West relations for Soviet–East European regional economic, political, and military ties in the Council for Mutual Economic Assistance and the Warsaw Treaty Organization. Parts Three and Four then discuss key facets of the national political and economic strategies of East European countries in the context of their regional and international relations.

This volume is one product of a research project on the world economy and Soviet–East European relations at The University of Michigan Center for Russian and East European Studies funded by the Rockefeller Foundation. Drafts of some of the chapters were presented and discussed intensively at a conference in June 1979 at the Rockefeller Foundation Study and Conference Center, Bellagio, Italy. The authors appreciate the many helpful comments at the conference from Franz Alting von Geusau, Zbigniew Kamecki, Marie Lavigne, Carl H. McMillan, Vladimir Pertot, and Sarah M. Terry.

We are grateful to the Rockefeller Foundation for financial support, and to John Stremlau, Associate Director for International Relations, for his advice and encouragement. We wish to thank Darlene Breitner for her assistance in the administration of the research project and the conference, and Jo Thomas for her meticulous editing of the manuscript for this book.

M.B.
Z.G.
W.Z.

The Authors

CORAL BELL is Senior Research Fellow in International Relations at the Australian National University in Canberra. She was previously Professor of International Relations at the University of Sussex, and earlier held academic posts at the London School of Economics and the Universities of Sydney and Manchester, after a period as an officer of the Australian Foreign Service. Her most recent books are *The Diplomacy of Détente* (1977) and *Agenda for the Eighties* (1980).

MORRIS BORNSTEIN is Professor of Economics at The University of Michigan, and a former Director of its Center for Russian and East European Studies. He has been a consultant to government agencies and foundations and has served on the executive committees of the Council for European Studies and the Association for Comparative Economic Studies and on the American Council of Learned Societies–Social Science Research Council Joint Committee on Eastern Europe. His publications include *Plan and Market* (1973), *Economic Planning, East and West* (1975), *Comparative Economic Systems* (4th edn, 1979), and many articles in economic journals and chapters in collective volumes.

STANISŁAW GEBETHNER is Associate Professor of Political Science at the University of Warsaw, where he teaches comparative government and political party systems and constitutional law. From 1956 to 1973 he taught constitutional law at the Law Faculty of the University of Warsaw. He was a visiting professor at the University of Florida (Gainesville) in 1974. He is currently deputy chairman of the Polish Political Science Association. His publications (in Polish) include *The Government and Opposition in the British Political System* (1967) and *The Political System of Poland* (1976) and numerous articles.

ZVI GITELMAN is Professor of Political Science and Director of the Center for Russian and East European Studies at The University of Michigan. His major research interests are nationality policy in the USSR, domestic politics in Eastern Europe, and Israeli politics. He is the author of *Jewish Nationality and Soviet Politics* (1972), co-author of *Public Opinion in European Socialist Systems* (1977), and author of the forthcoming *Becoming Israeli: Political Resocialization of Soviet and American Immigrants*. His articles have appeared in many professional journals.

FRIEDRICH LEVCIK is Director of the Vienna Institute for Comparative Economic Studies and Professor of Economics at the University of Vienna, where he teaches comparative economic policies. He formerly was a Head of Department at the Economics Institute of the Czechoslovak Academy of Sciences and a Chief of Section in the General Economic Analysis Division of the United Nations Economic Commission for Europe. His major research interests are economic planning, East–West economic relations, and industrial cooperation in CMEA countries. He is editor and co-author of *International Economics – Comparisons and Interdependences* (1978) and co-author of *Industrial Cooperation Between East and West* (1979) and has written many articles in economic journals.

ANDRÁS NAGY is Scientific Advisor in the Institute of Economics of the Hungarian Academy of Sciences, where he directs a research team on problems of growth and trade and of structural change in international trade. He has been a visiting professor at the Delhi School of Economics, the Johns Hopkins University, and the University of Grenoble. He has been a consultant to the United Nations Economic Commission for Europe, the United Nations

Conference on Trade and Development, and the International Institute of Applied Systems Analysis. His publications include 'Internal and International Consistency of Foreign Trade Estimations', in *Input–Output Techniques* (András Bródy and Anne P. Carter, eds, 1972), *The Structure and Future of World Trade* (in Hungarian, 1977), and *Methods of Structural Analysis and Projection of International Trade* (1979).

ALEX PRAVDA is Lecturer in Soviet and East European Politics at the University of Reading (England). His main research interests are political change in Soviet-type systems and the role of the working class in the political development of communist states. He is the author of *Reform and Change in the Czechoslovak Political System (January–August 1968)* (1975) and co-editor of *Czechoslovakia: The Party and the People* (1973), and has written a number of journal articles and chapters in collective volumes. He is currently completing a book entitled *Workers and Politics in Communist States*.

MÁRTON M. TARDOS is a Department Head in the Institute for Economic and Market Research in Budapest and also Professor of Economics at Karl Marx University. He is a consultant to the Hungarian Ministry of Foreign Trade and the National Planning Office and a member of several government commissions. His major research interests are foreign trade and macroeconomic regulation, He is the author of many articles in economic journals, a contributor to collective volumes published in France and the United States, and co-author of the forthcoming book (in Hungarian) *Enterprise Behavior and Environment*.

WITOLD TRZECIAKOWSKI is Professor of Economics at the Foreign Trade Research Institute in Warsaw and Head of the Foreign Trade Department of the University of Łódź. He is also Head of the Research Project on CMEA Economic Integration, conducted by leading Polish universities under the auspices of the Polish Ministry of Science. He has been director of the Foreign Trade Research Institute and a consultant to the United Nations Economic Commission for Europe and government agencies in Cuba and Algeria. He is a Fellow of the Econometric Society and a member of the executive committee of the Association Économique Européenne des Sciences Appliquées. He is the author of *Indirect Management in a Centrally Planned Economy* (1978), many articles in Western and Polish economic journals, and several books in Polish.

WILLIAM ZIMMERMAN is Professor of Political Science and a former Director of the Center for Russian and East European Studies at The University of Michigan. His major research interests include Soviet foreign policy, the international political economy of socialist states, and Yugoslav domestic politics and foreign policy. In addition to many articles in scholarly journals and collective volumes, he is the author of *Soviet Perspectives on International Relations* (1969) and co-author of *The Shaping of Foreign Policy* (1969).

Chapter 1

Introduction

ZVI GITELMAN

Research is often a collective enterprise for several reasons: a problem may be so complex as to require different kinds of expertise for its analysis; it may be of such magnitude as to require the work of several people; it may be of such complexity and intrinsic uncertainty that different approaches and points of view seem *a priori* equally legitimate. All these reasons apply to the research presented here. This volume assesses how Eastern Europe has been, and will be, affected by economic and political relations between the 'West' (the United States and its West European allies) and the 'East' (the Soviet Union and Eastern Europe). It is a collective effort in several senses. First, it involves analyses by professional economists and political scientists who are acutely aware of the importance of economic factors in political developments and of political considerations in economic ones. Second, among the authors are Americans, West Europeans, and East Europeans, who have met together to compare their different perspectives. Third, the chapters have been reviewed by experts who also come from several countries and represent different disciplines.

This collective enterprise aims to answer three questions. (1) How have world economic developments and East–West relations affected Eastern Europe in recent years, and how are they likely to do so in the 1980s? (2) What have been, and what are likely to be, the internal political determinants and the domestic consequences of East European foreign economic and political relations? (3) How have world economic changes and domestic politics in Eastern Europe affected the economic and political relations of Eastern Europe with the USSR, and what is the likely course of these relations in the 1980s?

Social scientists are not alone in finding the past easier to deal with than the future. Interpretations of the past may be as controversial and diverse as predictions for the future, but at least there appears to be 'solid' evidence for whatever point of view is adopted, whereas predictions of the future generally can marshall no better evidence than the extrapolation of present trends. But this does not mean that social science should exclude discussion about possible futures. Its purpose should be, not the prediction of discrete events, but the exposition of future possibilities with a reasoned account of which possibilities are more likely under what circumstances, and with some attempt to trace out the consequences of each contingency. The discourse should be in the nature of 'if . . . then' with some assessment of which 'ifs' are more likely and why. The logical starting point for such efforts must be the immediate past and the present, for the future grows directly out of them.

In this volume the economic and political evolution of East–West relations and Eastern Europe in the 1970s is analyzed with an eye toward the next decade. Some of the authors are bolder in looking ahead, while others are more concerned with a detailed understanding of the past decade. The past as well as the future are seen differently by scholars in the same discipline. But the diversity of viewpoints, the different political cultures from which the authors originate, and the perspectives of different disciplines fashion a richer, more problematic view of an intrinsically complex subject.

This volume rests on the assumption that Eastern Europe constitutes a region both from economic and political perspectives. Historically, the nations of the region share the experience of long-term domination by foreign empires, notably the Ottoman, Hapsburg, Russian, or German. They also have in common peasant-based societies and economies. Before 1939, only one country in the region, Czechoslovakia, had less than half its population directly dependent on agriculture for their livelihood. After the Second World War, when all the countries came to share a Communist system of government, they all experienced simultaneously the kind of rapid, forced-draft industrialization which the Soviet Union had introduced in the 1930s and which it then imposed upon Eastern Europe in the 1950s. Presently the countries of the region continue to share fundamentally similar political and economic systems, though over time each country has developed characteristics and nuances specific to itself. Institutionally they are all members of the Warsaw Treaty Organization (WTO) and the Council for Mutual Economic Assistance (CMEA or Comecon).

Twenty or thirty years ago the common Western view was that the states of Eastern Europe were mere extensions of the USSR, satrapies of a Soviet empire. Hence, separate analysis of these countries' policies was rather pointless, for one could generalize about them merely by following the evolution of Soviet policies. (The common phrase 'Soviet satellite' captured this notion precisely, for one predicts a moon's path by reference to that of the parent planet.) By the late 1950s it became clear that the relationship of Eastern Europe to the USSR had changed – a change that required an alteration of assessments of East European policies as well. Many observers judged that the trend toward differentiation in ideology, policy, and practice was a linear one and that, with time, Eastern Europe would become an entity to be treated completely separately from the USSR. Clearly, this has not happened, nor, according to the authors in this volume, is it likely to happen in the next decade. Rather Eastern Europe and the USSR constitute an organic region, and the relationships among the components of this region are not egalitarian but hierarchically organized. These relationships, however, are not frozen; instead they are affected increasingly by developments outside the region.

This broadens and complicates any analysis of intraregional trends. Consequently, we have been forced to exclude topics from this book that properly belong in any general analysis of the future of Eastern Europe. In particular, the authors take changes in the world economy as the starting point – the 'given,' or 'independent variable.' They do not seek the sources of those changes nor detail the economic problems of the West. This certainly does not mean that only the East has economic and political problems, merely that we assume the continuation of these Western problems into the 1980s and ask specifically how these will condition East–West relations and how those, in turn, influence domestic and international politics and economics in Eastern Europe.

Moreover, changes in the world economy have followed not a neat East–West division but rather what, to a great extent, many see as a North–South division, the former containing most of the economically developed countries, while the latter encompasses the less developed ones, including those who control much of the world's increasingly scarce natural resources. Eastern Europe's economic and political relations with the less developed countries have been profoundly affected by global economic changes. Until recently, East European involvement in the Third World generally resulted either from a Soviet desire to expand political and military influence there, partially through its East European allies, or from an ideological and national interest in spreading the Marxist–Leninist version of socialism and promoting goodwill toward the countries that practiced it. Both these reasons can explain the presence of thousands of East European experts and advisors in Africa and Asia, the supply of East European armaments to countries on those continents, cultural exchanges, and the like. To be sure, Third World countries became trading partners of East European nations, and were sometimes the recipients of East European economic aid, often to the dismay of people in Eastern Europe who felt their consumer needs ought to be served first. Now the need to purchase increasing amounts of petroleum from Iran, Libya, Iraq, and other countries affects not only economic relations with those countries but also elite and popular views of the Third World. Long-standing resentment of Arabs and Africans may grow among the East European masses even while their elites must try to draw closer to their counterparts in those countries out of economic necessity, not just because of ideological obligation or political choice. The authors of this book recognize the importance of the Third World for Eastern Europe in the 1980s. Precisely because of this, they believe that relationship deserves separate and detailed treatment.

The increasing interdependence of various regions of the world is a major underlying theme of the book. While generally global interdependence has become something of a shibboleth, one should remember that until recently the very notion of interdependence was highly controversial in East–West relations. The Soviet Union vigorously resisted any dependence on the West in the late 1940s and, for example, forced Czechoslovakia to renounce Marshall Plan aid and to isolate itself, along with the newly socialist countries, behind what was a real 'iron curtain'. This curtain was drawn along the full length of human contact. Not only was there a minimum of economic and political interchange, but there was very little cultural exchange. Even contacts within families who had been separated by the political division of the world were forbidden. The Soviet posture was matched by the American notion of 'containment', so that mutual isolation seemed to be desired by both East and West. Any notion that the two camps might be in any fashion dependent on each other would have been emphatically rejected by both as an attempt by one side to dominate the other.

These positions were modified in the post-Stalin period. Khrushchev's notion of 'coexistence' allowed for cultural and economic contact, while firmly resisting ideological encroachment. The two camps, whose lives were now complicated by the hitherto unacknowledged third camp of developing and mostly neutral nations, could no longer afford to ignore each other, if only because mutual ignorance might lead to mistakes and bring about their mutual destruction in a nuclear holocaust. For the sake of their own independent self-preservation East and West had to engage in at least a minimal dialogue. Some Western policy makers thought this would be a good time for 'bridge-building' to the East, expanding contacts beyond what was minimally necessary to avoid armed confrontation. By and large this was seen in the USSR as an insidious doctrine aimed at political penetration of the East and the reduction of the independence and cohesiveness of the socialist camp. But domestic economic and political pressures, along with global economic trends, impelled both West and East to expand economic and, to a lesser extent, political contacts with the other. In the 1970s business firms and governments in the industrialized capitalist countries showed a new willingness to expand trade with the East, to permit the previously banned export of advanced technology, and to grant the required credit on favorable terms. This led the USSR and East European countries to expand their economic ties with the West, while trying to control the extension of any concomitant political influence. How to import Western technology and goods without simultaneously importing Western political and social ideas has of course been a traditional dilemma for Russians. Thus far, the USSR has managed this task very successfully, though East European countries, especially those bordering directly on Western Europe, have juggled selective importation less well.

Interdependence itself is a very controversial idea. For some, it is a desirable goal because, they argue, mutual dependence creates stability, since no one wants to rock the boat in which he is a passenger. The more tightly the economies, polities, and cultures of East and West are linked, especially the economies, the less likelihood remains of a hostile confrontation between the two. For others, economic interdependence in the world is a reality to be regretted, as the West's dependence on Middle Eastern oil demonstrates. Therefore interdependence should be avoided if possible, because such relationships are not genuinely symmetrical or mutual and actually make one side more dependent on the other. Those in the West and East who assume that the ultimate aim of the other side is dominance or takeover, by whatever means, also reject the notion of interdependence, contending that interdependence would end with one side, not necessarily theirs, swallowing the other.

However one feels about East–West linkages, though, it is hard to imagine a Western leader speaking of Eastern Europe today as 'a faraway place . . . people of whom we know nothing,' as Neville Chamberlain did in 1938. But we still need to know much more about Eastern Europe than we do, and the purpose of this book is to expand our knowledge of the area and the relation of other areas to it.

Another form of linkage clearly does exist in Easten Europe, and that is between politics and economics. As befits states that claim to be guided by Marxism, to an increasing extent economic and political decisions seem to condition each other, especially in the more developed countries of the region. Gone are the days when economic decision makers could adopt a policy of 'damn the torpedoes, full speed ahead' – the torpedoes in this case being popular reactions to policy decisions. As workers in Poland and elsewhere have demonstrated on more than one occasion, the torpedoes can backfire to sink an elite decision. The political process in Eastern Europe used to be largely limited to elite politics, whereas today it involves elite–mass politics to a great extent. The reasons for this change are explored in the section on East European polities and societies, and need not be discussed here. But the political power of East European citizens, though perhaps more implicit than explicit, more of a veto power than a legitimated input into the regular decision-making process, has reached the point where some East European leaders cannot do what is economically necessary because it is politically dangerous. The contraints on economic decisions now arise not only in the domestic or foreign economic sphere or the international or regional political situation, but also in the domestic political arena. East European citizens have higher economic expectations than ever before; evidently their primary demand of the political system is that it satisfy those expectations. This is one reason that the working class has become such an important political actor. It represents the largest body of consumers; its demands are largely, though not exclusively, consumer demands; and it has emerged as a potential force for domestic change to no lesser extent than the intelligentsia, historically the prime mover of political change.

The organization of the book follows from the concerns outlined above. Part One consists of an overview of political and economic relations between East and West in the 1970s, with attempts to extrapolate to the following decade. Chapter 2, by Coral Bell, examines the relationship between the leading powers of East and West and the relations within the Western alliance. She is more optimistic about the latter than about the former. If she is correct in foreseeing continued tension between the United States and the Soviet Union, this will no doubt have a direct, and generally negative, effect on political and economic relations between Eastern Europe and the West. As Morris Bornstein's analysis in Chapter 3 demonstrates, only when the Soviet Union committed herself to significant expansion of commercial dealings with the West could the East European countries follow suit on a broad scale.

In the 1970s the economies and polities of Eastern Europe became demonstrably vulnerable to political and economic developments outside the region. Both domestic and foreign policy considerations prompted the more developed East European countries, along with the USSR, to involve their economies more deeply with nonsocialist countries. By the end of the 1970s, as Bornstein explains, it became apparent that, along with its benefits, this involvement brought trade deficits and Eastern indebtedness to the West, and sharpened the dilemma of whether to become even more involved in nonsocialist economies or more deeply integrated into the CMEA system. In Chapter 4 Friedrich Levcik attempts to calculate the prospects for East–West trade in the 1980s under different assumptions about economic growth, import and export possibilities, and balance-of-payment constraints. Which assumptions are most valid will be determined partly by how the East Europeans resolve the dilemma of the orientation of their economies. *That* will depend on the political climate in which economic policies – of Western private businesses as well as of Western governments – will be formulated. Dealing in political futures is at least as risky an enterprise as trying to forecast economic developments, but Chapter 2 by Bell and Chapter 5 by William Zimmerman at least array the possibilities for the 1980s created by the events of the 1970s.

The changing international system and, within it, East–West relations are concentric circles surrounding developments *within* the Soviet–East European region. In the past thirty years Soviet–East European relations have become more complex, less one-sided, and therefore less predictable, but more interesting. In the 1950s, when Soviet domination of Eastern Europe was challenged, at least rhetorically, by the United States and Western Europe, that domination was highly visible and not much restrained. Over time, that domination has changed under pressure from East European countries. The Soviet–East European relationship has evolved into a 'hierarchical regional system', in Zimmerman's characterization, and is likely to remain that in the 1980s. Zimmerman's judgment is that the 1980s will bring no great change in the degree of intraregional inequality, though Soviet–East European economic integration will increase, partly because of pressures stemming from the worldwide energy crisis. Nevertheless, there will not be an increase in the political and cultural integration of the East European states with the USSR. Indeed in some ways Eastern Europe will draw closer to Western Europe. Yet the region will remain militarily and politically unified *vis-à-vis* the external world with economics playing a larger role in making it so. As the major energy supplier of the region, the Soviet Union will loom larger than ever in East European economic calculations. Its role as a market for East European products, many of which cannot compete on world markets, will continue to be very significant. For a time in the 1960s and early 1970s, East European countries appeared to be 'exploiting' the USSR economically, but the pendulum has swung in the other direction. The reasons for this shift are explored by Bornstein in Chapter 6 on the economic aspects of the Soviet–East European relationship.

Economics and politics are inextricably linked not only on the international level, but also within individual countries. In Eastern Europe economic satisfaction has become politically crucial. The governments in the area no longer either will or can ignore consumer demands. Some of them have clearly made economic satisfaction the key element in what I have called their 'political strategies', that is, their attempts to gain short-term stability and long-term legitimacy. In Chapter 7 I compare the political strategies adopted by three of the economically more developed polities in the region, their treatment of consumers and 'consumerism', and their relative success in winning popular understanding and support. External economic developments have directly affected the internal economic and political capacities of the countries in question. As they enter the 1980s, the once despised Hungarian leadership appears the most successful in achieving relative economic prosperity, managing the disturbances created by world economic trends, and achieving political stability. The Polish government has been least successful in these respects. Only the Soviet presence and threat of active intervention keeps the Czechoslovak situation from becoming volatile. In all three countries the 1970s witnessed the emergence of the working class as a self-conscious group with impressive potential political power. No longer is the intelligentsia the primary initiator of political change 'from below', and no longer is the proletariat simply the object of 'mass mobilization' by a manipulative elite. Alex Pravda's comparative analysis of the working class in Chapter 8 explores how and why it has evolved in those three countries and East Germany, and attempts to assess the likely political and economic influence of the working class in the 1980s.

Part Four presents views of four East European authors on the impact of increased involvement with Western countries on East European economies and political institutions. In Chapter 9 the Hungarian economist András Nagy writes that at the onset of the 1980s Hungary faces the need to introduce considerable structural changes in its economy. The debate in Hungary ranges from those who favor an even greater opening to the West to those who point to the difficulties engendered by exposure to the uncertainties of Western economies, urging greater orientation to CMEA markets. Nagy explores in detail the implications of each option.

This overview of the strategic economic choices facing Hungary is complemented by Márton Tardos' detailed study in Chapter 10 of how Western technology imported to Hungary affects not only that country, but also her economic relations with other CMEA members. Tardos puts the options for the 1980s, described previously by Nagy, into the specific context of technology transfer. He concludes that only a further implementation of the 1968 economic reform would allow Hungary to take full advantage of the possibilities offered by importation of technology – and even then there would be serious constraints on the rate at which foreign technology is adopted.

Similarly, Chapter 11, by the Polish economist Witold Trzeciakowski, presents an argument that is similar in several respects to the two by the Hungarian economists Nagy and Tardos. He describes the problems that attended the growth of Polish foreign trade in the early 1970s, placing particular emphasis on the great imbalance between imports and exports to the West, which has produced an enormous Polish financial indebtedness to the West. Trzeciakowski argues forcefully for a strategy of export expansion *vis-à-vis* the West in the 1980s in which profit maximization would be the key.

In Chapter 12 the Polish political scientist Stanisław Gebethner considers some of the legal and institutional changes in socialist polities during the 1970s, tracing out their connections with domestic and foreign economic developments. Like Pravda, Gitelman, and some of the other authors, Gebethner concludes that the major political challenge of the 1980s for East European leaders will remain that of the 1970s – to raise substantially the standard of living. To achieve this, he argues, some decentralization of policy making and decision making is necessary, and the development of various forms of social self-management is urgently required.

The consensus of the volume is that East–West economic and political relations do alter East European economic and political policies but that their likely configuration in the 1980s will probably not lead to a fundamental reorientation of relationships within Eastern Europe or between Eastern Europe and either the USSR or the West. The impact of external economic developments and, perhaps to a lesser extent, political ones, will be felt more directly in the kinds of domestic economic policies East European governments will be able to pursue, policies that will in many cases have important repercussions for the political relationship between governments and populations.

A Talmudic sage warned long ago that after the destruction of the temple in Jerusalem, the gift of prophecy had been given to 'fools and children'. Yet another Talmudic passage defines the wise man as 'he who foresees what will come'. Neither children nor, one hopes, fools wrote this book. None of the authors claims to know with any certainty what will occur in the 1980s. But all have aspired to the status of wise persons by exploring the possibilities, more and less likely, for the future. They have tried to foresee, to describe the event before it actually happens. How accurate their visions are the reader can judge for himself, but only time can tell.

Part One

East–West Relations

Chapter 2

Soviet-American Strategic Balance, the Western Alliance, and East-West Relations

CORAL BELL

Lacking a gift of prophecy, I shall assume that the only mode by which one may forecast the probable course of a relationship is to look at the patterns of the present and immediate past, and assess which of those is most likely to persist. In this chapter I will concentrate on two relationships – that between the United States and other members of the Western alliance, and that between the United States and the Soviet Union. But since these two relationships are largely (though not wholly) interdependent, I shall look at them more or less simultaneously rather than in sequence. And I shall concentrate my attention mostly on decision makers and policy makers, and on articulate opinion as transmitted through the media. The deeper wells of feeling between peoples, important as they are, do not readily make themselves apparent in this kind of diplomatic context.

One initial point may perhaps be rather reassuring, as against any pessimistic conclusions that may emerge later. If in 1969 one had been set the task of forecasting Soviet-American relations in the 1970s, in the light of the past attitudes of the two policy makers then just come to office in Washington (President Nixon and Dr Kissinger), one might well have seemed possessed of an almost lunatic degree of optimism to predict that a marked improvement in American relations with both the Communist great powers would emerge during their stay in office. Yet it happened. The signals regarding prospective relations with both the Soviet Union and the Western alliance appeared in early 1980 still somewhat mixed and ambiguous, not to say confused and confusing. So anything seemed possible. But with that said, one still had to conclude that the auspices for the early 1980s were not particularly cheerful. Brezhnev, reviewing Soviet experience with Carter's Washington early in 1979, said frankly that there had been few encouraging moments in those two years; the earlier prospects for cooperation had 'marked time or reversed their course'.[1] In early 1980, the general situation appears to indicate not much impending change for the better, and quite possibly change for the worse, regardless of whether President Carter remains the chief Western decision maker until 1984 or is replaced by the Republican nominee, Ronald Reagan.

I Détente and its erosion

For an analysis of the reasons, one must look first at the nature and spirit of the Democratic administration that took office in January 1977. The initial outlook appeared to be that President Carter would combine much of the substance of the previous administration's policies with a marked change in the rhetoric of policy and in the moral assumptions behind policy. But a forecast of change in the rhetoric of policy might well have seemed then to the slightly cynical observer roughly equivalent to an announcement that nothing much would change. That proved by no means the case. If the Carter years established anything, they established that, in a decision maker, words are acts. The rhetoric of policy had real effects, some of them obviously quite unexpected.

International politics even at the topmost level rests on nothing more substantial than *a system of expectations*: expectations, essentially, as to what the power of a government is and how it will be used. Those expectations in turn are created by the signals that decision-making elites send each other. Some of these signals are conscious and deliberate, some involuntary or even insuppressible. The military capability of an adversary, in the form of actual hardware and troops and their state of deployment and alert, for instance, is always a forceful and persuasive signal, and one easily read these days by satellites and such. So are strategic and political arrangements and diplomatic connections. Words are by no means among the more powerful and convincing of signals; nevertheless, they *are* signals and must be read as such. The system of expectations concerning American policy undoubtedly changed, under the impact mostly of words, in the first few Carter months. To some of those reading the Washington signals from the world outside America, the changes seemed favorable: for instance, to black nationalists in Southern Africa, to 'opposition' parties in many parts of the world, and to some governments. To other governments the new signals clearly portended danger – to South Africa, for instance, to several Latin American governments, maybe to Iran or South Korea or the Philippines. To the Soviet Union's decision makers, it will be argued here, the changed Washington signals from the first aroused some irritation, even hinted at danger, but there also arose new opportunities, though not necessarily those that Washington hoped they would see. The combination of new American policy and the Soviet responses to both the irritation and the opportunities had, as the 1980s approached, eroded away a good deal of the détente of the early 1970s. The attitude of the European members of the Western alliance to this development had its own ambivalences, which will be examined later in this chapter.

To understand these shifts in position, we must begin by looking at Soviet–American relations at the time of President Carter's accession to power: that is, at the détente and what it was construed to mean by the spokesmen of various political forces concerned to uphold or modify it. The concept of détente had already suffered as much from ingenuous and disingenuous friends as from declared enemies. The ingenuous friends had equated it with peace, and seemed to use it as a reason to forget the balance of power. But détente, far from being synonymous with peace, is not even synonymous with 'peaceful coexistence'. (The Russian terms are *razriadka* or *oslablenie napriazheniia* for détente, and *mirnoe sosushchestvovanie* for peaceful coexistence.) The people who constructed the policy were not, of course, under that illusion, but perhaps the domestic political necessity of securing support for the policy led them to show it in a somewhat rosy light. Those who disliked the policy misrepresented it as appeasement. And even many of those prepared to see it as a bargaining strategy appeared to expect too advantageous a bargain: that the Soviet Union would or should bow out of the competition with the USA for power in the Middle East or Africa, for instance. I regard these views as misapprehensions, but I do not therefore assume they could have been prevented by consulting a dictionary. What was involved was something quite fundamental: a conflict between two sets of basic assumptions about the nature of international politics, traditionalist and moralist.[2]

At first sight it is a paradox that traditionalist assumptions about international politics, which rest on an axiom that inherent *conflict* of interests is the normal and basic stuff of international life, should have proved more friendly to détente than a set of assumptions which imply the possibility of an ultimate harmony of interests. Yet the paradox is only apparent; it masks a real logic. The traditionalist assumptions still include a strong echo of that very old diplomatic agreement, *'cuius regio, eius religio'*, which was the foundation of the Peace of Westphalia, which in turn created the European society of states in its modern form. In contemporary terms it implies that sovereign governments may expect to establish and maintain the domestic political *mores* of their respective societies without *official* lectures from the decision makers of other governments. That traditionalist assumption has been much eroded since 1917, and as often by the heirs of Lenin as by those of Woodrow Wilson. Yet it survives, and on the evidence it provided an easier basis for a diplomatic *modus vivendi*, and for bargaining within it, than did the alternate set of assumptions.

It is no coincidence that the word détente was first revived from the traditional French vocabulary of diplomacy by that highly traditionalist figure, President de Gaulle. Nor that the first notable Western voice to speak up strongly for détente with the Soviet Union in the postwar period was Winston Churchill (in a series of speeches from 1953 to 1955). Nor that the American policy maker who understood its requirements best was Henry Kissinger. What these three men had in common was that they were all conservatives by philosophy and temperament, steeped in balance-of-power theory and nineteenth-century diplomatic history.[3] With such sponsorship, it is somewhat surprising that détente could ever have been seen as a radical notion. What is *not* surprising, however, is that a concept or strategy found useful by those three conservatives should also have found favor with Soviet decision makers. It has often been remarked that Soviet leaders, from Stalin onward, have seemed more at ease with conservative leaders from Western Europe than with social democrats. Both conservatives and communists tend to be strongly oriented toward power, even obsessive about it; not inclined, at any rate, to doubt its importance or morally repudiate it. They are on opposite sides of the battle but they have essentially the same concept of the battlefield and its importance.

Almost any president attaining power in 1969 would have had a strong incentive toward détente, to relieve the pressures on American society created by the Vietnam war. But the two policy makers who then took office were particularly suited to the process. As a familiar political figure with strong anti-Communist credentials from his earliest days in politics, Richard Nixon did not have to fear, initially at least, any accusations from the far right (except the lunatic fringe) that he was 'soft on communism'. As an academic, Dr Kissinger was far more versed in the conventions and techniques of traditional European power politics than most secretaries of state have been.

Even in their time, there were of course many voices of dissent raised against détente with the Soviet Union; rather fewer, but some, were raised against détente with China. I have detailed elsewhere the rationales of these dissenters,[4] and will not repeat that examination here, save to say that the central charge that détente was 'amoral' or 'immoral' represented, in my view, a rejection of the traditionalist conventions and assumptions of diplomacy in favor of an alternate set of assumptions. That set of assumptions again became the dominant one in American foreign policy with the advent of President Carter.

Whatever else may have been thought from time to time about President Carter's diplomacy, I do not suppose anyone ever mistook him for an adherent of traditional balance-of-power analysis as the central component of foreign policy making. But even if he had had any leanings in that direction (which seems improbable), the circumstances in which he made his bid for power would have prescribed instead the sort of foreign policy with which he has in fact become identified. In the domestic debacle of the Nixon administration in 1974, its foreign policy successes were very generally seen as its only redeeming achievements and its only substantial legacy to the Ford administration. And these successes were widely (and to my view rightly) attributed to Henry Kissinger's intellectual understanding and diplomatic skills. So it was hard for the Democratic candidate to develop a plausible line of attack on the *competence* of Republican foreign policy. But a campaign already existed against Kissinger for his alleged lack of moral feeling or regard for the human consequences of foreign policy decisions. This campaign seems to have originated on the left of the American political spectrum, among academics and journalists concerned about Vietnam and Chile. But it was obviously susceptible to being borrowed by those (mostly on the right) averse for various reasons to America's cultivation of better relations with the Communist powers.

Thus there was, one may say, a foreign policy issue ready-made for Jimmy Carter when he first began campaigning for the presidential nomination. And it seemed positively tailor-made for the candidate's own personality. It was even more suited to the circumstances in which he was making his bid. For America was still at that time in the grip of a collective moral crisis, which was brought on by Vietnam and Watergate and affected particularly, on my observation, the younger members of the foreign policy elite. From the murders of Ngo Dinh Diem and John Kennedy in November 1963, to the election of Jimmy Carter in November 1976, political events had generated in Americans of sensitive conscience a high degree of grief, self-criticism, anger, disenchantment, self-doubt, guilt, resentment, anguish. The political melodrama of those thirteen years had had its moment of catharsis in the downfall of Richard Nixon, but it needed an 'upbeat' resolution with the emergence of a 'new face', untouched by the sordid affairs of that time of trouble. Jimmy Carter's great asset, as far as the winning of the presidency was concerned, was that he made Americans feel morally reassured about themselves and their society again at a time when moral reassurance was greatly needed. And, accidentally or by calculation, he seems to have managed this by encapsulating in his political image various traces of an earlier, more innocent America, nostalgically remembered: 'down-home folks' and small-town values. So the rise of Jimmy Carter, the 'born-again' Baptist, the man who bucked the machines, a real-life Mr Deeds gone to Washington, seemed in itself a reassertion, even proof, of the fundamental virtues of American life after a long period in which those virtues had seemed doubtful or flawed.

In domestic politics, to stand for virtue reasserted – indeed, virtue triumphant – is probably always an asset. In international politics, that is by no means the case. Perhaps one could even say that it has been disproved by Carter's experience. For an image of conspicuous virtue may be read by either adversaries or allies as signaling that the new man is naïve, inexperienced, 'doesn't know the score', especially among a group of other decision makers with long years of experience (Brezhnev, Schmidt, Callaghan, Giscard, Deng Xiao-ping). There is a saying in American sporting circles, 'Nice guys finish last'. Something of the same sort of expectation may be generated by a similar reputation in international politics.

Whatever personal handicap this represented to Carter in establishing himself *vis-à-vis* allies and adversaries was undoubtedly compounded by the erosion of presidential power at the hands of Congress and the media, which had been under way since 1973 as a direct consequence of the Vietnam experience, and which in some respects had disabled the presidential hand in foreign policy to a degree unparalleled since the early 1930s. In particular, the moral revulsion against presidential use of the Central Intelligence Agency for covert action seems retrospectively (judging by the agency's failures in Iran and Afghanistan) to have rendered it pretty ineffective also as an intelligence-gathering organization. One could hardly expect that the agency's general efficiency would not be diminished by the battering it took at various hands, 1974–78, and the consequential collapse in morale. The importance of this factor should not be underrated. By and large, the CIA conducted the combat operations of the Cold War on the West's behalf from 1947 onward. Doubtless, like other intelligence organizations, it did many stupid and wicked things in that process, but 'à la guerre comme à la guerre'. Since the Cold War eventuated at best in a stalemate, even given the lavish (probably overlavish) use of this instrumentality by successive presidents from

Truman onward, it should have been rather sobering to speculate on the likely course of covert battles for diplomatic influence once that instrumentality had been disabled, as the CIA visibly had been after the Angola resolutions of 1975–76.

So all in all, the new president as seen from without and with a somewhat adversary eye in January 1977 might reasonably have been judged not only as short on understanding and experience, but as essentially weaker than any of his predecessors since FDR (in terms of control of the various instrumentalities for projection of American power abroad). Indeed, among his predecessors the closest analogy, to European minds, seemed to be with Woodrow Wilson. There were a good many parallels. Carter's campaign for human rights (which at the end of 1978 he still insisted would continue to be the 'soul' of his diplomacy) offered clear comparisons with Wilson's campaign to make the world safe for democracy and national self-determination. Carter, like Wilson, appeared determined to be his own chief foreign policy maker, even though initially he had oddly little firsthand experience of the world outside America. (He seems not to have traveled abroad much, even as a tourist, which surely indicates a lower-than-usual level of curiosity about other peoples. Many Americans, much less prosperous, take to travelling abroad in their college days and never give up the habit.) Carter initially proclaimed also a return to the Wilsonian notion of 'open diplomacy', though he did give that up quite fast, after a couple of disasters *vis-à-vis* the Russians and the Middle East.

Wilson remains a hero to many, perhaps most, Americans, and to them these analogies probably appeared reassuring. But not so to the Russians, who still remembered the 1918 intervention. And not entirely so to the West Europeans, who tended to remember that twenty years after the crusade to make the world safe for democracy, the actual democracies in the world had been reduced to a small beleaguered band, fighting for their very lives. The American policies of the 1920s and early 1930s that provided the prologue to that disaster had been seen as a sort of backlash against the Wilson period. So European chancelleries could hardly fail to be afflicted by a sense of *déja vu* and a reinforced consciousness that morally admirable American sentiments and principles sometimes eventuated in diplomatically disastrous outcomes.

II   The 'Remoralizing' of American Foreign Policy

On the other hand, it became apparent early on that President Carter did not share any Wilsonian doubts about the concept of balance of power. His China policy, his attention to NATO, and his defense budgets were all testimonies to a considerable preoccupation with power relationships. So was the choice of Zbigniew Brzezinski as his chief diplomatic strategist. The evidence is rather of an assumption that the 'remoralizing' of American foreign policy, and especially a stress on human rights, could be combined with the balance-of-power preoccupations, so as to get the best of both worlds – to have the gratifying cake of moral approval, and yet eat it securely in the house of well-balanced power, so to speak. If the project had come off, it would undoubtedly have compelled applause. But the harsher of his critics would argue that instead of getting the best of both worlds, the Carter strategy perhaps got the worst of both worlds. The balance was not adequately secured, in that the erosion of Western power assets was considerable, as was the expansion of Soviet power assets. The détente was not developed, nor the prospects of peace enhanced. And such improvements as were made in the actual observance of human rights were not adequate recompense for this damage to the fabric of Western security, on which all sorts of human rights, including that to life, depended.

Those are judgments harsh enough to require a good deal of justification, and the evidence is not yet convincing. Nevertheless, there is some case for maintaining that the human rights campaign irritated Soviet decision makers enough to erode the détente, but without seriously eroding Soviet power. And unfortunately at the same time it eroded Western power positions in those parts of the world where the West was allied to regimes with dubious or poor records in this field. That covered quite a number of areas critically important to Western interests, most conspicuously Iran. To sum up, if one accepts the image of American–Soviet relations in the mid-1970s as consisting of a diplomatic 'superstructure', which was the détente, and a strategic 'infrastructure', which was the central balance of power, the remoralizing of policy may be judged to have operated as a sort of political sandstorm, abrasively eroding both superstructure and infrastructure. Of these two, the balance-of-power infrastructure was essentially the more important, since the détente superstructure is like a sort of diplomatic summerhouse that can always be reerected, provided the foundations are there and the conditions are right. By contrast, any undermining of the balance of power is a far more difficult matter to repair, and its repairing may even require dismantling what is left of détente.

The obvious but less important part of this double process of damage stemmed from the direct irritation induced in Soviet decision makers by matters like the American official feting of eminent Soviet dissidents such as Solzhenitsyn and Bukovsky. Given his earlier remarks about Ford's and Kissinger's caution on this matter, to do any less no doubt seemed politically impossible to Carter and his aides. But, obviously, in Moscow a presidential decision to publicize, endorse, 'legitimate' dissent in this fashion was bound to be interpreted as a deliberate campaign to focus American attention on the sins of the Soviet system. Of course, the Soviet press has often focused on analogous cases in the USA. The Soviet feting of Angela Davis, for instance, may be seen as a parallel to the Western feting of Solzhenitsyn. But the sensitivities of policy makers are not necessarily symmetrical. An open, pluralistic society like the United States is better fitted to shrug off such incidents than a tight autocracy, which holds that it has a monopoly of truth.

III The Brzezinski Strategy

How seriously ought one to take the view that Washington saw a tougher-minded American stance on détente as actually likely to exact change in important areas of Soviet policy, domestic or international? Here obviously one must consult the published views of Brzezinski, as Carter's chief diplomatic strategist. And those views had already conveyed a disconcerting level of apparent optimism as to what could be secured or, at any rate, might usefully be demanded. Here is Brzezinski in 1975, discussing the differences between his interpretation of détente, on the one hand, and Kissinger's and Brezhnev's, on the other:

> Brezhnev, too, prefers a limited, strictly compartmentalized, non-basic détente, especially in the economic and strategic fields which are, of course, inter-related, and in which the Soviet Union is extremely vulnerable. . . .
> . . . the Soviet leaders fear a truly comprehensive détente. They see in it a challenge to their legitimacy and thus to their very existence, and I must say their fears are justified. They are right in diagnosing the danger to them, they are wrong, however, in not realizing that their resistance to change is at odds with the facts of life at the end of the twentieth century. . . .
> . . . Nixon and Kissinger prided themselves on being less ideologically motivated and more pragmatic than the Kennedys. . . . [This] denies American foreign policy an asset which has made that policy so appealingly to many people throughout the world. . . .
> It seems to me that we should insist that certain forms of Soviet behaviour, none of them strictly economic, are themselves incompatible with better economic relations. . . .
> First . . .: ideological hostility. . . .
> Second: the secrecy surrounding Soviet strategic planning. . . .
> Third: indifference to global problems. . . .
> Fourth: the Soviet disregard of human rights. . . .
> Fifth: reciprocity of treatment. . . .
> These, then, are some of the areas of strain . . ., and it is here that we could use our economic leverage to best advantage. The Russians will not accommodate us willingly. . . .
> . . . some realistic encouragement of pluralism via nationalism and separatism may be our best answer to the Soviet challenge on the ideological front. . . .
> . . . My hope would be that after the disappearance of the communist state, a combination of residual socialism and internationalism would mitigate the power-oriented ambitions of extreme Russian nationalism. . . . it has to be our objective to try to promote, no matter how marginally, that more acceptable alternative.

These quotations are from a long interview, given of course before Brzezinski became a policy maker, and published in *Détente*, a volume edited by G. R. Urban from a set of discussions originally broadcast on Radio Free Europe.[5] For reasons of brevity I have omitted the interviewer's questions, and the phrases I have chosen have, deliberately, been those that would catch the eye of a reader in Moscow. That is, I have looked at the interview in search of a set of 'signals' that a Kremlin

'Americanologist' might derive from it, in his initial analysis of the prospects for détente in view of the new administration.

Obviously such expectations would be pessimistic. Speculations about a possible disappearance of the Soviet state, especially as broadcast to dissident audiences in Eastern Europe, are hardly likely to have appeared more palatable than lists of required improvements in Soviet behavior, to be demanded before the economic benefits of détente should be accorded.

The point I want chiefly to make about the interview, however, is that it defines the differences between the Kissinger and the Brzezinski interpretations of détente, and makes clear why the Russians found the Kissinger version so much more acceptable. In his time détente was seen as a mode of weaving a web of interconnections, whose benefits might in due course seem important enough to Soviet policy makers to warrant restraint in the pursuit of policies Washington would construe as undesirable. For Brzezinski, at least in this interview, détente was a benefit for which the Russians should be required to pay in advance. He did in fact say in the course of the interview that the Kissinger notion of détente was far more like Brezhnev's than his own. One may note, though, that while Kissinger was often accused of presenting an unduly optimistic account of what détente could do, Brzezinski here actually was more optimistic by far, putting forward quite unrealistic assumptions about détente's potential as an instrument of American foreign policy. If the Russians had indeed been induced to 'play ball' on the basis of the five conditions he outlined, a successful forcing of profound changes in Soviet theory and practice would surely have occurred.

But it takes two to make a bargain, and what the interview lacked was serious argument as to why Soviet decision makers would regard détente on this basis as any kind of a bargain at all. On the standard Western assumptions about their diplomatic and political priorities, they were logically likely to prefer a return to Cold War, if necessary, since that would clearly be far less incompatible with both their power interests and their ideological stance. And insofar as hope for economic advantages through the détente had earlier been a 'preferred option' of Soviet decision makers, as against other gains they could conceivably have extracted from various crisis situations, the downgrading of expectations from the détente operated, necessarily, *to reduce the reasons for Soviet restraint when other inviting options presented themselves, as for instance in Africa.* No one could say for certain that even a strongly maintained détente relationship could have restrained Soviet pursuit of the opportunities that were appearing, *vis-à-vis* Ethiopia for instance, in early 1977. But as matters by then stood, the Soviets certainly had no reason to feel they had anything much to lose in the prospective relationship with the USA.

It seems not unjust to regard the dominant ethos of the Carter foreign policy as a form of American messianism. By that term I mean the assumption that one's own society has a special role and duty to *redeem* the world, and that its *mores* and values have a universal relevance. On that definition messianism has been a recurrent strand in Russian as well as American policy. In the Russian case one can discern it in Czarist as well as Soviet times, and in the American case it has appeared quite frequently from the earliest days of the republic. In the Kissinger period, however, messianism had been so absent or *sotto voce* that its reappearance with Carter was widely greeted as something new.

The 'remoralizing' of American foreign policy (to employ the prevalent but rather inaccurate term) was undoubtedly popular with articulate intellectual opinion as well as with the electorate. Yet it seems to have been the chief factor on the Western side contributing to the erosion of the détente during the late 1970s – not, however, directly by creating resentment among Soviet decision makers, but indirectly, by eroding the stability of the central power balance. Since détente was primarily, from the West's point of view, a mode of management of balanced power, détente necessarily tended to become less useful insofar as power ceased to be balanced.

Though the erosion of the stability of the central balance proceeded most rapidly in the Carter period, it had begun in the Republican period. At that time its genesis was moral revulsion in Congress against the costs of using power. The two chief instances were the congressional sanctions against Turkey in the wake of the 1974 invasion of Cyprus and the 1975–76 congressional resolutions on Angola. The moves against Turkey, and the Turkish reactions to them, considerably damaged NATO's capacity in the eastern Mediterranean, and generated a Turkish resentment still potentially affecting the prospects of SALT II verification in late 1979. The Angola resolutions, by which Congress refused the use of CIA funds to compete for diplomatic influence in Angola, evidently provided a 'green light' for Soviet enterprises in Africa generally, signaling they were 'low-risk, low-cost options' entailing no danger of confrontation with the USA. The Soviet response to that signal, the Cuban involvement in Angola and Ethiopia and elsewhere, was the most important single episode in the downturn in Soviet–American relations.

Let me at this stage summarize my argument about the 1970s as that period serves to indicate the probabilities for the 1980s. My underlying premise is that international politics at the highest level rests essentially on *a system of expectations*; that these expectations are governed by the sets of signals that one decision-making elite receives, or believes it receives, from another; and that the most important content, or assumed content, of these signals concerns *what the power of a government is and how that power will be used*. Since the advent of Jimmy Carter as president, the Washington signals, as read in Moscow, for a variety of reasons had to be logically interpreted as conveying the reduced power of the presidential hand in the deployment of American strength in the world outside. In an essentially competitive relationship between the United States and the Soviet Union, that reduced power had equally to be read as conveying opportunity to the Soviet Union. At the same time, the replacement of the traditionalist assumptions characteristic of Dr Kissinger's diplomacy, with the moralist assumptions of President Carter's diplomacy, intimated to Soviet policy makers the likelihood of some irritations and even dangers – but also again opportunities – in possible impacts on the security of elites that were both vulnerable to human rights criticisms and allies or fellow travelers of the West (Iran, South Korea, Zaire, South Africa, etc.). It would take only a moderately cynical assessment to deduce that if the guns of the human rights campaign were to be directed against the plywood structures of authority in many Third World autocracies (mainly clients of the West), they might do real damage, whereas they were likely to prove about as effective as peashooters against the chilled-steel party autocracies of the Communist world. The signals from Washington also conveyed that even the assiduous pursuit of détente by the Soviet Union, if that objective were to be given high priority, would not necessarily produce the economic benefits for which it was in part initially undertaken, since Brzezinski's interpretation of what could be demanded in return would presumably be the ruling one within White House circles. And even if he or the president were inclined to yield a point, there would remain the Senate objections to MFN status and long-term credits and such. To sum up, if all diplomacy entails some use of both carrot and stick – coercion and benefit – the new administration's ability to deploy either appeared much reduced in early 1977, and this appearance matched the real experience of America's allies and the world in general up to mid-1980.

IV Armaments and Arms Control

American–Soviet relations in the arms control field at the end of the 1970s provided a sort of microcosm of the diplomatic relationship as a whole. The signing of the SALT II treaty in June 1979 constituted one signal of the possible future; the difficulty of getting it ratified provided another, and a conflicting one. Between the two, the auguries for the next decade remained ambivalent, as in other fields.

Again, as in other fields, the difficulties began during the Republican period, but were exacerbated in the Carter period, chiefly because of the individual concepts and strategies that the president brought to foreign policy making in general. The 'guidelines' initialed by Brezhnev and Ford at Vladivostok at the end of 1974 represented an effort on Kissinger's part to keep the arms control process in motion despite the fall of President Nixon. The treaty signed five years later departed only marginally from those guidelines. The lapse of time between the two points, and the fact that the diplomatic atmosphere had in the meantime chilled so much that ratification then appeared very doubtful (and in fact proved impossible) reflected the general erosion of détente. Administration officials disseminated the notion of 'arms control without détente' virtually as a 'selling point' for the treaty, because the human rights issue and other matters had made the Russians so unpopular. Yet in fact arms control had been useful because it created changes in the political relationship, rather than because it changed much in the strategic relationship. With or without SALT II, the strategic relationship remained of a monstrous 'overkill capacity' on both sides, though with some asymmetries of advantage for particular types of weapons and at particular periods. The episode as a whole confirms that the political relationship is anterior to the strategic one: a diplomatic relationship of reasonable ease creates the possibility of arms control, but the reverse does not necessarily hold.

The 1974 guidelines had been more or less enshrined in a fairly complete treaty by January 1976, but by then the presidential election campaign was under way, and Gerald Ford was so hard-pressed by right-wing Republican contenders for the nomination that he assumed it was impossible to sign the treaty. Had the same proposals been sent back to Moscow in March 1977, on Secretary Vance's first visit, they probably would have come to signature, and to ratification, since President Carter's standing in Congress was very high at that point. But relations between the United States and the Soviet Union were already in a state of increased tension by that time, chiefly because of the human rights campaign, and the proposals actually sent by Washington further exacerbated Russian resentments. Those porposals for 'deep cuts' were allegedly drafted by Senator Jackson, or at least formulated in order to appease him,[6] and as a serious negotiating bid they were nonstarters from the first. The Russian reaction to their presentation was so adverse that it barred even proceeding with the alternative offered, the Vladivostok proposals almost agreed upon previously. One may assume that the Russians reacted so strongly because they interpreted the new president's new proposals as a case of his deliberately making them an offer he knew they were bound to refuse, in order to gain a psychological point and to strike a pose as an enthusiastic peacemaker. The Russians are perhaps especially sensitive to that form of arms-control gamesmanship, because they have used it so often themselves. But the SALT I agreements had been reached because both sides eschewed that sort of ploy. Furthermore, Kissinger used to keep all the negotiations strictly secret, so that neither side would feel tempted to strike poses for publicity purposes. Jimmy Carter could hardly do that, however, after his denunciations of secret diplomacy, and told the world his proposals in a press conference before he officially told the Russians. This seems to have been the basis of Brezhnev's complaint to President Giscard a little later, on his visit to Paris, that Carter had broken the rules of conduct of détente. Since the French are traditionalists themselves in diplomatic matters, Giscard implied a considerable sympathy for the Russians at this American failure to adhere to the conventions.

Negotiations took a long time to recover from that initial setback, and as finally embodied in the treaty the proposals had not changed much from those of five years earlier. Moreover, in the meantime political anxiety over Russian diplomatic successes (or Western losses) in the Third World had grown acute, as had strategic anxiety over certain new Soviet weapon systems, so that the underlying confidence in the stability of the balance had been eroded too far to serve well as basis for agreement.

Even with SALT II, the level of 'overkill capacity' in the hands of American and Soviet decision makers in the mid-1980s will be formidable: about 20,000 warheads in toto, on a conservative estimate. This capacity will not be symmetrically distributed, in deliverable megatonnage: Soviet advantage in terms of ICBM payload will be of the order of two to one, and this may not be fully offset by American advantage in warhead numbers, carried in bombers and SLMBs. Consequently, some analysts argued that a Soviet 'first strike' would wipe out so substantial a proportion of American land-based missiles as to leave American policy makers unable to threaten with any credibility a reprisal strike of the same sort. That alleged imbalance, they argued, could prove a damaging influence on crisis decision making. Some in Western Europe also feared that the United States might sacrifice its ability to upgrade its own NATO forces, for instance, in nuclear-capable aircraft based in Europe, and long-range sea- and ground-launched cruise missiles based in Europe. Nevertheless European opinion, or at least official opinion as advanced by governmental spokesmen, favored the treaty fairly solidly. Its opposition lay in Washington.

V The Power Balance of the Early 1980s

Pessimism there concerning the 1980s arose chiefly from the probable, or at least potential, instability of the central balance, as it had begun to appear in analytical forecasts. And this in turn required compounding several factors: prospective counterforce capacities on the two sides, conventional military balances in various areas, apparent rates of growth and decline in diplomatic influence, the economic strength of the two sides. When one put these elements together, what seemed visible was a sort of 'capability gap', favorable to the Soviet Union, in the period roughly of 1982–87. Kissinger, not a representative of the alarmist sector of opinion, defined the nature of this gap in an *Economist* interview:

> Under current programmes, I do not see in the period 1980–87 an adequate emphasis on counterforce capability with or without SALT.... Of the various weapons we were considering, the two that would have been most useful for a counterforce role were the MX and to a lesser extent the B-1. The B-1 has been scrapped and the timetable for the MX has been stretched out so that it is unfortunately barely relevant to the period we are talking about.
> That bothers me because I also do not see an adequate development of forces for local defence by us or our allies. Therefore the 1980s could turn into a period of great instability. There is a growing gap between the global political alignment and its military capability . . . most major countries in the world (United States, western Europe, China and Japan) will be grouped on one side and the Soviet Union will be on the other. That may well be perceived in Moscow as a potential for encirclement. But for a period of five to seven years the Soviets may develop an advantage in power useful for political ends. On the one hand the Soviets may fear that if their opponents ever get their act together they will gain a rapid advantage even in military hardware. On the other hand the Soviet Union may perceive a period in which, though its political and economic instabilities are latent but not yet overwhelming, its military power is potentially dominant. If it is not used in that period, the Soviets' long-term fate is extremely uncertain. *Thus, we could be heading into a period of maximum peril.*[7] (Italics added.)

To these reasons for disquiet may be added some arising from the Soviet–Chinese relationship. The 'normalizing' of relations between the United States and China and the visit of Deng Xiao-ping to the United States were treated by sections of the Soviet press as indicating some sort of collusion by Washington in the Chinese attack on the Russians' Vietnamese allies.[8] There was probably not much substance to these allegations. Though the Chinese clearly signaled during the American visit that they intended the attack, and perhaps told their hosts a good deal about it, the evidence suggests that Carter attempted to discourage the idea. This would square with the rather irritable remarks about American 'weakness' that Deng was reported to have made in Tokyo on his way home.

Nevertheless, the nature of the visit, the prominence of Brzezinski's part in it and in the normalization process generally, the assorted remarks about 'playing the China card' and 'teaching the polar bear a lesson' then and during the earlier Brzezinski visit to Peking, and the indiscreet implication that the United States and China had the same 'essential interests' *vis-à-vis* the Soviet Union – all these may be argued as tending to reinforce the hand of any 'soon or never' contingent within the Kremlin. That is to say, from the point of view of Soviet policy makers, China probably appeared at the beginning of the 1980s to be still a very weak power militarily (in conventional terms), and the period of fighting in Vietnam would not have dispelled that impression. On the other hand, China had also demonstrated that it was conspicuously well endowed with the political will to pursue the quarrel with the Soviet Union and with Soviet allies, and that it was at last moving toward an ambitious modernization of Chinese armed forces by the acquisition of Western weapons systems. If a serious showdown with the Chinese leadership had to be contemplated by Soviet policy makers, the early 1980s might therefore logically seem to them a better period than the late 1980s or the 1990s, when those weapon systems would presumably be in Chinese hands. So again the early 1980s look like a crisis-prone period.

VI   Division of the Western Camp?

The crises will not occur in Western Europe. Since about the mid-1960s, policy makers and others have speculated that the central balance was about to transmute itself into a five-power system, with Japan and 'Europe' moving out of the American camp and setting up independent ones of their own. Both represent vastly greater agglomerations of immediate power (military and industrial) than China, which raised an independent banner years ago. And European chancelleries, of course, have a longer tradition of this technique than any other segment of the world's political elites. Yet both have stayed obstinately within the American sphere, with only occasional signals of restiveness, for more than three decades now. One has to ask what conditions maintained this state of affairs, against the expectations of some very shrewd observers, and whether these circumstances are likely to persist in the 1980s.

The answers are not far to seek. The powers concerned have stayed within the American camp because the policy makers involved (except President de Gaulle) have found it comfortable and advantageous to do so. It has served their respective national interests, as the policy makers in power to date in each country have defined the national interest. Also membership in the American camp is a good deal less expensive than keeping up an independent camp of one's own: compare the proportion of GNP devoted to defense by, for instance, Sweden (outside the NATO camp) and Norway (inside it). The United States, over the years, has spent about 7 percent of GNP for military purposes, as against 4 percent for the European members of NATO and less than 1 percent for Japan. The European members, moreover, are quite sophisticated enough in this diplomatic tradition to understand that their respective interests depend on keeping the Western camp looking as solid as possible to its only prospective challenger, the Soviet Union. French policy may often have seemed in contradiction to that observation, but actually has depended upon a slightly cynical calculation of its effectiveness. France's particular national advantages (well sheltered behind the Washington–Bonn axis, essential to the Western camp in providing the rear areas for the NATO armies, still with relics of the old imperial world role) have provided a basis solid enough for diplomatic finessing. And French policy makers have acted on that consciousness in their distinctive national initiatives *vis-à-vis* the Soviet Union, China, and Africa. They do not seem to have suffered any particular penalties, which is in itself a testimony to traditional French diplomatic skills. And though they have often caused irritation in Washington, on balance their efforts have mostly been useful to the West, especially in Africa.

If these are the reasons why Japan and 'Europe' (other than France) have shown little interest so far in moving out of the American camp, why should the situation be expected to change in the 1980s? Aside from some *sotto-voce* anxiety at aspects of President Carter's diplomacy, the level of conflict in the Western camp has been relatively low since the early 1970s. The European urge to 'distance itself' from the United States reached its peak in the Vietnam war years. No issue of equal moral power was in sight at the end of the 1970s. The nearest approximation would be the alleged overuse of the energy resources of the world by 'self-indulgent' American consumers. But this does not have the kind of dramatic impact on the TV news that Vietnam did. The American reconciliation with China removed a second major source of reproach to Americans. The West European student-left can still raise a protest about American interpretations of the interests of Palestinians, or Africans, or Iranians, or Latin Americans, but their banners do not carry much persuasion with average opinion. President Carter's championing of the cause of human rights has rather preempted the moral high-ground from under the feet of the European radicals, and by comparison with the 1960s and 1970s, they do not have clearly in view any good, brave anti-American cause.

Further, one might say, as the wolves look stronger the case for staying within the camp becomes logically more persuasive. The growth in strength of the Soviet Union and its Warsaw Pact adjutants had no doubt presented some version of that reflection to various West European minds by the late 1970s. And once the United States was no longer at war in Asia, American strategic priorities became much more like those of its European allies. The opposite was, of course, the case for Japan and Australia: American strategic priorities are now and for the future prospectively less close to their own. Ironically, China has seen matters the European way, and has thus become an enthusiast for more resources for NATO. Anything that focuses Soviet attention on its Western frontier (for instance, trouble with Romania or in Poland) may help reduce Soviet pressure against China.

Some obvious sets of circumstances could change this pattern. For instance, radical changes in the political elites in power in the countries concerned, through elections or otherwise, could conceivably produce new assessments of the usefulness and costs of the American connection, and possibly disavowal. However, it is uncommonly difficult in 1980 to see this happening either in Japan or in any of the major European countries. Even in Italy, Communist gains now appear stabilized, and the Communist party appears too little trustful of Soviet policy to campaign hard for the weakening of NATO should it become part of the government coalition. In Britain and Germany the notion of radical change in the political elite during the 1980s seems still less convincing. Only in Greece and Turkey can one make a plausible case. A radical change in either power would of course damage the southern wing of NATO and make a Mediterranean crisis (along lines sketched below, p. 28) still more probable and devastating.

VII   Some Possible Theaters of Crisis

As far as probable areas of danger are concerned, by 1980 one would readily agree with Brzezinski, who sees them primarily in what he has called the 'arc of crisis', a great crescent centered on the Persian Gulf–Middle East area, but stretching right over toward Indochina and down into Africa. If, as has been argued, Soviet policy is responsive to 'low-risk, low-cost options', or what look like them, this is clearly where such options have recently been found, and are likely to be found in future. Unless something very improbable happens to NATO, there do not appear to be many prospects of that sort in Western Europe, though in Southeastern Europe (the Balkans) one could discern the makings of a major crisis. That apart, both Soviet–American relations and relations within the Western alliance will probably find their storm centers of the 1980s in the non-European world, rather than in Europe itself.

At once the most probable and the most potentially dangerous center of crisis for the early and middle years of the decade seems to be the Middle East–Persian Gulf area. One might even call it a statistical near certainty, for considering that there were Middle Eastern wars in each of the last four decades – 1948, 1956, 1967, and 1973 – to assume the 1980s will be different would be an unwarranted piece of optimism. On the other hand, since Egypt and Israel have moved toward accommodation, the past scenarios featuring direct military encounters between Israel on one side, and Egypt (with variable assistance from other Arabs) on the other, do not seem likely to be repeated in the future. The focus of hostilities could be the Gulf rather than the Canal. According to many estimates, the competition for oil, and hence for diplomatic or political influence over oil-bearing real estate, will reach a peak toward the mid-1980s and will be as important for the Soviet Union and Eastern Europe as for the West. One might assume that Iran will then still be functioning as an Islamic Republic, but that the government will be not only nonaligned but relatively weak: torn by dissension between fundamentalist Islamic groups under the inspiration of the Ayatollah or his spiritual successors, on the one hand, and, on the other, radicals looking to a revived Tudeh party or other left-wing leaderships, and with some reemergence of separatist movements among Azerbaijanis, Kurds, and Baluchis.

Even without a precipitating event such as the seizure of the American hostages, these seem almost ideal conditions for some approximation of the Azerbaijan crisis of 1946, with the Soviets backing an 'autonomous' regime in the north, which would be parlayed into a dominant position in Iran generally, and thence into Soviet paramountcy in the Gulf area as a whole. That could portend a sort of 'Finlandization' of the Gulf states, a possibility vastly more feasible than the 'Finlandization' of Western Europe could ever be. Western Europe consists of tough, proud, sophisticated states with long historical and political identities, and vigorous military traditions. The Gulf states may be rich, but they are militarily negligible, now that the Iranian armed forces have been weakened, and their experience in preserving themselves diplomatically is very brief. Until 1971 they lived under the British protectorate, the full results of whose passing have only recently become apparent.

A crisis of this sort would be exceedingly dangerous. The United States will at that time probably still be 50 percent dependent on imported oil, much of it Middle Eastern. Japan and Western Europe will be even more dependent, unless there is an extraordinary rate of development of Chinese, Mexican, and other sources. So they will all have uncommonly strong reasons to risk even military action to keep the shadow of Soviet power off the source of their industrial life-blood. The scenario for this crisis could look very like the scenario for Armageddon.

Perhaps if that is understood it will not happen. A major Persian Gulf crisis might conceivably create a desperate sense of common interest between the United States and the rest of the Western alliance. On the other hand, arguments about the allocation of oil supplies are already a source of tension in the alliance (as also within the Warsaw Pact), and this might well be exacerbated in the subcritical period.[9]

An East Asian crisis that would react on the Western alliance and involved the Soviet–American relationship is at least equally likely early in the 1980s. In fact, given the Chinese readiness to use armed force in Vietnam and perhaps Laos, it might be described as more likely. Such a crisis would be a good deal more dangerous in Northeast Asia, at the meeting place of Soviet, American, Chinese, and Japanese interests, than it has been in Southeast Asia, and there is still the essential instability of the balance between North and South Korea to provide the occasion of crisis. A Soviet-Chinese confrontation here might rapidly become nuclear, and might also lead Soviet decision makers to envisage a chance of spoiling the China-Japan-USA-Europe relation, which would otherwise be more formidable by the 1990s.

An East European-Mediterranean crisis may require no more than Tito's mortality. The collective leadership that has assumed his role cannot hope to inherit his charisma. If the fragile amalgam of nationalities that he kept together begins to fall apart, there will be opportunities for Soviet initiatives to get Yugoslavia into the Warsaw Pact fold – for instance, by backing the central government should it wish to repress secessionist nationalism in the regions, or through Bulgarian claims on Macedonia. The prospective Soviet strategic and political/psychological gains here would be so large that they might be estimated to warrant the risks: the absorption of the original 'maverick' Communist Party, a window on the Mediterranean, perhaps revival of the Soviet grip on the whole of the Balkans, including Albania. Such a change would profoundly increase the danger to Greece and Turkey, and help squeeze them out of NATO and into nonalignment. Gains so large might induce the taking of even large risks. So one may argue this to be the most plausible of these potential crises. But history is apt to confound efforts at prophecy: the crises of the 1980s may come in quite unforeseen places.

VIII   Summation and Perspectives

In summary, I am relatively pessimistic about the Soviet-American relation for the early 1980s, but (in part for that reason) relatively optimistic about relationships within the Western alliance, using that term both in the smaller sense which confines it to NATO, and the larger sense in which it includes France, Spain, Japan, Australia, and other countries identifying their national interests with those of the United States. Even if SALT II is ratified, I expect somewhat abrasive Soviet-American relations chiefly because the terms of the dialogue have been altered. That dialogue has always been about both the conflict between power systems and the conflict between value systems. But the diplomacy of the Kissinger period tended to concentrate on restraining the power conflict, while that of the Carter period has tended to be more insistent about the value conflict. Since it is easier to share power than to reconcile values, that change has inevitably made the relationship more abrasive. At the same time, the change has coincided with or caused certain Western diplomatic losses, which have been equated with, and in some cases actually are, Soviet gains. Therefore the balance of power, to many Western eyes, has acquired an appearance of instability. Détente seems unlikely to reassert its earlier promise until the balance of power is judged as stable by both sides, and some rules are tacitly agreed upon to keep it stable. I am not speaking here of arms control, but of restraint or symmetry in diplomatic competitiveness.

The sense that the adversary coalition is now militarily strong, and getting stronger, has undoubtedly helped to maintain cohesion in the Western coalition. Only when the West's margin of advantage appears considerable does the luxury of faction-mindedness look 'affordable'. So I would expect the present low level of intra-alliance conflict generally to persist. Some of the factors that looked formidably divisive in the 1970s seem rather 'paper tigers' for the 1980s. This may prove true of 'Eurocommunism'. If SALT III eventuates, the arms control negotiations may still raise issues dividing European interests from American ones, but on the whole the chances of any substantial measure of arms control seem so slender that this does not at present appear a major danger to the Western alliance.

The only prospective reason I can see for serious dissension in the Western camp – and one for which there were some indications as the 1980s began – is a sense among European and other decision makers that the West as a whole is being 'outgeneralled', diplomatically and strategically, because of ill-considered policies originating in Washington. Restiveness on this point rose sharply at various times during the late 1970s, but was always 'taken off the boil' in the nick of time by some apparent success for President Carter, such as the Camp David negotiations. As anxiety about oil reasserted itself, even that success seemed rather hollow, since it was seen as probably contributing to the continued decay in Western diplomatic influence and strategic positions in the Persian Gulf, whence flows the very life-blood of the advanced industrial societies, in the form of oil. Looking back on the last few years of American diplomacy *vis-à-vis* the Soviet Union, one might regard them as a mordant illustration of the dangers of optimism and moral ambition in foreign-policy making. Looking forward, what seems most clearly in prospect is a period of considerable turbulence, perhaps building to a peak in the mid-1980s, and a pressing need for foresighted crisis-diplomacy by the decision makers of the dominant powers.

Notes: Chapter 2

1 Interview in *Time*, 22 January 1979, p. 22.
2 To give a really adequate account of the differences between these two sets of concepts and the history of their interaction in American and British foreign policies would require quite a lengthy essay. In brief, while foreign-policy making requires a blend of power calculations and value judgments in both cases, the proportions are quite different, and so are the priorities when values are in conflict.
3 In American politics the word 'conservative' is often reserved for political figures such as Ronald Reagan, very unfriendly to détente. I shall, however, use the term 'right-wingers' for that group since they do not seem to me to stand precisely in the tradition of Burke and Disraeli.
4 See the author's *The Diplomacy of Détente* (Oxford: Martin Robertson and New York: St Martin's Press, 1977), especially Ch. 11, 'The Enemies and Sceptics of Détente'.
5 Zbigniew Brzezinski, 'From Cold War to Cold Peace', in G. R. Urban (ed.), *Détente* (London: Temple Smith and New York: Universe Books, 1976), pp. 262–80.
6 According to a Washington columnist, Joseph Kraft. See *International Herald Tribune*, 20 June 1979.
7 *The Economist*, 3 February 1979, p. 20.
8 William Zimmerman informs me that the issue whether the USA was colluding with China

with respect to the latter's attack on Vietnam was a matter of explicit dispute between the political commentators of *Red Star* and *Izvestia*.

9 An area in which a build-up of frictions between European and American policy makers is even more likely is Southern Africa. In the 1980s, however, it appears probable that these will not be a source of fundamentally acute East–West crisis. There has been a foretaste of the possibilities here in the difficulty of maintaining a common Anglo–American front on Zimbabwe. Southern Africa is important strategically to the West as a whole, because of the commodities it produces and because its ports command the oil routes around the Cape. But it is considerably more important to the European members of NATO than to the United States. The Europeans are more dependent on those oil routes and commodities, and they have very large investments in the area. Besides, though the illiberal domestic policies of the Southern African regimes have made it impossible for liberal or social democratic governments in Europe to regard them as potential allies, they enjoy considerable sympathy at the level of the electorates. This is largely 'kith and kin' sentiment: a good many of the white residents of Zimbabwe (Rhodesia) are fairly recent migrants from Britain, and a substantial proportion of the white residents of South Africa are of British or Dutch descent. Popular attitudes in Europe are by no means as virtuously anti-racialist as official policy.

On Zimbabwe, the die must be cast by the very early 1980s, and perhaps compromises of sorts can be patched up there and on Namibia, since the white settler population involved is very small in total, its capacity for resistance cannot be indefinitely prolonged, and it could be reabsorbed elsewhere if worst comes to worst, from the point of view of the people concerned. As with the Portuguese settlers previously in Angola and Mozambique, the problem would be painful but finite. No such assumption could be made, however, about South Africa itself, which seems more likely to generate the crises of the middle or late 1980s. This is a white population more than the size of Israel, with an equally determined identity and an equally tough military tradition. What is more, it is a great deal richer than Israel, and less dependent on external powers. No government can exert on it the sort of diplomatic leverage that Washington in the last analysis can exert on Israel. Indeed, South Africa has been given strong motives to push for nuclear weapon status, by reason of its diplomatic isolation. South Africa's decision makers are likely to see their need for a last-ditch, that is, nuclear, capacity to threaten reprisal in much the same terms as Israeli decision makers, or still more strongly, since they have no great power protector. The conflict between South Africa and the black states may extend through the final decades of this century, in the same way as that between Israel and the Arabs has run through the middle decades, creating similar ambivalences in the Western camp.

Chapter 3

Issues in East–West Economic Relations

MORRIS BORNSTEIN

This chapter examines some of the most important developments, outstanding issues, and future prospects in East–West economic relations.

Section I reviews the factors responsible for the rapid expansion of East–West economic relations in the early 1970s and reasons for the subsequent loss of momentum in the mid-1970s in their further development. Section II analyzes the growth, composition, and burden of Eastern debt to the West resulting from Eastern trade deficits. Section III considers efforts to reduce these deficits by countertrade linking Eastern exports to Eastern imports. Section IV discusses East–West industrial cooperation as a basis for technology transfer, capital flows, and trade. Section V examines trade restrictions hampering the growth of East–West economic relations. Possibilities for greater Eastern participation in international economic organizations are considered in Section VI. Finally, some principal conclusions are summarized in Section VII.

In this chapter, the 'East' comprises the USSR and Eastern Europe, with the latter including Bulgaria, Czechoslovakia, the German Democratic Republic (GDR), Hungary, Poland, and Romania. In turn, the 'West' comprehends the developed market economies of Western Europe, the United States, Canada, and Japan. However, space limitations preclude separate discussion of the participation of each of these Eastern and Western countries in East–West economic relations, or a complementary analysis of economic relations of Eastern or Western countries with less developed countries of the 'South'.

I Evolution of East–West Economic Relations in the 1970s

For political reasons on both sides, East–West economic relations were severely limited during the 'Cold War' which soon followed the military cooperation of the USSR with the United States, Canada, and Great Britain during the Second World War. From 1948 to the mid-1950s, the

I wish to thank Dennis O'Hearn and John Attarian for assistance in research; and the International Research and Exchanges Board for assistance in connection with a research trip to the USSR and Eastern Europe. I am grateful for valuable comments (not all of which I was able to incorporate in this essay) from Zbigniew M. Fallenbuchl, Edward A. Hewett, Zbigniew Kamecki, Paul Marer, Jacques de Miramon Fitz-James, and Nicholas Plessz.

United States and its allies sought to restrain the growth of Soviet (and East European) economic and military potential by controls on the exports of 'strategic' goods, restrictions on credits, and other obstacles to economic relations.[1] In turn, the USSR undertook to form an economic bloc by linking the Eastern European economies to it through a network of bilateral trade agreements. Although the Council for Mutual Economic Assistance (CMEA) was formally established in 1949, it was not a vehicle for either multilateralism or region-wide integration.[2]

However, already by the mid-1950s a gradual 'thaw' in this 'Cold War' situation had begun, and East–West trade continued to grow steadily, if quietly, during the 1960s as a result of new attitudes on each side.

In the East, by the late 1950s or early 1960s (depending upon the country), rates of growth of industrial production, national product, and labor and capital productivity had begun to fall from the impressive figures achieved during the preceding decade. A common (and politically acceptable) diagnosis of economists and policy makers was that these economies were moving from the 'extensive' to the 'intensive' phase of economic development.

In the former phase, according to this analysis, it had been necessary to alter the structure of the economy drastically and rapidly, through industrialization, urbanization, and changes in the content and geographical orientation of foreign trade. The methods chosen for these tasks were socialization of the means of production, comprehensive and detailed central planning, rapid expansion of the industrial labor force (through increased participation of women and transfers from agriculture), and a sharp increase in the rate of investment.

In contrast, in the new 'intensive' phase the emphasis of economic policy was no longer primarily on politically determined rapid structural change, as much as on smaller, more economically based changes in the composition of output and methods of producing it. Because neither the labor force nor the capital stock could be increased at the former high rates, greater efficiency in the use of limited inputs was essential. Furthermore, in the consumer sector, for certain goods (including some clothing, footwear, and simpler consumer durables), a shift was occurring from a sellers' to a buyers' market, as a result of the rise in living standards and the availability of stocks.

This diagnosis led to the prescription that 'reform' of the domestic economic system could improve economic performance from available resources – through one or both of two kinds of 'decentralization'.[3]

On the one hand the 'administrative decentralization' approach involved partial devolution of authority over selected decisions from higher to lower tiers within the administrative hierarchy – for instance, from the ministry to an intermediate 'association' level supervising the producing enterprise. The idea was that lower administrative agencies could make more sensible and more timely decisions on some aspects of the composition of output and production methods, though subject to constraints in the form of centrally set global output assignments and input authorizations.

In contrast, the 'economic decentralization' approach envisioned a greater role for domestic and foreign market forces in determining the composition of output, the allocation of resources, and even the distribution of income. Enterprise activities would be coordinated through 'horizontal' market links rather than a 'vertical' administrative command chain. Supply and demand forces, expressed through more flexible domestic prices (in turn related to world market prices), would guide decisions on outputs and inputs by profit-seeking firms.

However, fearing a loss of control over the economy and society, most CMEA regimes proved in practice unwilling to accept much of either type of decentralization. Thus, economic reforms either were not undertaken or did not survive long, except in Hungary, where a reform of the economic decentralization type (the 'New Economic Mechanism') was implemented to a significant, though incomplete, extent.

With genuine systemic reform widely rejected as too risky, Eastern regimes paid greater attention to the potential contribution of more extensive trade and investment relations with Western developed capitalist market economies to solving Eastern countries' problems of sagging growth rates and popular dissatisfaction with the rate of improvement in living standards. East–West economic relations offer Eastern countries three means of enhancing economic performance. One is the acquisition of machinery and equipment – especially sophisticated, up-to-date models – not available in the CMEA region. The second is purchase, for example through licenses, of 'know-how' about production processes not directly embodied in machinery. The third is credit to cover two types of 'gaps'. One type is a 'foreign exchange gap' in the form of a shortage of hard currency to pay for such imports from the West. The other type is a 'domestic saving gap' which exists because the strained Eastern economies lack the capital and appropriate labor resources for additional investment projects (even if they had the technical know-how to carry them out).

All the Eastern countries believed that the benefits just mentioned justified an expansion of their economic relations with the West, although it is difficult to show statistically the impact of (imported or domestic) technology on a country's economic growth.[4] However, only Poland went so far as to adopt an 'economic strategy' based primarily on modernizing the economy with massive imports of Western technology, equipment, and industrial materials, financed by large credits, which it hoped to repay by future exports to the West of competitive industrial goods produced in the new plants.[5] Other Eastern countries assigned East–West economic relations a more modest, though important, role in their development plans.

A further impetus for Soviet interest in expanding its own and Eastern Europe's economic relations with the West was the USSR's conclusion that during the 1960s its trade with Eastern Europe had become economically less advantageous for the USSR. Because changes in world market prices were reflected incompletely and with a lag in intra-CMEA trade, the USSR was supplying Eastern Europe raw materials and fuels in return for outdated machinery and poor quality manufactures. Instead, the USSR could sell its primary products to the West for higher prices and payment in convertible currency which could be used to buy advanced

Western machinery and technology and, in bad harvest years, grain.

On the Western side, business firms and banks responded to the further opening of the 'Eastern market' with lively competition in goods, technology, and credit. The Federal Republic of Germany (FRG), France, Italy, Great Britain, and Austria led in these initiatives in the mid-1960s. Then the active participation of American firms and financial institutions in East–West trade received a political imprimatur and stimulus in Soviet–American efforts at rapprochement and détente culminating in SALT I and other agreements reached at a 'summit' meeting in Moscow in May 1972 and subsequent American–Soviet agreements in October 1972 about trade, shipping, and credit.[6] The implementation of these agreements was subsequently curtailed by disputes over Soviet emigration policies and other issues, but American trade with the USSR continued to grow, financed by private credits and Soviet hard-currency earnings.

Thus, during the early 1970s Eastern imports from the West increased much faster than Eastern exports to the West, leading to large trade deficits which (in the absence of significant surpluses on other current account transactions) were financed by substantial Western credits and the accumulation of significant net indebtedness to the West. For example, from 1970 to 1973 Soviet imports from the West rose from $2.8 billion to $6.2 billion, and Soviet exports to the West from $2.4 billion to $5.1 billion. The cumulative deficit for the three years 1971–73 was $2.3 billion. East European imports from the West climbed from $5.1 billion in 1970 to $11.1 billion in 1973, while exports to the West increased from $4.4 billion to $8.5 billion, and the cumulative deficit during 1971–73 totaled $4.6 billion. As a result, according to representative estimates, the net hard-currency debt of the six East European countries grew from $4.6 billion at the end of 1970 to $8.5 billion at the end of 1973, and for the USSR the corresponding increase was from $1.9 billion to about $4.0 billion.[7]

In the mid-1970s the development of East–West economic relations was interrupted by OPEC-led increases in world oil prices and subsequent inflation and recession in industrialized market economies.

According to estimates of the United Nations Economic Commission for Europe (UNECE), presented in Table 3.1, although the value of Soviet

Table 3.1   *Trends in East–West Trade, 1974–78*
(Percentage change over same period of preceding year)

Period	Eastern Imports from West			Eastern Exports to West		
	Value	Prices	Volume	Value	Prices	Volume
1974	40	30	8	42	62	–12
1975	31	8	21	6	0	6
1976	5.0	–4.7	10.0	17.0	8.9	7.4
1977	1.0	9.7	–8.0	12.0	10.9	1.0
January–September 1978	16	8	8	11	9	2

Source: United Nations Economic Commission for Europe (UNECE), *Economic Survey of Europe in 1978*, Part I: *The European Economy in 1978*, Ch. 3, 'Recent Economic Developments in Eastern Europe and the Soviet Union' (mimeographed prepublication text, 20 March 1979), section 6, table 6.5.

and East European imports from the West grew by 40 percent in 1974 compared with 1973, price changes were largely responsible, as Eastern import prices rose by 30 percent and real volume by 8 percent, while Eastern export prices rose by 62 percent (68 percent for the USSR) and volume fell by 12 percent. In 1975, the 31 percent increase in Eastern imports was due primarily to a big volume increase (63 percent for the USSR, reflecting large purchases of food products). In contrast, the value of Eastern exports rose by only 6 percent, entirely due to greater volume at the same prices. In 1976, as business conditions in the West improved, Eastern exports to the West rose by 7.4 percent in real terms and prices increased 8.9 percent, yielding an increase of 17 percent in value. With this growth in export earnings and a 4.7 percent decline in import prices, the East was able to achieve a 10 percent increase in the volume of imports from the West, although the corresponding value increment was only 5 percent. However, in 1977 the growth of imports into the Western market economies fell sharply, and Eastern exports to the West rose by only 1 percent in volume though, thanks to a 10.9 percent increase in prices, by 12 percent in value. In turn, Eastern imports from the West fell 8 percent in volume but rose 1 percent in value as a result of a 9.7 percent increase in prices. In the first nine months of 1978, the value of Eastern imports from the West climbed 16 percent, because of equal increases in volume and prices, but the value of Eastern exports to the West grew 11 percent, chiefly because of a 9 percent rise in prices. Thus the Eastern trade deficit, which had been reduced in 1976 and 1977, grew in 1978.

Initially, the USSR was far more successful than Eastern Europe in reducing the trade deficit with the West by expanding exports and curtailing imports. Soviet exports to the West rose from $8.4 billion in 1975 to $10.3 billion in 1976 and $12.2 billion in 1977, while imports grew only modestly from $13.5 billion in 1975 to $14.4 billion in 1976, and then were cut back in 1977 to $13.4 billion, the 1975 level. As a result, the Soviet trade deficit with the West fell from $5.1 billion in 1975 to $1.2 billion in 1977. However, in 1978 the USSR's imports rose to $16.1 billion, while exports grew to only $13.0 billion, leading to a deficit of $3.1 billion.

As a group, the six East European countries boosted exports from $11.3 billion in 1975 to $12.8 billion in 1976, $13.3 billion in 1977, and $15.2 billion in 1978. But their imports from the West increased from $17.7 billion in 1975 to $19.2 billion in 1976, stagnated at $19.3 billion in 1977, and then climbed to $21.6 billion in 1978. As a result, Eastern Europe's trade deficit with the West in 1978 was $6.4 billion, the same as in 1975.

Progress in reducing Eastern trade deficits with the West (or in arresting their growth) will be difficult. A recent econometric study by Vaňous[8] yields activity elasticities for CMEA imports from the West well above unity, indicating rising shares for these imports in CMEA countries' domestic supplies of machinery and equipment, fuels and non-food raw materials, food and raw materials for food, and industrial consumer goods. The relation of import prices from the West to CMEA contract prices does play some role in determining imports of manufactured goods from the West, but it is not significant for primary products, which must be imported from the West when they are not available inside CMEA. On the other hand, for CMEA exports to the West, Vaňous[9] finds that activity elasticities are generally close to unity, indicating relatively constant shares for CMEA countries in Western imports of different commodities from all regions of the world. Price elasticities for CMEA exports to the West tend to be rather high, especially for machinery and equipment. Thus, price-cutting may be the only effective way of increasing sales of manufactured goods to Western markets.[10]

In this connection it is important to note that East–West trade is much more significant for the East than for the West. At present, it accounts for one-third to one-half of the total trade of each of the Eastern countries, but only about 4 percent of the total trade of the Western countries as a group (although the share is somewhat higher for some individual Western countries, like the FRG and Austria).

II   Eastern Debt to the West

The substantial Eastern trade deficits of the 1970s were financed by large borrowings from the West. On the Eastern side, the deficits in part arose unexpectedly from increases in world market prices for imported oil, food, and raw materials; from food purchases in bad harvest years; and from the depressing effect of Western recession on Eastern exports. In part, however, the size of the deficits reflected Eastern countries' efforts to sustain the real volume of imports close to planned levels despite unfavorable developments in import prices and export earnings. On the Western side, recession stimulated a competitive effort, usually supported by Western government credits, to expand exports, especially of capital goods, to the East. At the same time, Western financial institutions, facing weak demand for loans by Western firms, were anxious to lend to Eastern Europe at favorable rates of interest and maturities.[11]

Despite the importance, to both sides, of the growing Eastern net debt to the West, the pertinent statistical information available is seriously deficient. The East European countries publish virtually no relevant data at all, and the statistical reports of Western governments and international organizations are quite incomplete.[12] As a result, specialists' estimates of the debt are imprecise and vary considerably in (1) what kinds of official and private credit are included; (2) the choice among commitments, actual drawings, and obligations outstanding after repayments; (3) the use of gross or net liabilities of Eastern countries to Western banks; (4) emphasis on stock figures (like liabilities at a given date) versus flow figures (such as loan drawings over a particular period); (5) attention to the maturity distribution of outstanding obligations; (6) treatment of CMEA banks' indebtedness (sometimes included in the figures for the USSR and sometimes simply omitted); (7) possible double counting, for example, of bonds and supplier credit paper held by banks; (8) inclusion of short-term securities of Western governments held by Eastern countries outside Western banks; (9) recognition that the GDR's liabilities to, and deposits with, FRG banks are not reported as 'external' positions by the FRG; and

(10)treatment of the official FRG 'swing' credit to the GDR (in some years more than $1.0 billion).[13]

Therefore, the estimates presented below, though representative, must be regarded as only very approximate, not necessarily mutually consistent, and subject to revision as additional data become available.

According to the estimates in Table 3.2, for the East European countries as a group, net debt to the West rose from $13.1 billion at the end of 1974 to $31.7 billion at the end of 1977. For Bulgaria, Czechoslovakia, the GDR, and Hungary, the estimated net debt slightly more than doubled over the period, but it more than tripled for Poland, while increasing only by half for Romania. The USSR's estimated year-end net debt also grew rapidly, from $5.0 billion in 1974 to $16.0 billion in 1977. In addition, as a result of their Eurocurrency borrowings, the net year-end debt to the West of the CMEA banks (the International Bank for Economic Cooperation, IBEC, and the International Investment Bank, IIB) rose from $0.1 billion in 1974 to $1.7 billion in 1977. Thus, total Eastern net debt to the West at the end of 1977 was estimated at $49.4 billion.

Table 3.2   *Estimated Net Hard-Currency Debt of Eastern Europe, USSR, and CMEA Banks, End of Year, 1970, 1974–77*
(US$b.)

	1970	1974	1975	1976	1977
Bulgaria	0.7	1.2	1.8	2.3	2.7
Czechoslovakia	0.3	1.1	1.5	2.1	2.7
GDR	1.0	2.8	3.8	6.0	5.9
Hungary	0.6	1.5	2.1	2.8	3.4
Poland	0.8	3.9	6.9	10.2	13.0
Romania	1.2	2.6	3.0	3.3	4.0
Total Eastern Europe	4.6	13.1	19.1	25.7	31.7
USSR	1.9	5.0	10.0	14.0	16.0
CMEA banks	0	0.1	0.5	1.1	1.7
Total	6.5	18.2	29.6	40.8	49.4

Source: Paul Marer, Statement in *US Policy Toward Eastern Europe* (Hearings Before the Subcommittee on Europe and the Middle East, Committee on International Relations, US House of Representatives, 95th Congress, 2nd Session, September 7 and 12, 1978) (Washington, D.C.: US. Government Printing Office, 1979), p. 100.

Table 3.3 presents estimates, from another source, of the composition of the Eastern net debt by type of obligation on 31 December 1977. (It will be noted that the country total figures in the last column in Table 3.3 differ somewhat from those for 1977 in Table 3.2.) (1) Official credits, estimated at $22.3 billion, are commonly for the purchase of plant and equipment, and include both loans directly from Western government credit institutions and government-guaranteed private credit. Under a not fully observed OECD 'consensus' agreement about official credit support, the maximum maturity should not exceed $8\frac{1}{2}$ years and the minimum rate of interest should be 7.25 percent for 2–5 year credits and 7.75 percent for longer periods. Thus some interest subsidy is involved for exports from

Table 3.3 Estimated Composition of Net Hard-Currency Debt of Eastern Europe, USSR, and CMEA Banks, 31 December, 1977
(US$m.)

	Debt on Official Credits	Supplier Credits[a]	Net Liabilities to Western Banks[b]	Outstanding Bonds and Notes	IMF and IBRD Drawings	Total
Bulgaria	798	100	2,065	0	0	2,963
Czechoslovakia	841	200	884	0	0	1,925
GDR	2,455	400	3,729[c]	0	0	6,584
Hungary	460	0	3,630	180	0	4,270
Poland	5,775	1,200	6,890	82	0	13,947
Romania	1,256	200	1,073	0	670	3,199
Total Eastern Europe	11,585	2,100	18,271	262	670	32,888
USSR	10,730	2,200	3,411	0	0	16,341
CMEA banks	0	0	3,500	0	0	3,500
Total	22,315	4,300	25,182	262	670	52,729

[a] Including outstanding à forfait obligations.
[b] Banks in Group of Ten countries, Switzerland, and foreign branches of US banks in the Caribbean and Far East.
[c] Excluding net liabilities of GDR to banks in Federal Republic of Germany.
Source: East–West Markets, 15 May 1978, pp. 3 and 10.

Western countries with higher domestic market rates of interest.[14] (2) Supplier credits are usually granted on the basis of commercial paper documenting the repayment obligation. Part of the paper may be held by the exporter or used for collateral for his own bank loans, but a major part is sold on a nonrecourse basis to banks and specialized dealers. Since the Western exporter seeks to recover refinancing costs in the contract price quoted his Eastern customer, supplier credits are a relatively expensive form of credit for CMEA countries and are ordinarily used only when official credit support is not available. (3) Net indebtedness to Western banks, estimated at $25.2 billion, is the difference between Eastern gross liabilities to Western banks and Eastern deposits in them. These gross liabilities are varied, including 6 month–5 year promissory notes bought by banks from exporters, 6–7 year syndicated Eurocurrency loans, and 8–15 year bonds. Eurocurrency loans and bonds provide untied balance-of-payments financing – unlike official and supplier credits tied to purchases of particular goods in specific countries. (4) The international bond market and (5) international financial institutions are other sources of credit.

As Table 3.3 shows, Eastern countries differ in the extent to which they rely upon the various types of credit. For example, the USSR prefers official credit, not only for its political implications but also because interest rates are fixed (not floating) and relatively low and maturities are longer than on Eurocurrency bank loans. Furthermore, one-third of the total Soviet debt to the West is in credits associated with compensation deals providing for repayment in kind in the early 1980s (see Section III below). In contrast, Hungary relies primarily on commercial bank credit, with relatively small use of official credits and no supplier credits at all. The Hungarian authorities believe that by paying cash, obtained from Eurocurrency loans, they have a better choice of suppliers and can obtain better prices and delivery terms than by getting goods and financing in a single package. In general, countries with relatively big deficits, such as Poland and Bulgaria, have a large portion of their debt in bank loans. Little use has been made of the international bond market, and only Romania, as a member of the IBRD and IMF, is entitled to borrow from them.[15]

Because adequate information is lacking on the maturity structure and interest rates for much of this debt, it is difficult to reach a reliable appraisal of Eastern countries' ability to service it by making scheduled payments of interest and repayment of principal, and the risk of default or need for refinancing to avoid it. One indicator used by some analysts[16] is the 'debt-export ratio', measuring how many years it would take the country to pay off its present debt if (1) convertible currency exports continued at the same rate and (2) all of these export proceeds were devoted to principal repayments. However, this ratio does not take into account interest payments or the term structure of the debt (in other words, what portion is due when). A conceptually superior indicator is the 'debt-service ratio' obtained by taking (1) annual interest on all debt plus repayments of principal on medium- and long-term debt as a percentage of (2) annual merchandise exports for convertible currency. This ratio more directly measures the pressure on Eastern borrower countries to meet debt-service obligations by reducing hard-currency imports and/or increasing hard-currency exports – at the expense of domestic absorption and/or intra-CMEA sales.

Table 3.4 presents estimates of such debt-service ratios for each Eastern country for 1970 and 1973–77. They show Bulgaria and Poland in the most unfavorable positions, while the USSR and Czechoslovakia are in the most favorable situations. However, one should keep in mind that only merchandise exports are included in the denominator of the ratio, which therefore omits convertible currency earnings from services, such as tourism (important for Bulgaria) and shipping (significant for Poland).

Table 3.4   *Estimated Debt–Service Ratios[a] of Eastern Europe and USSR, 1970, 1973–77*
(Percent)

	1970	1973	1974	1975	1976	1977
Bulgaria	35	35	45	66	75	85
Czechoslovakia	8	15	17	22	30	34
GDR	20	25	24	27	33	40
Hungary	20	20	24	35	39	44
Poland	20	21	27	43	49	60
Romania	36	35	29	42	41	42
USSR	18	17	15	22	26	28

[a]Ratio of (1) repayments of principal on medium- and long-term debt (i.e., obligations of one year and over) plus interest payments on all debt to (2) convertible currency merchandise exports (including gold sales).
Source: William F. Kolarik, Jr., 'Statistical Abstract of East–West Trade Finance', in *Issues in East–West Commercial Relations* (a compendium of papers submitted to the Joint Economic Committee, 95th Congress, 2nd Session) (Washington, D.C.: US Government Printing Office, 1979), table 10, p. 201.

Although commercial bankers are reported to regard a debt-service ratio of 25 percent as a signal for caution,[17] they take many other factors into account in assessing risk and 'creditworthiness' for future loans. These other factors include, for example, the borrower's (1) total and per capita GNP; (2) foreign exchange and gold reserves; (3) current and prospective composition and volume of convertible currency exports of goods and services; and, not least, (4) prospective use of new loan funds to earn (or save) convertible currency.

Differences among borrowers in these respects affect the amount of credit, the period, and the interest rate that can be obtained. By these measures, Eastern borrowers have been ranked by Western lenders approximately as follows in regard to creditworthiness: (1) the USSR; (2) the CMEA banks; (3) Hungary; (4) Czechoslovakia and Romania; (5) Bulgaria and the GDR; and (6) Poland.[18] This order presumably reflects such considerations as the USSR's gold reserves and the self-liquidating character of the part of its debt incurred to exploit natural resources under compensation agreements, on the one hand, and Poland's high debt-service ratio and internal political problems, on the other.

Such distinctions among Eastern borrowers are unfounded according to the 'umbrella theory', which asserts that Eastern debt to the West is really collective, because the USSR, alone or with some other CMEA countries, would assist any CMEA country facing default, lest such a default make it more difficult for other CMEA nations to borrow. Such a collective CMEA obligation is not formally acknowledged by the member countries, nor do they claim, or even appear, to coordinate closely their individual borrowing in the West, except for IBEC and IIB loans for joint investment projects. However, insofar as Western lenders attach any weight to the 'umbrella theory', this would tend to make credit terms less favorable for the USSR (as CMEA's 'lender of last resort') and more favorable for, say, Poland, than they would otherwise be.

On the whole, Western lenders rate Eastern countries favorably compared to most less developed countries (LDCs). Eastern countries have lower debt/GNP and debt/convertible-currency–merchandise–export ratios than most LDCs and pay smaller interest rate spreads over LIBOR (the floating London Interbank Offered Rate) than most LDCs.[19]

As stressed above, the figures in Tables 3.2, 3.3, and 3.4 must be considered only approximate and tentative. Thus, a recently published study by US Central Intelligence Agency (CIA) economists concludes that previous Western estimates seriously overstated Soviet gross and net hard-currency indebtedness, particularly outstanding debt on official credits. The new CIA estimates, characterized by the authors as approximate 'mid-points' within a significant range, are summarized in Table 3.5. They put Soviet net debt at the end of 1977 at only $11.2 billion, compared with $16.0 billion in Table 3.2 and $16.3 billion in Table 3.3. Soviet debt on official credits at the end of 1977 is only $5.9 billion in Table 3.5, compared with $10.7 billion in Table 3.3. Furthermore, the CIA

Table 3.5 *Estimated Hard-Currency Debt of the USSR, End of Year, 1971–78*
(US$b.)

	Debt on Official Credits (1)	Commercial Debt[a] (2)	Deposits in Foreign Banks (3)	Total Net Debt[b] (Col. 1 + Col. 2 – Col. 3) (4)
1971	1.4	0.4	1.2	0.6
1972	1.6	0.9	1.9	0.6
1973	1.7	2.0	2.6	1.2
1974	2.4	2.8	3.5	1.7
1975	3.6	6.9	3.1	7.5
1976	5.2	9.7	4.7	10.1
1977	5.9	9.9	4.5	11.2
1978	6.9	10.3	6.0	11.2

[a]Sum of (1) claims, exclusive of government-supported credits, of banks of Group of Ten countries, Austria, Switzerland, Japan, and countries not reporting to the BIS, and (2) Soviet promissory notes held in the West but not included in reporting to the BIS.
[b]Components may not sum to total because of rounding.
Source: Paul G. Ericson and Ronald S. Miller, 'Soviet Foreign Economic Behavior: A Balance of Payments Perspective', in *Soviet Economy in a Time of Change* (a compendium of papers submitted to the Joint Economic Committee, 96th Congress, 1st Session) (Washington, D.C.: US Government Printing Office, 1979), Vol. 2, pp. 217–24.

estimates in Table 3.5 show no increase in total Soviet net hard-currency debt from the end of 1977 to the end of 1978. These figures in turn lead to a lower estimate of the Soviet debt-service ratio, for example, 24 percent in 1978, compared with the 28 percent shown in Table 3.4.

Finally, Table 3.6 presents recent estimates for the end of 1978 for each of the East European countries, the USSR, and the CMEA banks. The net figure for the USSR, $11.6 billion, is very close to the $11.2 billion in Table 3.5. However, in the absence of detailed explanations of the coverage and derivation of the figures in Tables 3.2, 3.3, and 3.6, one should not assume that they attempt to measure the same debt components and concepts.

Table 3.6 *Estimated Total Foreign Liabilities and Deposits in Foreign Banks of Eastern Europe, USSR, and CMEA Banks, 31 December, 1978* (US$b.)

	Total Foreign Liabilities	Deposits in Foreign Banks	Total Foreign Liabilities less Deposits in Foreign Banks
Bulgaria	4.0	0.6	3.4
Czechoslovakia	3.5	0.6	2.9
GDR	9.0	1.2	7.8
Hungary	7.3	0.9	6.4
Poland	17.5	0.8	16.7
Romania	4.4	0.2	4.2
Total Eastern Europe	45.7	4.3	41.4
USSR	17.2	5.6	11.6
CMEA Banks	5.8	0.4	5.4
Total	68.7	10.3	58.4

Source: Lawrence Brainard, 'East–West Financial Relations Prospects for the 1980s', in *Economic and Financial Aspects of East–West Cooperation* (Vienna: Zentralsparkasse und Kommerzbank, 1979), p. 31.

Western credit is likely to continue to be available to finance future Eastern trade deficits with the West, but it unlikely that the net debt outstanding will grow as dramatically as in the mid-1970s. The liquidity of Western banks, due to OPEC deposits, on the one hand, and weak business conditions in various Western countries, on the other, makes them willing to grant credit to Eastern borrowers. Also, it has proved very difficult to enforce OECD 'consensus' (or 'gentlemen's') agreements covering such aspects of official credit as the share of local cost financing, down payments, interest rates, and maturities.[20] Finally, Western banks strive hard to avoid default by refinancing debt, as shown by the experience of various LDCs and by a syndicated loan of $550 million to Poland in early 1979. But new Western credit is likely to be more selective, as lenders, concerned about Eastern debt-service ratios, require from Eastern borrowers (1) more information about their balance of payments and foreign exchange reserves, (2) greater restraint on imports, and (3) more evidence that Western loans will increase the Eastern country's hard-currency export potential.

III Countertrade

Their trade deficits and debt help explain Eastern countries' interest in 'countertrade' by which imports are financed through paired current or future exports. Several types of countertrade are usually distinguished, according to such criteria as (1) the duration of the agreement; (2) the size of the transactions; (3) the relative shares of credit, payments in cash, and payments in goods; (4) the kind of goods involved, including the extent to which the Eastern export is a 'resultant' product from an earlier Western export; (5) the 'counterdelivery ratio' expressing the value of Western purchases as a percentage of Eastern purchases; and (6) the legal forms of contract.[21]

Compensation agreements involve long-term (often 10–20 year) deals of relatively large value (hundreds of millions of dollars) providing for Eastern imports of equipment and technology from the West largely on credit and with subsequent repayment chiefly (but not necessarily exclusively) in 'resultant' products. The Western 'buyback' of 'reciprocal deliveries' usually begins at least several years after the Western exports, and the cumulative value of Western purchases may equal or even exceed the value of the Western exports (i.e. for a counterdelivery ratio of 100 percent or more). These 'product payback' deliveries are usually valued (annually) at the then prevailing world market prices less a discount to the Western firm to compensate it for marketing the product. Separate contracts cover the Eastern purchase of the Western equipment and the Western purchase of the Eastern product. Also, the Eastern obligation to repay Western credits is not conditional on the progress of counter-deliveries, although these of course earn convertible currencies which can be used for debt service.

Counterpurchase agreements, in contrast, are shorter-term (usually 3–5 year) deals (for machinery, semimanufactures, or raw materials) of smaller magnitude in which (1) technology transfer is not a major element, (2) the Eastern exports commonly have no intrinsic link to the Western exports, (3) there is little or no time lag between Eastern imports and Eastern exports, and (4) the counterdelivery ratio is usually less than 100 percent. The two legally separate contracts customarily provide for full cash payment at delivery, but in some cases the Eastern partner pays partly in cash and partly in goods, which must then be resold by the Western partner.

Less common in East–West trade are straight *barter* agreements consisting of one-time deals with a single contract covering offsetting deliveries over a relatively short period of a few years.

Finally, countertrade may also involve industrial cooperation, discussed below in Section IV. Countertrade arrangements appeal to Eastern countries as a way to finance imports, either by providing credit against future exports (as under compensation agreements) or by placing exports currently (as under counterpurchase agreements). When counterdelivery ratios exceed 100 percent (as for some Soviet and Polish natural resource projects), the Eastern country gets a surplus of convertible currency, above the cost of the linked imports, which is available to pay for other imports or debt service. Also, through Western partners Eastern countries often gain access to new markets which the Eastern countries could not successfully enter by themselves because they lack the necessary market information and sales and service units. Furthermore, central planning agencies look favorably on countertrade as a basis for multiyear planning of at least some imports and exports and related domestic production. These agencies believe that countertrade reduces fluctuations in, and uncertainty about, foreign trade, which they consider more difficult to plan and control than domestic economic activities.

In turn, Western firms engage in countertrade for two principal reasons. First, countertrade may be the only way to make export sales to Eastern customers lacking convertible currency. Second, through countertrade the Western firm can obtain assured supplies of raw materials, intermediate goods, components, or finished products on advantageous terms. Sometimes the countertrade deal may serve both objectives, but often the Western firm considers that the benefit comes from its export sale, while the linked import transaction must be accepted as a necessary cost.

Because countertrade is not explicitly so recorded in trade statistics, available data on countertrade are obtained chiefly from surveys of agreements by Western firms. This information is incomplete with regard to the magnitude, composition, and partners of countertrade agreements signed, on the one hand, and the actual subsequent flows of goods and services from West to East and from East to West, on the other hand. Also, the amount of credit associated with countertrade cannot be precisely identified.

There is more (though still rather incomplete) published information on compensation agreements than on counterpurchase deals, because the large size of the former usually requires some political and financial support by Western governments. A very rough estimate is that during 1969–77 compensation agreements providing for Western exports of at least $15 billion and perhaps as much as $22 billion were signed. New compensation agreements signed in 1977 provided for about $1.5 billion of Western exports to the East annually. Reverse flows are still small, because most of the Eastern projects have not yet been completed. However, a larger and increasing contribution to Eastern exports comes from counterpurchase deals, estimated to have been responsible for about one-fifth of Eastern exports to Western countries in recent years.[22]

On the Eastern side, the USSR accounts for two-thirds of the estimated total value of East–West compensation agreements, chiefly in natural gas, chemicals, and semifinished products.[23] Poland is responsible, in raw materials, metals, and manufactures, for about one-fourth of the Eastern total. The other East European countries' agreements are relatively small and concentrated in manufacturing. On the Western side, Italy, France, and the Federal Republic of Germany each account for about one-fourth of the estimated total value of compensation agreements.

The role of counterpurchase agreements in Eastern countries' trade varies both by the country and by the Western import commodity involved. For example, Bulgaria, with a relatively large hard-currency trade deficit, routinely requires a 40–50 percent counterdelivery ratio for

Western import transactions exceeding $1.0 million, while for chemical products a 100 percent counterdelivery ratio is sought. In the case of Hungary, imports for which hard currency has been allocated by planning agencies usually do not involve countertrade, whereas other imports normally require 100 percent counterdelivery ratios. In contrast, Romania seeks 100 percent counterdelivery ratios for nearly all imports from the West, even those in the five-year and annual foreign trade plans. Both the USSR and the GDR have stressed compensation rather than counterpurchase deals, while Poland has pursued both.[24]

Although there are some striking examples of large compensation agreements with high counterdelivery ratios – for instance, the USSR's multibillion dollar arrrangement covering the import of pipe, machinery, and equipment for a trans-European gas pipeline, to be repaid by natural gas deliveries to Western Europe – it is questionable how far countertrade can ease the East's hard-currency balance-of-payments problems.

First, the raw materials deals of greatest interest to Western partners are relevant only for a few Eastern countries. In the case of the USSR, they are typically of a magnitude requiring extensive negotiation and considerable Western official credit support. Construction times are long and projects are often completed behind schedule, with a considerable lag (of five or more years) before payback deliveries of resultant products begin.

Second, counterpurchase deals in manufactures are sometimes difficult to negotiate because of coordination problems on the Eastern side. The foreign trade organization (FTO) or ministry handling Eastern imports may have a small range or volume of suitable goods available for counterdeliveries. The Western partner may instead want – or at least be willing to accept – goods produced by other ministries, or sold by other FTOs, in the Eastern country.

Third, the manufactures that the East offers for countertrade are frequently hard to sell in the West. Their deficiencies in style, quality, and availability of spare parts and service are long-standing and well known and have proved hard to overcome. In addition, it is difficult to sell new Eastern products in Western markets when business conditions are sluggish and competition from aggressive and experienced Asian rivals like Taiwan and South Korea is severe. Furthermore (as discussed in Section V below) there is growing protectionism in Western developed countries affecting such current and potential Eastern exports as clothing, footwear, electronics, chemicals, steel, rubber tires, electric motors, and metal products.

Although Eastern countries press for wider use of counterpurchases, and higher counterdelivery ratios, countertrade can do little to overcome the shortcomings of Eastern products and weak domestic demand conditions and trade restrictions in Western markets.

IV Industrial Cooperation

Some countertrade, especially of the compensation type, is linked to 'industrial cooperation agreements' (ICAs). They establish a contractual relationship between Eastern and Western firms under which they pool certain assets and jointly coordinate their use in mutual pursuit of complementary objectives. The pooled assets may be tangible (plant or equipment) or intangible (patents or know-how). They may be transferred between the partners or remain in place. The agreement may involve a fee basis, an income-sharing scheme, or formal equity ties. Cooperation may cover production, investment, marketing, financing, and/or research and development. Thus, the range of activities included under the rubric of 'industrial cooperation' varies from one expert study to another.[25] As many as fourteen different activities can be distinguished, as shown in Table 3.7.

Table 3.7 *Types of Contractual Arrangements Included in Different Definitions of 'Industrial Cooperation'*

1 *Sale of equipment for complete production systems*
   Such as 'turnkey' plants (usually including technical assistance).
2 *Licensing*
   Of patents, copyrights, and production know-how.
3 *Franchising*
   Of trademarks and marketing know-how.
4 *Licensing or franchising*
   With provision also for *market-sharing and quality control.*
5 *Cooperative sourcing*
   This involves long-term agreements for purchases and sales *between partners* (especially exchanges of industrial raw materials and intermediate products).
6 *Subcontracting*
   Under a short-term (e.g., renewed annually) agreement, the subcontractor, *with existing facilities*, makes a product *to the specifications of the contractor*, who often also supplies materials or components.
7 *Sale of plant, equipment, and/or technology*
   Including 1–3 (above) but *with* complete or partial *repayment in resultant products.*
8 *Production contracting*
   This agreement provides for production, on a continuing basis to the partner's specifications, of intermediate or final goods to be incorporated into the partner's product or to be marketed by him. In contrast to (6) subcontracting, production contracting involves some *transfer of production capability*, in the form of capital equipment and/or technology (through a license or technical assistance contract).
9 *Coproduction*
   Usually on the basis of some shared technology and agreed specifications, the partners *specialize in producing and then exchange components*, so each makes the same final product for sale in his own market area. Usually the Eastern partner makes the simpler or more labor-intensive components, and the Western partner the more complicated or capital-intensive parts.
10 *Product specialization*
   The partners specialize *in making end products* and then exchange them so each has a full line for sale in his market area. In contrast to (5) cooperative sourcing, product specialization involves changes in existing end product lines.

(Table 3.7, *cont.*)

11 *Comarketing*

The partners (a) divide up market areas for some products, (b) sell and service each other's products in their respective market areas, and/or (c) sell jointly in third markets the products of one or both partners. In practice comarketing occurs together with other forms of industrial cooperation, like (4), (8), (9), and (10), or through (14), a separate joint venture marketing company.

12 *Project cooperation*

Often called 'joint tendering', this involves *East–West cooperation* in building plants, developing natural resources, and/or providing infra-structure facilities *in third (usually less developed) countries.* It is sometimes labeled 'tripartite' to acknowledge the participation of the host country.

13 *Joint research and development* (R & D)

The agreement provides for joint planning and conduct of R & D, and joint commercial rights to the resulting product or process technology.

14 *Joint venture*

For any of the above activities the partners form a special mixed company, ordinarily with joint equity participation, management, and risk- and profit-sharing.

Source: Carl H. McMillan, 'East–West Industrial Cooperation', in *East European Economies Post-Helsinki* (a compendium of papers submitted to the Joint Economic Committee, 95th Congress, 1st Session) (Washington, D.C.: US Government Printing Office, 1977), p. 1182.

The broadest definitions of ICAs, such as those commonly used by Soviet and East European authors, comprehend all or nearly all of these fourteen types. Intermediate definitions, employed for example by the United Nations Economic Commission for Europe, encompass types (6) through (14), but exclude types (1) through (5) as essentially straight commercial transactions. Finally, a still narrower conception includes only types (8) through (13), omitting types (6) and (7) as basically forms of countertrade and type (14) as a particular vehicle for conducting one or more of activities (1) through (13).

The activities in the commonly used intermediate, and even in the narrow, conception of ICAs appeal to Eastern countries as a way of obtaining Western equipment and technology without the expenditure of convertible currency. Furthermore, industrial cooperation is considered a more effective vehicle of technology transfer than, say, straight licensing, because the Western partner has a continuing interest in the production methods, cost, quality control, and product characteristics of Eastern output which the Western partner must absorb or market to others. In joint ventures the Western partner also contributes capital and manage-ment services. Finally, Eastern countries hope that deliveries under co-operation agreements can escape Western quantitative restrictions to which the goods involved would otherwise be subject (see Section V below).

In turn, ICAs often enable the Western partners to make otherwise impossible export sales – to Eastern partners, through them to other CMEA countries, or (in the case of joint tendering) with them outside CMEA to less developed countries. In some cases, industrial cooperation is a superior alternative to counterpurchases demanded by the East, because an industrial cooperation arrangement enables the Western partner to influence the quality and product mix of Eastern output to make it easier for the Western partner to absorb it or resell it without a loss. Also, through ICAs Western firms can effectively increase their production capacity by obtaining components or end products from their Eastern partners. Western firms consider the labor force in Eastern countries well trained, relatively cheap, and not likely to strike. Specialization by partners in different components or end products reduces costs through economies of scale and longer production runs. By selling Eastern partners' output, Western firms can expand the product lines they offer, without incurring new fixed investments in their own production facilities. Through comarketing, the Western firm can obtain market-sharing or representation arrangements which prevent prospective competition by the Eastern firm.[26]

Unfortunately, published information on East–West ICAs is incomplete and often not mutually consistent. As noted above, national governments, international agencies, and private scholars do not agree about the types or forms to be included, or how to classify a given set of activities. Because of the large size of some turnkey projects and compensation agreements, their inclusion or exclusion can significantly affect ICA statistics. Neither Western nor Eastern governments, nor international agencies, regularly collect and publish statistics on ICAs. Therefore, the available published information has been compiled (with different definitions and methods in different studies) chiefly from press reports and sample surveys of private Western firms. These estimates report the *number of agreements signed*, often including not only active agreements but also unimplemented and expired agreements. But the estimates do not tell the *value of the contracts*, progress in their actual *implementation*, or their *effect* on the volume and composition of the partners' output and sales or on international flows of goods and services.

Although the published estimates about ICAs signed are not fully comparable because of differences in the types included, the samples of firms surveyed, and the time period covered, they nonetheless indicate some of the main characteristics of East–West industrial cooperation so far.[27] By the end of 1976 about 1,200 ICAs had been signed between Western and Eastern partners (excluding Yugoslavia), and the number presumably is larger now. In the extent of participation in ICAs, the Eastern countries may be ranked roughly as follows: Hungary and Poland; the USSR and Romania; and Bulgaria, Czechoslovakia, and the German Democratic Republic. On the Western side, the order is the Federal Republic of Germany, Austria, and France; Italy, Sweden, and the United Kingdom; and Japan and the United States.

About three-fourths of ICAs concern producer goods and one-fourth consumer goods. Machine building is the leading branch of industry for ICAs, followed closely by chemicals and electronics and electrical equipment, with smaller but significant shares for transport equipment and metallurgy.

The most common form of ICA, accounting for almost half of the total, is coproduction involving coordinated specialization in production components to Western specifications on the basis of Western technology. Sale of plant, equipment, and technology with repayment in resultant products and joint ventures each represent about one-seventh of all ICAs. Other types, such as subcontracting and project cooperation, are of minor importance.

Certain forms of cooperation are especially common in particular branches of industry – for example, coproduction in machine building and chemicals; supply of plants in chemicals; licensing in electronics and electrical equipment, transport equipment, and machine building; and subcontracting in light industry, machinery, and transport equipment.[28]

Despite the number and variety of ICAs, in 1978 they were responsible for only 3–4 percent of total East–West trade flows and 10–15 percent of East–West trade in manufactures, according to UNECE estimates.[29]

Various problems hamper the negotiation of ICAs, on the one hand, and their implementation, on the other.[30]

In the *negotiation* process, the Western partner must deal not only (or even chiefly) with an Eastern firm but also with the appropriate branch ministry and various central agencies responsible for foreign economic relations, technology, foreign exchange, investment, etc. The interests and objectives of all the Eastern actors seldom coincide. In particular, although a high-level political decision may cause (some or most) organizations above the firm to pursue ICAs actively, enterprise managements are often disinterested in, and tacitly opposed to, industrial cooperation. Managers fear it will require new investment and technology, upset established input and output programs, lead to unattainable output and export assignments, and thus jeopardize their bonuses and job security.

The Eastern and Western sides often disagree over the content of the ICA, including the varieties and models to be made and the standards and supervision of quality control. In regard to the choice of technology, the East usually seeks to obtain the latest technology in capital-intensive industries, while Western firms often prefer to transfer more labor-intensive processes based on standard (or even aging) technology. The two sides may also disagree on the scale of operation and volume of output, as well as on the life of the ICA.

Pricing in ICAs is often troublesome. In the internal price systems of CMEA countries, administratively set producer prices do not incorporate all relevant costs or measure relative scarcities of inputs and outputs. In turn, arbitrary Eastern official exchange rates do not reflect relative price and cost levels compared with other countries. Thus, ICAs must find some agreed pricing scheme involving world market prices in convertible currencies to value different kinds of East–West deliveries over a number of years.

Joint ventures located in Eastern countries are the most difficult form of ICA to negotiate, on both political and economic grounds.[31] Insofar as they appear to involve foreign private ownership of (some of) the means of production – and foreign participation in the management of labor and capital – in a socialist country, joint ventures face serious ideological and constitutional obstacles on the Eastern side. Also, the calculation, sharing, and taxation of profits and their remittance to the West must be settled.

Thus, most of the existing East–West joint ventures are sales and service companies located in the West. Only Romania and Hungary have followed the Yugoslav precedent by establishing East–West joint ventures inside a socialist country, and both their number (nine in Romania and three in Hungary) and their capitalizations are small.[32]

Nor is the *implementation* of signed ICAs always smooth. In surveys Western partners express various complaints. Construction schedules for new facilities in Eastern countries often are not met. The transfer of technology is sometimes hampered by the Eastern practice of assigning R & D and production responsibilities to different organizations. Many important decisions affecting the Eastern partner's production and sales are made not by the enterprise itself but by supervising agencies controlling the allocation of inputs, the distribution of output, and pricing. In the 'tautly planned' Eastern economies, shortages of materials and spare parts are not unusual. Finally, Eastern partners, used to supplying CMEA customers, frequently find it difficult to meet quality standards under ICAs.

Eastern partners' dissatisfaction with ICA experience focuses on the marketing of cooperative deliveries in the West. Accustomed to the more stable controlled domestic and CMEA markets, they dislike the fluctuations in volume and prices of sales, and in exchange rates, that occur on the world market. They would like deliveries under ICAs to be exempt from Western tariffs and quantitative restrictions. The East believes that Western customs duties on Eastern shipments under production contracting or subcontracting should be levied only on the value added in the East, not on the total value including materials originally supplied by the Western partner. Finally, Eastern partners sometimes complain that there is an excessive marketing margin for the Western partner between what it pays for Eastern goods and what it earns by reselling them in the West.

So far industrial cooperation has been of greater qualitative than quantitative significance in the development of East–West economic relations. Industrial cooperation provides a potential basis for close long-term links between Eastern and Western partners in technology transfer, production, and marketing. But up to now ICAs have consisted chiefly of simpler types like coproduction, rather than more complex kinds like production specialization and joint ventures, and they have played a relatively small role in East–West trade.

Several factors will influence the future growth of East–West industrial cooperation. One is Eastern governments' decisions about the nature of their economic development plans and the distribution of their foreign trade among the CMEA nations, the industrialized West, and the less developed countries. Another is the speed with which the Western and Eastern sides in ICA negotiations learn to adapt to differences in their respective objectives, management methods, and government regulations. Finally, it has been suggested that the progress of industrial cooperation may be sensitive to Western business cycles.[33] In the expansion phase, Western firms are likely to be interested in raising their sales capacity through short-term ICAs for subcontracting and production contracting (and to a lesser extent coproduction and product specialization). In the recession phase, Western firms will not seek such capacity-raising arrangements, and may even try to reduce commitments under earlier agreements. But Western firms will then have a greater interest in longer-term ICAs for sales of plant and equipment, joint tendering, and joint ventures – under which Eastern reciprocal deliveries (if any) will start some years later.

V Trade Controls

Four kinds of trade restrictions affect East–West trade: (1) Eastern export restrictions, (2) Eastern import restrictions, (3) Western export restrictions, and (4) Western import restrictions.

Eastern Export and Import Restrictions
In Eastern planned economies, both exports and imports are subject to comprehensive quantitative controls as part of the system of central economic planning of production and its disposition. Thus foreign trade plans regulate the quantity, composition, and destination of exports, on the one hand, and the quantity, composition, and origin of imports, on the other. Import tariffs play only a nominal role, because changes in customs duties do not necessarily lead to corresponding changes in domestic selling prices, nor to changes in foreign exchange allocations by planning agencies.

Through these quantitative restrictions, Eastern governments limit exports to the West in order to satisfy domestic requirements and meet CMEA commitments, both of which have high priorities for political as well as economic reasons. In turn, quantitative controls curtail imports from the West to what the East's limited resources of convertible currencies permit.[34]

Western Export Restrictions
Western restrictions on exports to the East are primarily of a political–military, rather than an economic–commercial, origin. Therefore, these restrictions have been reduced markedly as East–West political relations have improved in the last fifteen to twenty years.

The multilateral framework for Western export restrictions is provided by the Coordinating Committee (Cocom) established in 1949 at the instance of the United States.[35] It includes the NATO countries (except Iceland) and Japan and is located in Paris. Cocom maintains a 'control' list of items not to be exported to Communist countries because (1) they are weapons or equipment for producing weapons, (2) they contain unique technology of military significance, or (3) they are materials whose scarcity affects Communist countries' military potential. However, the Cocom member countries must agree unanimously to put an item on the control list. Also, member countries decide individually if a proposed sale by one of their firms involves an embargoed item, and, if so, whether to submit an 'exception request' to Cocom for unanimous approval by the member countries.

The United States has long sought a more restrictive Cocom embargo than the other members desired. The latter are much more dependent on exports, are more involved in trade with the East, and tend to separate trade from politics to a greater extent. In the first decade of Cocom, the United States could secure compliance with its views from allies dependent on American aid for recovery from the Second World War. But by the 1960s American leverage had declined considerably, and both the scope of the embargo list and adherence to it by other member countries were reduced. Thus in practice the United States has often applied stricter controls than most other Cocom members on exports to the East.

However, discussions preceding revision of the US Export Administration Act in 1979 showed growing acceptance by American policy makers of the following propositions:[36] (1) Only a relatively very small range of goods can be included in an embargo list acceptable to, and observed by, all Cocom members. (2) Denial of these goods to the East will have little effect on the development of Eastern economic, as distinct from narrowly military, potential. (3) An American policy on exports to the East more restrictive than the effective policies of the other Cocom members can succeed in denying only very few goods and technologies to the East. More often, such a more restrictive American policy – about the embargo list and/or licensing procedures – simply puts American firms at a disadvantage in competition with West European and Japanese rivals. (4) Thus, American export restrictions to express disapproval of another country's domestic or foreign policies (e.g. 'human rights' or involvement in Africa) are usually only symbolic gestures, and the goods withheld by the United States (or a satisfactory substitute) will be supplied by other Western countries. (5) To increase its exports, the United States should make its export controls more like those of other Western countries, by interpreting the list of embargoed items in the same way and by simplifying and speeding export licensing procedures. This new perspective is reflected in the provisions of the new US Export Administration Act, enacted 29 September 1979.[37]

Western Import Restrictions

Because Eastern quantitative restrictions on exports to and imports from the West are considered inherent in the nature of Eastern economic systems, while Western export controls are very limited, most of the attention to restrictions in East–West trade has been directed to Western constraints on imports from the East.

Eastern exports already encountering strong protectionist actions in the West include textile yarns and fabrics, clothing, footwear, and iron and steel products. Less severe, or only incipient, are Western restrictions on Eastern textile fibers, chemicals, manufactured fertilizer, plastic materials, metal manufactures, electrical equipment and electronic products, and transport equipment.[38]

Western governments limit imports from the East in various ways. In regard to tarriffs, West European countries have granted *de jure* or *de facto* most-favored-nation (MFN) treatment to the East, but the United States currently accords MFN treatment only to Poland, Romania, and

Hungary. The East complains that the common external tariff of the European Economic Community (EEC) puts Eastern exports of manufactured goods at a disadvantage in competition with goods (a) produced in EEC countries or (b) covered by free trade arrangements between the EEC and the European Free Trade Association. But these are basic relationships which cannot be altered by negotiations between Eastern countries and the EEC (see below).

'Variable levies' imposed by the EEC under its Common Agricultural Policy severely limit exports of agricultural products by Bulgaria, Hungary, Poland, and Romania.

Quotas have long been used by Western countries to limit imports of particular goods from the East. From the early 1960s to the mid-1970s West European import quotas on Eastern products were gradually but steadily relaxed by raising the amount of the quota, by freeing some goods completely from quota restrictions, or by eliminating quotas altogether. However, under recession conditions in the mid-1970s, this 'liberalization' process slowed down, and new 'safeguard' actions were taken by various Western countries to restrict imports from the East of such goods as glass, synthetic textile fibers, clothing, and steel.

Eastern countries are especially vulnerable to charges of 'dumping' through sales at 'less than fair value', defined as an export price below the cost of production, because (as explained in Section IV above) Eastern costing, pricing, and exchange rates are all deemed arbitrary by Western standards. Thus, Western governments may levy countervailing duties if the price of the Eastern good is less than the cost of production, or export price, in some market economy judged to be at a comparable level of economic development, or if the Eastern price is less than an officially established 'reference price'. However, Western anti-dumping charges and countervailing duties against Eastern products were rare until the mid-1970s. Since then, anti-dumping actions have been taken by the EEC against Eastern exports of steel, and threatened for some other products, including chemicals, rubber tires, electric motors, and paper. In the United States, anti-dumping actions have been sought against ammonia, steel, and other products from the East.[39]

To avoid Western import quotas and anti-dumping measures, Eastern countries have signed 'export restraint agreements' establishing maximum quantities, and sometimes also minimum prices, for their exports to Western countries. For example, Poland and Romania have agreed to limit exports of textiles and apparel to the EEC and the United States. Recent agreements between the EEC and Czechoslovakia, Hungary, Poland, and Romania fix the volumes and also set minimum prices for their steel exports to the EEC.

Thus in recent years Western import restrictions have grown both in the number of products covered and in the sophistication of the measures used. These restrictions can, of course, affect all potential sources of imports, including not only the East but also less developed countries and even other industrialized capitalist market economies.

Both structural and cyclical factors are responsible for the increase in Western protectionism. Structural causes include the slow growth in labor productivity, compared to wages, in more labor-intensive industries like clothing and footwear, and difficulties in reallocating labor and capital to other branches in which industrialized Western economies possess a comparative advantage. Trade unions and business usually prefer protection to preserve their present markets for existing products, rather than 'adjustment assistance' to help them shift to new products. Cyclical factors exacerbate the situation. First, structural changes are always more difficult when aggregate demand is weak and unemployment is high. Second, in cyclically sensitive industries like steel, excess capacity leads to severe competition, price-cutting, charges of dumping, and petitions for protection against imports.

Protection is likely to grow if Western economies continue, into the 1980s, to restrain aggregate demand in their efforts to curb domestic inflation due, in part, to rising world oil prices. And when import quotas are imposed – unilaterally or through nominally 'voluntary' bilateral or multilateral export restraint agreements – on the basis of historical market shares for particular products, newer suppliers, including Eastern countries, will be at a disadvantage compared to more established suppliers, like Taiwan, South Korea, and Brazil.

It is not clear to what extent Eastern exports to the West would be aided by the conclusion of an agreement between the CMEA and the EEC, under discussion since 1975.[40]

Until 1973, the EEC states concluded bilateral trade agreements with individual Eastern countries. But under the EEC's Common Commercial Policy, since 1 January, 1973, only the Commission of the European Communities (or EC, consisting of the EEC, the European Coal and Steel Community, and the European Atomic Energy Commission) has the right to negotiate trade agreements with nonmember countries. The Commission is also responsible for establishing common rules and procedures for the application of quantitative restrictions by EEC member countries against state-trading countries, for conducting import surveillance, and for carrying out anti-dumping actions. However, individual EEC states continue to set the actual import quotas for specific goods from particular Eastern countries; to negotiate 'economic cooperation' (as distinct from 'trade') agreements with Eastern countries; and to decide their own policies for official credits to the East.

Since the expiration of existing bilateral trade agreements at the end of 1974, there have been no formal trade agreements between the EEC and the Eastern countries, because the latter so far have been unwilling to sign such agreements with the EC Commission. In practice this has meant that earlier arrangements have been continued, but that no progress can be made by the East (with the exception of Romania, as explained below) in securing from the EEC tariff cuts, concessions in the application of the Common Agricultural Policy, or an EEC-wide commitment to reduce quantitative restrictions. These are much more important questions for the East than for the EEC, because EEC–East trade represents more than half of the East's total trade with the West but only about 4 percent of the EEC's total external trade. And they are much more significant for the six small East European countries than for the USSR. The former find their exports of agricultural products and manufactured goods limited by EEC trade restrictions, while Soviet exports to the EEC consist chiefly of primary products not subject to tariffs or import quotas.

In 1974 the EC Commission proposed separate negotiations with each Eastern country on tariffs, import quotas, 'safeguard' mechanisms in emergency situations, and problems of payments and financing of trade. In 1976, the East responded with a counterproposal for negotiations with the EEC not by the Eastern countries individually but on their behalf by the CMEA (whose statutes had been amended in June 1974 to give the CMEA Council explicit authority to conclude international agreements with nonmember nations and international organizations). The EC replied that trade negotiations had to be conducted separately with each Eastern country because the CMEA (unlike the EC) did not have supranational authority over the trade of its members. However, the EC expressed a willingness to conclude an agreement with the CMEA on subjects other than commercial policy, for example, the exchange of statistical data and forecasts. Despite subsequent meetings of EC and CMEA representatives in Brussels and Moscow, the gap between the two positions has apparently not been narrowed significantly. Although it may take some years, a compromise may be found whereby the EC and the CMEA would conclude a broad and vague framework agreement which would provide for official recognition of the EC by the CMEA and under which the CMEA would then acquiesce in subsequent negotiations with the EC by individual Eastern countries belonging to the CMEA.[41]

However, the results of such negotiations might be limited. First, the EC has only partial control over EEC quotas and no effective jurisdiction over official export credit programs and various aspects of East–West bilateral governmental 'economic cooperation' agreements. Second, the East is unlikely to get from the EC any significant concessions in its Common Agricultural Policy. Finally, various concrete issues in EEC–East economic relations are being tackled in the absence of formal trade agreements. For example, in 1974 the EC included Romania in the 'generalized system of tariff preferences' for less developed countries and granted it concessions on various nonagricultural products, and in February 1979 the EC opened negotiations to raise or eliminate quotas on a wide range of industrial products from Romania. Also, the EC has made 'technical agreements' covering agricultural products with Bulgaria, Poland, Hungary, and Romania, and export restraint accords for textiles with Poland and Romania and for steel with Czechoslovakia, Hungary, Poland, and Romania. Thus, individual Eastern countries have de facto contact with the EEC despite the lack of de jure recognition.

VI Eastern Participation in International Economic Organizations

The Eastern countries could increase their involvement in the world economy by joining international economic organizations like the General Agreement on Tariffs and Trade (GATT) and the International Monetary

Fund (IMF) and International Bank for Reconstruction and Development (IBRD, or World Bank).

GATT

The extent of Eastern participation in GATT is varied. Czechoslovakia was one of the original contracting parties in 1948. Poland, Romania, and Hungary became full members, respectively, in 1967, 1971, and 1973. Bulgaria has been an observer since 1967. The USSR and the German Democratic Republic have never belonged to GATT.[42]

Because (as explained in Section V above) in centrally planned economies (CPEs) tariff concessions ordinarily do not assure a corresponding increase in imports, GATT's policy has been to admit CPEs (after Czechoslovakia) only through special protocols in which they make commitments to increase imports in return for MFN treatment and other privileges of GATT. Poland agreed to a 7 percent annual increase in the value of imports from GATT members as a group, and Romania promised to raise imports from GATT countries at least as fast as the rate of growth of total imports specified in the Romanian five-year plan. The protocol with Hungary contains no such explicit commitment, apparently because the Hungarian negotiators convinced GATT that under Hungary's 'New Economic Mechanism' changes in its customs tariffs did affect the volume of imports.

GATT membership is advantageous to Eastern countries for several reasons. The Eastern country gets MFN treatment for all tariff cuts previously negotiated and to be negotiated by GATT. GATT also provides a forum to discuss nontariff barriers to Eastern exports, such as quantitative restrictions. Despite their aggregate commitment to increase imports from GATT as a whole, Eastern countries can still favor one Western country over another in the allocation of Eastern import quotas. In biennial discussions and annual questionnaires, GATT does not press Eastern countries for information on prices, quantities, and other aspects of trade which they do not wish to disclose.

Although in economic terms the benefits appear to outweigh the costs of GATT membership, the USSR has shown no interest in joining GATT, perhaps because it is unwilling to accept the qualified membership status for CPEs. In turn, the Soviet position has influenced the attitudes toward GATT of Bulgaria, Czechoslovakia, and the German Democratic Republic.

IMF and IBRD

To countries with balance-of-payments problems, the IMF and IBRD are important potential sources, respectively, of short-term and long-term convertible currency credit. However, membership in the IMF and IBRD involves obligations to supply information on foreign trade, gold and foreign exchange reserves, and domestic economic activity, and also to work toward reducing foreign exchange restrictions and making the national currency convertible.

Although the USSR participated in the Bretton Woods Conference establishing the IMF and IBRD, it did not sign the resulting agreement.

Poland and Czechoslovakia did join, but withdrew in 1950 and 1954, respectively.

Romania became a member of the IMF and IBRD in 1972 under a special agreement by which the data it submits to them are kept confidential. So far Romania has borrowed over $300 million from the Fund and over $1.1 billion from the Bank.

It does not seem likely that other Eastern countries, except possibly Hungary and Poland, will follow Romania into the IMF and IBRD in the near future. There are various obstacles to the entry of the USSR, whose position in turn affects that of other Eastern countries.[43] The USSR has advocated basing the world monetary system on gold, presumably with fixed exchange rates, rather than on the IMF's 'special drawing rights', which are linked to a basket of convertible currencies under a scheme of floating (though still managed) exchange rates. Under the IMF charter, member countries' shares in voting rights and control depend upon the size of their contributions in gold and convertible currencies. With the ruble inconvertible, it is unlikely that the USSR could make a contribution large enough to give it the voice in the IMF it would want in view of its status as a world power. It is questionable whether, for prestige reasons, the USSR could join the IMF with the kind of exceptions regarding convertibility and the disclosure of information granted to a small country like Romania. Finally, the USSR may believe that it does not need access to IMF and IBRD resources because, with a good debt service record and potential natural resource exports, it can obtain adequate convertible currency financing from official export credits, supplier credits, and Eurocurrency loans.

VII Conclusion

The critical element in the development of East–West economic relations in the 1980s is the East's ability to finance imports from the West. Eastern convertible currency earnings will depend on (1) the goods available for export to the world market after domestic requirements and CMEA commitments are satisfied, (2) the demand for these goods in the West and in oil-exporting LDCs, and (3) their world market prices. But only part of these hard-currency revenues will be available for imports from the West after the East meets debt service obligations and buys oil from OPEC. Additional imports from the West must then be covered by new credits, including the recycling of OPEC deposits in Western countries.

Weak demand conditions in Western countries and rising protectionism will make it difficult to boost Eastern exports to the West, even through countertrade or on the basis of industrial cooperation agreements. Although Western official and private banks will extend further credit to the East, they are likely to be more selective than in the past.

The general picture for East–West economic relations in the early 1980s is thus somber, although the situation of particular Eastern countries will necessarily vary according to such important factors as the composition of exports, the debt service ratio, access to international credit institutions, and political relationships.

For example, the USSR's ability to expand imports from the West will depend both upon economic factors, notably the size of Soviet oil production and exports to the world market, and upon political factors, like the response of major Western powers to the Soviet invasion of Afghanistan in December 1979. Of the East European countries, Hungary may have the best prospects because of the greater flexibility of its economic system under the 'New Economic Mechanism' and its commitment to integration with the world economy. (These are discussed below in Chapters 9 and 10.) Romania has the advantage of access to credit from the IMF and IBRD. Because of its special relationship with the Federal Republic of Germany, the German Democratic Republic has access to EEC markets as well as favorable official credit from the Federal Republic of Germany. In contrast, Poland will have the greatest difficulties in economic relations with the West, as it will require periodic refinancing of its debt, despite stringent measures to limit its hard-currency imports and the resulting decline in its economic growth. Bulgaria and Czechoslovakia are in an intermediate position – in a less serious situation than Poland but without special favorable factors like Hungary, Romania, or the German Democratic Republic.

Finally, both the East's interest in developing economic relations with the West and its ability to do so are closely linked to the evolution of Soviet–East European economic relations, discussed below in Chapter 6.

Notes: Chapter 3

1 Gunnar Adler-Karlsson, *Western Economic Warfare, 1947–1967* (Stockholm: Almqvist & Wiksell, 1968), provides a detailed account.
2 See, for example, Michael Kaser, *Comecon*, 2nd edn (London: Oxford University Press, 1967).
3 For a detailed analysis, see Morris Bornstein, 'Economic Reform in Eastern Europe', in *East European Economies Post-Helsinki* (a compendium of papers submitted to the Joint Economic Committee, 95th Congress, 1st Session) (Washington, D.C.: US Government Printing Office, 1977), pp. 102–34.
4 See, for example, Donald W. Green and Herbert S. Levine, 'Macroeconometric Evidence of the Value of Machinery Imports to the Soviet Union', in John R. Thomas and Ursula Kruse-Vaucienne (eds), *Soviet Science and Technology: Domestic and Foreign Perspectives* (Washington, D.C.: The George Washington University for the National Science Foundation), pp. 394–425; and Stanislaw Gomulka, 'Growth and the Import of Technology: Poland, 1971–1980', *Cambridge Journal of Economics*, Vol. 2, No. 1 (March 1978), pp. 1–16.
5 Zbigniew M. Fallenbuchl, 'The Polish Economy in the 1970s', in *East European Economies Post-Helsinki*, op. cit., pp. 826–38.
6 Edward T. Wilson, David K. Katz, Suzanne F. Porter, Bonnie M. Pounds, and Gilbert M. Rodgers, 'US–Soviet Commercial Relations', in *Soviet Economic Prospects for the Seventies* (a compendium of papers submitted to the Joint Economic Committee, 93rd Congress, 1st Session) (Washington, D.C.: US Government Printing Office, 1973), pp. 638–59.
7 Joan Parpart Zoeter, 'Eastern Europe: The Growing Hard Currency Debt', in *East European Economies Post-Helsinki*, op. cit., p. 1352; and Paul Marer, 'Indebtedness, Credit Policies, and New Sources of Financing', in Carl H. McMillan (ed.), *Changing Perspectives in East–West Commerce* (Lexington, Mass.: D. C. Heath, 1974), p. 129. Reasons for differences in Western estimates of Eastern indebtedness are discussed in Section II below.

8 Jan Vaňous, 'The Determinants of Imports of the CMEA Countries from the West', Discussion Paper No. 78–34 (Vancouver, British Columbia: Department of Economics, University of British Columbia, 1978; mimeo).
9 Jan Vaňous, 'The Determinants of Exports from the CMEA Countries to the West', Discussion Paper No. 78–35 (Vancouver, British Columbia: Department of Economics, University of British Columbia, 1978; mimeo).
10 However, these calculations involve a high degree of aggregation, and calculations with more disaggregated product groups may show lower price elasticities for Eastern exports.
11 The origin and nature of the Eastern debt to the West are examined in detail in Richard Portes, 'East Europe's Debt to the West: Interdependence Is a Two-Way Street', *Foreign Affairs*, Vol. 55, No. 4 (July 1977), pp. 751–82.
12 Bank for International Settlements (BIS), *Manual on Statistics Compiled by International Organisations on Countries' External Indebtedness* (Basle: BIS, 1979), explains in detail what is included and excluded in statistics compiled by the BIS, International Bank for Reconstruction and Development (IBRD, or World Bank), International Monetary Fund (IMF), and Organization for Economic Cooperation and Development (OECD).
13 On these issues, see, for example, Kathryn Melson and Edwin M. Snell, 'Estimating East European Indebtedness to the West', in *East European Economies Post-Helsinki*, op. cit., pp. 1369–95.
14 However, the significance of interest rate differences is diminished by inflation, which reduces the real burden of payments of both interest and principal. Also, under a regime of floating exchange rates, lower (higher) interest rates can be offset by appreciation (depreciation) of the lender's currency.
15 For a more detailed discussion of differences in country borrowing practices and reasons for them, see 'Comecon Borrowing on International Credit Markets', in OECD, *Financial Market Trends*, No. 2 (December 1977), pp. 63–74. This source (p. 79) reports different figures for international bond offerings, namely, as follows (in millions of US dollars): Hungary, 289; Poland, 133; and Romania, 100.
16 For instance, Benedykt Askanas, Halina Askanas, and Friedrich Levcik, 'East–West Trade and CMEA Indebtedness up to 1980', in Friedrich Levcik (ed.), *International Economics – Comparisons and Interdependences: Festschrift for Franz Nemschak* (Vienna and New York: Springer-Verlag, 1978), pp. 183–97.
17 *Economic Relations between East and West: Prospects and Problems* (a tripartite report by fifteen experts from the European Community, Japan, and North America) (Washington, D.C.: Brookings Institution, 1978), p. 24.
18 Cf. OECD, 'Comecon Borrowing', op. cit., pp. 63–74.
19 Lawrence H. Theriot, 'Communist Country Hard Currency Debt in Perspective', in *Issues in East–West Commercial Relations* (a compendium of papers submitted to the Joint Economic Committee, 95th Congress, 2nd Session) (Washington, D.C.: US Government Printing Office, 1979), pp. 179–85.
20 See, for example, *East–West Markets*, 17 October 1977, pp. 5–6; 23 January 1978, pp. 9–10; 12 June 1978, pp. 7–8; and 30 October 1978, p. 8.
21 Comprehensive recent surveys of East–West countertrade include US Department of Commerce, Industry and Trade Administration, *East–West Countertrade Practices*, by Pompiliu Verzariu, Scott Bozek, and JeNelle Matheson (Washington, D.C.: US Government Printing Office, 1978); JeNelle Matheson, Paul McCarthy, and Steven Flanders, 'Countertrade Practices in Eastern Europe', in *East European Economies Post-Helsinki*, op. cit., pp. 1277–1311; Organization for Economic Cooperation and Development (OECD), *Countertrade Practices in East–West Economic Relations* (Paris: OECD, 1979); and United Nations Economic Commission for Europe (UNECE), *Countertrade Practices in the ECE Region* (Trade/R. 385, 9 November 1979).
22 UNECE, *Economic Survey of Europe in 1978*, Part I: *The European Economy in 1978*, Ch. 3, 'Recent Economic Developments in Eastern Europe and the Soviet Union' (mimeographed prepublication text, 20 March 1979), p. 129.
23 Dennis J. Barclay, 'USSR: The Role of Compensation Agreements in Trade with the West', in *Soviet Economy in a Time of Change* (a compendium of papers submitted to the Joint Economic Committee, 96th Congress, 1st Session) (Washington, D.C.: US Government Printing Office, 1979), Vol. 2, pp. 462–81.
24 On differences in countertrade practices among Eastern countries, see US Department of Commerce, *East–West Countertrade Practices*, op. cit., Ch. 5.

25 Major sources on East–West industrial cooperation include Carl H. McMillan, 'East–West Industrial Cooperation', in *East European Economies Post-Helsinki*, op. cit., pp. 1175–1224; C. T. Saunders (ed.), *East–West Cooperation in Business: Inter-Firm Studies* (Vienna and New York: Springer-Verlag, 1977); and Friedrich Levcik and Jan Stankovsky, *Industrielle Kooperation zwischen Ost und West* (Vienna and New York: Springer-Verlag, 1977), translated into English by Michel Vale as *Industrial Cooperation Between East and West* (White Plains, N.Y.: M. E. Sharpe, 1979). The preceding definition of industrial cooperation is from McMillan, op. cit., p. 1178. Alternative useful classifications are presented in Levcik and Stankovsky, op. cit., Ch. 3.
26 Motives for Eastern and Western participation in ICAs are discussed further in Levcik and Stankovsky, op. cit., Ch. 4.
27 See McMillan, op. cit.; Levcik and Stankovsky, op. cit., Ch. 10; UNECE, *Recent Trends in East–West Industrial Cooperation* (Trade/R. 373, 31 August 1978); and UNECE, *Statistical Outline of Recent Trends in Industrial Cooperation* (Trade/R. 373/Add. 5, 19 October 1978).
28 Space limitations preclude a separate discussion of the participation of each Eastern country in ICAs by type of agreement and branch of industry. For this, see the sources cited in n27.
29 UNECE, *Recent Trends*, op. cit., p. 33.
30 McMillan, op. cit., esp. pp. 1218–33; Levcik and Stankovsky, op. cit., Ch. 11; UNECE, *Recent Trends*, op. cit.; UNECE, *Case Studies in Industrial Cooperation: Results of a Survey of Five Western Enterprises* (Trade/R. 373/Add. 3, 18 September 1978); UNECE, *The Experience of Selected Western Enterprises Engaging in East–West Industrial Cooperation: Results of a Survey of Fifteen Firms in the Machine-Tool Sector* (Trade/R. 373/Add. 4, 14 August 1978).
31 Theoretical and empirical analyses of East–West joint ventures include Josef C. Brada, 'Markets, Property Rights, and the Economics of Joint Ventures in Socialist Countries', *Journal of Comparative Economics*, Vol. 1, No. 2 (June 1977), pp. 167–81; Levcik and Stankovsky, op. cit., Ch. 6; and Iancu Spigler, *Direct Western Investment in Eastern Europe* (Oxford: St Antony's College, Oxford University, Centre for Soviet and East European Studies, 1975).
32 In 1976 Poland authorized a limited form of joint venture in certain kinds of consumer services, but only about a dozen very small-scale ventures have been established.
33 Levcik and Stankovsky, op. cit., Ch. 9.
34 The administration of import quotas by central agencies in Eastern planned economies is discussed in Edward A. Hewett, 'Most-Favored-Nation Treatment in Trade under Central Planning', *Slavic Review*, Vol. 37, No. 1 (March 1978), esp. pp. 29–33. Some recent changes in Eastern trade practices are reviewed in UNECE, *Review of Recent Trends, Policies, and Problems in Intra-Regional Trade* (Trade/R. 366, 9 October 1978), pp. 10–15.
35 The following analysis of Cocom operations is based on Jonathan B. Bingham and Victor C. Johnson, 'A Rational Approach to Export Controls', *Foreign Affairs*, Vol. 57, No. 4 (Spring 1979), pp. 903–7; and US Congress, Office of Technology Assessment (OTA), *Technology and East–West Trade* (Washington, D.C.: US Government Printing Office, 1979), Chs. 8–9.
36 Cf. Bingham and Johnson, op. cit., esp. pp. 907–14.
37 The text appears in US Congress, OTA, op. cit., pp. 287–303.
38 Relevant US anti-dumping laws and procedures are explained in Paul Marer, 'US Restrictions and Safeguard Procedures against Imports from Eastern Europe', in Herbert Giersch (ed.), *International Economic Development and Resource Transfer* (Tubingen: J. C. B. Mohr-Paul Siebeck, 1979), pp. 273–92.
39 The main features of recent protectionist measures by industrialized Western countries are analyzed in detail in International Monetary Fund (IMF), Trade and Payments Division, *The Rise in Protectionism*, IMF Pamphlet Series No. 24 (Washington D.C.: IMF, 1978); and Bela Balassa, 'The "New Protectionism" and the International Economy', *Journal of World Trade Law*, Vol. 12, No. 5 (September–October 1978), pp. 409–36. The implications of these measures for Eastern Europe are examined in Karen C. Taylor, 'Import Protection and East–West Trade: A Survey of Industrialized Country Practices', in *East European Economies Post-Helsinki*, op. cit., pp. 1132–74; and Karen Taylor and Deborah Lamb, 'Communist Exports to the West in Import-Sensitive

Sectors', in *Issues in East–West Commercial Relations*, op. cit., pp. 125–67. The last-named source discusses how protectionist measures of particular Western countries affect exports of specific goods by individual Eastern countries.

40 On CMEA–EEC relations, see Levcik and Stankovsky, op. cit., pp. 106–18; John Pinder, 'Economic Integration and East–West Trade: Conflict of Interests or Comedy of Errors?' *Journal of Common Market Studies*, Vol. 16, No. 1 (September 1977), pp. 1–21; Peter Marsh, 'The Development of Relations between the EEC and the CMEA', in Avi Shlaim and G. N. Yannopoulos (eds), *The EEC and Eastern Europe* (Cambridge: Cambridge University Press, 1978), Ch. 2; Edward A. Hewett, 'Recent Developments in East–West European Economic Relations and Their Implications for US–East European Relations', in *East European Economies Post-Helsinki*, op. cit., pp. 174–98; European Communities, European Parliament, *Report on the State of Relations between the EEC and East European State Trading Countries and Comecon* (Working Document No. 89/78, 11 May 1978); and András Inotai, *The EEC at the End of the Seventies: Western European Integration in the New World Economic Environment*, Trends in World Economy, No. 28 (Budapest: Hungarian Scientific Council for World Economy, 1979), pp. 82–90.

41 This might be interpreted as consistent with Article 11 of the Draft Proposal for a CMEA–EEC agreement submitted to the EC by CMEA in 1976. The text was never officially published by either side, but an unauthorized and condensed English translation of the original Russian text appeared in *East–West* (Brussels), No. 151 (8 April 1976) and is reproduced in Levcik and Stankovsky, op. cit., pp. 265–8. According to this version, Article 11 states (emphasis added):

Individual questions of commercial-economic relations for the realization of the provisions of this Agreement related to cooperation between member countries of the CMEA, and member countries of the EEC may be regulated by bilateral and multilateral agreements between these countries.

Individual concrete questions may also be solved on the basis of the accepted principles of the Agreement in the way of direct contacts, understandings and *agreements between member countries of the CMEA and organs of the European Economic Community*, between member countries of the EEC and organs of the CMEA, and also between the competent economic organizations.

42 The most comprehensive account of East European countries' relations with GATT is M. M. Kostecki, *East–West Trade and the GATT System* (London: Macmillan, 1979). See also John W. Evans, 'GATT as a Framework for East–West Trade', in The Atlantic Council Committee on East–West Trade, *East–West Trade: Managing Encounter and Accommodation* (Boulder, Colorado: Westview Press, 1977), pp. 122–38; and Roy Baban, 'State Trading and the GATT', *Journal of World Trade Law*, Vol. 11, No. 4 (July–August 1977), pp. 334–53.

43 Marie Lavigne, 'The International Monetary Fund and the Soviet Union', in Levcik (ed.), op. cit., esp. pp. 377–9; and Boris S. Fomin, 'Monetary and Financial Aspects of East–West Cooperation', in C. T. Saunders (ed.), *Money and Finance in East and West* (Vienna and New York: Springer-Verlag, 1978), esp. pp. 106–8.

Chapter 4

The Prospects for East–West Trade in the 1980s

FRIEDRICH LEVCIK

One can use two distinct approaches in discussing East–West trade prospects. One approach consists of identifying policy issues, analyzing factors affecting East–West trade, exposing barriers to trade, and recommending ways, means, and methods for overcoming obstacles and for making a sustained expansion of East–West economic relations possible. Another approach consists of using past trends of East–West trade in order to analyze the determining factors of this development and to attempt projections, in quantitative terms, of the future growth potential of mutual trade under certain assumptions. It would be futile to debate the relative importance of these two approaches. In our opinion both approaches are not only legitimate but indispensable and supplement each other. A macroeconomic framework seems to be necessary to lend perspective to the discussion of policy issues and to the scope of actions required. On the other hand, a perception of the policy issues at stake and a realistic assessment of possible developments and of actions required are indispensable to lead trade projections beyond the two diverse dangers of either making mere extrapolations of past trends or reliance on wishful thinking.

This chapter draws upon a study of East–West trade projections up to 1990 elaborated by the Vienna Institute for Comparative Economic Studies for the Austrian Federal Ministry for Commerce, Trade and Industry.[1]

I The Conceptual Framework

In discussing future trade prospects between the East and the West one ought to take into account differing interests within and between East and West. In the West one can discern the following interests:

(1) The CMEA countries ought to be able to service the debt now and in the future.
(2) Exports from the West to the East should continue to grow.
(3) Imports from the East should not hurt domestic industries and the labor market.

In the East the following interests can be identified:

(1) The CMEA countries should step up exports to the West considerably to be able to close the trade gap and to service the debt.
(2) Growth of indebtedness should come to a halt, and for this purpose some import management is indispensable.
(3) The rate of growth of the economy should remain at a high level.

One can easily see that it is impossible to pursue all these incompatible interests with equal intensity. While there is an identity of interests on both sides about the necessity to control and to contain the future development of the East's indebtedness, most of the other interests seem to clash. The Eastern interest in expanding exports to the West is in direct conflict with the Western interest in protecting home industries and jobs. The Western interest in increased protection of the home market clashes with its own interest in assuring a continuous servicing of the debt. Indirectly protectionism hurts the interests of Western exporters, because the East cannot buy more goods without earning more hard currency. Likewise, the East cannot keep up a high growth of its national production simultaneously with severe restrictions of imports from the West.

The study attempts to trace possible paths of development of East–West trade capable of reconciling to some extent the conflicting interests by

(1) allowing Western exports to the East to grow at a reasonable rate;
(2) closing the trade gap and balancing trade of the CMEA countries within a reasonable period of time;
(3) avoiding undue disturbance of Western markets by excessive imports from the East;
(4) enabling access of Eastern products to Western markets under similar conditions as in the early 1970s before the recession in the West.

Thus the projections have more the character of scenarios of possible future developments under certain conditions than of deterministic forecasts of what will happen to East–West trade irrespective of the policy actions of the agents involved. Whether our projections will be verified by actual events is a judgment not so much of the soundness of our calculations as of the soundness of the actual policies pursued. The projections therefore provide a framework for the ongoing discussion on East–West trade, and on policies that ought to be taken. More is not intended.

II Past Developments

In its first part the study analyzes past developments of East–West trade, especially in the second half of the 1960s and the first half of the 1970s. In this decade East–West trade expanded vigorously – even faster than other trade flows – under the influence of steady growth in the world economy, an opening of the economies of the CMEA countries to foreign trade under the impact of economic reforms, gradual liberalization of measures against Eastern imports on the part of the developed market economies, and last but not least because of the political atmosphere of détente. Exports from

Table 4.1 *CMEA Countries' Foreign Trade with the Industrial West, 1970–78*[a]
(US$m.)

		1970	1971	1972	1973	1974	1975	1976	1977	1978[b]
Bulgaria	E	258.1	300.7	343.0	440.6	448.2	434.5	562.3	608.0	676.7
	I	349.9	357.1	384.3	517.7	973.9	1278.4	1037.5	996.0	1277.9
	B	-64.8	-56.4	-41.3	-77.1	-525.7	-843.9	-475.2	-388.0	-601.2
Czechoslovakia	E	771.5	846.4	962.0	1321.1	1691.8	1656.4	1647.1	1899.6	2101.5
	I	904.7	992.5	1084.0	1556.9	2085.7	2236.9	2420.3	2633.8	2898.5
	B	-133.2	-146.1	-122.0	-235.8	-393.9	-580.5	-773.2	-734.2	-797.0
GDR	E	1002.8	1070.3	1295.6	1725.9	2393.1	2259.6	2760.7	2477.1	2625.7
	I	1296.2	1374.4	1817.8	2556.9	3293.8	3274.1	4196.3	3784.1	4162.5
	B	-293.4	-304.1	-522.2	-831.0	-900.7	-1014.5	-1435.6	-1307.0	-1536.8
Hungary	E	629.8	617.3	824.0	1193.5	1363.0	1327.3	1551.2	1711.3	1903.4
	I	678.6	836.3	890.5	1193.3	1965.7	1965.0	2023.9	2439.5	3063.4
	B	-48.8	-219.0	-66.5	+0.2	-602.7	-637.7	-472.7	-728.2	-1160.0
Poland	E	1006.9	1155.5	1498.6	2186.0	3013.9	3241.0	3525.0	3834.1	4202.2
	I	930.3	1101.9	1815.1	3471.1	5322.1	6182.3	6781.1	6330.0	6235.1
	B	+76.6	+53.6	-316.5	-1285.1	-2308.2	-2941.3	-3256.1	-2495.9	-2032.9
Romania	E	590.4	716.4	888.9	1435.0	2052.1	1853.5	2129.8	2127.3	2512.3
	I	774.3	832.7	1069.9	1553.6	2499.8	2318.3	2206.6	2575.6	3278.7
	B	-183.9	-116.3	-181.0	-118.6	-447.7	-464.8	-76.8	-448.3	-766.4

(Table 4.1, *cont.*)

		1970	1971	1972	1973	1974	1975	1976	1977	1978[b]
European CMEA countries without USSR	E	4286.5	4706.6	5812.1	8302.1	10962.1	10772.2	12176.1	12657.4	14021.8
	I	4934.0	5494.9	7061.9	10849.5	16141.0	17254.9	18665.7	18759.0	20916.1
	B	-647.5	-788.3	-1249.5	-2547.4	-5178.9	-6482.7	-6489.6	-6101.6	-6894.3
USSR	E	2393.4	2758.1	2944.4	5093.2	8269.4	8511.1	10391.5	11958.0	12603.9
	I	2822.3	2889.9	4150.4	6232.9	8116.1	13451.7	14356.6	13459.3	15907.7
	B	-428.9	-131.8	-1206.0	-1139.7	+153.3	-4940.6	-3965.1	-1501.3	-3303.8
CMEA total	E	6679.9	7464.7	8756.5	13395.3	19231.5	19283.3	22567.6	24615.4	26625.7
	I	7756.3	8284.8	11212.0	17802.4	24257.1	30706.6	33022.3	32218.3	36823.8
	B	-1076.4	-920.1	-2455.5	-3687.1	-5025.6	-11423.3	-10454.7	-7602.9	-10198.1

[a]E = exports, I = imports, B = balance.
[b]Partly estimated.
Source: 'Die Wirtschaft der RGW-Länder zur Jahreswende 1978/79', *Monatsberichte des Österreichischen Institutes für Wirtschaftsforschung*, No. 4, 1979.

West to East, however, grew faster than imports from the CMEA countries and some trade surpluses of the OECD countries started to accumulate already in the late 1960s. The trade deficits of the CMEA countries, which remained at a reasonable level in the beginning, started to explode in connection with a prolonged recession in the West triggered by the startling increase of the oil prices. Over two-thirds of the debt of the CMEA countries, defined here as a first approximation by the cumulative adverse trade balances from 1959 onward, was incurred in the years 1975 to 1978 because export possibilities of the CMEA countries deteriorated due to the weak economic activity in the OECD area (see Table 4.1).

It is more the fast growth of the indebtedness in the last years than its absolute level (over $56 billion at the end of 1978) that leads to a certain apprehension both in the West and in the East. In most Eastern countries corrective measures have been initiated since the middle of the 1970s to slow down imports from the Western market economies and to keep trade deficits within certain limits. But there is more to watch than merchandise trade. By cumulating the trade balances over a longer time period to make inferences about the size of the debt, one disregards the balances of invisible trade, such as insurance, transport charges, interest payments, license fees, royalties, net proceeds from tourism, and unrequited transfer payments. While the study used the official trade statistics of the CMEA countries for analyzing the development of East–West trade, this path was not open for assessing the invisibles, as the CMEA countries do not publish statistics of the balances of payments. Regional 'mirror' balances of payments of Western industrialized countries (excluding Japan) with the European CMEA countries, published for the years 1965 through 1977 by the Secretariat of the UNECE in Geneva, were used instead.

An analysis of these data shows that up to 1973 the CMEA countries could somewhat diminish the deficit on trade accounts through a net surplus in invisibles (by 5 to 10 percent). But from 1974 onward the balance-of-payments deficit becomes increasingly higher than the mere trade deficit as interest payments on loans incurred substantially overreach other invisible surpluses of the CMEA countries, such as travel and unrequited transfer payments. The conclusion can be drawn that any assessment of the future path of East–West trade will have to take into account also the present state and future development of the balance of payments (see Table 4.2).

III   Projections of East–West Trade, 1978–90

The projections of East–West trade are based on the conviction that sooner or later the CMEA countries' trade and payments accounts with the West will have to be balanced and that this is also the wish of both the Eastern and Western trade partners.[2] But such a development should not lead to a collapse of East–West trade: both East and West are interested in maintaining and further extending it. A sudden curtailment of mutual shipments would hurt both sides, though the immediate damage for the CMEA countries may be graver as the OECD share in the CMEA trade is much bigger than vice versa. But in the long run the huge potential of the CMEA market, both as an importer (mainly of capital goods) and at least of the USSR as a supplier (mainly of fuels and energy) cannot be easily forgone by the West, both for economic and political reasons.

This is why scenarios that envisage the speedy elimination of present imbalances by drastic reduction of Western exports to the CMEA countries were not taken into account. Instead, several variants were computed that allow for a further expansion of East–West trade and at the same time for a step-by-step reduction of the balance-of-payments deficits of the CMEA countries by allowing CMEA exports to grow faster than imports from the West.

Basic Assumptions of Projections: Economic Growth, Import and Export Possibilities, and Balance-of-Payments Constraints
The development of CMEA exports is determined, on the one hand, by the CMEA countries' export potential and, on the other, by the Western markets' propensity to import. The CMEA export potential is probably on the increase, aided by increased imports of capital goods and technology from the West. But the slowing down of import growth from the West observed in recent years may impair the ability to expand exports in the years to come, since exports to the West, especially of manufactured goods made with the aid of plant and equipment imported recently from the West, are dependent, to a very high degree, on imports of materials, parts, and components from the West. The effects of these two factors affecting the export potential of CMEA countries are operating in opposite directions and can hardly be assessed in quantitative terms; they are therefore left out of account in our estimates.

In the projections the future development of CMEA exports to the West has been derived from the presumed import propensity of the Western markets, because a close connection could be observed between the Western conjunctural fluctuations from 1965 to 1976 and CMEA export growth. CMEA exports to the West were projected through 1990 assuming unchanged historically observed elasticity between growth of the volume of CMEA (East European, Soviet) exports to the West and the OECD countries' economic growth, estimating and annual 4 percent rise of foreign trade prices in both directions. One might also postulate different (higher or lower) price rises in both directions, but such variances would not materially affect the results because higher or lower figures of projected indebtedness would be matched by higher or lower figures for CMEA exports. However, a substantially higher general inflation rate would somewhat lower the burden of the debt since the already accumulated debt remains unaffected by future inflation. Different price rises for CMEA imports and exports implying a change in the terms of trade would, at least in variants 2 and 3 (see pp. 75, 76), likewise not affect the nominal results, which assume equal amounts for imports and exports in 1985 or 1990, respectively.

Estimated OECD economic growth is based on World Bank projections operating with two growth variants, of 3.5 percent and 4.1 percent annually, respectively. These growth rates were weighted in the projections

Table 4.2   Estimated Balance of Payments of Industrialized Market Economies (excluding Japan) with Eastern Europe and the USSR, 1965–77[a] (US$m.)

| Years | Total (1–10) | Trade Balance fob-fob (1–2) | Current Account | | | | Transfers (9–10) | Capital (11–19) | Multilateral Settlements and Net Errors and Omissions |
| | | | Net Services and Income | | | | | | |
			Total (3–8)	Transport and Insurance (3–4)	Travel (5)	Income (6–8)			
1965	218	242	38	11	-52	79	-62	-272	54
1966	280	322	20	4	-66	82	-62	-11	-269
1967	413	488	-8	-44	-71	107	-67	-334	-79
1968	479	549	42	-7	-72	121	-112	-147	-332
1969	575	620	67	-12	-74	153	-112	-183	-392
1970	831	890	79	-6	-114	192	-138	-623	-208
1971	527	581	156	16	-152	292	-210	-196	-331
1972	1465	1662	106	31	-212	287	-303	-1095	-370
1973	2718	2836	231	17	-292	506	-349	-3243	525

(Table 4.2, cont.)

1965–73	7506	8190	731	10	-1105	1819	-1415	-6104	-1402
1974	3388	3209	553	123	-332	762	-374	-2409	-979
1975	8793	8255	890	25	-430	1295	-352	-5715	-3078
1976	6617	5827	1190	20	-480	1650	-400	-4917	-1700
1977	4711	3641	1570		-530	2100	-500	-4711	
1974–77	23509	20932	4902	168	-1772	5807	-1626	-23509	
1965–77	31015	29122	4934	178	-2877	7626	-3041	-31015	

[a]Numbers in parentheses under column headings are the IMF item numbers.
Sources: Economic Bulletin for Europe, Vols 28, 29, and 30.

with the individual OECD countries' shares in CMEA (East European, Soviet) exports to the West.

For the USSR and for Eastern Europe respectively, too, a higher and a lower NMP growth rate were assumed; in both cases values were set down that lie somewhat below the growth targets for the current five-year plans. We assume a continuation of trends toward reduced growth rates noted in the USSR since the 1960s and in Eastern Europe since the mid-1970s. The actual economic performance between 1976 and 1978 gives added weight to this reasoning. A further slowdown may be expected due to a number of internal and external factors. The labor force will grow much more slowly during the 1980s than previously, and a faster growth of labor productivity cannot be expected to compensate for this. Besides, the long-term trend toward growing capital coefficients will be at least maintained during the 1980s and may even become more pronounced, since a shift of investments in the direction of more capital-intensive projects in the fields of energy and raw materials is to be expected. Under these circumstances, the maintenance of previous growth rates would presuppose a further increase of the investment ratio with concomitant decrease of the consumption ratio, which seems hardly feasible in view of the consumers' still deferred expectations.

However, it must be assumed that in the years to come the development of CMEA imports will be determined by the exigencies of the balance of payments rather than by the requirements of economic growth. This new orientation of import policies began to be evident, in most CMEA countries, in the last years when they started to put the brake on import growth from the industrialized West. We assume that they will attempt also in the next few years to reduce the deficits in their foreign trade with the West step by step through curbs on imports in order to achieve balanced trade in the 1980s. The degree of import restraint will vary from country to country, according to the extent of the balance-of-payment deficits.

In addition to merchandise trade, other items of the balance of payments will also be taken into account. The regional balance-of-payments positions of Western industrialized countries *vis-à-vis* the CMEA countries as computed for the years 1965 to 1977 by the ECE secretariat were used as the sources of data to determine the net positions pertaining to transport, insurance, travel, and transfers. These balance-of-payments positions had, until now, in the aggregate shown positive balances in favor of the CMEA countries – balances that rose from $103 million to about $1 billion between 1965 and 1977. For purposes of the projections, the 1976/77 total CMEA value was apportioned to Eastern Europe and the USSR (proportionately to their shares in total CMEA Western merchandise exports) and its growth until 1990 estimated according to projected growth of their national product, inflated by the assumed change in foreign trade prices (4 percent annually).

Interest payments constitute an important item of the CMEA countries' balance-of-payments accounts *vis-à-vis* the West. Interest rates vary from country to country subject to the liquidity of the credit market and the volume and maturity structure of loans granted. In the projections a uniform rate of interest of 7 percent was assumed for both outstanding debts and newly granted credits, and a uniform rate of repayment of 14 percent. This implies an average maturity of seven years for all types of loans. Since no reliable information is available concerning the maturity structure of the outstanding debt and since possible future changes in the repayment periods cannot be assessed, the validity of the estimated loan maturity is certainly debatable.

But while a change in maturity structure does affect the yearly amount of repayment, new credit drawings, and the debt service ratio, it does not affect interest payments, the size and growth of the debt, and the debt-to-export relation. This fact was shown in the projection study by increasing the rate of repayment from 14 to 30 percent of the debt at the end of the previous year corresponding to a shortening of the average loan maturity from seven to between three and four years. One could also deduce from the alternative computations that changes in the ratio of repayment to debt are not likely to affect the liquidity on the international money market. While larger amounts of new credits will have to be raised, larger repayments fall due in respect of old liabilities. The only effect is that at higher repayment the CMEA countries appear more often in the international credit markets, repaying outstanding and drawing new credits.

Whether this does affect CMEA countries' creditworthiness in a positive or a negative way is difficult to assess. On the one hand they will impress as being debtors who redeem their debts punctually; on the other hand they will lay claim to a bigger proportion of newly granted loans. Therefore we regard changes in the relation between debt and exports as a more reliable measure of the debt burden than the debt service ratio, which, in any case, varies depending on the method of computation.[3]

This is not to suggest that monitoring the development of debt service ratios of individual clients of banks is without any value, nor that a lengthening of the maturities could not positively affect the time of readjustment, but only that it is of little value for macroeconomic exercises.

Three variants were computed for the projection of East–West trade to 1990. A synopsis of assumptions of the varying scenarios is given in Table 4.3, and a synopsis of the results in Table 4.4. The study itself has sixteen appendix tables for all three variants, for Eastern Europe and the USSR separately, and for the entire European CMEA area, as well as for the subvariants (a) and (b), alternating higher or lower projected gross domestic product (GDP) growth rates for the OECD countries.[4]

The main determinant for the projected CMEA exports to the industrialized West is the OECD areas' propensity to import, which depends, according to the projections, on the economic growth prospects of the area. The projections imply that the conditions of access to Western markets will not change radically in comparison with the period of reference (expressed by the elasticities for 1966–77; see Table 4.3). Substantial liberalization measures or an increase in market protection do, of course, positively or negatively affect the projected import propensity of Western countries, and the periods of achieving balanced trade given in the projection variants would be shortened or lengthened accordingly. The question as to whether a development of liberalization or protection is more likely in our opinion depends more on the level of economic activity of the OECD economies in the years to come than on good or bad intentions.

Imports into the CMEA area from the West are determined mainly by the balance-of-payment constraints. The projection variants vary according to the time in which the trade deficits of the CMEA countries could be eliminated and the balance-of-payments equilibrium restored during the 1980s. Accordingly the projected growth rates of CMEA imports from the West are derived from projected growth rates of CMEA

Table 4.3   *East–West Trade Projections, 1978–90:*
Synopsis of Assumptions

1   Economic growth of OECD area[a]

	Average Annual Rate of Growth (%)	
	1966–77	1978–90
GDP growth	3.9	(a) 3.5
		(b) 4.1
GDP of OECD, growth weighted by the shares of individual OECD countries in CMEA exports		
East European weights	4.0	(a) 3.59
		(b) 4.21
USSR weights	4.34	(a) 3.9
		(b) 4.56
Total CMEA weights	4.18	(a) 3.75
		(b) 4.39

2   Economic growth of CMEA area[a]

	Average Annual Rate of Growth (%)		
	1966–77	1978–80[b]	1981–90
Growth of NMP			
Eastern Europe	7.2	(a) 5.7	(a) 5.2
		(b) 6.2	(b) 5.7
USSR	6.5	(a) 4.0	(a) 3.5
		(b) 4.5	(b) 4.0
European CMEA	6.7	(a) 4.5	(a) 4.0
		(b) 5.0	(b) 4.5

3   Foreign trade elasticities

	1966–77	1978–90
Elasticity of exports to the OECD area[c]		
Eastern Europe	1.87	1.87
USSR	1.31	1.31
Elasticity of total imports[d]		
Eastern Europe	1.39	1.39
USSR	1.35	1.35

4   Foreign trade prices

Annual change in percent	4

exports to the West and from the implied development of the other components of the balance-of-payments accounts.

In the following a brief account of the main results of the projection variants will be given.

Variant 1: CMEA Imports from the West Grow at Same Rates as CMEA Total Imports

This variant assumes that CMEA exports to the West will continue to develop at unchanged export elasticity, while CMEA imports from the West will grow in proportion with total imports. This implies an unchanging Western share in CMEA imports in years to come. That variant was based only on the higher OECD growth and lower CMEA growth given in the assumptions, this being the most favorable combination taking into account the balance-of-payments position of the CMEA countries.

Under these conditions CMEA exports to the West would grow a little faster in real terms until 1990 (Eastern Europe, 8 percent; USSR, 6 percent annually) than during the period 1966–77 (Eastern Europe, 7.5 percent; USSR, 5.7 percent), since economic growth assumed for OECD is somewhat above that of recent years. Conversely, CMEA imports from the West would grow at a slower rate than during the preceding period, in keeping with the assumed decelerated economic development in the CMEA area.

Variant 1 has different effects on the balance of payments of Eastern Europe, on the one hand, and on that of the USSR, on the other. As far as *Eastern Europe* is concerned the variant is unrealistic in terms of the balance of payments, for a growth of imports from the West equal to total imports growth would effect a drastic deterioration of the balance of payments by 1990. The trade deficits, and even more so the payments deficits, would grow rapidly and with them indebtedness too. By 1990 the debt would have climbed to $300 billion at current prices ($180 billion at 1977 prices). The debt burden, measured by annual exports, would then have grown from 2.6:1 to 5:1. The debt-service ratio (repayments of

---

^{a}(a) Lower growth rate.

(b) Higher growth rate.

^{b}Current five-year plans adjusted by actual performance, 1976–78, assuming that in the remaining years the average yearly growth rate planned for the entire period 1976–80 will be achieved.

^{c}Growth of CMEA exports to OECD GDP.

$$\epsilon_x = \frac{\sqrt[11]{\frac{x_{77}}{x_{66}}} - 1}{\sqrt[11]{\frac{y_{77}}{y_{66}}} - 1}$$

x = CMEA exports to the West at constant prices

y = GDP of OECD at constant prices

^{d}Growth of total imports to CMEA NMP.

$$\epsilon_m = \frac{\sqrt[11]{\frac{m_{77}}{m_{66}}} - 1}{\sqrt[11]{\frac{p_{77}}{p_{66}}} - 1}$$

m = CMEA imports from the West at constant prices

p = NMP of CMEA at constant prices

GDP – Gross Domestic Product

NMP – Net Material Product

Table 4.4   *East–West Trade Projections, 1978–90:*
Synopsis of Results

| | Exports to the West | | Imports from the West | |
	Constant Prices	Current Prices	Constant Prices	Current Prices
	Average Annual Rate of Growth (%)			
	Variant 1			
Eastern Europe (without USSR)	7.9	12.2	7.4	11.7
USSR	6.0	10.2	4.9	9.1
	Variant 2a			
Eastern Europe	6.7	11.0	1.7	5.8
USSR	5.1	9.3	3.6	7.7
CMEA total	6.0	10.2	2.5	6.6
	Variant 2b			
Eastern Europe	7.9	12.2	2.9	7.0
USSR	6.0	10.2	4.4	8.6
CMEA total	7.0	11.3	3.6	7.7
	Variant 3a			
Eastern Europe	6.7	11.0	3.6	7.8
USSR	5.1	9.3	4.1	8.3
CMEA total	6.0	10.2	3.8	8.0
	Variant 3b			
Eastern Europe	7.9	12.2	4.8	9.0
USSR	6.0	10.2	5.0	9.2
CMEA total	7.0	11.3	4.9	9.1

principal and interest on all types of loans in proportion to annual exports), which amounted to 43 percent of export earnings in 1977, would almost swallow the total of export earnings by 1990.

Under less favorable assumptions, that is, assuming slower OECD economic growth (3.5 percent annually), and, on the other hand, a somewhat faster economic growth in Eastern Europe, an even worse development of the balance of payments would have to be expected. A growth of imports from the West equaling the rate of total imports growth would therefore be economically insupportable for Eastern Europe as a whole (though the situation may vary from country to country).

Under assumptions of variant 1 the *Soviet Union's* balance-of-payments perspective would appear more favorable than Eastern Europe's. The foreign trade deficit *vis-à-vis* the West, after a slow increase until 1980, would gradually decrease in the following years to give place, by 1988, to a positive balance. However, since interest payments would surpass the positive balances of other incomes even after 1988, the debt would continue to grow, reaching the sum of $45 billion ($27 billion at 1977 prices) by 1990. The debt-service ratio will increase until 1984 from 22.8 percent to 27 percent, to return, by 1990, to the initial level of over 22 percent. The relation of debt to exports will amount to 1.0 in 1990, as against 1.3 in 1977. Thus there is no cause for the USSR to reduce imports from the West below the overall import level to initiate an improvement of her balance of payments.

Under slightly less favorable circumstances (either higher or lower growth rate in both regions) the development of the Soviet balance of payments would very likely deteriorate somewhat as her trade deficits with the West would increase until 1990.[5]

Variant 2: Balanced East–West Foreign Trade by 1985
Considering East–West foreign trade developments under variant 2, the CMEA countries are assumed to follow restrictive import policies aimed at balancing their foreign trade accounts by 1985. To achieve this, the CMEA countries would have to restrain the growth of their imports from the West considerably – though this applies to Eastern Europe in a much higher degree than to the USSR.

If 'traditional' export elasticities continue, exports to the West would grow in accordance with OECD economic growth. Two subvariants each were calculated on this basis for Eastern Europe and for the USSR. In *Eastern Europe*, exports to the West will increase until 1990 at annual growth rates of 11 percent or 12.2 percent (at current prices) respectively. To eliminate the deficit *vis-à-vis* the West by 1985, the growth of imports from the West would not be allowed to exceed an annual rate of 1.7 percent or 2.9 percent respectively at constant prices, or of 5.8 percent and 7 percent respectively at current prices.

Were East–West trade to develop according to this pattern, then this would bring about a comparatively quick improvement of Eastern Europe's balance of payments. The debt-service ratio and the debt-to-export relation would reach the peak before the middle of the 1980s and would return to the level of 1977 in the second half of the decade. The growth of the debt would stop soon after the mid-1980s and start diminishing near the end of the decade.

However, in view of overall economic considerations, it may be over-optimistic to anticipate such developments of the balance of payments of Eastern Europe. Remembering that Eastern Europe's total import elasticity is 1.35 (based on the link between import growth and economic growth, statistically evidenced for the period 1966 to 1977), import totals from all regions in real terms would have to grow at annual rates of no less than 7.4–8 percent. A real growth of imports from the West of only 1.7–2.9 percent annually would presuppose the appropriate substitution of imports from the West through vastly increased imports from the CMEA region and the developing countries.

Substitution feasibilities are generally limited and they vary greatly in individual commodity groups. Raw materials and fuels, as well as semifinished products that are imported from the West, are hardly replaceable. The USSR may be thought the main source of substitute deliveries; but the chances of increased Soviet exports of raw materials and fuels to Eastern Europe are rather limited. Only partial substitution of machinery and installations appears feasible. Some of the machines imported from the West are irreplaceable in view of their technological characteristics, and not available within the CMEA. Since all CMEA countries are presently attempting to maximize their exports to the West and at the same time to replace imports from the West with increased imports from other CMEA countries, supply in the intra-CMEA market must necessarily lag behind demand. One could hardly envisage that the development of exports of the CMEA countries could be accelerated in face of a slowed-down growth of imports from the West. And it could hardly be supposed that the OECD countries would be willing to absorb quickly growing imports from the CMEA region without hindrance for a period of at least seven years without being given an opportunity for substantially increasing, on their part, exports to Eastern Europe.

The *USSR* is in a different position; her foreign trade with the West could be balanced by 1985 without any drastic reduction in the growth rate of her imports from the West. Besides, foreign trade is of relatively little significance in the USSR, measured by the volume of the national product and in comparison to other industrialized countries. Thus a moderate deceleration of import growth from the West need have no grave consequences for the country's economic growth. The Soviet balance of payments would improve at a faster rate under variant 2 than it would for variant 1. The debt-service ratio and the debt-to-export relation would vary within fairly narrow limits, and would be below the value of 1977 by the mid-1980s. The debt would reach its peak in 1987, when it would amount to $31 billion ($18 billion at 1977 prices), and it would recede in the years thereafter.

Variant 3: Balanced East–West Foreign Trade by 1990
A further variant 3 was computed under the assumption of achieving balanced trade by 1990 only. With this concept higher import growth than under variant 2 is possible for Eastern Europe. While overall imports according to the elasticity assumptions would grow at an annual rate of 7.4–8 percent, imports from the West could grow at 3.6–4.9 percent annually in real terms, which is two percentage points more than under variant 2. The debt-service ratio and relation of debt to exports would attain higher values than under variant 2. However, both coefficients would also begin to decline in the middle of the 1980s. Since growth of indebtedness would decelerate more slowly than under variant 2, the debt volume would be almost twice as large by 1990 as against variant 2; its absolute decrease could only be expected to take place in the 1990s.

For the *USSR* variant 3 yields results very similar to those of variant 1. In both cases trade would be balanced by the end of the 1980s.

IV   Conclusion

The projections are based on restrictive assumptions, some of which need not conform to realities. The projected steady development, not taking into account possible growth fluctuations, is certainly unrealistic, but there were no techniques available to simulate fluctuations. It is also assumed that there will be no changes in the terms of trade between East and West up to 1990, by assuming an annual 4 percent rise of both import and export prices in East–West trade. The supposition concerning the import capacities of Western markets is also not unassailable. Even accepting the likelihood of the projected (relatively high) economic growth in the OECD countries, unemployment in the West will subside only slowly. In view of possible measures in the West for the protection of jobs, CMEA exports to the West may well grow at a lower rate than could be deduced from the historically evidenced tie-up between OECD growth and OECD imports from the CMEA region.

Balanced trade by 1990 would appear to be the most favorable solution both for East and West, allowing the Western industrial countries to increase their exports to the East reasonably quickly, yet at the same time eliminating the balance-of-payments deficits of the CMEA countries in the long run. But this variant presupposes willingness on the part of the West to grant further credits to the CMEA countries throughout the 1980s, reasonable growth prospects for the OECD area, and avoidance of increased protection in the OECD countries' import policies. The advantage for the CMEA countries would lie in not having to curtail their imports from the West drastically – something they could only do by accepting also considerable cuts of their economic growth. However, to implement an export growth envisaged by this variant, the CMEA countries would have to make considerable efforts to improve the structure and quality of their exports.

At this stage of the study, the position of the individual CMEA countries was not examined in detail. Ability to cope with debt service depends, in each country, on the extent of its indebtedness, on the rate of interest, possibly on the maturity structure, on export prospects, and on the possibilities for reducing imports. Economic policy in each CMEA country must take these differences into account, and while some of them will follow a more restrictive course in their import policies, others will be able to follow a more open course toward the West. In further phases of this project differences between countries and trade prospects according to commodity groups will be analyzed.

Appendix

Table 4.A1 *Projection of East–West Trade and Indebtedness to 1990 – Variant 3a:
Eastern Europe*[a]

(Current prices, in US$b. assuming an annual 4 percent inflation rate)

	Revenue				Expenditure		
	Exports	Other Revenue	Total Revenue	Imports	Debt Service		Total Expenditure
					Repayments	Interest	
Year	(1)	(2)	(3)	(4)	(5)	(6)	(7)
1977	12.828	.556	13.384	18.754	3.707	1.854	24.315
1978	14.235	.606	14.841	20.212	4.719	2.359	27.290
1979	15.796	.660	16.456	21.783	5.801	2.900	30.484
1980	17.528	.720	18.248	23.476	6.953	3.476	33.905
1981	19.451	.785	20.236	25.301	8.171	4.086	37.557
1982	21.584	.855	22.440	27.267	9.452	4.726	41.446
1983	23.952	.932	24.884	29.387	10.790	5.395	45.571
1984	26.579	1.016	27.595	31.671	12.175	6.088	49.934
1985	29.494	1.108	30.601	34.133	13.598	6.799	54.530
1986	32.729	1.207	33.936	36.786	15.045	7.522	59.353
1987	36.318	1.316	37.634	39.645	16.497	8.248	64.390
1988	40.302	1.434	41.736	42.727	17.933	8.967	69.626
1989	44.722	1.564	46.286	46.048	19.327	9.664	75.038
1990	49.627	1.704	51.331	49.627	20.647	10.323	80.597

[a]Export growth: 11.0 percent annually.
Import growth: 7.8 percent annually.
Explanation of columns:
(1) Annual growth 11.0 percent (export elasticity 1.87; OECD growth 1978–90: 3.5 percent; OECD growth weighted by export shares of Eastern Europe; 3.59 percent).
(2) Net revenue from transport, tourism, and unilateral transfers; partly estimated.

(Table 4.A1, cont.)

Year	Balance of Trade	New Credit Drawings	Increase in Debt	Debt: Total Debt	Debt Service Ratio	Growth of Indebtedness in %	Debt to Exports
	(8)	(9)	(10)	(11)	(12)	(13)	(14)
1977	-5.926	10.931	7.224	33.705	43.4	27.3	2.63
1978	-5.977	12.449	7.730	41.435	49.7	22.9	2.91
1979	-5.987	14.028	8.227	49.662	55.1	19.9	3.14
1980	-5.947	15.657	8.704	58.366	59.5	17.5	3.33
1981	-5.850	17.322	9.151	67.516	63.0	15.7	3.47
1982	-5.683	19.006	9.554	77.070	65.7	14.2	3.57
1983	-5.435	20.687	9.898	86.968	67.6	12.8	3.63
1984	-5.092	22.339	10.164	97.131	68.7	11.7	3.65
1985	-4.639	23.929	10.330	107.462	69.2	10.6	3.64
1986	-4.057	25.417	10.372	117.834	69.0	9.7	3.60
1987	-3.327	26.756	10.259	128.093	68.1	8.7	3.53
1988	-2.425	27.890	9.957	138.050	66.7	7.8	3.42
1989	-1.326	28.753	9.426	147.476	64.8	6.8	3.30
1990	0	29.266	8.619	156.095	62.4	5.8	3.14

(3) (1) + (2).
(4) Balanced trade projected for 1990.
(5) 14 percent of debt at end of preceding year (average seven-year term assumed).
(6) 7 percent of debt at the end of preceding year.
(7) (4) + (5) + (6).
(8) (1) − (4).
(9) (7) − (3).
(10) (9) − (5) = balance-of-payments deficit.
(11) (10) + debt at the end of preceding year.
(12) [(5) + (6)]/(1).
(13) [(10)/debt at end of preceding year] × 100.
(14) (11)/(1).

Table 4.A2 Projection of East–West Trade and Indebtedness to 1990 – Variant 3a: Soviet Union[a]

(Current prices, in US$b. assuming an annual 4 percent inflation rate)

	Revenue				Expenditure		
					Debt Service		
Year	Exports	Other Revenue	Total Revenue	Imports	Repayments	Interest	Total Expenditure
	(1)	(2)	(3)	(4)	(5)	(6)	(7)
1977	11.843	.378	12.221	13.337	1.800	.900	16.036
1978	12.945	.408	13.353	14.445	2.082	1.041	17.568
1979	14.149	.441	14.590	15.646	2.380	1.190	19.216
1980	15.465	.476	15.942	16.946	2.695	1.347	20.988
1981	16.904	.514	17.419	18.354	3.024	1.512	22.890
1982	18.477	.555	19.033	19.879	3.367	1.683	24.929
1983	20.196	.600	20.796	21.531	3.721	1.860	27.112
1984	22.075	.648	22.723	23.320	4.084	2.042	29.446
1985	24.129	.700	24.829	25.258	4.454	2.227	31.938
1986	26.374	.756	27.130	27.356	4.825	2.413	34.594
1987	28.828	.816	29.644	29.629	5.195	2.597	37.422
1988	31.510	.881	32.392	32.092	5.557	2.778	40.426
1989	34.442	.952	35.394	34.758	5.903	2.952	43.613
1990	37.646	1.028	38.674	37.646	6.228	3.114	46.988

[a] Export growth: 9.3 percent annually.
Import growth: 8.3 percent annually.
Explanation of columns:
(1) Annual growth 9.3 percent (export elasticity 1.31; OECD growth 1978–90: 3.5 percent, OECD growth weighted by export shares of the USSR: 3.9 percent).
(2) Net revenue from transport, tourism, and unilateral transfers; partly estimated.
(3) (1) + (2).

(Table 4.A2 cont.)

Year	Balance of Trade (8)	New Credit Drawings (9)	Increase in Debt (10)	Debt — Total Debt (11)	Debt Service Ratio (12)	Growth of Indebtedness in % (13)	Debt to Exports (14)
	(8)	(9)	(10)	(11)	(12)	(13)	(14)
1977	-1.494	3.816	2.016	14.870	22.8	15.7	1.26
1978	-1.501	4.215	2.133	17.003	24.3	14.3	1.31
1979	-1.497	4.626	2.246	19.249	25.2	13.2	1.36
1980	-1.480	5.046	2.352	21.601	26.1	12.2	1.40
1981	-1.449	5.471	2.447	24.048	26.8	11.3	1.42
1982	-1.402	5.896	2.530	26.578	27.3	10.5	1.44
1983	-1.334	6.316	2.595	29.173	27.6	9.8	1.44
1984	-1.245	6.723	2.639	31.812	27.8	8.7	1.44
1985	-1.128	7.109	2.656	34.467	27.7	8.3	1.43
1986	-.982	7.465	2.639	37.107	27.4	7.7	1.41
1987	-.801	7.778	2.583	39.689	27.0	7.0	1.38
1988	-.581	8.035	2.478	42.168	26.5	6.2	1.34
1989	-.316	8.220	2.316	44.484	25.7	5.5	1.29
1990	0	8.314	2.086	46.570	24.8	4.7	1.24

(4) Balanced trade projected for 1990.
(5) 14 percent of debt at end of preceding year (average seven-year term assumed).
(6) 7 percent of debt at the end of preceding year.
(7) (4) + (5) + (6).
(8) (1) – (4).
(9) (7) – (3).
(10) (9) – (5) = balance-of-payments deficit.
(11) (10) + debt at the end of preceding year.
(12) [(5) + (6)]/(1).
(13) [(10)/debt at end of preceding year] × 100.
(14) (11)/(1).

Table 4.A3 *Projection of East–West Trade and Indebtedness to 1990 – Variant 3a: CMEA[a]* (Current prices, in US$b. assuming an annual 4 percent inflation rate)

	Revenue				Expenditure		
	Exports	Other Revenue	Total Revenue	Imports	Debt Service		Total Expenditure
Year					Repayments	Interest	
	(1)	(2)	(3)	(4)	(5)	(6)	(7)
1977	24.670	.934	25.604	32.091	5.507	2.753	40.351
1978	27.179	1.014	28.193	34.657	6.800	3.400	44.858
1979	29.945	1.101	31.046	37.428	8.181	4.091	49.700
1980	32.994	1.196	34.190	40.422	9.648	4.824	54.893
1981	36.355	1.299	37.654	43.654	11.195	5.598	60.447
1982	40.061	1.411	41.472	47.146	12.819	6.410	66.375
1983	44.148	1.532	45.680	50.917	14.511	7.255	72.683
1984	48.654	1.664	50.318	54.991	16.260	8.130	79.380
1985	53.623	1.807	55.430	59.390	18.052	9.026	86.468
1986	59.103	1.963	61.066	64.142	19.870	9.935	93.947
1987	65.146	2.132	67.278	69.275	21.692	10.846	101.812
1988	71.812	2.316	74.128	74.818	23.490	11.745	110.053
1989	79.164	2.515	81.679	80.806	25.230	12.615	118.652
1990	87.274	2.732	90.006	87.274	26.874	13.437	127.585

[a] Export growth: 11.0 percent annually.
Import growth: 7.8 percent annually.

Explanation of columns:
(1) Annual growth 10.2 percent (export elasticity 1.60; OECD growth 1978–90: 3.5 percent, OECD growth weighted by export shares of CMEA countries: 3.75 percent).
(2) Net revenue from transport, tourism, and unilateral transfers; partly estimated.
(3) (1) + (2).
(4) Balanced trade projected for 1990.

(Table 4.A3 cont.)

Year	Balance of Trade (8)	New Credit Drawings (9)	Increase in Debt (10)	Debt Total Debt (11)	Debt Service Ratio (12)	Growth of Indebtedness (%) (13)	Debt to Exports (14)
1977	-7.420	14.747	9.240	48.575	33.5	23.5	1.97
1978	-7.478	16.664	9.864	58.438	37.5	20.3	2.15
1979	-7.483	18.654	10.473	68.911	41.0	17.9	2.30
1980	-7.428	20.703	11.055	79.966	43.9	16.0	2.42
1981	-7.299	22.793	11.598	91.564	46.2	14.5	2.52
1982	-7.085	24.902	12.083	103.648	48.0	13.2	2.59
1983	-6.770	27.003	12.493	116.141	49.3	12.1	2.63
1984	-6.337	29.062	12.803	128.943	50.1	11.0	2.65
1985	-5.767	31.038	12.986	141.929	50.5	10.1	2.65
1986	-5.039	32.881	13.011	154.940	50.4	9.2	2.62
1987	-4.128	34.534	12.842	167.782	49.9	8.3	2.85
1988	-3.006	35.925	12.435	180.218	49.1	7.4	2.51
1989	-1.642	36.972	11.742	191.960	47.8	6.5	2.43
1990	0	37.579	10.705	202.664	46.2	5.6	2.32

(5) 14 percent of debt at end of preceding year (average seven-year term assumed).
(6) 7 percent of debt at the end of preceding year.
(7) (4) + (5) + (6).
(8) (1) − (4).
(9) (7) − (3).
(10) (9) − (5) = balance-of-payments deficit.
(11) (10) + debt at the end of preceding year.
(12) [(5) + (6)]/(1).
(13) [(10)/debt at end of preceding year] × 100.
(14) (11)/(1).

Notes: Chapter 4

1   The full study, 'Projektionen des Ost-West-Handels und der RGW-Verschuldung 1978–1990', which was elaborated by the Vienna Institute for Comparative Economic Studies for the Austrian Federal Ministry for Commerce, Trade, and Industry, appears in Benedikt Askansas, Gerhard Fink, and Friedrich Levcik, *East–West Trade and CMEA Indebtedness in the Seventies and Eighties*, in the series 'Perspektiven' (Vienna: Zentralsparkasse und Kommerzbank, 1979). The author of this chapter would like to express his appreciation to the co-authors of the original study for their permission to use the main findings of the study.
2   Direct capital imports that could offset trade deficits and deficits in the current account of the balance of payment in general are not possible in CMEA countries. Here such deficits can be covered only by new borrowing that increases the indebtedness, which may become unmanageable if not curbed in time.
3   In the literature the debt-service ratio is calculated differently than in this study. In most cases maturities up to and including one year are excluded from the calculations, because it is assumed that short-term credits will be rolled over automatically. This does not seem to be very meaningful, because short-term obligations also have to be repaid. According to Bank for International Settlements publications, short-term obligations amount to at least 30 percent of the total debt.
4   To give an illustration of the techniques used the computations for variant 3a are reproduced in the Appendix tables.
5   Earnings from gold sales and balances accruing from hard-currency deals with developing countries were not considered in this study because the appropriate data were not available in a suitable form. Hard-currency deals among CMEA countries are evidently irrelevant to the issue of indebtedness of total CMEA toward the West.

Part Two

Soviet–East European Regional Relations

Soviet–East European Relations in the 1980s and the Changing International System

WILLIAM ZIMMERMAN

This chapter attempts to characterize the nature of future Soviet–East European relations. It is not the first such effort. In a recent paper, Jan F. Triska has speculated specifically about the impact of material, manpower, and energy shortages on Soviet–East European relations in the 1980s.[1] Archie Brown has in effect bypassed the 1980s by speculating on 'Eastern Europe: 1968, 1978, 1998'.[2] Each has paid greatest attention to the likely impact on Eastern Europe of changes in the Soviet Union. In this chapter I assume no basic changes in the Soviet Union during the 1980s and focus more on the impact of likely attributes of the evolving global system on Soviet–East European relations in the 1980s. The bases for my projections are not entirely confined to omphaloskepsis; previous papers have analyzed the changing pattern of Soviet–East European relations in the 1960s and 1970s.[3] Nevertheless, I am engaged basically in crystal-ball gazing, an endeavor meriting a healthy skepticism, especially in reference to Soviet–East European relations.

A literature search with the advantage of hindsight would reveal an impressive array of misplaced conjectures were we to examine comparable projections of the 1950s written in 1949, the 1960s written in 1959, and the 1970s in 1969. The list of specialists who in the late 1940s contemplated the decompression and recompression in East Europe of the mid-1950s, or who in 1959 envisaged a set of occurrences such as the Prague Spring and the intervention in Czechoslovakia by Warsaw Treaty Organization forces in 1968, or who in the late 1960s contemplated that the 1970s would bring such a burgeoning of East–West trade and East European indebtedness to the West, is vanishingly small. More typically, we have been surprised by events in Soviet–East European relations. The Twentieth Congress of the Communist Party of the Soviet Union (CPSU) occurred only months after conceptions of Soviet politics premised on the purge as a permanent feature of Soviet life were articulated. Leading Western specialists on communism contended in 1960 that predictions of an imminent major Sino-Soviet rupture revealed a misunderstanding of the nature of communism. A conference of Western specialists on change in Communist systems held in the summer of 1968 was virtually (though not totally) unanimous in predicting that the Soviet Union would not intervene militarily in Czechoslovakia. The point should thus be clear: one prediction that can be made with great certainty is that many of our predictions about Soviet–East European relations in the 1980s will be wrong.

Caveats having been entered, I am obliged to assert that I do not foresee progress in our ability to specify the likelihood of social phenomena unless we persist in our efforts to project such phenomena as explicitly as possible. In so doing we make clear the assumptions that organize our conception of those phenomena, assumptions that can then be modified if projections are disconfirmed. Since, however, my conception of Soviet–East European relations in the 1980s is rooted fundamentally in my understanding of the 1960s and 1970s, I must beg the reader's indulgence if we arrive at the future via an excursion into the present and recent past of Soviet–East European relations.

I   Soviet–East European Relations: 1960–79

In the 1960s and 1970s, the essential attributes of Soviet–East European relations were most appropriately grasped if they were conceived as constituting a hierarchical regional system; that is, a regional interstate system made up of a single great power, the regional hegemon, and a number of relatively small states.

Such a perspective was consistent with the evolution of relations among Communist states in the post-Second World War period. From 1948 to 1953 it had been largely appropriate to think of the set of Communist states as making up 'the Soviet bloc' – although the exclusion of Yugoslavia from the Cominform in 1948 was testimony that, virtually from the outset, not all Communist states were a part of that bloc. Indeed, the Stalin–Tito clash revealed that Communist states created more or less in imitation of the Soviet model were highly capable of repulsing the imperial blandishments – short of actual armed force – of all states, including the Soviet Union. The emergence of China as a significant force in the 1950s, the reemergence of interstate relations among the European Communist states after Stalin's death in 1953, and Khrushchev's secret speech at the Twentieth CPSU Congress suggested the transformation of Communist relations from those of a bloc to those of an international system constituting a potential world system.

The 1960s, however, lent little support to the idea widespread at the beginning of that decade that there would emerge by the end of the 1970s a global international order dominated by the Soviet Union and governed by 'scientific socialist' norms. Nor did the 1960s show that it made sense to set off relations between Communist states and nonruling Communist parties from the general international system. Changes in trade and transaction flows, the evolving pattern of organizational memberships, and, most notably, the failure of the Communist states to contain conflict within the set of Communist states all served to undermine the utility of postulating a general Communist international system. Instead it became increasingly appropriate in the 1960s to define Soviet–East European relations in regionally specific terms, to differentiate between relations among these states and other states, whether the latter were non-Communist or Communist.

Institutionally, the 'boundaries' of that regional system were defined by membership in the Warsaw Treaty Organization and Comecon (CMEA), each of which in the 1960s was almost exclusively East European in composition. (Mongolia was a member of Comecon.) Trade patterns among the East European states, with the exception of Romania, in the 1960s and early 1970s were distinctive from those of other states, capitalist or Communist. The trade of the USSR and the East European states other than Romania was overwhelmingly with each other and remarkably constant throughout the period, as Table 5.1 shows. Communist elites

Table 5.1   *East European Intra-CMEA Trade as a Proportion of Total Trade, 1960–72*
(In percent)

	1960	1972
Bulgaria		
Turnover	80	80
Imports	80	80
Exports	80	80
Czechoslovakia		
Turnover	63	66
Imports	64	65
Exports	63	66
German Democratic Republic		
Turnover	67	67
Imports	66	63
Exports	69	65
Hungary		
Turnover	62	64
Imports	64	63
Exports	61	65
Poland		
Turnover	56	59
Imports	58	58
Exports	55	60
Romania		
Turnover	67	46
Imports	68	45
Exports	66	47

Source: J. T. Crawford and John Haberstroh, 'Survey of Economic Policy Issues in Eastern Europe', in *Reorientation and Commercial Relations of the Economies of Eastern Europe* (a compendium of papers submitted to the Joint Economic Committee, 93rd Congress, 2nd Session) (Washington, D.C.: US Government Printing Office, 1974), p. 41.

themselves displayed a growing propensity to confine references to the concept 'socialist community' to the USSR and Eastern Europe. Viewed from the perspective of behavior norms, finally, it was increasingly evident that 'proletarian internationalism' had clear behavioral consequences only for Soviet–East European relations and not for relations with other Communist states, much less nonruling parties.

At the outset of the 1970s, Soviet–East European relations could thus be appropriately distinguished from relations with other states, Communist or non-Communist. Several developments in the 1970s, however, made the distinction less obvious. The salience of the boundaries of the Soviet–East European regional system diminished. Against the background of détente East–West tourism grew rapidly. Not only was there an immense burgeoning of Western tourism in Eastern Europe but East European tourism in Western Europe became substantial as well; by the mid-1970s more than a million tourists from Czechoslovakia, Hungary, and Poland annually visited the West. Similarly a veritable flood of Western tourists descended on East Germany, largely from West Germany; 6.8 million West German tourists visited the German Democratic Republic in 1977, and 1.3 million older East Germans visited West Germany in the same year.[4]

Likewise in the 1970s there was an immense burgeoning of trade with the West on the part of all the European members of Comecon, a burgeoning that would have been even more extensive except for the impact on East–West trade of the OPEC oil price rise and subsequent Western stagflation. (Poland in particular underwent a trade reorientation in the 1970s paralleled only by the Romanian reorientation of the 1960s.) Indeed, while the energy crisis generally dampened East–West trade and accelerated intra-Comecon integration, the conditions that the Soviet Union exacted from the East European states in the mid-1970s in return for energy-source security reduced the distinctions between Soviet–East European trade conditions and those of the world market. Institutionally, too, Comecon lost its regional distinctiveness. First, Cuba became a member. Affiliations were worked out with Iraq, Finland, and Mexico. More important, Vietnam became a full member in June 1978. Should Angola and Ethiopia acquire full membership in place of the observer status they occupied (together with Yugoslavia and North Korea) at recent annual meetings of the Comecon Council, 'Eastern Europe' will have become the world.

Consequently, there was somewhat more reason at the end of the 1970s than at the beginning of the decade to suppose a global system of socialist states headed by the USSR might ultimately emerge. For the first time, the term 'socialist commonwealth' (which had been around for decades) bore some analogue to its British namesake. In general, however, the distinctiveness of Soviet–East European relations remained. Non-Soviet Communist elites continued to perceive Soviet–East European relations as distinct from other relations. While the Soviet invasion of Afghanistan in December 1979 provided an indication that the Soviet leadership had elected to treat a state on the USSR's southern border as being little different from Eastern Europe, it remains doubtful whether in practice Soviet decision makers regard proletarian internationalism as applying with equal force to all Marxist states or even Comecon members, that is, as implying that the USSR's commitment to preserve socialism was as great for Vietnam or Cuba or other future members of Comecon as it was for Eastern Europe. The organizational distinctiveness of the Warsaw Treaty Organization had not changed by the end of the 1970s. On the occasion of the Chinese invasion of Vietnam in 1979, Romania was as successful in limiting the *domain* of the WTO commitment as it had been in 1969–70, when the Soviet leadership had apparently urged that the Mongolian People's Republic be made a member of the pact and called for the stationing of East European troops along the Ussuri River. But Romania, at the end of the 1970s, was also as unsuccessful as it had been at the beginning of the decade in asserting that the idealized *norms* of the international system ought to obtain for all interstate relations including Soviet–East European relations. The Soviet Union continued to maintain a crucial distinction between the norms that govern Soviet–East European relations and all other relations.

Conceiving relations among the Soviet Union and Eastern Europe in the 1960s and 1970s as a hierarchical regional system has, moreover, several advantages. Emphasizing the hierarchical nature of the system summarizes the general pattern of asymmetry that has typified Soviet–East European relations throughout the period since the Communist takeovers at the end of the Second World War. This conveys some sense of the distinct limits on the behavior of the small states, while still allowing for some independent behavior on the part of all the states in the system. That asymmetry has been such an essential aspect of Soviet–East European relations as to warrant somewhat greater detail.

Assuming, for instance, as a first approximation that gross national product summarizes the power of a state, one can employ a measure suggested by James Caporaso to describe more specifically the inequality of the Soviet–East European system.[5] Caporaso's equation is

$$\text{Con} = \sqrt{\frac{\sum_{i=1}^{n} P_i^2 - 1/N}{1 - 1/N}}$$

where concentration is represented by Con, P_i stands for the proportion of GNP of each state in the total gross product of the regional system, and N is the number of actors in the system. Higher system inequality will result in scores that are nearer to unity. Using Caporaso's measure, it turns out, not surprisingly, that the Soviet–East European regional system (here defined as the members of the WTO and the European members of Comecon) is somewhat less unequal than the Western hemispheric system (i.e. the Organization of American States) and somewhat more unequal than the North Atlantic community (NATO). There was some indication of a trend toward greater concentration in the 1960s, but in general the overall pattern of asymmetry was relatively stable throughout the 1960s and 1970s. (See Table 5.2.)

The asymmetry in Soviet–East European relations was also reflected in the extent to which the East European states were penetrated by the Soviet Union. In the years of high Stalinism, the East European states, like the republics of the Soviet Union, were national in form and socialist in content; they were totally penetrated systems that were little more than transmission belt organizations. The death of Stalin and the ramifications in East Europe of the Twentieth CPSU Congress produced important changes in the penetration of the East European states. The most obvious forms of penetration were eliminated. After 1956 Soviet citizens were no longer members of the Polish Central Committee, and East European budgets in the 1960s and 1970s were much less directly correlated with 'the Soviet pattern of social expenditures' than they had been in the 1950s.[6]

Table 5.2   *Measures of Interstate Inequality in Regional Systems*

International Organization	1957	1965	1972
Organization of American States	.882	.877	.867
	.891[a]		.877[a]
North Atlantic Treaty Organization	.618	.615	.584
	.616[a]		.485[a]
Warsaw Treaty Organization	.685	.712	.717
	.678[b]		

[a] Inequality scores for the seven members with the largest gross national product from each alliance.
[b] Includes Albania.
Sources: Gross national product figures are drawn from: Bruce Russett *et al.*, *World Handbook of Political and Social Indicators* (New Haven: Yale University Press, 1964); Charles L. Taylor and Michael C. Hudson, *World Handbook of Political and Social Indicators*, 2nd edn (New Haven: Yale University Press, 1972); and US Arms Control and Disarmament Agency, *World Military Expenditures and Arms Trade, 1963-73* (Washington, D.C.: US Government Printing Office, 1974).

Indeed, for the 1960s and early 1970s, the data suggested that the free rider problem – that expenditures per capita on a public good, defense, are disproportionately borne by the larger members of an alliance – was a phenomenon observable both in the WTO and NATO contexts. Nor did the increased leverage that the USSR was able to exercise on the East European states in the mid-1970s as a result of the direct and indirect consequences of the energy crisis alter the situation substantially. The East European states as a whole evidently did not assume an increasingly greater share of the burden of defense for the alliance in the 1970s. Bulgaria increased somewhat its contribution to defense procurements. The German Democratic Republic probably increased its contribution. The Czechoslovak budget shares for defense remained constant. Hungary, Poland, and Romania reduced the proportion allocated for defense, in the Polish case rather substantially. In the 1970s détente apparently allowed Poland to find in its defense allocations some of the funds with which to buy the consumer goods, the *importing* of which has been made more difficult by Western inflation, and the *importance* of which has become crucial in the evolving pattern of Polish elite/mass relations. (See Table 5.3.)

Similarly, the constitutions adopted after 1956 suggested that there were ranges in the degree of penetration. Constitutions adopted in the 1960s and 1970s varied in their evidence of deference to the Soviet Union. The 1965 Romanian Constitution made no mention of the USSR by name; the 1971 Bulgarian Constitution and the 1974 East German Constitution did. The last affirms that the German Democratic Republic is 'forever and irrevocably allied with the USSR and is an inseparable component of the socialist community of states.' It was initially proposed that the 1975 Polish Constitution contain a phrase referring to Poland's 'unshakable

Table 5.3 *Defense Expenditure by East European States, 1970–77, as Percentage of GNP, Domestic Currencies*

	1970	1971	1972	1973	1974	1975	1976	1977
Bulgaria	2.4	2.6	2.7	2.7	2.8	3.0	3.0	
					(2.7)	(2.7)	(2.4)	(2.5)
Czechoslovakia	3.9	3.9	3.7	3.6	3.6	3.5	3.8	
					(3.8)	(3.8)	(3.9)	(3.8)
German Democratic Republic	4.5	4.4	4.4	4.4	4.3	4.3	4.4	
					(5.4)	(5.5)	(5.7)	(5.9)
Hungary	2.8	2.7	2.4	2.2	2.3	2.4	2.4	
					(2.4)	(2.4)	(2.5)	(2.6)
Poland	4.0	3.8	3.4	3.2	3.0	2.9	3.0	
					(3.0)	(3.1)	(3.0)	(3.0)
Romania	2.1	2.0	1.9	1.7	1.7	1.7	1.7	
					(1.7)	(1.7)	(1.7)	(1.7)

Sources: The numbers *not* in parentheses are from Thad P. Alton *et al.*, 'Defense Expenditures in Eastern Europe, 1965–76', in *East European Economies Post-Helsinki* (a compendium of papers submitted to the Joint Economic Committee, 95th Congress, 1st Session) (Washington, D.C.: US Government Printing Office, 1977), p. 270. The numbers in parentheses are from International Institute of Strategic Studies, *The Military Balance 1978–79* (London: ISS, 1978), p. 88. While these numbers should be treated with some skepticism, they are less suspect than, for instance, estimates of Soviet military expenditures which must include quite rough estimates for R & D and missiles.

fraternal bond with the Soviet Union'; protests by elites with aspirations to see Poland less explicitly linked to the USSR resulted in a final text simply declaring that 'Poland strengthens its friendship and cooperation with the Soviet Union and other socialist states'.[7]

More generally, however, knowledge of the extent of the overall penetration of East European parties, economy, and society by the CPSU and the Soviet military through the WTO during the 1960s and 1970s leaves a lot to be desired. One can nevertheless obtain a reasonable approximation of the evolving overall Soviet presence in Eastern Europe by focusing on the degree of cultural penetration by the Soviet Union. A comparison of the expected frequency with which East European states translate books from Russian and English, were it a random occurrence, with the observed pattern at a given year in time reveals the extent of the continued Soviet cultural presence in Eastern Europe. Similarly, a longitudinal analysis of translations from Russian as a proportion of all books translated indicates a steady decrease in the Soviet cultural presence in Eastern Europe over time. (See Table 5.4.)

The inequality in the power of the member states of a hierarchical regional system and the concomitant penetration of the lesser states have often led specialists to regard the exploitation of the East European states as an essential feature of Soviet–East European relations. One man's exploitation is another's mutually advantageous sharing of resources, know-how, or capital: perceptions and frame of reference are crucial. The consensus of specialists, however, is that, while in the early post-Second World War period the Soviet Union used its preeminent political and military status to exploit its East European clients economically (particularly disadvantaging what became the German Democratic Republic), the issue of who was exploiting whom in Soviet–East European relations from 1956 to 1973 was at least an open question.[8] If one employs the criterion favored by most Marxists and dependency theorists – terms of trade – the general disposition of economists has been that the developed, manufactured goods-producing East European states were the exploiter states, a situation that provoked largely ineffectual protests by the USSR. (Soviet objections, however, were evidently not too strenuously advanced since the economic disadvantages to the Soviet Union were compensated for in considerable measure by such political gains as bloc loyalty and cohesion.) After the OPEC price increases began to affect the structure of Soviet–East European trade, the situation changed significantly. The terms of trade shifted in favor of the Soviet Union, and in addition its improved bargaining position allowed the USSR increasingly to insist on higher quality products from its East European sellers. Consequently, one could no longer speak of East European exploitation of the Soviet Union, with the important qualification that in the last years of the 1970s the East European states were able to trade on ('exploit', as it were) their respective weaknesses – economic, in Hungary's case; political, in the case of Poland. Some observers contend that by the end of the 1970s the tables had been so reversed that the Soviet Union was once again (as in the immediate post-Second World War years) exploiting Eastern Europe. This judgment turns largely on the assessment one makes of East European investment in the

Table 5.4   Russian Language Books as a Percentage of the Total Number of Books Translated in East European Countries[a]

	Albania[b]	Bulgaria	Czecho-slovakia	GDR	Hungary	Poland	Romania	Yugo-slavia
1954	NA	66	64	NA	59	70	NA	7
1955	NA	69	52	NA	48	57	47	21
1956	NA	63	47	NA	40	47	53	23
1957	NA	63	31	NA	16	30	32	10
1958	57	50	24	NA	27	22	43	10
1959	44	49	26	NA	25	20	44	10
1960	61	54	26	NA	30	23	44	10
1961	48	57	24	NA	23	26	49	13
1962	39	51	24	NA	30	27	37	9
1963	34	53	23	NA	22	23	34	13
1964	58	46	16	NA	20	23	24	13
1965	26	43	16	NA	16	23	11	NA
1966	16	37	11	NA	13	25	9	11[c]
1967	26	33	12	NA	15	23	8	11
1968	19	34	15	NA	13	20	8	12
1969	25	37	8	NA	10	19	5	8
1970	28	39	9	NA	11	21	10	13
1971	17	36	13	41	10	19	5	12
1972	7	44	18	73	11	17	10	8
1973	10	44	24	42	11	16	6	7

[a] While there are a number of possible explanations for the above figures, the trend over time seem unmistakably linked to changes in Soviet relations with particular European Communist states, especially when one compares the impact of truly significant events (Hungary, Poland in 1956, Czechoslovakia in 1968) lagged a year.
[b] NA = Not available.
[c] 1965–66 combined.
Source: United Nations, Statistical Office, Statistical Yearbooks.

Soviet Union, substantial amounts of which were only forthcoming after the energy crisis. The derivative impact of the global jump in commodity prices in the mid-1970s certainly rendered the East European states more dependent on the USSR; whether that will result in exploitation – manifestly unequal exchange – remains very much to be seen.

Just as emphasizing the *hierarchical* nature of the regional international system highlights the essential asymmetry in Soviet–East European relations, there are distinct advantages to defining these relations as a *regional international system*. Specifically, this perspective prompts attention to the ways in which linkages between the dominant international system and the regional system can influence the maneuvering capacity of the member states of that regional system.

Elsewhere I have used the phrase 'the politics of system boundaries' to describe the effort by decision makers of a regional system's member states to exploit the linkages between the regional and dominant international system in order to enhance their capacity for maneuver.[9] Generally, for instance, the regional hegemon is disposed toward, and pursues, policies that seek to maintain or increase the barriers (system boundaries) separating the regional system from the outside world. The Soviet Union in particular has traditionally cared intensely about maintaining the distinctions between Soviet–East European relations and all other relations.

Yet by the 1960s and early 1970s the USSR was no longer a mere regional great power but had become a world power as well. This had consequences for Soviet behavior. The Soviet leadership was increasingly torn between regional-system and dominant-system goals. As a world power, increasingly concerned with events outside the region, the USSR was increasingly drawn to viewing the regional system as a resource to be mobilized against an extra-regional rival. In the 1970s especially it became evident, moreover, that in some instances the Soviet Union might at the margin trade off reduced intraregional system cohesion for gains elsewhere. Ironically, however, the more or less parallel occurrence of détente, the minimization of Soviet security concerns in Europe, and the reversal of the long-term trend in the global terms of trade combined to reduce the Soviet need to make those hard choices during the 1970s. As a result, the Soviet Union was not obliged to choose between actions that encourage alliance cohesion and stability and those that address Soviet economic priorities which can only be properly achieved outside their region. In the 1970s Moscow did not feel intensely the potentially acute tension between political security (i.e. regional) and economic (i.e. global) concerns.

Just as the regional hegemon has the option of pursuing policies that increase or maintain the barriers separating the regional system from the outside world or, alternatively, of seeking to reduce the salience of the regional system boundaries, so, too, do the lesser states within a regional system. In the 1960s, for instance, in Eastern Europe (as in Latin America) the states most likely to define national security in a manner similar to the regional hegemon were those relatively small powers whose regimes had not sought to achieve a sense of legitimacy in the eyes of key social groups by engendering in them a sense of participation in the political system. Like the regional hegemon, they tended to emphasize the distinctions between the regional system and the outside world.

Other small powers, by contrast, seek to alter the foreign policy environment in which they operate by reducing the salience of a regional system's boundaries. Archetypically, the small states in a hierarchical regional system drawn to such policies are attempting to achieve a basic legitimacy *vis-à-vis* society either by approximating a pluralist or conciliationist model *or* through more typically totalitarian, mobilizational methods. In the Soviet–East European hierarchical regional system, Czechoslovakia in 1968 and Romania in the 1960s were the prototypes of such regimes and such boundary-reducing strategies. Both the Czechoslovak and Romanian stories are oft-told tales and need not detain us here. For our purposes, however, several points are notable. (1) Romania managed, over approximately a decade, to accomplish a dramatic reorientation in its trade patterns and international institutional affiliation, even joining the International Monetary Fund in 1973. (2) Romania achieved considerable success in implementing its claims to treatment as simultaneously a member of the socialist camp *and* a developing country. (3) Romania received formal recognition in the 1971 Comecon Comprehensive Program that East European integration would proceed on the basis of respect for national independence and sovereignty and that Comecon 'reaffirmed the commitment . . . to equalize economic development levels as a precondition of full integration'.[10] (4) Throughout the 1970s, Romania persisted in efforts to reduce the salience of the regional system boundaries. It has continued to maintain its claim to simultaneous status as a socialist state allied to the Soviet Union and as an independently oriented developing country, and has institutionalized that claim in the context of Western stagflation by impressively redirecting its trade from the global West to the global South.

Moreover, our limiting cases of conciliationist 1968 Czechoslovakia and mobilizational Romania have not stood alone in seeking to reduce the salience of the East European regional system's boundaries. Hungary sought to implement the New Economic Mechanism by becoming increasingly integrated with the world economy. More broadly, from 1965 on, Hungarian foreign policy followed the guiding motif that the class principle did not exclude geographical considerations, that Hungary's 'identity references' (in Kenneth Jowitt's felicitous term[11]) could extend across regional system boundaries, that Hungary could be both socialist and Danubian.

Hungary pursued this policy throughout the 1970s, despite impressive economic hurdles. As the most open economy among the East European states, Hungary felt most acutely the direct impact of the Western stagflation following the 1973 OPEC oil price rise, and as one of the most energy-deficient countries in Eastern Europe, Hungary also felt acutely the indirect impact (as mediated by Soviet policies) of the 1973 OPEC oil price rise. Yet in 1977 the Hungarian Foreign Minister, Frigyes Puja, reiterated Hungary's commitment to a policy grounded both in geographical and class considerations. The response of Hungarian commentators to Western economic difficulties has been substantially to reaffirm, indeed stress, Hungary's foreign trade orientation, to the extent of making public references to a 'civic duty' of increasing foreign trade.[12]

Poland, too, engaged in analogous policies throughout the 1970s. The ouster of Gomulka following the December 1970 riots was the precipitating event leading to a dramatic reversal of attitude toward the world economy, but improved East–West relations, particularly Soviet–East European relations with the Federal Republic of Germany, also were an important backdrop for the Polish actions. As in the case of Hungary, Poland persisted in its policies throughout the 1970s. The dramatic reorientation in trade has been mentioned. What bears stressing is how much this fits into an overall tactic of reducing the salience of the boundaries setting off the East European regional system from the rest of the world. In response to Western stagflation the East European nations have generally increased their indebtedness to, and dependence on, the West. They have also permitted increased Western economic penetration, even granting Western banks access to data, the gathering of which in another time would have been characterized as espionage.

The underlying motif of the Polish reorientation was epitomized by a Polish Central Committee member who in 1976 said, in words faintly echoing the 1968 Czechoslovak Action Program, 'We Polish Communists have an ambition to play an important role in Europe, creating a mode of socialism acceptable to everyone, including comrades in both directions'.[13]

II   Soviet–East European Relations in the 1980s

What then about the 1980s? Will the past, as exemplified by Soviet–East European relations in the 1960s and 1970s, be prologue? Or are the 1980s more likely to illustrate that sage, if doubtless apocryphal, remark of the Washington cab driver who was asked by a tourist to explain the meaning of the statement 'What is past is prologue' emblazoned on the face of the National Archives: 'It means you ain't seen nothing yet'. Will the defining features of Soviet–East European relations remain essentially as they were? Will the hierarchical cast to the relationship be altered substantially? Will integration progress to such an extent as to raise the issue whether it is still appropriate to view the set of relations as an international system? Or will increased Soviet penetration in the context of greater plan coordination make the putative independence of the East European states largely symbolic? Will the change in the global system – shifts in the Soviet–American distribution of strategic power, East–West relations,[14] changes in global North–South relations of the magnitude of the 1973 OPEC oil price rise – alter the rules of the game so fundamentally that East European elites who previously advocated system-boundary permeability and greater independence from the Soviet Union will seek the security of a system marked off from the external environment? Will the Soviet leadership pressure its East European allies to fend increasingly for themselves? Will the Soviet Union once again resort to force in order to protect socialism in Eastern Europe, this time in possible disregard of an explicit Soviet–American arrangement for the withdrawal of forces in the center of Europe? What developments in Soviet–East European relations are most likely to occur? What occurrences and what possible patterns of Soviet–East European relations can be excluded for the 1980s?

A central point about Soviet–East European relations in the 1980s is that in the coming decade they will still be most appropriately treated as a hierarchical regional international system. This is a nontrivial proposition, more for the possibilities excluded than for those envisaged.

It assumes, for instance, that the kinds of change that could alter the hierarchical structure of the system are not options for the 1980s. To produce such a transformation would require the introduction of one or more additional great powers into the system. The prospects for that occurrence are negligible. Even were there a Sino-Soviet reconciliation, for example, Soviet–East European relations would still be distinctively separable from general intra-Communist relations. Other possibilities – a unified Communist Germany or a Communist East Europe unified without the Soviet Union in such a way as to create a bipolar or multipolar Soviet–East European regional system – strain credulity.

Some have seen the emergence in recent years of economic institutions in Eastern Europe that parallel Soviet institutions, the emphasis attached within Comecon to increased plan coordination, and Soviet rhetoric about the relevance of Soviet internal nationality policies to relations within Comecon as steps towards the achievement of a single economic 'complex' in the 1980s. My position assumes that they have missed the point, that in fact all these developments are relevant to increased economic integration of independent states and economies.

The proposition affirms, furthermore, the expectation that even though the Soviet Union's global role will increase in the 1980s, the priorities of the Soviet leadership will not change so greatly that they blur completely the distinction between Soviet–East European relations and other relations. Eastern Europe will not become the world: the probable expansion of Comecon's domain will not find its counterpart in the expansion of the Warsaw Treaty Organization. To be more precise, the Soviet commitment to, and integration with the military forces of, non-East European states will not approach that of the current Soviet commitment to, and integration with the military forces of, East European states. Doctrinally, no imaginable Soviet leadership in the 1980s will offer to place Soviet–East European relations on the same plane as relations with non-East European states, Communist or non-Communist. No Soviet leadership in the 1980s will propose to a recalcitrant Polish leadership, as the current Soviet leadership has proposed to the Chinese, that peaceful coexistence be the basis of their bilateral relations.

Assuming, moreover, that the composition of the Soviet–East European regional system remains more or less constant (though the defection or agglutination of one or more states is entirely conceivable) we can state with reasonable confidence that the degree of interstate inequality will not alter significantly in the 1980s. If we extrapolate to the 1980s on the basis of likely ranges in differential growth rates and employ the measure of inequality used above, the interstate inequality for the Soviet–East European regional system will not be greater than the inequality score for the Organization of American States in the early 1970s (1972 = .867), or lower than that for NATO in the early 1970s (1972 = .584).

At the same time, it seems safe to predict that Soviet–East European economic integration will increase, though very likely differentially across states and sectors, in the 1980s. Although the evidence available does not suggest that the direct and indirect consequences of the energy crisis have had substantial impact on the general cast of Soviet–East European relations, the energy crisis has accelerated intra-Comecon integration. The developing practice of intra-Comecon coordination of overall plans; the development of long-term coordination in specific areas, energy most notably; the propensity of East European states to invest in the Soviet Union – all will intensify. These processes appear ineluctable. Despite Soviet encouragement of East Europeans to look elsewhere for energy, in the intermediate run – the 1980s – the East European states will have to import energy largely from the USSR, a concomitant of which will be greater intra-Comecon integration. Indeed the mere implementation of decisions already taken will result in greater economic integration.

The increase in Soviet–East European economic integration, however, will not be paralleled by increased Soviet cultural and political penetration of Eastern Europe as a whole. (There may very well be detectable increases in particular states that currently constitute the Soviet–East European regional system. Generalizations about overall trends in Soviet presence in the 1960s were small comfort for Czechoslovak elites in 1968.) Instead, I anticipate that the steady trend toward a reduction in the Soviet cultural presence in Eastern Europe will continue, but that the rate of that decrease will itself continue to decrease and may be rapidly approaching a limit.[15] As such, this would seem to be an instance, barring societal shocks, where the past is prologue, where the 1960s and 1970s do adumbrate the 1980s. The insidious cultural Europeanization of Eastern Europe is likely to continue as is the equally insidious Americanization of Europe. Further decreases in Soviet political penetration will result, to use an old phrase from Zbigniew K. Brzezinski, in greater 'domesticism', that is, further internal autonomy and greater differentiation within the East European states. This in turn will make it more difficult in the future to generalize about the internal behavioral norms, and conceivably the institutions, of the one-party states of Eastern Europe. Internal behavioral differentiation is almost certain to spill over into the foreign policy domain, or into what is likely to be perceived by other, most notably, Soviet elites as the foreign policy domain. Resource allocation decisions, for instance – the proportion of zlotys for guns and margarine – are intimately linked to foreign policy. When an East European state reduces the shares of the budget for defense in order to procure consumer goods, that action in the context of alliance politics is very likely to be construed, often quite properly (viz. Romania in 1979), as deliberately nonsupportive of the alliance.

Nor will increased Soviet–East European economic integration be at the cost of reduced intra-European integration. Rather, the East European states and, to a lesser extent, the Soviet Union will be more linked with Europe and the larger international economic system than in the 1970s. In fact, increased Soviet–East European integration will require greater East European ties with the world economy.

Part of the rationale for this somewhat paradoxical assertion (paradoxical if one assumes that increased regional integration is incompatible with increased ties between that region and its external environment) depends on the credence given to various projections of Soviet oil production in the early 1980s. The major estimates[16] are listed in Table 5.5.

Table 5.5 *Soviet Oil Output*
(Million metric tons)

	CIA High	Oil and Gas Journal	Dienes Low	Dienes High	Official Soviet
1975 (actual)	491	491	491	491	491
1980	590	600	605	605	620–640
1985	500	550	605	655	750
1990	500	550	605	710	

If the low Western estimates (especially those of the United States Central Intelligence Agency) are correct, there will be a greater likelihood that East European purchases of Soviet oil will be accomplished in ways that necessitate extensive linkages with the West. This could produce a situation in which East European states purchase Soviet oil increasingly with hard currency, with goods obtained from Western Europe by the East European states, or in exchange for East European products (in short supply domestically) that are of a quality that they *could* be sold in the West. (Examples of all the above, of course, already exist.) In the 1980s East European masses and, conceivably, elites would increasingly perceive such a situation as exploitation. Should the Soviet projections be correct, the pressure on Eastern Europe from the Soviet side to reduce the distinctions between the regional market and the international market will be lessened. In either event, though, there are lots of reasons why Soviet–East European integration is conducive to increased East European ties with the world economy. (Should the Soviet Union reduce its sales to Eastern Europe, of course, the East European states would have to obtain their oil on the world market.) Moreover, at least the Romanian, Polish, and Hungarian elites give every indication of persisting in their commitment to expand economic ties with the West.

In general, the markers – the transnational flows, identity references, institutional memberships, behavioral norms – that set off the Soviet–East European regional system from the rest of the world are likely to decrease in the 1980s. Both for the economic reasons explained in the previous paragraph and for reasons related to the USSR's increased global political role, the Soviet Union will engage in some policies that reduce the differentiation between the Soviet–East European and other relations. The greater integration of Eastern Europe in the world economy will be paralleled by efforts by elites in some East European states to reduce the salience of the boundaries separating the regional system from the general international system to an extent greater than contemplated by Soviet elites. The most obvious choice of states likely to pursue such policies are those East European states that engaged in such efforts throughout the 1970s. Leadership changes and changes in the external environment may result in such moves by other East European states as well. Moreover, external powers – the United States, the West generally, and China – will all pursue, perhaps more than in the 1970s, what were in the 1960s called 'bridge building activities'.

The generally increased domestic differentiation and the reduced salience of the regional system boundaries will very likely increase the tendency of the Soviet leadership to engage in differentiated policies *vis-à-vis* the East European states. Foreign and domestic behavior of Poland, say, which the USSR will tolerate will not be tolerated elsewhere – in Hungary or Czechoslovakia, for instance. In this sense, the rules of the game for the regional system will be less clear in the beginning of the 1980s than they were in the early 1970s. Certain East European domestic and international actions constitute serious irritants but are not sufficient to provoke Soviet reprisals. The incidence of controversies between the Soviet Union and particular East European states over such actions is likely to increase.

It is, nevertheless, entirely possible that in at least one East European state the 1980s will bring domestic transformations or changes in foreign policy that elites in the USSR will find entirely intolerable. The possibility that the USSR will use military force in or against one East European state during the 1980s therefore also exists, regardless of the ultimate outcome of the 1980 strikes in Poland.

Both the incidence of conflict and the intensity of conflict within the Soviet–East European regional system will be influenced by the state of relations between the Soviet Union and the United States and Soviet–Western relations generally. The level of East–West political tension will affect substantially the penetrability of Eastern Europe by the West; to the extent that East–West relations are less tense than in the 1970s the rate of penetration will increase. Given the likely range of possible degrees of East–West tension, however, the prospects are for some increase in penetration in comparison with the 1970s in any event. The Soviet Union's acquiescence in the expected increase in the differentiation among the behaviors of East European states in marginal cases will be strongly conditioned by the state of Soviet relations with the West. The number and range of issues that produce overt Soviet–East European clashes will fluctuate in part at least according to overall relations with the West.

Disputes, for instance, over the burden of defense within the Warsaw Treaty Organization are more likely to the extent that Soviet–Western relations improve. Disputes over East European investments in the Soviet Union and Soviet supplies of energy to Eastern Europe would follow the same pattern. The intensity of disputes among member states of the Soviet–East European regional system, however, will be greater, the greater the tension between the Soviet Union and the major actors in the external environment.

On the other hand, within the range of East–West distributions of power conceivable in the 1980s, the East–West military balance will probably not substantially affect relations within the Soviet–East European regional system. What would have a dramatic effect on the evolution of Soviet–East European relations would be a negotiated and dramatic decrease in the disposition of Soviet–American forces in the center of Europe. Thirty-five years after the Second World War, the location of American, British, and Soviet troops at the end of that war is still the central fact in explaining the nature of the domestic political systems of Europe. Even in the aftermath of the Soviet invasion of Afghanistan, it may well be that at some juncture in the 1980s, Soviet–American troop reductions in the center of Europe may occur. Should such an arrangement take place, the degree of maneuver for the East European states would be greatly enhanced, and the impact of developments outside the region on Eastern Europe would be intensified as well.

This in turn could encourage masses and elites within one or more East European countries to act in such conflict with Soviet interests as to provoke a Soviet intervention. But this time such an intervention would contravene an explicit Soviet–Western agreement with all the attendant consequences. While such a possibility must not be dismissed (there is no end to our worries) the more likely prospect in the context of Soviet–American troop reductions, given the increased economic dependence of the East European states on the Soviet Union and forty years of elite socialization, would be something approximating the Finlandization of parts of Eastern Europe. Such an outcome would imply that the boundaries setting off the Soviet–East European regional system from the world would have become obscured. All things considered, though, such a development, however, desirable, is merely a possibility and not at all a probability for the 1980s.

Were it to occur, however, the inevitable paper written in *1989* about the future of Soviet–East European relations in the 1990s would not begin with what is axiomatic in 1979 about the 1980s: namely, that througout the coming decade, Soviet–East European relations will be most appropriately characterized (as in the 1960s and 1970s) as a hierarchical regional international system set off from the general international system by discontinuities in trade, tourism, institutional memberships, and most of all, behavioral norms. Rather, in this optimistic scenario, Eastern Europe would not become the world, as it would in scenarios that contemplate the transformation of the Soviet–East European regional system into an alternative global system. Instead, we would once again begin to think less of 'Eastern' Europe and more of *Central* Europe. And in the 1990s, there is some hope that Eastern Europe will have become a part of Europe.

Notes: Chapter 5

1 Jan F. Triska, 'Future Soviet–East European Relations'. Paper prepared for the Conference on the Future of the Soviet Union, Stanford University; Palo Alto, California; September 1978.
2 Archie Brown, 'Eastern Europe: 1968, 1978, 1998', *Daedalus*, Vol. 108, No. 1 (Winter 1979), esp. pp. 164–71.

3 William Zimmerman, 'Hierarchical Regional Systems and the Politics of System Boundaries', *International Organization*, Vol. 26, No. 1 (Winter 1972), pp. 18–36; 'Dependency Theory and the Soviet–East European Hierarchical Regional System: Initial Tests', *Slavic Review*, Vol. 37, No. 4 (December 1978), pp. 604–23; 'The Energy Crisis, Western "Stagflation" and the Evolution of Soviet–East European Relations', in Egon Neuberger and Laura D. Tyson (eds), *Impact of International Economic Disturbances on the Soviet Union and Eastern Europe* (Elmsford, N.Y.: Pergamon Press, 1980), pp. 409–37. What follows draws heavily on these articles.

4 I am indebted to Alex Pravda for these figures. On the notion of 'boundaries' in a hierarchical regional system, see Zimmerman, op. cit.

5 James Caporaso, 'Methodological Issues in the Measurement of Inequality, Dependence and Exploitation', in Steven J. Rosen and James R. Kurth (eds), *Testing Theories of Economic Imperialism* (Lexington, Mass.: D. C. Heath, 1974), p. 100.

6 Valerie Bunce and John Echols, 'Aggregate Data in the Study of Policy Change in Communist Systems'. Paper presented at the 1975 Annual Meeting of the American Association for the Advancement of Slavic Studies; Atlanta, Georgia; October 1975.

7 As cited by Thomas Heneghan in Radio Free Europe (hereafter RFE), *Background Report (Poland)*, 1975, No. 158.

8 The best treatment is Edward Hewett, *Foreign Trade Prices in the Council for Mutual Economic Assistance* (London: Cambridge University Press, 1974).

9 Zimmerman, op. cit.

10 Peter Marsh, 'The Integration Process in Eastern Europe, 1968–1975', *Journal of Common Market Studies*, Vol. 14, No. 4 (June 1976), pp. 311–35.

11 As cited by Sarah Meiklejohn Terry, 'External Influences on Political Change in Eastern Europe', in Jan F. Triska and Paul M. Cocks (eds), *Political Development in Eastern Europe* (New York: Praeger, 1977), pp. 277–314.

12 Deputy Foreign Trade Minister Gyula Kovacs, Radio Budapest, 10 May 1975, as cited by William F. Robinson in RFE, *Background Report (Eastern Europe)*, 1975, No. 116.

13 As reported by Malcolm Browne, *New York Times*, 10 August 1976.

14 See also Coral Bell's discussion of this topic in Chapter 2 of this volume.

15 My research assistant Marita Kaw extrapolated Russian translations as a proportion of all text translations for various East European states in the 1980s. Were the past pattern to continue, Romania would already be translating a 'negative percentage' of Russian language books. A more serious estimate would be that the Romanian pattern of translation of Russian books, as with so many other measures of Romanian autonomy of the USSR, will parallel that of Yugoslavia in the 1980s. Romanian propensity to diverge from Soviet voting patterns in the United Nations General Assembly now almost precisely parallels that of Yugloslavia.

16 This table is adapted from Daniel L. Bond and Herbert S. Levine, 'Energy and Grain in Soviet Hard Currency Trade', in *Soviet Economy in a Time of Change* (a compendium of papers submitted to the Joint Economic Committee, 96th Congress, 1st Session) (Washington, D.C.: US Government Printing Office, 1979), Vol. 2, pp. 244–89. See also Levine's discussion in 'The USSR and the Sources of Soviet Policy' (Summary Report of a seminar sponsored by the Council on Foreign Relations and the Kennan Institute for Advanced Russian Studies, The Wilson Center), Occasional Paper No. 34 (Washington, D.C.: The Kennan Institute, The Wilson Center, Smithsonian Institution, 1978; mimeo), p. 73.

Chapter 6

Soviet–East European Economic Relations

MORRIS BORNSTEIN

Despite their efforts in the 1970s to expand trade with the West, virtually all of the East European countries continue, for both economic and political reasons, to concentrate the bulk of their trade inside the CMEA. This chapter examines some key features of Soviet–East European economic relations that affect the regional versus international orientation of the East European economies and their future prospects.

Section I analyzes the pattern and recent development of trade between Eastern Europe and the USSR. Section II considers the most critical aspect of their economic relations – the supply of energy from the USSR to Eastern Europe. Section III discusses the nature and problems of Soviet–East European 'economic integration' in CMEA. Finally, Section IV draws some conclusions about the implications for Eastern Europe's economic orientation toward CMEA versus the West.

I Trade

The USSR is the dominant trading partner of all the East European countries except Romania. As Table 6.1 shows, in 1977 the USSR absorbed more than half of Bulgaria's exports and furnished over half of its imports. For Czechoslovakia, the GDR, Hungary, and Poland, the Soviet share in both exports and imports was about a third. In contrast, the USSR accounted for only about a fifth of Romania's total trade.

However, to assess their involvement in the Soviet-led regional bloc, one must also consider trade by East European countries with each other. When the shares of exports to, and imports from, other East European countries are added to the USSR's share, the proportion of intraregional trade in total trade rises to three-fourths for Bulgaria; two-thirds for Czechoslovakia, the GDR, and Hungary; half for Poland; and more than one-third for Romania.[1]

Among the European CMEA countries,[2] the commodity composition of trade follows fairly well defined lines. The East European countries import chiefly fuels and nonfood raw materials from the USSR. In return

I wish to thank Dennis O'Hearn and John Attarian for assistance in research; the International Research and Exchanges Board for aid in connection with a research trip to the USSR and Eastern Europe; and Zbigniew M. Fallenbuchl for helpful comments on an earlier version.

they export to the USSR machinery and equipment, industrial consumer goods, and some food products. Among themselves, however, the six East European countries exchange mostly manufactured products, including semifabricates, machinery and equipment, and consumer goods.

Table 6.1   *Shares of USSR and of Other East European Countries in Total Exports and Imports of Individual East European Countries, 1977* [a]
(Percent)

Country	Exports to		Imports from	
	USSR	Other East European Countries	USSR	Other East European Countries
Bulgaria	54.0	21.9	58.4	20.1
Czechoslovakia	39.6	33.7	33.4	30.8
GDR[b]	32.8	33.1	33.5	27.9
Hungary	35.4	29.7	33.4	26.6
Poland	31.2	25.4	29.2	20.6
Romania	18.9	20.4	19.1	22.5

[a]Imports are f.o.b. except for Hungary, which is on a c.i.f. basis. Dollar values for trade were derived by converting the value of trade expressed in the currency of each East European country to rubles and then to dollars at the prevailing foreign exchange rates, except as noted for the GDR.
[b]The official FRG deutsche mark–US dollar rate was used to convert intra-German trade in GDR marks to US dollars because using the GDR mark–US dollar rate understates the value of this trade. The GDR converts FRG marks at parity, but the GDR mark is actually worth less than the FRG mark.
Source: Computed from values in millions of US dollars in US Central Intelligence Agency, *Handbook of Economic Statistics 1979* (Washington, D.C.: Library of Congress Photoduplication Service, 1979), tables 67–68, pp. 106–7.

Thus, in Soviet–East European trade relations the USSR plays a dominant role for purely economic (as well as also political–military) reasons. First, the enormous difference in the size of the Soviet economy compared with the economies of the East European six (individually and collectively) makes the USSR the big regional supplier and customer. The result is a 'radial' pattern of bilateral trade between the USSR and each of the East European countries, in which the trade of each of the latter is oriented toward the USSR.[3]

Second, to a considerable extent Soviet exports to Eastern Europe consist of 'hard' goods, such as fuels and raw materials, which, for lack of convertible currency, Eastern Europe cannot purchase on the world market. In contrast, the USSR takes from Eastern Europe 'soft' goods, such as outdated machinery and poor quality consumer goods, which Eastern Europe cannot easily sell to the West, for reasons explained in Chapter 3.

As a result, while trade with Eastern Europe does not play a decisive role in Soviet economic growth, all aspects of trade with the USSR – the level, the composition, the terms, and the balance and how it is financed – are critical for the economic development of Eastern Europe.[4]

In the first decade after the Second World War, the USSR enjoyed substantial net benefits from its economic relations with Eastern Europe as a result of reparations, deliveries by Soviet-controlled 'joint' enterprises, and favorable terms of trade. However, the consensus view of Western specialists is that by the mid-1950s the situation began to change, and that in the 1960s and 1970s the East European countries turned into an economic 'liability' to the USSR for two reasons. First, the terms of Soviet–East European trade became unfavorable to the USSR as a result of the lag of intra-CMEA prices for fuels and raw materials behind rising world market prices. Second, Moscow found it necessary at various times to grant credit to dependent nations in economic and/or political difficulties, notably Poland and the GDR but also most of the other East European countries as well.[5]

After the quadrupling of Middle Eastern oil prices in 1973–74, the system of relating intra-CMEA foreign trade prices to world market prices was drastically changed. Previously, intra-CMEA foreign trade prices for a five-year period were supposed to be based on average world market prices for a preceding five-year period. For example, intra-CMEA prices in 1971–75 were to be related to average world market prices in 1965–69. The new formula, imposed by the USSR, provided instead for *annual* adjustments on the basis of *moving* averages. In principle, 1975 intra-CMEA prices were to be based on average 1970–74 world prices, 1976 intra-CMEA prices on average 1971–75 world prices, and so on. However, for oil and some other commodities, 1975 prices were supposed to be based on average 1972–74 world prices, which for oil were about 8 percent less than average 1971–75 prices.[6]

According to recent calculations by Vaňous,[7] the application of this new formula led to the following approximate percentage increases in intra-CMEA prices in 1975 relative to 1974: fuels, 100; raw materials, 8–50; food, 15; machinery and equipment, 11; and industrial consumer goods, 13. The result was a sharp improvement in the USSR's terms of trade with Eastern Europe, estimated by Kohn and Lang at about 12 percent for trade with the six East European countries as a group, and *vis-à-vis* individual countries as follows (in percent): Bulgaria, 9; Czechoslovakia, 17; GDR, 23; Hungary, 13; Poland, 3; and Romania, 3.[8] Thus, the impact was greatest on the heavy raw material importers (Bulgaria, Czechoslovakia, the GDR, and Hungary) and much more modest for the countries more generously endowed with raw materials and/or fuels (Poland and Romania). Other calculations by Vaňous[9] show that these trends persisted into 1976, when the terms of trade with 'socialist' countries continued to decline for Bulgaria, Czechoslovakia, the GDR, and Hungary, but improved for Poland, Romania, and the USSR.

Table 6.2 presents recent calculations by N. Mitrofanova, a leading Soviet specialist on intra-CMEA contract prices. For fuels, raw materials, and metals, she finds that Soviet export prices to CMEA kept pace with world market price increases from 1970 to 1972, fell far behind in 1973 and 1974, rose sharply in 1975, but then leveled off in 1976. For unprocessed and processed agricultural products, world market prices climbed sharply in 1973 and 1974 and then declined in 1975 and approximately stabilized in 1976, while Soviet export prices to CMEA rose less rapidly but more steadily. For machinery and equipment, the increase in Soviet export prices to CMEA

Table 6.2 Indexes of World Market Prices, Soviet Export Prices to CMEA, and Soviet Domestic Wholesale Prices, by Commodity Groups, 1960, 1966, and 1971–76 (1970 = 100)

Year	Fuels, Raw Materials, and Metals			Unprocessed and Processed Agricultural Products			Machinery and Equipment		
	World Market Prices	Soviet Export Prices to CMEA	Soviet Domestic Wholesale Prices	World Market Prices	Soviet Export Prices to CMEA	Soviet Domestic Wholesale Prices	World Market Prices	Soviet Export Prices to CMEA	Soviet Domestic Wholesale Prices
1960	94	131	58	89	97	86	78	85	74
1966	94	101	60	101	100	93	89	100	76
1971	108	105	99	103	96	103	103	101	97
1972	111	110	99	121	107	104	112	108	106
1973	168	113	99	176	108	106	117	105	105
1974	243	119	96	216	111	107	128	116	117
1975	247	175	96	201	135	111	141	127	119
1976	258	177	96	203	148	109	148	145	122

Source: N. Mitrofanova, 'Tendentsii dvizheniia kontraktnykh tsen v torgovle stran SEV' [Tendencies in movements of contract prices in trade of CMEA countries], *Voprosy ekonomiki*, 1978, No. 8, p. 103.

was much closer to world market price movements, with approximately the same change from 1970 to 1976. These figures support the Soviet argument that within CMEA since the early 1970s the exporters of fuels, raw materials, and agricultural products ('hard' goods) failed to get price increases justified by world market price movements, whereas export prices of machinery and equipment ('soft' goods) on balance kept up with world market trends. Finally, the isolation of Soviet domestic wholesale prices from both world market prices and CMEA contract prices is strikingly confirmed by these calculations.[10]

These changes in intra-CMEA foreign trade prices beginning in 1974 were reflected in rising trade deficits with the USSR for all of the East European countries except Romania, which continued to have a trade surplus with the USSR. Table 6.3, based on official Soviet statistics, shows how quickly and dramatically the balance in Soviet–East European trade altered. In 1973, the Soviet deficit (equal to the East European surplus) was almost a billion dollars. In 1974, the balance changed by $1.1 billion in favor of the USSR, as the Soviet trade deficit was eliminated and replaced by a small surplus of $139 million. The Soviet surplus then climbed sharply to $1.9 billion in 1977, and the cumulative Soviet surplus (East European deficit) during 1974–77 totaled about $4 billion. However, in 1978 Soviet imports from Eastern Europe grew faster than Soviet exports to Eastern Europe, and the Soviet surplus was cut to $249 million.

Table 6.3   *Soviet Foreign Trade with Eastern Europe, 1970–78[a]*
(US$m.)

Year	Soviet Exports to Eastern Europe	Soviet Imports from Eastern Europe	Balance (Exports – Imports)
1970	6,752	6,627	125
1971	7,234	7,250	−16
1972	8,139	9,301	−1,162
1973	9,964	10,925	−961
1974	11,491	11,352	139
1975	16,494	15,723	771
1976	17,432	16,261	1,171
1977	20,762	18,839	1,923
1978	24,910	24,661	249

[a]Official Soviet statistics using US dollar exchange rates for the Soviet foreign exchange ruble as announced by the USSR State Bank. Exports and imports are f.o.b. Eastern Europe includes Bulgaria, Czechoslovakia, the GDR, Hungary, Poland, and Romania.
Source: US Central Intelligence Agency, *Handbook of Economic Statistics 1979*, table 60, p. 99.

Because neither the USSR nor any of the East European countries publishes comprehensive balance-of-payments statistics, one cannot tell to what extent these East European deficits were covered by Soviet credits. Part of their trade deficits may have been offset by net East European surpluses on the other current account items, such as services. Also, part of the USSR's trade surplus beginning in 1974 may have been to repay debts it incurred because of its substantial trade deficits with Eastern Europe in 1972–73. Finally, it is not clear how flows of goods connected with joint investment projects, such as the Soyuz (Orenburg) natural gas pipeline,[11] are reflected in these trade statistics.

Nevertheless, it is likely that the USSR did – as it promised when the new intra-CMEA prices were introduced in 1975 – extend significant credits to East European countries to help them finance their imports of Soviet fuels and raw materials. A Soviet loan of 1 billion rubles to Poland was announced in 1976, and credits were probably granted also to at least the GDR and possibly other countries as well.[12]

Although such credits, and perhaps other Soviet concessions, have eased the burden on Eastern Europe from rising prices of Soviet primary products in the second half of the 1970s, one of the most severe problems for Eastern Europe in the 1980s will be the quantity and price of energy imports from the USSR.

II   Energy Problems

On the whole, Eastern Europe is poorly endowed with energy resources. Only Poland and the GDR have important coal deposits, and only Romania is a significant producer of oil (though a net importer beginning in 1976).

As part of the drive to modernize their economies, since the early 1960s Eastern Europe has been shifting from primary reliance on high-cost domestic coal to greater use of imported oil and natural gas, almost all of it from the USSR.

Table 6.4 shows the contribution of energy imports to energy consumption in 1977 in each of the East European countries and in the area as a whole. The share of energy imports from all other countries in total energy consumption ranged from 75 percent for Bulgaria down to 20 percent for Poland and Romania. To all countries except Romania, the USSR provided 75 percent or more of their energy imports. As a result, the share of energy imports from the USSR in national energy consumption, presented in the last column of the table, was almost three-fourths for Bulgaria, half for Hungary, a third for Czechoslovakia, a fourth for the GDR, a sixth for Poland, and negligible for Romania. Thus, for most, although not all, of the East European countries a steadily growing supply of Soviet oil, and to a lesser extent natural gas, plays a critical role in their economic development.

As Table 6.5 indicates, in 1978 Soviet oil production was 11.4 million barrels per day (b/d) and imports only 0.2 million b/d. Domestic consumption absorbed 8.4 million b/d, or about three-fourths of the total supply. The remaining one-fourth was exported, almost half of it to Eastern Europe.

It is questionable whether Soviet oil production can grow fast enough in the 1980s to meet rising domestic demand and to increase, or even maintain, net exports, because the Soviet oil industry faces a number of difficult problems.[13]

First, the Soviet oil industry uses production techniques, such as rapid water injection methods, which boost output in the short run but

Table 6.4 *Eastern Europe: Energy Imports as a Share of Energy Consumption, 1977*
(Percent)

	Energy Imports as a Share of Energy Consumption	Energy Imports from the USSR as a Share of Total Energy Imports	Energy Imports from the USSR as a Share of Energy Consumption
Bulgaria	75	93	70
Czechoslovakia	42	85	35
GDR	35	80	28
Hungary	54	82	44
Poland	20	75	15
Romania	21	9	2
Total, six countries	34[a]	76	26

[a] The quotient of 2,674 thousand barrels per day (b/d) oil equivalent of imports divided by 7,846 thousand b/d oil equivalent of consumption. The former figure includes 224 thousand b/d oil equivalent imported by Eastern European countries from each other.

Souce: US Central Intelligence Agency, *Energy Supplies in Eastern Europe: A Statistical Compilation* (Washington, D.C.: Library of Congress Photoduplication Service, 1979), tables 14, 15, 16, and 18, pp. 11–12.

which ultimately achieve the recovery of less of the oil in a field.

Second, drilling has emphasized exploitation of known fields rather than exploration for new sources. As a result, proved oil reserves have been falling in recent years, and the reserves-to-production ratio will probably deteriorate further in the next five to ten years.

Table 6.5   *Soviet Oil Production, Imports, Consumption, and Exports, 1970–79[a]*
(Million Barrels per Day)

Year	Production[b]	Imports	Consumption	Exports To East European Countries	To Other Countries	Total
1970	7.1	0.1	5.2	0.8	1.1	1.9
1971	7.5	0.1	5.5	0.9	1.2	2.1
1972	8.0	0.2	5.9	1.0	1.1	2.1
1973	8.6	0.3	6.3	1.1	1.3	2.4
1974	9.2	0.1	6.8	1.2	1.1	2.3
1975	9.8	0.2	7.2	1.3	1.3	2.6
1976	10.4	0.1	7.6	1.4	1.6	3.0
1977	10.9	0.1	7.9[c]	1.4	1.7	3.1
1978	11.4	0.2	8.4[c]	1.5	1.7	3.2
1979	11.7[c]	n.a.[d]	8.9[c]	n.a.	n.a.	n.a.

[a]Because of rounding, production plus imports may not equal consumption plus exports.
[b]Crude oil, including natural gas liquids.
[c]Preliminary estimate.
[d]Not available.

Source: US Central Intelligence Agency, *International Energy Statistical Review*, 13 February 1980 (Washington, D. C.: Library of Congress Photoduplication Service, 1980), pp. 22–3.

Since 1970, nearly all output growth has come from West Siberian fields, as production fell in the Ukraine, North Caucasus, and Azerbaidzhan, and leveled off in the Urals–Volga area. It is doubtful that in the next decade Siberian production can increase sufficiently to offset the decline in output west of the Urals.

Geological conditions are favorable to future discoveries in East Siberia, offshore regions in the Arctic and Caspian, and off Kamchatka and Sakhalin in the Sea of Okhotsk. However, exploration and development of these areas will require many years, very large outlays, and foreign equipment. In East Siberia, production and transportation are hampered by vast distances, forbidding terrain, and severe climate. The technology to cope with pack ice in the offshore Arctic has not yet been developed even in the West. Weather and ice conditions in the Sakhalin area are harsher than in the North Sea, where development of commercial-scale production took ten years. Climatic conditions are more favorable in the Caspian region, but difficult deep drilling is required.

Third, exploration for and exploitation of new oil reserves has been hampered by shortages, outdated design, and inferior quality of equipment available to the Soviet oil industry. For example, most Soviet seismic recording uses a technology employed in the United States twenty years ago. There is a shortage of drilling rigs, the service life of components is short, and the quality of bits is much inferior to those produced in the West. Soviet pumps are inferior to American units in efficiency, capacity, and service life. Domestic production of large-diameter pipe meets about two-thirds of Soviet requirements, with the remainder imported. Finally, a serious deficiency for the future is lack of modern offshore technology using mobile (including submersible) drilling platforms. Some indication of Soviet needs for foreign equipment and technology is given by Soviet orders for Western oil and gas equipment and technology (excluding large-diameter line pipe) in 1972–76 totaling about $3.1 billion.

Western specialists' assessments of the negative impact of these problems on Soviet oil production and exports differ, depending upon their assumptions about various key factors, including the following: (a) Will the Soviet authorities expand oil production through a crash program of exploration and development? (b) What will be the effectiveness of Soviet efforts to restrain domestic oil consumption through conservation programs and the substitution of coal and gas for oil? (c) To what extent will OPEC-led price increases on the world market offset possible decreases in the quantity of Soviet oil exports, thus sustaining or even raising Soviet hard-currency earnings from a smaller quantity of exports?

A now widespread (but not universal) view among specialists is that Soviet oil production may peak in the early 1980s in the neighborhood of 12 million b/d(600 million metric tons per year), and then level off or perhaps even decline. If so, it would be very difficult for the USSR to continue to meet its own requirements and those of Eastern Europe, and to send non-Communist countries the quantity of oil exports which has recently been the USSR's largest single source (about half) of convertible currency. Unless domestic consumption and/or oil exports to Eastern Europe could be curtailed sufficiently, hard-currency exports of oil would fall. However, sustaining and raising Soviet oil production over the longer run will require large imports of Western equipment and know-how.

The prospects for conserving oil by shifting to coal are limited. In the Soviet energy balance, coal is important primarily for use in boilers to produce electricity, steam, and hot water, which together account for two-fifths of total Soviet energy consumption. In these uses, the technical and economic advantages of oil and natural gas over solid fuel are minimal. Plans to substitute coal for oil and gas in existing power stations have been announced, but it is questionable how far they can be implemented, because the massive amounts of new specialized equipment required to convert the stations are not available. In turn, the expansion of coal production for use in new facilities faces formidable obstacles. Coal production west of the Urals is constrained by the exhaustion of old seams, unfavorable and even dangerous geological conditions, labor force problems, and lack of mechanization of many operations. Thus, more than three-fourths of additional coal output must come from strip mines in Siberia. Although surface operations are cheaper than underground mining, the Siberian deposits are located far from consumers in the

Western USSR and the poor physical properties (such as high ash content) of some of the coal preclude its shipment over long distances.[14]

Table 6.6   *Soviet Natural Gas Production, Imports, Consumption, and Exports, 1970–79[a]*
(Billion Cubic Feet per Day)

				Exports		
				To East European	To Other	
Year	Production	Imports	Consumption	Countries	Countries	Total
1970	19.2	0.3	19.2	0.2	0.1	0.3
1971	20.5	0.8	20.9	0.3	0.1	0.4
1972	21.4	1.1	21.9	0.3	0.2	0.5
1973	22.9	1.1	23.3	0.5	0.2	0.7
1974	25.2	1.2	25.0	0.8	0.6	1.4
1975	28.0	1.2	27.3	1.1	0.8	1.9
1976	31.1	1.1	29.6	1.2	1.3	2.5
1977	33.5	1.3	31.6	1.7	1.5	3.2
1978	36.0	0.9[b]	33.4	1.8	1.8	3.6
1979	39.4[b]	n.a.[c]	n.a.	n.a.	n.a.	n.a.

[a]Because of rounding, production plus imports may not equal consumption plus exports.
[b]Preliminary estimate.
[c]Not available.
Source: US Central Intelligence Agency, *International Energy Statistical Review*, 13 February 1980, pp. 24–5.

The picture for natural gas is brighter. Table 6.6 shows Soviet production, imports, consumption, and exports of natural gas. In 1978 only about 10 percent of total output was exported, with half of it going to Eastern Europe. The start-up of the Soyuz pipeline will raise Soviet gas exports to Eastern Europe sharply in 1980, to about double the 1978 level. The longer-term growth of Soviet natural gas production faces some problems similar to those of the oil industry. Most new gasfield development and pipeline construction will be in the permafrost areas of West Siberia. In addition, there are serious shortages of large-diameter pipe and ancillary equipment such as compressors, valves, and turbines. Yet gas production is likely to grow steadily, perhaps at an average annual rate of about 6 percent in the 1980s, permitting increased exports to both Eastern Europe and Western Europe.[15]

However, it is not clear to what extent these additional shipments of Soviet natural gas will substitute for or add to increments in supplies of Soviet oil to Eastern Europe. In the early 1970s, Moscow told the East European countries that Soviet oil deliveries would not grow after 1975 and that the East European countries therefore should seek additional oil on the world market. The East European countries could not do so when (1) oil prices quadrupled in 1973–74, and (2) world market prices also rose sharply for raw materials they import, while (3) slow growth in the West held down their hard-currency exports. In these circumstances, the USSR reconsidered and increased its oil deliveries to Eastern Europe, but more slowly than previously – at an average annual rate of about 4.3 percent in 1976–78, compared with 8.9 percent in 1971–75.[16]

As the expansion of Soviet oil production slows, Soviet oil shipments to Eastern Europe will in turn grow more slowly in the early 1980s, perhaps at only 3 percent per year. So far the USSR has announced publicly only a general commitment that in 1981–85 total deliveries (expressed in tons of standard fuel equivalent) of oil, natural gas, coal, and electricity to all CMEA countries as a group will be 20 percent above deliveries in 1976–80, compared with an increase of nearly 50 percent in 1976–80 over 1971–75.[17] Moreover, Soviet energy exports will be supplied at sharply rising prices and in return for commitments of East European countries to participate in projects to develop Soviet natural resources under CMEA integration plans.

III Economic Integration

The conception of 'economic integration' in CMEA is much narrower than, for example, in the European Community.[18] In the latter, integration involves the elimination of tariffs, quotas, and other restrictions on trade among member countries; the establishment of common trade restrictions against nonmember countries; the liberalization of factor movements among member countries; and the harmonization of national economic policies. In contrast, in CMEA, integration is to be accomplished by greater coordination of member countries' national economic plans.

However, CMEA's coordination of national plans is evolving slowly in various dimensions.[19] For two decades, it occurred chiefly through bilateral trade agreements covering planned exports and imports. Then in 1971 CMEA approved a Comprehensive Program for the Further Intensification and Improvement of Collaboration and the Development of Socialist Economic Integration of CMEA Countries. This Comprehensive Program proposed to achieve closer economic integration, over a twenty-year period, through (1) joint efforts at forecasting economic trends and scientific developments; (2) joint scientific and technical research in selected economic branches; (3) more *ex ante* coordination of medium-term (five-year) and long-term (fifteen- to twenty-year) plans; and (4) joint planning of research and development, investment, production, and trade for selected products, such as metal-cutting lathes and transport containers.[20]

The Comprehensive Program also promised to improve the mechanism for setting intra-CMEA prices, to establish more realistic exchange rates, and to increase convertibility and multilateral settlements. But subsequent efforts to implement the Comprehensive Program have stressed 'production integration' through closer plan coordination, rather than 'turnover integration' through improved pricing and payments arrangements.[21]

Thus, in accordance with a decision at the Twenty-seventh Session of the CMEA Council in 1973, each member country established a special department in its national planning agency to coordinate with other

CMEA countries important aspects of five-year plans for 1976–80. The results of this joint work were approved at the Twenty-ninth Session in 1975, as a Coordinated Plan of Multilateral Integration Measures *(soglasovannyi plan mnogostoronnikh integratsionnykh meropriatii)* for 1976–80. It included (1) joint investment projects, primarily in fuels, raw materials, and electric power, located, or originating in, the USSR; (2) specialization and cooperation assignments in machinery and chemicals; (3) various science and technology projects; and (4) cooperation in the development of the Mongolian People's Republic.

The Thirtieth CMEA Session in 1976 extended the time horizon for plan coordination to 1990 and focused it on five 'leading' sectors for which Long-Term Special [or Target] Programs of Cooperation *(dolgosrochnye tselevye programmy sotrudnichestva*; hereafter, LTSPs) were to be elaborated: (1) fuel, energy, and raw materials; (2) machine building; (3) agriculture and food industry; (4) consumer goods of industrial origin; and (5) transportation. For these sectors, the member countries were to make bilateral and multilateral agreements covering production, consumption, exports and imports, and investment projects for specific product groups.

The Thirty-first CMEA Session in 1977 concentrated the work on LTSPs in the first three sectors: fuel, energy, and raw materials; agriculture; and machine building; and the Thirty-second Session in 1978 approved programs in these fields.[22] The LTSP for fuel, energy, and raw materials emphasizes projects to develop natural resources in the USSR.[23] The agricultural program calls for expansion of output of grain, meat, and other farm products, but primarily to meet each country's own domestic requirements rather than for export to other CMEA nations.[24] The program for machine building is apparently chiefly to support the other LTSPs, especially for fuel, energy, and raw materials, rather than an independent and equal effort.[25]

The Thirty-third Session in 1979 approved the LTSPs for industrial consumer goods and transportation. The former involves specialization in production of furniture, household appliances, and other products. The latter includes modernization of selected regional rail lines, expansion of the CMEA pools of freight cars and containers, and port development.[26]

However, the number of high-priority output categories (almost 100) is too large to be meaningful, in the opinion of a leading Hungarian specialist on CMEA, Kálmán Pécsi:

. . . the individual countries . . . wanted to be members of as many organizations as possible or to recommend the joint implementation of as many special-purpose programs as possible. The danger of being left out and the knowledge that they will not share in the subsequent results and distribution of the market act as a strong incentive to participate and to locate more and more possibilities. However, once they are members, they have difficulty in coordinating the development investment requirements and objectives with the possibilities and tasks of their national plans, and their behavior becomes cautious and uncertain when giving concrete form to their ideas for the development of production integration and making resources available.[27]

... we can see that we are trying to solve almost all of the problems of the CMEA within the framework of the special-purpose programs. The realistic nature of this is obviously in contradiction with experiences to date.[28]

If the special-purpose programs are clearly defined and directed at the solution of one or two major tasks on the basis of the decisive link principle, they make it possible to combine resources to attain the goal set . . . Obviously, if all tasks become top-priority ones, then we are giving priority to none.[29]

It is questionable too how far the LTSPs can advance economic integration in CMEA, because thirty years of experience show that the obstacles are serious and very difficult to overcome.

First, national interests of the CMEA member countries conflict. The less developed countries oppose 'integration' which would retard their industrialization by assigning them relative specialization in primary production of foodstuffs and raw materials. Romania has been the most prominent and most successful exponent of this view. More developed countries, such as Czechoslovakia and Hungary, desire to produce modern machinery and equipment that can be sold for hard currency in the West and at the same time to sell inside CMEA lower-quality producer and consumer manufactures. The GDR wishes to exploit its special relationship with West Germany, through which it gains access to the markets of the European Community. And the USSR wants to allocate its fuels and raw materials to domestic use and to hard-currency exports, through which it can import better machinery and equipment and more food than Eastern Europe can supply. In the face of the overwhelming economic, political, and military power of the USSR, the East European members of CMEA have opposed the creation of supranational CMEA agencies and have insisted upon a rule of unanimity on the part of countries involved in CMEA decisions.[30]

Second, there are serious technical problems in determining an economically sound pattern of specialization in production and trade in CMEA. Calculations of (static or dynamic) comparative advantage involve comparisons of relative costs at home and abroad. But the internal price systems of the CMEA countries cannot provide the necessary information on domestic costs, because administratively set producer prices do not incorporate all relevant costs or measure relative scarcities of inputs and outputs.

Third, in turn arbitrary official exchange rates imperfectly reflect relative price (and cost) levels among CMEA countries.

Fourth, as a result, intra-CMEA trade must be conducted on the basis of world market prices. Various CMEA economists have proposed basing intra-CMEA contract prices on 'regional socially necessary labor costs',[31] but this approach is hardly feasible. As Pécsi has pointed out:

... socially necessary inputs should be correctly reflected in the internal prices of the different countries and the establishment of economically sound and mutually agreed national exchange rates and currency factors for transfer of the national currencies from one to another and to the collective currency and for determining economically sound foreign trade prices . . .[32]

Thus, most CMEA economists accept the need to base CMEA contract prices on world market prices. However, controversy continues on how to adjust world market prices to obtain fair 'purified' CMEA prices. The discussion currently focuses on four problems:[33]

(1) How long a base period should be used to obtain an 'average' world market price? A five-year period is convenient because it corresponds to the length of national medium-term plans and trade agreements based on them. But a shorter period may be preferable for fuels and raw materials, whose world market prices have increased markedly in the 1970s, as well as for machinery and equipment, whose changing product characteristics make it difficult to obtain a comparable price series for the 'same' item for more than two or three years.
(2) Should base periods of different length therefore be used for different product groups?
(3) Should 'extreme price intervals' – of abnormally high or rapidly rising prices – be omitted in calculating the average for the base period chosen?
(4) How can a 'representative world price' be identified, particularly for manufactured products, in view of the multiplicity of prices arising from differences in quality, quantities sold, export taxes and subsidies and import duties, terms of payment and delivery, etc.?

Finally, inconvertibility and bilateralism predominate in intra-CMEA trade, despite the establishment of the 'transferable ruble' (TR) in 1964 as an 'international socialist collective currency'.[34] Intra-CMEA trade transactions are denominated in TRs after world market prices (expressed in internationally traded currencies) are converted into TRs on the basis of the official ruble–dollar exchange rate specified by the USSR. CMEA countries make a great effort to balance trade bilaterally and avoid surpluses, because a credit balance in TRs in CMEA's International Bank for Economic Cooperation is in fact *not* usually transferable. Instead, the creditor country must hold the balance until it can arrange to run an offsetting deficit with the original debtor country.

Thus, TRs do not have 'currency convertibility' into convertible currencies, gold, or even national CMEA currencies (such as the Soviet domestic ruble). Nor do TRs have 'commodity convertibility' at the holder's option into goods of its free choice from other CMEA countries. Hence, multilateral settlements through TRs have constituted in recent years no more than 2 percent of total CMEA trade turnover accounted in TRs.

Instead, bilateralism is still the rule inside CMEA. Bilateral balancing in intra-CMEA trade is pursued not only globally for the total exports and total imports of one country with another. It is also done by individual commodity groups (different 'hard' goods for each other and different 'soft' goods for each other), because CMEA contract prices do not reflect to the same degree the scarcities inside CMEA for different categories of goods. In this balancing process, bilateral bargaining leads to many deviations of CMEA contract prices from the world market prices upon which they are supposedly based. The price for the same commodity often varies by trading partner, because of the commodity against which it has been traded.[35]

To a small extent, estimated at 5–10 percent of total intra-CMEA trade turnover, bilateral balances are settled outside the TR system by payments in convertible Western currencies. This occurs primarily in two cases: (1) when above-plan deliveries of 'hard' goods are made; and (2) when an export to CMEA contains inputs purchased for convertible currency, or when an import from CMEA will be incorporated by the buyer in a subsequent export for convertible currency.[36]

Little change should be expected in the CMEA settlements system, because it reflects the arrangements for planning, pricing, and exchange rates in CMEA. In Pécsi's opinion:

> . . . plan coordination and the order of signing agreements on mutual deliveries in themselves limit the use of the transferable ruble.[37]
>
> Little progress has been made in the question of the usability of the transferable ruble and particularly in its transferability. In view of the predominant concept of the form of integration, transferability is only of limited, secondary importance, and no change should be expected for a long while yet.[38]
>
> . . . we can expect the system of payments within the CMEA to remain unchanged in the coming years . . . I consider the establishment of a mutual settlements system based on some form of combination of the national currencies and the common currency to be practically out of the question for the period under consideration [to 1990].[39]

Some of the difficulties involved in securing greater economic integration in CMEA are illustrated by experience in machine building, in which production does not depend primarily on natural resource endowment, unlike fuel and raw material industries.

> Between 1956 and 1973 the CMEA standing committees formulated and adopted 5,300 recommendations for engineering industry specialization. It is also known that the CMEA production specialization recommendations have not exercised any significant influence on the development of the engineering industry in the member countries.[40]

CMEA has made slow progress in 'specialization and cooperation' in machine building for a number of reasons.

First, the committees preparing specialization recommendations did not take into account their effects on the domestic production and supply plans of the affected countries and on their determination to achieve a bilateral balance in machinery trade.

. . . all such recommendations [for specialization and cooperation in machinery production] come up against the 'quota approach' arising from . . . the fact that in the structure of foreign trade the countries strive for equilibrium in the volume of their two-way machinery deliveries. This makes production specialization possible only within given limits. When they come up against this limitation, the recommendations taper off, since they are practically impossible to apply.[41]

Second, one CMEA country is reluctant to become dependent on another for components and parts, for fear that foreign suppliers will not meet their commitments, thus imperiling the fulfillment of national plan assignments for end products. Hence, a Soviet specialist reports:

For the USSR's industrial ministries and departments that plan the development of international specialization and cooperation, the chief criterion in selecting an object of international specialization or cooperation is a current shortage of a particular product. Given this approach, questions of economic efficiency either are not considered at all or are worked in as 'afterthoughts' to already developed proposals.[42]

Third, according to another Soviet expert, when planning commissions, branch ministries, and foreign trade agencies decide to import machines, prospective user enterprises are often not anxious to buy them because they are priced much higher than comparable domestic products.[43]

Finally, under the 'foreign trade monopoly' system prevailing in CMEA countries, there is a lack of direct contacts between domestic producer enterprises and foreign customers, and between domestic user enterprises and foreign suppliers. This is especially disadvantageous to specialization and trade in machine building, where product specifications are complex and individualized.

Another example of the problems of integration is provided by the experience of the international economic organizations (IEOs) assigned a prominent role in the Comprehensive Program. Although some types of IEOs, for example, 'international economic associations' and 'international economic unions', exchange technical information and coordinate production assignments to promote specialization, there are very few genuine 'joint enterprises' involving joint investments, production, and marketing by enterprises and industrial associations in different CMEA countries. There is no common CMEA-wide legislation covering joint enterprises, and each such venture must be worked out individually by the (usually only two) participating countries.

No participant accepts the internal prices of the others as appropriate for calculating costs, revenues, profits, and profit shares in a joint venture. Therefore, initial contributions of capital and subsequent inputs, outputs, and deliveries must be valued both in the currency and prices of the supplier country and also in transferable rubles at corresponding intra-CMEA trade prices based (with a lag) on world market prices. However, this principle cannot be easily applied in practice. First, there is no such intra-CMEA trade price for some inputs (such as labor and land). Second, there is no single intra-CMEA trade price for a particular good but rather various prices reached in different bilateral negotiations between different countries over different bundles of goods. Hence, for each joint enterprise it is necessary to negotiate a separate and extremely complicated set of coefficients to convert prices of goods and services in national currencies into mutually acceptable prices in TRs.[44] As a result, the number of joint enterprises in operation is estimated, on the basis of fragmentary information, at only between five and ten.[45]

On balance, it appears that CMEA 'integration' efforts are more likely to produce results in two rather different dimensions: (1) joint investments in Soviet fuel and raw material resources, and (2) narrow technical questions, such as coordination of selected research projects[46] and agreements on product standards.[47] On the other hand, the prospects are much weaker for (3) effective coordination of industrial or agricultural production; (4) greater convertibility and multilateralism in trade and payments; or (5) more mobility of labor across national boundaries.[48]

IV Conclusion

All of the East European countries are heavily involved, though to varying degrees, in economic ties with the CMEA regional bloc and in particular with its dominant member, the USSR. Eastern Europe has found this association advantageous because it could get Soviet fuels and raw materials at considerably less than world market prices and in return for East European machinery and manufactured consumer goods that were often hard to sell on the world market.

However, Soviet energy deliveries to Eastern Europe will grow much more slowly in 1981–85 than in 1976–80, and the lag in adjusting CMEA contract prices to changes in world market prices may be further reduced. The many serious obstacles to effective economic integration in CMEA continue. Finally, as its economic growth slackens to about 3 percent per year in the early 1980s, Eastern Europe badly needs the potential benefits of technology transfer from trade and industrial cooperation with advanced Western market economies.

As a result, the East European nations want to expand their economic relations with developed and less developed non-Communist countries, despite Eastern Europe's sobering experience with inflation and recession on the world market in the 1970s. There is little evidence that in response to the difficulties encountered on the world market Eastern Europe (or the USSR either) has reacted by deliberately 'turning inward' toward a greater commitment to its regional economic bloc at the expense of ties with the rest of the world.[49]

Although some countries like Hungary (see Chapters 9 and 10) pursue this goal more aggressively than others, all of the East European nations want to enlarge their economic relations with the West in the 1980s. Their ability to do so depends primarily, not upon constraints imposed by the USSR, but upon the determination and skill of both Eastern Europe and the West in overcoming the trade and credit problems discussed in Chapter 3.

Notes: Chapter 6

1 These shares are calculated from official statistics of the East European countries. As explained below, intra-CMEA prices are supposed to be set on the basis of average world market prices in an earlier period, and thus changes in prices in intra-CMEA trade lag changes in world market prices. In a period of sustained inflation on the world market, intra-CMEA trade takes place at lower prices than trade with non-CMEA countries. Therefore, the share of intra-CMEA trade in total trade volume at comparable prices is understated by official statistics.

2 That is, excluding the three other members of CMEA – Cuba, Mongolia, and Vietnam. On Soviet economic relations with these countries, see Lawrence H. Theriot and JeNelle Matheson, 'Soviet Economic Relations with Non-European CMEA: Cuba, Vietnam, and Mongolia', in *Soviet Economy in a Time of Change* (a compendium of papers submitted to the Joint Economic Committee, 96th Congress, 1st Session) (Washington, D.C.: US Government Printing Office, 1979), Vol. 2, pp. 551–81.

3 Zbigniew M. Fallenbuchl, 'The Commodity Composition of Intra-Comecon Trade and the Industrial Structure of the Member Countries', in North Atlantic Treaty Organization (NATO), *Comecon: Progress and Prospects* (Brussels: NATO, 1977), pp. 104–5.

4 Marie Lavigne, 'La commerce intra-CAEM et son influence sur le développement économique soviétique', in North Atlantic Treaty Organization (NATO), *The USSR in the 1980s: Economic Growth and the Role of Foreign Trade* (Brussels: NATO, 1978), pp. 185–96.

5 Evidence on the change of Eastern Europe from 'asset' to 'liability' to the USSR is assembled and evaluated in Paul Marer, 'Has Eastern Europe Become a Liability to the Soviet Union? The Economic Aspect', in Charles Gati (ed.), *The International Politics of Eastern Europe* (New York: Praeger, 1976), pp. 59–81.

6 See Martin J. Kohn and Nicholas R. Lang, 'The Intra-CMEA Foreign Trade System', in *East European Economies Post-Helsinki* (a compendium of papers submitted to the Joint Economic Committee, 95th Congress, 1st Session) (Washington, D.C.: US Government Printing Office, 1977), pp. 135–51; and Raymond Dietz, 'Price Changes in Soviet Trade with CMEA and the Rest of the World Since 1975', in *Soviet Economy in a Time of Change*, Vol. 1, pp. 263–90.

7 Jan Vaňous, 'The East European Recession: Did It Come from the West or Was It Sent from Russia with Love?', Discussion Paper No. 78–8 (Vancouver, British Columbia: Department of Economics, University of British Columbia, 1978; mimeo), p. 9.

8 Kohn and Lang, op. cit., p. 141. These figures are geometric averages of their results with 1974 and 1975 weights.

9 Vaňous, op. cit., p. 38.

10 It should be noted that Mitrofanova's indexes for Soviet domestic wholesale prices differ substantially from the official statistics. For example, she shows domestic wholesale prices for machinery and equipment rising, while the official series reports them to be falling. On the official series and its shortcomings, see Morris Bornstein, 'Soviet Price Policy in the 1970s', in *Soviet Economy in a New Perspective* (a compendium of papers submitted to the Joint Economic Committee, 94th Congress, 2nd Session) (Washington, D.C.: US Government Printing Office, 1976), pp. 20–6.

11 Commitments of the participating countries are summarized in Viktor Petrenko, 'Soyuz Gas Pipeline in Service', *Foreign Trade* [Moscow], 1979, No. 8 pp. 26–9.

12 Martin J. Kohn, 'Soviet-Eastern European Economic Relations, 1975–78', in *Soviet Economy in a Time of Change*, Vol. 1, pp. 250–3.

13 This summary draws on Morris Bornstein, 'Soviet Economic Growth and Foreign Policy', in Seweryn Bialer (ed.), *Domestic Context of Soviet Foreign Policy* (Boulder, Colorado: Westview Press, 1981, pp. 238–40). For detailed data on production problems and the regional distribution of production, see J. Richard Lee and James R. Lecky, 'Soviet Oil Developments', in *Soviet Economy in a Time of Change*, Vol. 1, pp. 581–99.

14 Leslie Dienes, 'The Soviet Union: An Energy Crunch Ahead?' *Problems of Communism*, Vol. 26, No. 5 (September–October 1977), pp. 51–6; and Leslie Dienes, 'The Soviet Energy Policy', in *Soviet Economy in a Time of Change*, Vol. 1, pp. 200–12.

15 Leslie Dienes, *Soviet Energy Policy and the Hydrocarbons* (Washington, D.C.: Association of American Geographers, 1978; processed), p. 42.

16 These rates were calculated from the following data in thousands of barrels per day in the source for Table 6.5: 1971 – 895; 1975 – 1,260; 1976 – 1,370; and 1978 – 1,490. In Table 6.5, these figures are rounded to millions of barrels per day.

17 Mikhail Loshakov and Alexander Poliyenko, 'USSR Trade with CMEA Countries', *Foreign Trade* [Moscow], 1979, No. 11, p. 5.

18 E. S. Kirschen, 'Origins, Aims, and Objectives of the EEC and the CMEA', in E. S. Kirschen (ed.), *Economic Policies Compared: West and East* (Amsterdam: North-Holland, 1975), Vol. 2, pp. 243–56.

19 The following discussion draws on Morris Bornstein, 'East–West Economic Relations and Soviet–East European Economic Relations', in *Soviet Economy in a Time of Change*, Vol. 1, pp. 302–8.

20 Administrative procedures for 'plan coordination' and 'joint planning' are described in R. Petrosian, 'Pravovye voprosy sovmestnoi planovoi deiatel'nosti' [Legal questions of joint planning activity], *Khoziaistvo i pravo*, 1977, No. 9, pp. 93–7.

21 K. Pécsi, *Economic Questions of Production Integration Within the CMEA*, Trends in World Economy, No. 24 (Budapest: Hungarian Scientific Council for World Economy, 1978), p. 14.

22 Procedures for preparing LTSPs and linking them with national economic plans are discussed in E. O. Gavrilov and I. F. Motorin, 'Vzaimosviaz' dolgosrochnykh tselevykh programm sotrudnichestva stran SEV s natsional'nym planirovaniem' [Relationship of long-term special programs of cooperation of CMEA countries with national planning], *Izvestiia Akademii Nauk SSSR, Seriia ekonomicheskaia*, 1979, No. 3, pp. 79–89.

23 A. Iakushkin, 'Sotrudnichestvo stran SEV v toplivno-energeticheskom komplekse' [Cooperation of CMEA countries in the fuel-energy complex], *Voprosy ekonomiki*, 1979, No. 6, pp. 92–100.

24 Iu. Pekshev, 'The CMEA Countries: Integration in Agriculture and the Food Industry', *Foreign Trade* [Moscow], 1979, No. 7, pp. 2–7. Previous CMEA cooperation in agriculture is described in *Agrarnopromyshlennaia integratsiia stran SEV* [Agricultural-industrial integration of CMEA countries] (Moscow:Nauka, 1976), Part III. For a critical evaluation of this experience, see Chantal Beaucourt, 'L'agriculture et la politique d'intégration économique des pays socialistes européens dans le plans 1976-80', *Revue d'Études Comparatives Est-Ouest*, Vol. 9, No. 3 (Septembre 1978), pp. 7–61.

25 According to Pécsi (op. cit., p. 37): 'It is hardly probable that with the attempts to solve much more pressing materials supply problems, sufficient energy will remain for independent attention to the idea of specialization and cooperation [in engineering industries].' See also Iu. Pekshev, 'Spetsializatsiia i kooperatsiia mashinostroitel'nogo proizvodstva stran-chlenov SEV' [Specialization and cooperation in machine building Production of CMEA Member Countries], *Planovoe khoziaistvo*, 1978, No. 6, p. 89.

26 Nikolai Mozharov, 'Long-Term Special Purpose Program for Cooperation in Developing Transport Links Between the CMEA Countries', *Foreign Trade* [Moscow], 1979, No. 11, pp. 36–9. On previous experience in CMEA cooperation in transportation, see Bogdan Mieczkowski, *Transportation in Eastern Europe: Empirical Findings* (Boulder, Colorado: East European Quarterly, 1978), Ch. 6.

27 Pécsi, op. cit., p. 38.

28 Ibid., p. 40.

29 Ibid., p. 60.

30 On the failure of the USSR's effort in 1962–63 to establish supranational planning in CMEA, see Robert S. Jaster, 'The Defeat of Khrushchev's Plan to Integrate Eastern Europe', *World Today*, Vol. 19, No. 12 (December 1963), pp. 514–22.

31 For recent Soviet suggestions, see Pekshev, op. cit., and N. M. Mitrofanova, 'Ob ekonomicheskoi prirode kontraktnykh tsen vo vzaimnom sotrudnichestve stran SEV' [On the economic nature of contract prices in mutual cooperation of CMEA countries], *Izvestiia Akademii Nauk SSR, Seriia ekonomicheskaia*, 1977, No. 5, pp. 116–24.

32 Pécsi, op. cit., p. 68.

33 Yu. Shamrai, 'Problems Bearing on the Planned Use of World Market Prices in the USSR's Trade with the CMEA Member Countries', *Foreign Trade* [Moscow], 1978, No. 11, pp. 33–42.

34 On the TR and the CMEA payments system, see I. Vincze, 'On the Common Currency and the System of International Payments within the CMEA', *Acta Oeconomica* [Budapest], Vol. 19 (1977), No. 1, pp. 1–17; Jozef M. van Brabant, *East European*

Cooperation: The Role of Money and Finance (New York: Praeger, 1977), pp. 108–16 and 312–42; and Freidrich Levcik, 'Transferable Rouble and Convertibility', in J.-L. Guglielmi and Marie Lavigne (eds), *Unités et monnaies de compte* (Paris: Economica, 1978), pp. 111–17.

35 Many examples are given in Françoise Lemoine, 'Les prix des échances a l'intérieur du Conseil d'Aide Économique Mutuelle', in NATO, *Comecon*, pp. 135–76.

36 Pécsi, op. cit., p. 94.

37 Ibid., p. 49.

38 Ibid., p. 11.

39 Ibid., p. 52.

40 Ibid., p. 21.

41 Ibid., p. 19.

42 A. Leznik, 'Mezhdunarodnaia spetsializatsiia i kooperatsiia v mashinostroenii' [International specialization and cooperation in machine building], *Planovoe khoziaistvo,* 1978, No. 7, p. 114.

43 Pekshev, op. cit., p. 88. See also Iu. Kormnov, 'Mezhdunarodnaia kooperatsiia i proizvodstvenno-eksportnyi profil' [International cooperation and production-export assortment], *Planovoe khoziaistvo*, 1979, No. 1, pp. 34–5; and Yu. Medvedkov, 'Programmes for Specialization and Cooperation in Production up to 1990 and Some Questions of Organization of Socialist Countries' Foreign Trade', *Foreign Trade* [Moscow], 1979, No. 2, p. 33.

44 'Thus, in one of the enterprises, capital investments and current expenses are calculated with the aid of 14 basic and more than 30 supplementary coefficients. That circumstance complicates joint activity.' A. I. Zubkov, 'Mezhdunarodnye sotsialisticheskie sovmestnye proizvodstva' [International socialist joint production], *Izvestiia Akademii Nauk SSSR, Seriia Ekonomicheskaia*, 1978, No. 4, p. 79.

45 Zubkov, op. cit.; Marie Lavigne, 'The Problem of the Multinational Socialist Enterprise', *The ACES Bulletin*, Vol. 17, No. 1 (Summer 1975), pp. 33–61; Heinrich Machowski, 'International Economic Organizations Within Comecon: Status, Problems, and Prospects', in NATO, *Comecon*, pp. 187–200; and N. Ivanov and N. Markicheva, 'International Economic Organizations: An Important Form of Cooperation Between the Socialist Countries', *Foreign Trade* [Moscow], 1977, No. 7, pp. 31–8.

46 For a recent survey of these efforts, see Stanislaw Stepanenko, 'Scientific and Technical Cooperation and Trade Between the CMEA Member Countries', *Foreign Trade* [Moscow], 1979, No. 11, pp. 15–19.

47 Eastern and Western appraisals of the standardization program are provided, respectively, by S. Stepanenko, 'CMEA Standards and Their Role in the Development of Production Specialization and Cooperation in the CMEA Member Countries', *Foreign Trade* [Moscow], 1978, No. 7, pp. 36–41, and Philip Joseph, 'Comecon Integration: The Place of Standardization', in NATO, *Comecon*, pp. 59–74.

48 The obstacles to labor mobility in CMEA are discussed in Friedrich Levcik, 'Migration and Employment of Foreign Workers in the CMEA Countries and Their Problems', in *East European Economies Post-Helsinki*, pp. 458–76.

49 Cf. Kohn, 'Soviet-Eastern European Economic Relations', pp. 254–8.

Part Three

East European Polity and Society

Chapter 7

The World Economy and Elite Political Strategies in Czechoslovakia, Hungary, and Poland

ZVI GITELMAN

The expansion of economic relations between the advanced capitalist states of the West and the socialist countries of Eastern Europe that took place in the 1970s led many to speculate on its political consequences. Indeed, the expansion was 'sold' to some Western publics and politicians not only as an economic end in itself but also as a means of promoting 'mutual understanding', at the very least, and, hopefully, even 'democratization' or 'liberalization' of Soviet-type political systems. This assertion was matched by Soviet and East European warnings, and sometimes assurances, that Western trade or aid should not entail the import of influence, whether political or cultural, but would require increased vigilance to prevent pernicious materials and ideas from being smuggled in with Western goods and services. Neither the assertion that increased economic ties would lead to 'liberalization', nor the insistence that it would not, has been proved. Western influence on East European mass and 'high' cultures is obvious and considerable, but Western political influence is problematic. Impressions of the political consequences of increased economic contacts diverge widely.[1]

Expanded economic relations have clearly exposed the socialist economies to economic developments in the West. The initial smugness of Soviet and East European observers of skyrocketing energy prices, Western recession, unemployment, and inflation was replaced by a realization, admitted publicly, that economic adversity in the West could have a harmful influence in the East. 'The worse, the better' did not necessarily hold in an increasingly interdependent world. The Soviet press, not surprisingly, was slower than its East European counterparts to admit this.[2] The Hungarian media, followed by the Polish and Czechoslovak, discussed the subject at an earlier date than the Soviet, and did so in far greater detail.[3] But subsequently, first in the specialized journals (e.g. *Voprosy ekonomiki*) and then in the popular press, the Soviet media admitted that changes in world prices of raw materials and fuels demanded adaptation of domestic wholesale prices and affected the allied socialist countries even more.[4] By 1976 the political leaders of Eastern Europe were publicly admitting that Western inflation raised the prices of imported goods and changed the terms of trade within CMEA.

Economists have detailed and analyzed the economic impacts on

Eastern Europe of world economic difficulties, and they need be only briefly mentioned here: (1) the rise in OPEC petroleum prices led to an increase of Soviet fuel prices, forcing East European customers to pay more for Soviet fuels; (2) food shortages in Eastern Europe and a commitment to the consumer necessitated the import of grains at a time when the USSR, formerly a grain supplier itself, was importing large quantities from the West; (3) recession in Western Europe and North America made it harder for East European goods to penetrate those markets; (4) at the same time, inflation in the capitalist countries raised the prices of goods imported to Eastern Europe from those countries.

Soviet and East European sources either deny that economic trade with the West is having political effects or stress that such possibilities must be averted. A Soviet writer, acknowledging that Western technology should play 'an important but not determining role' in the development of the CMEA countries, warns that 'the expected expansion of economic links with developed capitalist countries should not lead to the creation of strategically or technically vulnerable loci in the CMEA community'.[5] The Soviet Union has shown itself sensitive to any possible infringements of its sovereignty or what it sees as attempts at influencing its domestic affairs – as in the case of the 'Jackson Amendment' to the US Trade Reform Act or attempts by American officials to influence the treatment of Soviet dissidents – and the primary constraint on trade, according to one analyst, is 'the determination not to give hostages to fortune'.[6] This is at least equally true of the East European countries, since they must also remember that the USSR would undoubtedly take measures to prevent a 'penetration' of Eastern Europe that would result in Western political leverage there. Moreover, the USSR is willing to pay a heavy economic price to maintain political control in Eastern Europe. World economic changes have led the Soviet Union to adjust its economic relationship with Eastern Europe in a direction more favorable to itself, but even the renegotiation of intra-CMEA trade prices in 1975 'reduce[s] substantially but [does] not eliminate, the economic disadvantage to the Soviets'.[7] By the late 1970s, however, the USSR seemed once again to be enjoying a net benefit in its economic relations with Eastern Europe. Still, the question remains whether attempts to insulate socialist countries from political influence while opening them to economic interaction with the West will be successful.

While the economic consequences for Eastern Europe of global economic changes may be observed and measured, the possible political effects of these changes are far more difficult to assess. As Terry and Korbonski point out, 'There is no political equivalent of the economists' "transmission and response" model by which to distinguish, measure, and analyze the generation, channels of impact, transmission, and policy response measures, whereby an international disturbance affects a national economy.'[8] Moreover, given our inadequate knowledge of East European decision-making processes and the complex relationships between Moscow's wishes and domestic forces in determining domestic change, it is 'highly unlikely that we could discover a predictable pattern of linkages between external influences and internal effects'.[9] Yet we may at least conclude that external economic changes 'have brought old issues to the fore with a new sense of urgency, and have narrowed the options open to the regime in dealing with these issues and increased the penalties of inaction'.[10] External economic changes are therefore not only a factor influencing political strategies and decisions, but have a catalytic effect in speeding up the reactions and interactions of other political forces.

Western technology has had a direct and differential *economic* impact on Eastern Europe. The Czechoslovak computer industry, once the supplier of large computers to the rest of the bloc, has been hurt by the importation of Western computers; on the other hand, the Poles 'are beginning to reap the benefits of technology transfer from the West in their exports of machinery and equipment, consumer goods, and other products'.[11] I would argue that recent external economic difficulties have had a *differential* impact not only on the economies of the East European countries, but also on their politics. They have served to sharpen the political issues confronting these nations, and they are influential in shaping the choices elites must make in their quite different attempts to achieve common goals: the political integration of their societies, the establishment of long-term political legitimacy, which will be the guarantor of short-run political stability. Elite talents, behavior, and choices are increasingly important in shaping the politics of Eastern Europe. We believed in the 1950s that these were secondary to choices made in Moscow; some of us believed in the 1960s that these were secondary to ineluctable rquirements of political development. A case study of three relatively developed East European states' reactions to world economic changes will show that different political strategies are currently being pursued in Eastern Europe and that these strategies can be attributed primarily, though not exclusively, to elite choices interacting with responses and predispositions of decreasingly malleable publics.

I   Strategies of Political Integration in Eastern Europe

For about two decades most of the regimes in Eastern Europe have been seeking to establish their political authority on a base other than coercive power. They have tried to promote the process of political integration wherein those who physically inhabit a political system develop a firm sense of identity with it and commitment to its political culture.[12] While each regime has adopted different tactics, and the same regime has shifted tactics over time, some common factors influence the choice of tactics. In recent years the developed countries of Eastern Europe, Czechoslovakia, the German Democratic Republic, Hungary, and Poland, seem to have adopted a common general strategy for political integration, one of gaining the people's trust and support by providing them with a rising standard of living. There are three common influences on the governments' strategic choices, which can be grouped as historical, developmental, and situational.

In Czechoslovakia, Hungary, and Poland, the three countries with which we shall be concerned, traumatic domestic disturbances are the proximate historical influences on contemporary political strategies.[13] I have in mind specifically the events of 1956 in Hungary, the 1968 reforms and the reaction to them in Czechoslovakia, and the 1968 'events', the 1970 and 1976 riots, and the 1980 strikes in Poland. The Hungarian regime, remarkably stable since 1957, has worked hard and seemingly successfully to restore a shattered polity. The Czechoslovak party leadership is also engaged in a process of socialist restoration, though its initial situation and present course differ considerably from the Hungarian. While the Polish party has experienced several political cataclysms, from 1956 through 1976, it seems to be reacting primarily to the events of December 1970, which catapulted the present leadership into power.

The historical origins of a leadership group influence its tactics and behavior. After the Hungarian 'counterrevolution' was suppressed, the complete purge of Imre Nagy and his associates permitted an almost completely new leadership to take the helm, thus making possible a fresh start. In a way, the 1956 collapse of the Communist Party worked to the advantage of the present leaders by facilitating a relatively free hand in personnel and other policies. The post-1957 leaders, if not· politically homogenous, have been able to cooperate and work together. It is widely agreed that the ruling group has worked well as a coalition, not of interest groups or of factions, but of politicians with somewhat different outlooks united by a fundamental commitment to the political course articulated by Janos Kádár. This allows the Hungarian party to pursue more innovative policies and to pursue them more consistently.

The differences between the Hungarians and the Poles or Czechoslovaks are illustrated by their respective policies toward economic reform. 'The Hungarian approach was to reject gradual and piecemeal reforms as futile, and to move boldly to simultaneous major revision of most of the traditional mechanisms for directing the economy.'[14] No doubt, Hungarian 'boldness' was encouraged by the favorable publicity given at that time to the 'Liberman reforms' in the Soviet Union. In contrast, the Poles have launched five major reform proposals in two decades, none of them as comprehensive, nor as effective, as the Hungarian. At least one reason for this Polish pattern can be found in the political sphere. Elite factionalism in the 1960s (Gomułka, Moczar, Gierek *et al.*) weakened the party so that it could never make a decisive choice for reform. As one analyst of Polish attempts at reform notes, 'The history of the reform movement in Eastern Europe indicates the crucial importance of party unity for the success of reform', and such unity was never achieved in the Polish United Workers Party.[15]

Under the pressure of widespread strikes in the late summer of 1980, the unity of the party cracked and, ultimately, Stanisław Kania replaced Edward Gierek as party leader, much as a decade earlier Gierek had replaced Władysław Gomułka following workers' riots. Gierek came to power on a platform of immediate and substantial payoffs to the Polish consumer, and he and the people were intensely aware, especially after the price riots of 1976, of the contingent nature of his tenure, dependent on consumer satisfaction. Thus far, the new Polish leadership has not been able to persuade the population to give it political credits, to make short-term sacrifices for long-term gains. The Polish regime has less 'slack' in its support than the Hungarian one. And so both the Gomułka and Gierek groups felt it impossible to make major structural changes, though there is no evidence that either really desired to do so.

In Czechoslovakia the leadership is split. The 1968 Soviet intervention, unlike the 1956 invasion of Hungary, did not lead to a decisive break with the past, at least insofar as personnel is concerned. The present leadership includes different historical–political strata: for example, at least one Politburo member (Lenart) was a member of the 1966 Novotný Politburo; the Politburo in April 1968, the high point of the Dubček period, included two men from the Novotný period (Dubček, who became a reformer, and Kolder, who did not); and the Politburo formed after Gustav Husák became First Secretary included Vasil Bilak, a member of the Politburos of April 1968 and March 1969. The small number of changes in the ruling group since 1971 may be attributed not to its inner harmony but to a deadlock, perhaps imposed by the Soviet Union, among politicians who have serious differences over policy but who cannot marshall enough political support, inside and outside the country, to defeat their rivals and remove them from power. Whatever the actual divisions, they may constrain Husák's ability to strike out on a less cautious and conservative course than he has thus far pursued. Although there have been hints that professional economists are thinking about reforms, economic reform is taboo on political–historical grounds because it was one of the hallmarks of the 1968 changes. In contrast, economic reform was not a prominent part of Imre Nagy's program and therefore could be experimented with in Hungary. As David Granick has stated, 'The fact that the Hungarian economy has evolved differently from that of its allies must be explained on political rather than on economic grounds.'[16] In sum, the differences observed in the present-day political–economic strategies of the socialist countries may be explained partly by the differences in their recent political histories.

Developmental influences on political strategies and tactics include rising consumer expectations, changing consumption patterns, a mature and self-conscious working class whose standards of comparison are no longer village life, articulate intelligentsias, which in Eastern Europe are increasingly aware of developments outside the region, and increasing awareness of the world outside by mass publics as well. The 'revolution of rising expectations' is a concomitant of modernization in Eastern Europe and the world over. Consumer expectations rise, not only as a result of increases in the standard of living, but also because of explicit leadership commitments to such development, increasing awareness and knowledge of more affluent Western societies, and secular political trends that permit greater aspirations and greater scope for the articulation and pursuit of those aspirations. Kenneth Jowitt describes the development of regime–society relations in 'European Leninist regimes' as involving a (reversible) shift from domination to manipulation. 'Manipulation . . . is not simply a more economical and clever mode of domination. It allows for a certain measure of recognition and influence to aspiring social strata that have felt relatively deprived of status, influence and economic well-being.'[17] Prominent among such strata is the industrial working class. This class, originating in the peasantry, has been sizable for several generations in industrialized Czechoslovakia (though much more recently in Slovakia), and has grown in Hungary and Poland to the point where 'workers are not as easily satisfied as ex-peasants might be, and they are organizationally more astute'.[18] In Poland the number of industrial workers more than doubled between 1950 and 1970; they and their families now make up about half the nation's population. While in 1962 only 17 percent of industrial workers had been in that category of employment before the war,[19] by 1980 the working class has become 'increasingly hereditary in composition. The sons of ex-peasants, who themselves have known only industrial–urban life, are now coming to replace their fathers behind the benches and machines.'[20] These people are more involved, at least formally, in the exercise of political power, since the percentage of workers in the Polish United Workers Party has risen from 40.6 in 1975 to 44.7 in 1977, the highest percentage of workers in the party since 1955. But the workers have little positive influence in political decision making, though they have gained a tacit veto power over fundamental domestic decisions in those areas directly affecting them. Should the new independent trade unions gain legitimacy, and should the Soviet Union give its tacit acquiescence to their existence, the workers will have institutionalized and activated their latent political power.

A third indication of economic development is the change in consumption patterns. A Polish study found that food is declining as a proportion of total consumption. In 1975 the lowest income group spent 55 percent of its budget on food while the highest group spent 34 percent. The structure of food consumption was also changing, with a decrease of expenditures on grain products, potatoes, and fats, and an increase in spending on fruits, vegetables, and meat. Expenditure on transportation increased substantially between 1970 and 1975, as private cars became more available. People are spending a greater proportion of their money on those items which a better educated population and one with greater consumer aspirations might be expected to favor. This means that expectations and demands of the consumer market are greater and more difficult to meet.

The political importance of the intelligentsia in Eastern Europe has been pointed out many times and need not be detailed here. But its role as an agent of social change may have diminished, as the role of the working class has expanded. One astute East European social scientist suggests that the working class now is the most sensitive to 'misdeeds' and the group with the most 'social power' in the society.[21] However, the *institutional*, regularized means for integrating this power into the established political system do not exist in any of the socialist countries. This seems to be one of the greatest weaknesses of the East European systems at the present time, as I shall argue in more detail.

Finally, heightened awareness of Western society's high levels of consumption has whetted consumer appetites in Eastern Europe. This awareness has increased because of greater access to Western television programs and magazines and because of increased tourism in both directions, especially in Hungary and Poland, which encourage Western tourism to bolster their hard currency holdings. Hungary allows its own citizens to go abroad more than any other CMEA country (300,000 Hungarians traveled to Western countries in 1978).

We turn now to the common situational influences, before examining those factors differentiating the political strategies of each of the three countries. The obvious common situational influence is that of the USSR. One should not assume that their ties with the Soviet Union are weakening, simply because the East European countries are currently pursuing different political strategies. Precisely because of the difficulties created in the world economy, on the economic plane the East European countries are anxious to draw closer to their best customer and supplier, the Soviet Union. The political diversity of Eastern Europe can be accounted for by a combination of East European domestic considerations coupled with what must be a Soviet decision to allow such diversity while defining its limits from time to time as the need arises. Soviet leaders have apparently recognized that limited autonomy is needed by East European leaders if they are to succeed politically and economically. Failure would impose burdens not only on the East Europeans, but also on the Soviets, given their commitment to maintaining a socialist Eastern Europe. In return for limited domestic autonomy, the socialist countries are expected to support the Soviet position in world affairs and to maintain their political and economic allegiance to the socialist bloc. The Soviet Union's own increased attention to the world market has facilitated parallel moves by the East Europeans. Moreover, the USSR has bailed out the three countries economically during their times of troubles. Extensive Soviet aid was rendered to Hungary after 1956, probably to Czechoslovakia in 1969, and to Poland in 1971, 1976, and 1980. Certainly the immediate beneficiaries of political and military aid within the East European regimes would rank it no less important than the economic. Even critics of the regimes have accepted Soviet domination as a *fait accompli* and, by and large, seek only to soften, not to remove it. Political strategies in Eastern Europe are designed, therefore, on the premise that the alliance with the USSR will remain.

The second common situational factor in the developed countries of Eastern Europe is the use of consumer satisfaction as the justification of the leadership's existence and the vindication of its policies. This has been widely discussed. A Czechoslovak commentator notes that 'citizens don't judge our progress by . . . statistics but according to what they experience as consumers. From this . . . follows the political importance of the availability of goods and the sales environment.'[22] For certain elements in Eastern Europe – the intelligentsia, religious believers, some young people – consumer satisfaction is not an acceptable yardstick by which to judge the leadership, but for the large majority consumer satisfaction is the most important influence on their attitudes toward the leadership and the political system generally. A second concern of many is to participate in and truly influence decisions affecting their work situations and local conditions, and studies of *West* European societies have led some to conclude that consumer satisfaction is no longer the universal goal. Eastern

Europe, however, is still in its industrializing stage, and people are striving to acquire consumer goods, unlike 'the German and American publics who have become less "thing-minded" and more concerned with self-actualization through meaningful work'.[23] While these kinds of attitudes are characteristic of a small minority in Eastern Europe, the great majority are certainly still very materialistic.

Even if consumer satisfaction is presently the basis of political stability and possibly even legitimacy, it depends on two factors beyond the control of the political elites, and on their own proclivities as well. These are, first, the subjective perception by consumers of their lot – and consumers' attitudes are generally of the 'what-have-you-done-for-me-lately' variety. Consumer satisfaction depends also on the state of the economy, never fully controllable even in a centrally directed economy, and even less so at present when world economic developments affect Eastern Europe more than ever before. Moreover, Communist elites have traditionally favored production of capital goods and investment in heavy industry over production for consumer use. Mieczkowski offers the interesting hypothesis that in Poland 'growth of consumption has been inversely proportional to the power of the Communist Party' and that possibly the Polish experience can be generalized to other countries of Eastern Europe. That is, the Polish leadership promotes consumption only to bolster its political power; once that power is perceived as enhanced, the leadership returns to the traditional, and preferred, policy of investment in heavy industry. Thus there is a 'cyclical character of the consumption–politics syndrome' as investment in heavy industry leads to consumer dissatisfaction, threat to the leadership, and a return to increasing consumption. Mieczkowski sees these cycles as self-sustaining, and suggests that since 'consumption and the material satisfaction of the population replace free voting, political opposition, and other indices of the degree of popular support of the government', one can measure the power of the Communist party at any given time by observing its consumption policies. The traditional policy of favoring capital goods indicates that the party considers itself in a solid political position, whereas a pro-consumer policy betrays the party's perception of its own weakness.[24]

This intriguing thesis may not really offer a satisfactory explanation. It is an oversimplification to substitute consumption and material satisfaction for other indices of public support because, ingrates that they are, East European (and other) citizens may not translate their satisfaction as consumers into political support for the elites or the system that brought them the satisfaction. The objective improvement in the Polish consumer's lot in the 1970s was impressive: real wages increased by 7.2 percent annually in 1971–75 (while the planned rate was only 3.4 percent), and the growth of personal consumption outlays was higher than in any other period since 1950.[25] Yet 1976 saw riots directed against the leadership's attempt to increase retail prices, a step with which few would argue on economic grounds alone. So even the most dramatic improvement in the lot of the Polish consumer was insufficient to induce acknowledgment of satisfaction with the system on this score, let alone in a more general way. Certainly, few would contend that Czechoslovak consumers, who enjoy perhaps the second highest standard of living in Eastern Europe, have become supporters of the present regime.

A second caveat is that not all Communist leaders or parties are quick to return to investment in capital goods. Mieczkowski himself points out that 'unlike Gomułka in 1970, Gierek did not seem consciously to revert to the traditional planners' preference for investment'. Rather, the boom got out of hand, and Poland's domestic and foreign economic difficulties gave rise to a situation where 'something had to give' and consumer prices were chosen as the best solution. 'Thus consumption proved once again to be an underdog' under Communist rule.[26] But this shows that the Polish leader did not choose to turn away from consumption as soon as his power had been consolidated; he raised prices, or attempted to do so, in order to keep the consumer boom going. Polish workers obviously did not appreciate the subtlety of the economic logic. Furthermore, other Communist leaders have adopted consumption-oriented policies out of strength rather than weakness. Janos Kádár moved to a consumer-oriented policy in the late 1960s, *after* the party had consolidated itself and the disaster of 1956 had been overcome. In fact, when the Hungarian Communist Party was at its weakest, in the late 1950s, it pursued the more traditional economic policy, and only later began to favor the consumer. It has shown no sign of turning away from this policy now that popular support seems to be substantial. Kádár and his colleagues may have lost the congenital Communist reflex toward heavy emphasis on capital investment.

Despite these objections, Mieczkowski's thesis alerts us to a possible relationship between economic policies and elite–mass politics. We now turn to these relationships, examining Hungarian, Czechoslovak, and Polish strategies, with particular attention to the effects on them of problems arising in the world economy.

II Domestic Crisis and Political Reintegration in Hungary, Czechoslovakia, and Poland

The current leaders in the three countries came to power as the result of a domestic crisis leading to Soviet invasion, or, in the case of Poland, to civil strife and rebellion. Thus, more than the other Communist elites in Europe, their task has been one of restoration, reconstruction, and reconciliation. In Hungary and Czechoslovakia, political restoration involved military intervention to halt ongoing trends and permit a Soviet-approved leadership to take control; a massive infusion of economic aid, which gave the new leadership time to reorganize (this was also true of Poland in 1970, 1976, and 1980); the reconstitution of the party elite followed by a 'consolidation' of the rank and file; and, finally, beginning the process of at least neutralizing, if not reconciling, the population.[27] The last process has been going on in Poland as well, and we can compare the reconciliation attempts of all three leaderships, beginning with the Hungarian and Czechoslovak cases.

The approaches of the Hungarian and Czechoslovak leaderships and the differences between them are best summarized by the formulas of Kádár and Husák. In December 1961, Janos Kádár declared, 'He who is not against us, is with us'; less publicized and less often quoted was Gustav Husák's statement of January 1970, 'He who is not against us is our potential ally.' These, of course, were conscious variations – or even reversals – of the Leninist theme of demanding total commitment, at least from party members. Kádár has assumed that popular passivity should not be interpreted as muted hostility but as tacit acceptance and *de facto* cooperation. Husák has not taken quite so sanguine a view. For him, neutrality cannot be assumed to be benevolent, but it does open the possibility that through conscious efforts the individual might be won over to the cause. Kádár's formula implies a more optimistic assessment of the Hungarian public, while Husák's indicates less trust in the people, yet hope that they can be won over by hard work.

The difference in slogans reflects the different approaches to the question of bringing state and society together in a harmonious working relationship. There is, first, the matter of style. Kádár is more relaxed, more earthy, and speaks in rather plain language, whereas Husák tends to repeat well-worn political cliches and favors the use of abstract terms, eschewing earthy illustrations.

Substance matches style. Asked in 1969 whether he still held to his formulation, 'He who is not against us is with us', Kádár replied that it was 'suitable and valid for today too' and explained his intent. 'Under our socialist conditions, anyone who is not engaged in conspiracy or subversive activities against the regime, but is performing socially useful work in whatever sphere, is taking part in socialist construction. In other words, whoever is not against us, is with us!'[28] Thus, anyone gainfully employed could be considered 'with us'.

This assumption is linked to Kádár's stated belief that 'people can be changed, i.e., that ideology influences people, and if ten years ago someone was not a supporter of the socialist idea, he could have changed in ten years'. From this belief in the malleability of the individual and his political commitment, Kádár draws two conclusions. First, the party followed the right policy in differentiating among those who seemed to oppose the regime and even socialism and 'split the people who were temporarily gathered on the other side, and . . . [led] those whose real place was on this side to the right road'. Second, past positions and errors can be overcome and forgiven; there is no use in 'deal[ing] with who did what nine, fourteen, or twenty-seven years ago'. 'We are firmly convinced,' said Kádár in Prague, 'that only on the basis of mutual trust is it possible to work, only if the working people have confidence in the Party and the Party has faith in the masses.'[29]

Husák, much closer in time to the crisis than Kádár, is also much more likely to warn against 'opportunists' and 'enemies' and to mention the dangers that face the nation. In 1969 Husák stressed the need for a 'revival of our Party's unity', for 'the renewal of the leading role of the Communist Party in our society', and for the solution of 'grave economic problems'. 'Our concern,' he said, 'is to strengthen the entire system of state coercive organs, national committees, the security corps and the army.' By 1971, with the party purged and matters seemingly in control, Husák could turn his attention to less forbidding matters. He claimed in 1975 that 'after April 1969 we decided to solve matters not by administrative methods but by political ones. I think we made the correct decision.'[30] By late 1970 the emphasis was on 'constructive work' and the need to establish close relations with the 'broad masses' of the population. Even such a staunch opponent of liberalization as Viliam Šalgović contended, 'It is . . . impossible to build socialism merely with the force of the communists or of the working class. The construction of socialism, if it is to be successful, must become the cause of the widest possible strata.'[31]

But this does not mean 'he who is not against us is with us'. For there are two essential differences between the Czechoslovak and Hungarian assessments of their respective situations. The Hungarians assume that the great majority *already* support the party's vision of socialism, while the Czechoslovaks explicitly say that they must still fight to achieve this. The contrast is especially visible in regard to the intelligentsia. Whereas Kádár consistently lists the intelligentsia along with the proletariat and peasantry as supporters of the system, the Czechoslovaks stress that the intelligentsia lags behind the proletariat in reconciling itself to the new political situation (and most outside observers agree). Thus, while rejecting the 'opinion that the intelligentsia as a whole had turned traitor', the party press describes the intelligentsia as having 'illusions about itself' and displaying tendencies toward individualism, 'the rejection of discipline'. Therefore the intelligentsia must adopt 'unconditional loyalty to the cause of the socialist revolution, a self-critical attitude and discipline'.[32] In other words, the loyalty of the intelligentsia is yet to be won.

A second difference is that in Hungary the struggle was 'on two fronts' (against the 'dogmatism' of Matyas Rakosi and against the 'liberalism' of Imre Nagy), and the struggle has been declared successfully concluded. In Czechoslovakia, by contrast, the struggle 'against rightist opportunism, as the principal danger, was and is correct and necessary', in the words of Gustav Husák.[33] This means both that the struggle continues and that the party is committed to a one-sided struggle against 'right revisionism and opportunism' rather than to a 'middle way', which would permit considerable maneuver and flexibility. Some even claim that 'our building process is taking place in sharp ideological combat against counter-revolutionary ideology which is being smuggled in',[34] a claim that even more 'vigilant' Hungarian comrades would not be likely to make.

On the other hand, just as Kádár constantly refers to the policy of 'alliances', Husák also refers approvingly to the 'Leninist policy of alliance' and argues that no one need be written off as politically hopeless and beyond rehabilitation. The Czechoslovak media call for differentiating among the reformers of 1968, separating the hard-core revisionists from their misguided followers. Echoing the kinds of sentiments expressed by Kádár, *Rudé právo* stresses that 'it is imperative not only to act on the basis of the degree of the guilt of one or another individual but also on . . . whether or not an individual has adapted to the Party's policy and on how he makes good his past mistakes and errors'.[35] At the Fifteenth Party Congress (1976) Husák justified the 'differentiated approach' to those not yet won over and asserted that 'there is no need to change anything in this policy', possibly hinting that 'some comrades' might be urging a less discriminating policy, perhaps going back to the 'methods of the 1950s', which Husák has explicitly renounced. Although Husák is not quite as enthusiastic as Kádár about the 'Leninist policy of alliances', in the Czechoslovak context his stress on working with the masses should be seen as conciliatory. Kádár goes further, arguing that the masses will be convinced of the party's policy 'on the basis of their own experience'. Husák is less eager to let experience be the best teacher, arguing forcefully that the masses must be taught the proper lessons.

This difference in emphasis is related to seemingly different conceptions of the relationship of Marxist–Leninist theory to the lot of the individual. The Czechoslovak experience is seen as part of a larger phenomenon, the development of societies along lines postulated by the authoritative interpreters of the doctrine. Individual satisfaction is not a priority. Kádár, on the other hand, stresses the utility of the doctrine and its system for the Hungarian people specifically. 'The relationship between Marxism–Leninism, socialism, communism and the . . . Hungarian people is not that we have an excellent theory and we are going to test it on, say, ten million guinea-pigs. . . . I think that it is the other way around; Marxism–Leninism, the whole idea of communism, is *for the sake* of a better life for ten million Hungarians.'[36] For Kádár, consumer satisfaction in the present is the aim of the doctrine and the system born of it. Consumption is not a tactic to which one resorts out of weakness but a legitimate and immediate goal.

A policy of alliances and of bringing benefits to the nation leads to tactics of compromise and even negotiation. As Kádár reflected, 'Nothing happens the way it is first imagined. . . . Life does force compromise on us . . . in the good sense of the word. . . . Our theory cannot go against common sense.'[37] The history of Hungarian economic, political, and social evolution in recent years reveals careful compromise, constant adjustment, flexibility, a willingness to face up to difficulties, and, to a greater extent than in most socialist countries, even to discuss such difficulties publicly and privately. A Hungarian social scientist has written, 'Today, the science of correct compromises is the chief "branch of science" of domestic politics (including economic and standard of living policy, and social and cultural policy).'[38] Such a statement could not appear in a Czechoslovak journal. Compromise is precisely one of the sins attributed both to Novotný and his immediate successors, and is blamed for much of what went wrong in 1968. Alliances can be made, but compromises cannot. While the Hungarian leadership has compromised its policies in the face of popular opposition, such compromise is not evident in Czechoslovakia.

A more specific tactical difference, indicating contrasting degrees of trust in the people, is that within five years after the 1956 crisis, class criteria were no longer employed in admission to higher education in Hungary. In Czechoslovakia they were introduced after 1968 in order to rid society of the pernicious influence of revisionist intellectuals and introduce a 'healthier' element into the schools.[39] At this point Czechoslovak policy is more restrictive and less trusting than Hungarian policy was at a parallel point in time.

In Poland the post-1970 government and party leadership acknow-ledged publicly that the crisis which had brought it to power resulted from a communications gap both between the party and the people and even within the party itself. Two basic strategies were proposed to close the elite–mass gap. The first was to change the institutional machinery linking elites and masses, and the second was to change the 'manner of ruling', or political style of leadership. But, aside from a reform of government administrative structures below the national level, the Gierek leadership showed no intention of changing Poland's institutional structure,[40] and its successors have been struggling to keep the independent trade unions within the framework of the present one. Poland suffers from 'overinstitutionalization', whereby its institutions are stable and unchang-ing, but their stability derives not from their efficiency or being valued by the population, but from bureaucratic inertia and political paralysis.[41] No new institutions for linking masses and elites effectively have been established, and the failure of the traditional institutions – party cells, national councils, trade unions, workers' management conferences – to link them is most dramatically illustrated by the enormous miscalculation of public reaction to the 1976 price rises, to the proposed changes in the constitution, and, most vividly, to the strikes in 1980.

The changes made in Poland under Gierek were largely in style, and consisted of the adoption of a kind of populist approach by the leadership. Gierek and other top officials frequently met with workers and citizens, to try to discuss their problems and desires frankly. A Central Committee lecturer was assigned to each one of 164 major plants, which account for about a quarter of the labor force, of party members in industry, and of industrial output. The lecturer was obliged to consult directly with workers and party activists in his enterprises and was supposed to report in detail to the Central Committee, which, in turn, was obligated to respond promptly to the concerns expressed at the plant level. These measures and other minor institutional rearrangements proved ineffective in bringing elites and masses closer together. One is inclined to agree with the judgment of Vincent Chrypinski: 'More than efficient authoritarianism and psychic stimuli, Poland needs a basic reform of the centralized bureaucratic system of government. . . . Real reform requires a break with old authoritarian tendencies and the acceptance of genuine democratic participation with individuals convinced of their influence on the decision makers.'[42] This is precisely what Poland has not achieved.

Some observers continue to see signs of impending change in the extensive public discussions of participation and involvement in decision making. But such discussions have gone on for so long and with such intensity, with absolutely no visible practical effect, that either this is all a cynical exercise or, more likely, the leadership recognizes the problem and therefore permits, perhaps even encourages, such discussion, but lacks either the will or the power (or both) to draw practical conclusions from the prescriptions for change. Although the Conferences of Workers' Self-Management have existed for twenty years, not until 1978 was a national meeting of representatives from the Conferences called. In an address that covered sixteen pages, not once did Secretary Gierek mention giving workers more control over management decisions in the workplace. His entire speech was devoted to the role of the Conferences in improving production and mobilizing the proletariat toward better work. The Conferences were to remain nothing more than transmission belts, another (ineffective) instrument for raising productivity, while keeping participation and influence at a minimum. In sum, the consultative leadership style did not mean any devolution of real power to the working people. Alex Pravda points to the 'clear line drawn by the regime between the opening up of channels for consultative access to policy makers and the devolution of real decision-making influence and power'.[43] The present leaders are afraid to allow more participation in decision making. It seems that in the 1950s many people feared the party; now the party fears the people.

Instead of expanding participation, the Polish regime, even more than the Hungarian and Czechoslovak, has emphasized material incentives for political compliance and economic development. Reacting to Gomułka's blithe disregard for the consumer, his fear of borrowing from the West or becoming involved with extra-CMEA trade, and his conservative economic policies generally, his successors determined to increase both investment and consumption simultaneously on an unparalleled scale. Such expansion would be accomplished by increases in the productivity of inputs, rather than in their quantities, as well as by massive importation of foreign credits, products, and licenses. Total trade turnover increased by 165 percent between 1971 and 1975, with imports from the West increasing by 452 percent and exports growing by 167 percent. By 1974 Poland's trade with the West had almost pulled even with her CMEA trade, but had also resulted in a hard-currency debt of $7 billion by the end of 1975 (and about $15 billion by mid-1979).[44] Nevertheless, the short-run gains were extremely impressive. To cite only one well-known example, in 1976 half of Poland's existing industrial capacity had been installed in 1971–75. This frenzied growth seems to have enjoyed wide approval in Polish society, though some Polish functionaries expressed fears that traditional ideological goals were lost sight of in the mad rush to acquisition.[45]

Like the Czechoslovak leaders, Gierek and his successors were aware of the gulf separating the *pays légal* and *pays réel*, especially because the church drives this point home, but have tried to bridge the gap by bringing material satisfaction to the population. In the short run, both the Polish and Czechoslovak leaderships hope that consumer satisfaction will result in political quiescence. The Prime Minister of the Czech Republic noted, 'A balanced market contributes to people's happiness. The recent fluctuations in retail turnover once again confirmed what a sensitive barometer this is also of the political situation.'[46] The Polish leadership also openly acknowledges the linkage between consumer satisfaction and politics, while political analysts point out that rapid growth and a rise in living standards lead to increases in income inequalities and cause social tensions.[47]

Indeed this is a very serious problem for the Polish ruling group. Since the previous leadership fell from power over the issue of consumer (dis)satisfaction, the public is acutely aware of the issue. Even the casual reader of *Polityka* is impressed by the generous space devoted to consumer complaints and problems. This focus on the consumer makes it extraordinarily difficult, especially for a leadership with little accumulated credit in the eyes of the population, to take measures that may result in short-term losses to the consumer, though they might have long-range benefits. Gierek's room for maneuver was painfully limited, as is Kania's, yet external and internal economic difficulties strongly suggest that decisive steps must be taken if Poland is to avoid severe difficulty in the future. 'Gierek purchased the workers' political support by mortgaging Poland's economic future.'[48] But by 1980 he had lost that support, and developments in the world economy raise serious questions about the future.

III   World Economic Changes and Political Strategies in Eastern Europe

Since the political strategies of the developed East European countries emphasize consumer satisfaction, whatever has an economic impact on consumers affects the political situation as well. Initially, the Hungarians and Poles viewed the West as playing a useful economic role in supplying consumer goods and some of the wherewithal to aid the development of the local economy (redounding also to the benefit of the local consumers). But recession, inflation, and unemployment in the West have had negative effects on the East European economies, and hence on the consumers. Terry asserts that 'where the opening to the West was originally pursued as a means of overcoming the bottlenecks and inadequacies of their domestic economy, it is now in large part the urgency of coping with the strains produced by expanded external ties which is increasing the pressures for domestic change'.[49] Though there are few signs of fundamental systemic change in any of the countries, consumer prices have risen in all of them, attempts are being made to conserve energy, and, as a consequence, production targets of automobiles have been lowered. 'In the overall allocation of resources under the 1976–80 plans the consumer is to do less well than he did in 1971–75. Everywhere, the rates of growth of real wages are below those achieved in the previous five years.'[50] Great stress is laid on the need to expand exports more rapidly than imports.

Hungary was the first to acknowledge publicly the negative impact of world economic developments and to prepare the population for the consequences. A deterioration in Hungary's terms of trade with both the dollar markets and CMEA began in 1973, leading to increases in both producer and consumer prices. Subsidies for consumer goods were doubled in 1974 over 1973.[51] There is no doubt that world trends have had a negative effect on the situation of the Hungarian economy. Terry and Korbonski claim that 'the impact of external economic dislocations, whether transmitted from East or West, has been significantly greater on the Hungarian than on the Polish economy', but there have been no 'marked repercussions in the domestic political environment' because of, among other reasons, the 'more moderate and balanced development strategy' of the Hungarians compared to the Poles.[52]

One important additional factor is the relative success of Hungarian agriculture, which has adequately supplied the Hungarian consumer and has helped the country's export effort. Hungarian collectives have flourished partially because of the government's willingness to tolerate a significant private sector, which is aided by legal and illegal acquisition of materials from the collective sector. The heads of the collectives and those who farm the private plots intensively often help each other, with the prosperous farmers joining the party and even constituting a kind of local elite. On the other hand, because successful peasants cannot buy land or machinery for their private plots, they spend their money on color television sets, extravagant houses (I am informed that some build three-story houses, with the top two floors remaining empty but there 'in case of need'), large automobiles, some to be put on blocks for use by a teen-age son later on, etc. Some even go on ten-day excursions to Japan! But there is no doubt that a successful agriculture contributes a great deal to the standard of living and partially compensates for the problems caused by world economic trends.

Politically, for reasons we have explored, the Hungarians have been more successful than the Poles in gaining the understanding of the population for the painful economic decisions that must be made. With a united leadership and a First Secretary who seems genuinely popular and whose personal style is appealing, the government has more room for maneuver than the Polish government. Moreover, the Hungarian people, seared by the events of 1956, are no doubt wary of upsetting the political situation to the point that a Soviet intervention might ensue. Besides, they do not assume that a successor to Kádár will 'do better' for them than the present leader.[53]

Hungary, then, is better able to absorb blows dealt by the world economy, both because of its more flexible economic system and because the absorptive capacity of the Hungarian political system is greater than that of the Polish or Czechoslovak. Nevertheless, by 1979 the country had reached a crossroads where hard choices had to be made; economic problems either created or exacerbated by external economic developments, could no longer be avoided or deferred. (For 1979 the Hungarians planned an overall consumer price rise of nearly 5 percent, up from 4.6 percent in 1978, and an increase in real wages of only 1 percent, down from 3 percent in 1978.) The state provided a buffer against externally and internally produced inflation (blaming all inflation on external forces), but with the end of the Western 'credit boom' and a poor balance of trade (at the end of 1978 Hungary had a foreign trade deficit of 55.5 million forint), it would seem that consumer prices have to be raised considerably. But what is economically necessary is politically dangerous. There are no reliable feedback mechanisms (in Hungary or in any other socialist country) to warn political leaders how far they can go without encountering significant resistance. By the same token, no one can predict how the leadership would react to manifest popular discontent. Even the economists who agree on the need to raise food prices and to make exchange rates more realistic disagree about how this should be accomplished, whether incrementally, say with a 10 percent annual inflation, or at one blow. In any case, they claim, the politicians are reluctant to do what is economically necessary because they are uncertain of the political repercussions.

The Czechoslovak consumer also experienced some 'good years' in the early 1970s, but personal consumption slowed and real wages declined in 1975 and thereafter. The leadership tries to keep the economy going without reform, though occasionally there appear cautious discussions by professional economists which sound like hints for reform, a subject tainted by the association of economic reforms with the Dubček period. Czechoslovakia has managed to keep its net indebtedness to the West lower than the other CMEA countries and has floated only three Western loans, totaling $410 million, in Western money markets. But, of course, this restraint has not immunized the economy from infection by world trends. In January 1975 Husák claimed that 'our people did not feel in any form the burdens of the crisis manifestations of the capitalist world and of increased raw materials prices'; but, almost in the same breath, he said that, although the CSSR economy is based primarily on cooperation with the USSR and other socialist countries, 'the effect of increased prices of raw materials and imported foodstuffs was for us considerable'. Exactly two years later he repeated this, adding that bad weather, drought, and fuel shortages had further complicated the situation. However, 'the policy of our Party and the state tried to insure that the impact of these negative influences would not affect the living standard of our people. This course of action required a great deal of strength and means. Everybody will understand this.'[54] By March 1978 Husák noted that 'external economic conditions . . . have become exacerbated in a pronounced manner', attributing this to the 'general crisis of capitalism', which, however, leads to 'discriminatory and protectionist policy'. This would necessitate improved quality of Czechoslovak exports, a reduction in delivery times, and better 'after-sales service'.[55] The Czechoslovak leadership has also emphasized that the difficulties created by external economic developments necessitate closer economic cooperation with the USSR and other socialist states and higher productivity by Czechoslovak workers.[56]

Apparently, engineered products are not being sold abroad because of their poor quality. One study showed that of 311 products of the Ministry of General Engineering, only twenty-four attained the 'first degree of quality', 262 the second, and thirty-two the third.[57] In 1977, engineering imports exceeded exports. 'It should be exactly the other way around,' complained a Czechoslovak newspaper, noting that in the first half of the year the foreign trade plan had been overfulfilled in regard to the socialist countries, but unfulfilled with capitalist states.[58] This may be a symptom of increasing difficulties facing the economy, which thus far has been less affected by global economic change than Hungary or Poland, but which still has seen price rises. Moreover, in March 1979 Prime Minister Štrougal, seen by some as an advocate of substantial economic changes, called for 'a speedier and more flexible adjustment to world conditions. . . .

Foreign economic relations have extraordinary importance in our national economy. Some 30 percent of our national income is created by . . . international exchange and by 1990 it will be almost 50 percent. This is why a high and effective export performance must be one of the cornerstones of our strategy for the coming period.'[59] Some economists see 'serious symptoms that the economy is moving on a path similar to that which led to the slump in the early 1960s'.[60] That slump was, of course, a key element in the move toward economic and political reform.

The impact of external economic developments on Poland has been well documented.[61] Poland's own soaring domestic needs have complicated efforts to control imports, to expand exports, or to take maximum advantage of higher prices for Polish coal. Poland continues to suffer from problems of meeting world standards for exported goods. Meanwhile the Poles have been hit with higher prices for imported Soviet oil, the breakdown in Soviet wheat shipments as a result of the USSR's own problems, and the need to compete for the *Soviet* market with Western industrial technology and manufactures.

However, 'the fundamental reason for Poland's economic and political difficulties today lies not in the external economic environment, but in the excessively ambitious and unbalanced development strategy pursued by the Gierek regime since 1971'.[62] Polish sources point to a drop in the rate of increase in the labor force, the rigidity of the financial system, agricultural problems, and administrative problems in industry as well as other economic problems.[63] The chairman of a committee for domestic market affairs admitted serious shortages of goods in the first quarter of 1978, wage increases exceeding the plan, and a resulting demand that outstripped supply significantly.[64] A group of dissident Polish economists add other problems to the list: work is poorly organized; wage differentials are growing, and social benefits do not compensate for growing inequalities; alcohol consumption is increasing; working hours are increasing; yet housing remains poor in quality and in short supply. Party leaders continued to claim, in the summer of 1980, that communication between workers and political leaders had improved,[65] but the economists contended that the population has limited access to information and no opportunity to present independent ideas. Therefore, according to the latter, 'the only way people could react to economic policy was through spontaneous display of their dissatisfaction. Economic policy in Poland has been molded by the fear of social explosion, on the one side, and by the pressures from individual powers, on the other. Thus, economic development itself has been shaped by decisions taken by the pressure group that happened at the time to wield greater influence.'[66] The events of 1980 proved that the economists, not the party leaders, were right.

An immediate problem is that Poland is due to start repaying her considerable foreign debts in 1980–81, which means that real wages must be held down unless the debts can be rescheduled or another way out found.[67] Moreover, if the USSR will indeed face a fuel crisis in the early 1980s, Poland might have to import more energy from hard-currency areas. Declining labor reserves will further exacerbate the situation.

Should the working class, and the population generally, protest the decline in real wages (or their slowed growth), other centers of discontent – the church, dissident intellectuals – will join in a general manifestation of political protest, as they have done in the latter half of 1980. In this sense the external economic situation bears on the internal political one and creates pressures for political change. In fact, these pressures probably produced the reported freezing of defense expenditures.

Is Hungary the future of Poland and Czechoslovakia? If it is true that the Hungarian political strategy has been more successful and that Hungary has adjusted fairly well to the conditions imposed by world economic changes, might Hungary not serve as a model for the others? Probably not, and for several reasons. First, as indicated earlier, Hungary now faces difficult economic choices, which are not so different from those confronting Poland and Czechoslovakia. Second, though the Polish media have reported extensively about the Hungarian economic system,[68] East Europeans admit their reluctance to model themselves after other socialist states and sometimes display an impressive lack of knowledge (and interest?) regarding other countries in the area. There are also specific reasons why Poland and Czechoslovakia are unlikely to pattern themselves after Hungary. Czechoslovakia's leadership is not as cohesive as the Hungarian and not likely to make the type of bold moves exemplified by the 1968 introduction of a New Economic Mechanism in Hungary. Over the years Kádár has also built up a degree of trust among the Soviet leaders not enjoyed by the other leaders, whose tenure has been shorter. Kádár has proved that he is able to accomplish economic reform without political reform (though with policy adjustments), that he can trim his sails if need be and control the reform process, that he has the fundamental confidence of the population. Having been burned once by a Czechoslovak leadership, which promised to curb reform several times but failed to do so, the Soviet elite is not likely to extend too much credit to the present ruling group. Finally, there is the crucial matter of elite choices and popular inclinations. Husák simply makes different assumptions about elite–mass relations than Kádár, and, as will be pointed out, each is probably correct. The Czechoslovak public is not likely to see Husák and his colleagues in the way the Hungarians see Kádár and his – as a group that led them from initial catastrophe and has earned their respect, if not their affection, by consistent performance at least since 1961. The Polish public is probably so cynical by now about elite promises, and so conscious of its power to frustrate elite moves, that only the most talented of leaders could win its confidence, and that over a long period. But, as Zielinski points out, 'The political precondition of successful economic reform is effective consolidation of power in the hands of *one* faction of the . . . party.' Zielinski also argues that reform should never be initiated in the midst of economic difficulties, so it should not be undertaken for the foreseeable future in Poland. Since any reform would entail short-run difficulties, 'there is a need for a special determination and sense of purpose on the part of party and government and at least a measure of popular support'.[69] None of these currently seem to exist in sufficient measure to undertake a change as great as that launched in Hungary in 1968.

IV   East European Responses to World Economic Changes: the Case of Consumer Prices

The political situations and strategies of the three regimes are vividly illustrated by the ways in which they have handled the perceived necessity to raise consumer prices, deriving in large part from the changes in the external economic world.

In Hungary, consumer prices rose at least 5 percent in 1976, with meat rising 20–40 percent. This cut down the planned rise in real wages from 3.5–4 percent to 0.8 percent.[70] For 1976–80 the Hungarians expect a 19 percent rise in prices, with nominal income to rise by 7.4 percent per capita per annum, meaning that consumption and real income in the fifth five-year plan are to rise more slowly than they have in the past fifteen years.[71] How are these realities presented to the public? First, the most significant price increases are usually announced well in advance, so that the public can assimilate the news and prepare for the rises. Second, money income changes are used to compensate for serious distributional effects. Third, there is extensive public presentation of the reasons for the price rises. Bela Csikos-Nagy, head of the National Material and Price Control Office, writes and is interviewed extensively in all large circulation newspapers, so that the discussion of prices is well in the public domain and not only in the specialized journals of the economists and planners. The Prime Minister has assured the people that the government is not exaggerating the seriousness of world inflation and has reminded them, in a rare admission by so high an official in Eastern Europe, that there is inflation in the CMEA countries independent of developments outside.[72] Thus, without pulling many punches, the government informs the public of the realities confronting both of them, and so far the public has accepted the government's policy and, presumably, its rationale for it.[73]

Czechoslovak officials have understandably been more skittish about price increases. They have been able to delay them longer than the Hungarians or Poles and have tried to compensate for them by lowering the prices of commodities such as color television sets, refrigerators, and pocket calculators. There is a highly defensive air about the Czechoslovak announcements, which are linked to discourses about the 'deepening crisis of capitalism'. The public seems fearful of the government's intentions, giving credence to all sorts of rumors about price rises and acting accordingly. There have been reports of runs on certain stores and on gasoline stations. Typically, the following themes are emphasized in Czechoslovak discussions of price changes: prices have been very stable; prices are actually being reduced on some items; those rises that occur are due to 'complicated foreign influences on our economy'; do not be misled by rumors and by those who would spread panic ('we possess a system and latent reserves enable us to successfully counter these outside influences').[74] In August 1976 Husák even reassured the public that it should not draw conclusions from the way in which 'certain states resolve their retail price problem' (an obvious reference to Poland) and that Czechoslovakia would keep prices stable.[75] More than the Hungarians and Poles, the Czechoslovaks emphasize how cheaply they obtain supplies, especially fuel, from the USSR and how the Western countries pursue 'a policy dating back to the period of the cold war . . . Czechoslovak goods are discriminated against through the imposition of the highest customs duties on them'.[76]

Like the other countries, Poland subsidizes food prices substantially. From 1971 to 1976 food subsidies rose at an annual rate of 20–40 percent as a result of increasing consumption and the widening gap between retail prices, which remained fairly stable, and prices paid to farmers, which rose considerably.[77] In 1977, for every 10 zlotys spent by a consumer on food, the state was adding 7 zlotys.[78]

The attempt to raise prices suddenly in 1976 and the reaction to it need no recounting here. What is not often realized is that, in contrast to the Hungarians, the Poles did little to prepare the population for the necessity of price rises, betraying the lack of trust the elite has in the masses. Ignoring the lessons of December 1970, which it claims to have learned so well, the leadership made a discussion of price increases taboo and tried to sneak them past a public obviously on guard against a regime it trusts very little.[79] *Polityka's* editor-in-chief explained lamely that since the need for price changes was discussed at the party congress, 'this fact alone has served to discredit the claim that there was an element of surprise in all this'.[80] But a deputy editor took a more realistic view. Zygmunt Szeliga wrote of the need for 'economic education of society'. 'The practice so far has led to the extremely widespread conviction that in Poland . . . the state sets prices in a completely arbitrary way. . . .' In another article Szeliga called for giving the public more information 'on the state of the nation and the economy, on plans and intentions. In such an atmosphere of, to put it diplomatically, mutual trust and understanding the leadership will not be caught unawares by hasty public reactions, nor will the public be surprised by decisions.'[81] Obviously, Szeliga's advice was not needed.

The level of trust the Gierek leadership had in the population is discernible from the book of instructions to Polish censors. Among other prohibitions, the instructions say that any information about price changes of market commodities should be cleared first with the State Price Commission, and no criticism is to be allowed of the prices of new items on the market. A favorite means of raising prices is to withdraw items from the market and replace them with higher-priced equivalents. Almost incredibly, given the scope of Polish license importation from the West, a ban is placed on information regarding it, though short notices about widely known products manufactured on license (Fiat cars, Berliet buses, Grundig tape recorders) are allowed. Data on coffee consumption cannot be published in order to prevent disclosure of the extent of reexportation, and data on sales of meat to the USSR, or purchase of meat from the German Democratic Republic, are also banned from publication,[82] as well as information on the true state of certain Polish industries and of agriculture, along with information on the terms of foreign trade agreements. All of this contrasts sharply with the Hungarian policy of relative openness. Even the Polish leadership must have realized the absurdity of pretending the obvious did not exist. By 1977, one could find data on Poland's foreign debt, and the government apparently decided that the Polish producer might be induced to work harder and more effectively if shown the seriousness of the problem.[83] Despite calls for 'rational management' and oblique suggestions for allowing workers to regard themselves as genuine 'co-managers', no real changes were made until workers took matters into their own hands in 1980. As Mieczyslaw Rakowski observed in 1977, people become 'pessimistic', nervous, and edgy about the future. 'Supply troubles . . . exert a negative influence on the public perception of stability.'[84]

The strategies, strengths, and weaknesses of the Hungarian, Czechoslovak, and Polish leaderships are revealed in the policies they have adopted to cope with the necessity for increasing consumer prices. This necessity, partly a result of world economic trends, has hampered attempts at achieving political integration on the basis of consumer satisfaction.

V   Popular Response to East European Political Strategies

The relative success of the political integration attempts described here can be ascertained only indirectly.[85] A major target of the regimes is the proletariat. The evidence is that the Czechoslovak and Polish working classes have not responded very positively, with the former expressing its lack of enthusiasm largely through apathy and minimal performance, and the latter giving vent to its feelings in more dramatic and directly political ways. Worker morale seems somewhat better in Hungary and the leadership more responsive to the desires and complaints of the workers, who have expressed them quite openly. In none of the countries has there been any real attempt to give the working class greater political input and more effective institutional channels to the political elite. In the face of the growing maturity and self-consciousness of the proletariat and its own realization of its social, economic, and political potential, the failure to develop institutions to absorb this force may be a costly political weakness.

Some of the indirect indications of the proletariat's view of the political system reported in the Czechoslovak press are low morale, wasted working time, absenteeism, and violations of work discipline. While the economic reform brought about a sharp increase in labor productivity, efficiency has declined considerably since, as output per man-hour has tailed off.[86] This may be symptomatic of the failure of the leadership to win the hearts of the working class even as it has filled their stomachs. The link between low productivity and political attitudes is hinted at by the fact that in the CSSR only one-fourth of the workers and one-half of the apprentices between the ages of 15 and 26 are members of the Socialist Youth Union; in Slovakia, a survey showed that only 30 percent are 'politically active' and about 25 percent 'show no interest at all in public affairs'.[87] Not surprisingly, the Czechoslovaks, in contrast to the Hungarians, implicitly acknowledge that the working class is not yet won over. Presidium (Politburo) member Alois Indra has stated that 'a great emphasis is being placed on the methods of contact with the workers, on how to gain them over to our side and how to convince them'.[88]

The Hungarian public, including the working class, seems to be more supportive of the political course set by the leaders, though not enthusiastically so. Political indifference is a problem also in Hungary.[89] University students are said to be concerned more with material matters than with 'higher' ones. While 'most of our students approve and endorse the socialist system – it never enters their minds to seek an alternative', they are indifferent to everyday political issues and make invidious comparisons between Hungary and advanced capitalist countries insofar as consumer opportunities are concerned.[90] The official youth organization has enrolled fewer than 40 percent of those eligible to join. According to one report on a nationwide poll of Hungarian youth, 70 percent of the respondents were indifferent to politics and 10 percent openly hostile. 'Of the respondents who were members of the Communist Youth League, half said they felt there could be no open discussion of anything meaningful at League meetings.'[91]

While there are labor problems analogous to those in Czechoslovakia – surveys show that 15–20 percent of working time is wasted and many people call in sick when they are in fact healthy[92] – labor productivity seems to be relatively high.[93] The leadership has been sensitive to workers' concerns. When forced to choose between efficiency in production and avoiding unemployment, 'Kádár came down decisively for the workers, as he saw it. . . . He stressed the relative drop in the position of industrial workers, argued that equality had to take precedence over efficiency, and criticized petit-bourgeois excesses.'[94]

In sum, the general reaction to Czechoslovakia's political strategy seems to be a mutedly hostile indifference, while in Hungary it is at least a grudging acceptance. As Portes notes regarding the latter, 'It is difficult to judge how much this may be due to rising living standards, a less bureaucratic atmosphere in economic life, the bitter experience of 1956, Kádár's political acumen, or Hungarian pragmatism and sophistication.'[95]

There are indications of poor labor morale in Poland similar to those in the other two countries. The number of sick days and hours lost per worker has grown steadily, according to official Polish statistics. Research done in 1972 concluded that about 30 percent of working time in some industries was being lost because of 'organizational deficiencies', and workers were responsible for the loss of another 15 percent. Skills were underutilized, and engineers, especially, were spending far too much time on paper work.[96] It was calculated that in 1974 over 9 percent of the national income generated in the socialized economy was lost 'because of unjustified absenteeism and irrationally used work time'.[97]

Labor turnover is another indication of poor morale, according to some industrial sociologists in Poland. In 1974 and 1975 nearly half a million workers in each year left their jobs without notice (in 1969 in Hungary, 42 percent of workers in state and cooperative jobs changed their places of work).[98] As one manager remarked, 'Born on Sunday, they come in for a few days, and disappear after receiving work clothes. The clothes find their way to Rozycki's Bazaar [the local black market]. . . .' Comparing local workers with Polish workers on contract abroad the manager observed that 'the true reason for successes, about which journalists . . . do not write' is that the workers have a 'personal economic interest' in their work and also that the managers have the right to send slackers back to Poland. 'As a result, Polish workers on construction sites abroad are not the same people as those in the country.'[99]

It is not possible to establish with certainty what causes poor labor morale, whether it is lack of economic incentives, the near impossibility of being fired, political alienation, or a sense that workers are not masters in their own house and have little say over what goes on in their place of work. In any case, poor labor morale and high turnover have political significance because the dominant ideology assigns work such significance: a good worker is a good citizen helping to build socialism and a poor worker is politically derelict. But, in none of the countries are the authorities willing to change the traditional function of the trade unions as an instrument of the state in boosting production rather than as a means for workers to transmit their opinions and needs to the authorities. The Czechoslovaks have reaffirmed the traditional view many times. The workers' councils which sprang up in 1968–69 (some 300 were in existence by June 1969, and they were supposed to represent over 800,000 people) were first ignored and then banned altogether by the post-1968 leadership,[100] just as their predecessors in Hungary and Poland were abolished or absorbed into a party-controlled framework. These councils were not necessarily spontaneous, valued alternatives to the trade unions, created by the proletariat. In most cases they were dominated by white-collar workers, and it is not clear whose interests they would ultimately serve. The Yugoslav experience also shows that they do not necessarily reduce workers' alienation, nor, according to some, do they offer genuine industrial democracy. Nevertheless, the councils in Poland, Hungary, and Czechoslovakia were the creation of blue- and white-collar workers themselves, not of the authorities, and offered the potential, at least, for becoming a genuine voice of the proletariat. Even if white-collar workers dominated, they were chosen by blue-collar workers.

The Hungarian NEM gave the workers veto powers over management decisions that violate rules or contract provisions, but 'these many opportunities are not being used to the full. . . . So far, the unions use their veto right only to ban overtime over and above prescribed norms, or when management violates contract provisions on work quotas and wages.'[101] The Hungarians acknowledge an unresolved tension between economic goals requiring discipline and 'unconditional subordination to managerial competence' and the goal of factory democracy, which would require increased involvement of workers in decision making. While asserting that the 'simplistic view of the unions as mere "transmission belts"' has been overcome, the Hungarians clearly state that in the clash between economic and sociopolitical goals, the former must take priority, leaving improvement of labor discipline and production as the unions' main task.[102] Some experiments in expanding worker influence have been undertaken on a very limited scale, but Hungarian sources admit that 'many formal elements have crept into the work' of various committees and conferences involving workers, meaning that they have become as ineffective as the unions in truly representing the workers.[103] Overall, the dominant theme in Hungarian writings on the subject is the justification of 'the Lenin principle of the "transmission" role of the trade unions' which is 'generally valid for the period of the full building of socialism'.[104] The trade unions are admonished to be selective in choosing which opinions of the workers are to be represented to the government, to avoid pitting the interests of the workers against those of the state organs, and not to allow the workers to participate directly in planning, though it is admitted that many trade union meetings lead to 'alienation of the masses from the trade union apparatus'.[105] Economic priorities thus rank ahead of sociopolitical ones, leaving the trade unions and the workers where they have always been. But the unions have failed to promote even *economic* goals well. To date no effective means of improving their work in this regard has been devised.

In Poland the situation is much the same. Until the 1980 strikes, there was a curious non-dialogue between social scientists and commentators, on the one hand, and party leaders, on the other. While the former wrote extensively about the gap between the nominal and real roles of the trade unions and other workers' organizations,[106] the latter doggedly insisted that 'the prime interest of workers' self-government should revolve around work effectiveness and productivity. . . . The principle of one-man management remains unchanged.'[107] Shortly after the riots of 1970–71, the journals, including the most important party organ, were asserting that the workers had no confidence in the unions, which had failed in their tasks and must be reformed. Such assertions appeared throughout 1980, but nothing changed until the mass strikes. In this light, and in view of the growth of Polish dissidence generally, it is not surprising that a 'Workers' Committee' was formed in early 1978 in Katowice, appealing to Polish workers to form 'free national trade unions'. Despite repressions, a similar group was formed in the Baltic,[108] and efforts to organize free trade unions quickly multiplied throughout the country. Such unions were formed in 1980, and a struggle ensued between 'official' and 'independent' unions, the outcome of which is not clear at this writing. In any case, many Poles are extremely alienated from anything that smacks of official sponsorship. As dissident Jacek Kuroń observed, when attractive hopscotch squares were painted in the courtyards of new housing developments children stopped playing the game there, preferring their own designs. 'The same holds for official forms of self-management.'[109]

What is true of the workers is true of the citizenry as a whole. Opinion research in Czechoslovakia[110] bears out Jan Triska's assessment:

> The citizens seem to feel that they are subject to a kind of historical fate against which any application of will is useless and ineffective. Widespread lethargy, social and political apathy, a mental state devoid of any alternative perspective, pervade the nation. The leadership knows this well. . . . But it chooses to interpret the national mood of passivity as a political and ideological victory, maintaining that the population stands steadfastly behind the new socialist order.[111]

The Hungarian people, by contrast, seem more positively responsive to their leadership, but it is hard to assess to what extent their support is conditional on continued relative prosperity and whether a serious economic downturn might not lead, if not to rebellion, to retreat into the kind of sullen passivity characteristic of the Czechs (though not so much the Slovaks). The Polish public appears less supportive of its leaders than the Hungarians are of theirs and provides cynical interpretations of government moves. The distrust in the people displayed by the government is reciprocated in full measure. Widespread grumbling about shortages in consumer goods and about the poor quality of the goods elicits countercomplaints about the people's refusal to acknowledge that *they* are producing the shoddy goods.[112] The highly publicized shortages of meat have become as much a symbolic issue as a substantive one, though food shortages are a genuine issue in 'medium-developed' countries such as those discussed here. The elite–mass gap is so wide that rumors gain credence rapidly, while information released by the government is suspect. Former Politburo member Jan Szydlak admitted that 'rumor has become an important tool of the anti-social diversion' and called upon all party members to fight this phenomenon so that the society would be 'immunized' against rumors.[113] That a leader should specifically seek to mobilize the party to help official information gain more public credence than rumor is a comment on the success of the Communist Party's attempts to draw the population closer to itself and its ideals. Moreover, data gathered by Polish social scientists point to the conclusion that the Polish population has accepted many fundamentals of socialism, but focuses its attention on the satisfaction of individual, private, and economic needs, and is highly apathetic toward the broader social and political goals posited by the party.[114]

VI   Conclusion

Changes in the world economy have had both beneficial and harmful effects on the domestic political situation in Eastern Europe, but the latter are likely to prevail in the near future. On the one hand, the greater openness of both superpowers to trade with each other and with each other's allies allowed Hungary and Poland to expand their economic ties with the West. These ties make a direct contribution to consumer satisfaction and hence to political stability, and perhaps longer-term legitimacy. However, this may have led to increased citizens' *expectations* of their governments and not necessarily to increased *support* for them. Czechoslovakia chose to abstain pretty much from the opening to the West, perhaps fearful that with the task of political consolidation still only partially accomplished, the risks of involvement with the Western economies (regarding both domestic and Soviet reactions) were too high. However, there are increasing and acknowledged economic pressures on Czechoslovakia to improve her products, both for the Western markets, from which unavoidable imports have become considerably more expensive, and for the CMEA market, which has become more demanding as consumer and producer expectations rise and as available Western products expand the range of choice. With low worker morale and severe political constraints on economic reform, the CSSR probably cannot turn the necessity for increased ties with the West to the leadership's advantage.

Might the increased importance of exports lead to some accretion of political power in the hands of those running export industries? In order to produce more for export they might demand higher wages and other benefits for their workers and also constitute a lobby for the importation of materials needed for their production. The 'export sector' might then become a political force to be reckoned with. As yet there is no clear evidence of this, though only detailed case studies of the relationships between managers and other party and government officials could clarify this question. (Such studies have not come to my attention.) Some observers contend that these relationships have not changed because the primacy of the party is accepted, and the managers will not confront the political leadership over such issues.

Clearly in all three countries the present and future effect of global economic trends is to exacerbate political difficulties. But external economic factors are only part of the forces determining the political situation (as Terry and Korbonski point out), and other factors mediate the impact of the external economic influences. To assess the overall near-term prospects for political stability in the area, one would have to take into account the economic situation, the political dispositions of the working class, the nature of dissent and the intelligentsia's role in it, and, finally, the nature of the Communist Party leadership.

Without trying to decide which country faces more serious economic difficulties, a task best left to the economists, we would hazard a suggestion that, of the three, Hungary is *politically* best able to cope with economic difficulties, and Poland least able to do so. The Hungarian party has built up enough confidence among the population in its intentions and abilities that short-term reverses will be better accepted. By involving the masses in its dilemmas to a considerable extent, the party is able to demonstrate the reasonableness of its policies. Should they ultimately be perceived as unreasonable, the traumatic memory of 1956, punctuated by the later invasion of neighboring Czechoslovakia, may serve as an effective barrier against hasty actions. Within Czechoslovakia, the unhappy Czechs are blocked from active attempts to destabilize the political situation by the continued presence of Soviet troops and the absence of any clear alternative to the present course, especially because the Slovaks, who have achieved federalization and a greater relative improvement in their economic situation, are less likely to seek a change in their status quo.

The Poles face the most serious short-term difficulty. They bear the largest external debt burden, appear to have little diffuse political support, and seem to lack a decisive, courageous political leadership. Moreover, they are the only ones faced with a competing authority structure, the Catholic church, whose social role is increasing. The unprecedented meeting of Gierek and Cardinal Wyszynski, followed by a meeting in October 1980 between Kania and Wyszynski, is perhaps the party's acknowledgment of the church's expanded role. In addition the election and visit to Poland of a Polish pope also demonstrate that the church is a force to be reckoned with. Thus far, however, the church has acted to restrain 'political adventurism'. Because it shares with the government a desire to avoid

Soviet intervention, the church may be an important force for stability. At the same time, the dissident movement has revived to a considerable extent in recent years, making Polish dissidence the largest such phenomenon in Eastern Europe. Moreover, whereas dissent in Hungary has not had much resonance in society and has been curbed rather effectively by a combination of exile, imprisonment, and simple disregard, Polish dissidence has been addressed to less abstract and intellectual issues and has had wider appeal.

The Czechoslovak signers of 'Charter 77' were largely from the intelligentsia and overwhelmingly identified with the reformers of the 1968 period. Official reaction to Charter 77 was somewhat vague and inconsistent, but the movement seems to have been successfully confined. Dissent in Poland is far more complex and wide-ranging. There are about twenty-five dissident periodicals, which claim a circulation of thousands, with some addressed to workers and others to the politically minded and to literati. A 'flying university', modeled after the underground institution of the tsarist and later occupations, has involved some prominent intellectuals.

Student solidarity committees have been formed in at least six towns. The opposition – and it really is that, rather than merely a small group of dissenters who opt out of the system rather than try to change it – includes people who are active in unofficial organizations, those who are associated with recognized nonparty organizations (largely Catholic), and perhaps even some in the party. Unofficial organizations range from KOR (Workers' Defense Committee), which has a liberal orientation, to the more nationalistic Movement for the Defense of Human Rights. The opposition aims at concrete change, is organized formally, and has an extensive publication apparatus. Though instances of police brutality and even murder are not unknown, the opposition is pretty much tolerated and has achieved a kind of *de facto* recognition by the regime.

Oppositionists in Poland have addressed many of the issues raised here. Even the more cautious elements have rejected trading consumer satisfaction for political quiescence and have called for independent workers' councils and 'co-management'.[115] Adam Michnik, a prominent oppositionist for a decade, observed:

> The emphasis on consumption has given rise to new desires. People . . . expect constant improvement in their standards. The revolt of June 1976 was not one of people who were starving, but of people who had had enough of being treated like sheep. It arose as a reaction not only to the increase in prices, but also to the manner of its justification by the propaganda machine. The people no longer trust the verbal assurances of those in power. . . . During the June events the fictitious nature of the official trade unions was once again demonstrated.[116]

In 1980 those unions were rejected by great numbers of Polish workers who founded new ones not controlled by the party or state.

It is striking that the opposition is operating relatively openly in Poland at the very time that dissidents are hounded in the USSR. The trials of

Soviet dissidents, along with accusations against foreign newsmen and businessmen, came about as the flow of Polish *samizdat* increased and as both church figures and cultural–political oppositionists made bolder criticisms of the situation. Apparently, the Soviet authorities are not pressing their Polish comrades to take firmer repressive steps. Perhaps both the Soviet and Polish authorities believe that repression would only boomerang (which it does not do in the USSR), as an alienated population is feeling its power and may wish to test it out. The Hungarian and Czechoslovak leaders have the consolation of knowing that their people might be more reluctant to engage in 'adventures', in light of their recent experiences, and consumer satisfaction is in any case higher than in Poland. (Polish tourists in Czechoslovakia are very impressed by the availability of meat there.) The working classes seem more content in Poland's neighbors, and they probably hold the key to the dimensions of any possible future political crisis.

Since the working class is the key consumer group from a political point of view, and likely to feel any economic pinch most (whether externally or internally caused), its strengths and weaknesses as a force for political change should be examined. It has the advantage of numbers, of course, as well as of geographic scope. It has physical power, and it has economic power in the sense that it can withhold services and thereby disrupt the economy. Since the proletariat enjoys high standing in the official mythology, antigovernment actions by it are highly embarrassing and less easily explained than the deviance of 'a few misguided intellectuals'. On the other hand, except in Poland, the working class has no identifiable leaders (except after a crisis has already broken out) and does not have a specific program for change (though its pursuit of concrete goals, such as rescinding prices, can be an advantage). The proletariat may lack the political sophistication to deal with party leaders on an ongoing basis, and it can be bought off in the short run, though that may be decreasingly the case. Moreover, the working class in Eastern Europe (and perhaps in many capitalist countries as well) seems to be quite 'conservative' in the sense that it is negatively disposed toward change. Proposed political and economic innovations are often greeted hesitantly or with skepticism. For example, it resists attempts to move away from wage egalitarianism. The Czechoslovak working class greeted the economic reforms proposed in 1968–69 with great suspicion, and the Hungarian workers also displayed little enthusiasm about some aspects of NEM. When given a chance to elect representatives freely, the workers show considerable deference to white-collar employees and those with better education. So one should not see the proletariat as the spearhead of change if left to itself, though the Polish case may be the harbinger of things to come elsewhere.

However, when moved by economic discontent, the working class can supply the energy and the sheer manpower for a drive toward change. For significant political change to occur in a Marxist–Leninist system, the necessary but not sufficient ingredients have been a mass social base, such as the proletariat, an intelligentsia to give it direction, and a catalytic event to unite the different elements. The key ingredient is a split in the ranks of the party, with one group supporting those who demand change. Because the Communist Party holds a monopoly of political power, and because change without at least some party support would mean the intervention of the USSR, only with at least partial party support is there a chance for lasting change, if it can be tolerated by the USSR, which still holds a veto over political change in Eastern Europe.

In sum, from the point of view of the domestic political situation in the three countries, Poland is the most likely to be hard pressed by the consequences of world economic trends. While the direct economic impact on Hungary may be greater, the Hungarian leadership seems to have a greater political capacity for controlling its consequences. There is a serious debate going on in Hungary between those who think the economic situation dictates a further implementation of the NEM and those who say it demands a drawing back from the Western economies and a return to greater involvement with CMEA. But most of those involved in the discussion seem acutely aware of the domestic political constraints on economic policy decisions.[117] Czechoslovakia is in a different position from either Hungary or Poland: it is not yet as deeply affected by external economic trends, but lacks Hungary's political capacity. On the other hand, the Czechoslovak leadership is not faced with a situation as volatile as the Polish, and the presence of Soviet troops serves as a reminder of the dangers of reform. Thus world economic trends serve both to bring into sharper relief the realities of the East European political situation and to affect those realities directly.

Notes: Chapter 7

1 For example, Roger Kanet asserts that 'the assumption that expanded East–West contacts are likely to result in a greater degree of economic and political autonomy for Eastern Europe does not appear to be warranted' ('East–West Trade and the Limits of Western Influence', in Charles Gati (ed.), *The International Politics of Eastern Europe* (New York: Praeger, 1976), p. 212). By contrast, Sverre Lodgaard contends that economic relations with the West, because they vary considerable from country to country, contribute to the ongoing differentiation among the socialist countries. He also claims that 'the introduction of Western technology encourages individualism, fragmentation, and verticalization. . . . It contributes to the growth of a new managerial elite, which becomes increasingly opposed to the old style bureaucracy. . . .' ('On the Relationship between East–West Economic Cooperation and Political Change in Eastern Europe', *Journal of Peace Research*, Vol. 11, No. 4 (1974), p. 335.)
2 In 1974, for example, *Izvestiia* claimed that 'bourgeois propaganda is attempting to prove that even the socialist countries are affected by the energy crisis, that their economic integration allegedly will not withstand the mega-calorie and megawatt test. The recent session of the CMEA executive committee is a convincing and well-reasoned reply to these fantasies'. B. Rodionov, 'Scope and Effectiveness', *Izvestiia*, 5 March 1974, p. 2, translated in *Current Digest of the Soviet Press (CDSP)*, Vol. 26, No. 9 (27 March 1974), pp. 12–13.
3 Andrzej Wasilkowski, 'In the Countries of the Socialist Community: Facing Changes in World Markets', *Trybuna Ludu*, 23 June 1975, translated in *Polish News Bulletin*, 27 June 1975, pp. V–VIII.
4 Speeches on the subject by party secretaries Gierek of Poland and Kádár of Hungary were reprinted in *Izvestiia*, and Soviet commentators themselves dealt with the topic.
5 Y. Kormanov, 'Scientific-Technological Progress and Integration of the CMEA Member Countries in Machine Building', *Planovoe khoziastvo*, 1977, No. 5, p. 73, quoted in Alfred Zauberman, 'The East European Economies', *Problems of Communism*, Vol. 27, No. 2 (March–April 1978), p. 60.

6 William N. Turpin, *Soviet Foreign Trade* (Lexington, Mass.: Lexington Books, 1977), p. 10.
7 Paul Marer, 'Has Eastern Europe Become a Liability to the Soviet Union? The Economic Aspect', in Gati (ed.), op. cit., p. 61.
8 Sarah Meiklejohn Terry and Andrzej Korbonski, 'The Impact of External Economic Disturbances on the Internal Politics of Eastern Europe: The Polish and Hungarian Cases', in Egon Neuberger and Laura D'Andrea Tyson (eds), *The Impact of International Economic Disturbances on the Soviet Union and Eastern Europe: Transmission and Response* (New York: Pergamon Press, 1980), p. 377.
9 Ibid., p. 377.
10 Ibid., p. 388.
11 Sarah Meiklejohn Terry, 'The Implications of Interdependence for Soviet–East European Relations: A Preliminary Analysis of the Polish Case' (Cambridge, Mass.: Russian Research Center, Harvard University, June 1977), p. 33.
12 For an elaboration of this point, see Zvi Gitelman, 'Power and Authority in Eastern Europe', in Chalmers Johnson (ed.), *Change in Communist Systems* (Stanford: Stanford University Press, 1970).
13 For a discussion of the German Democratic Republic, see Alex Pravda's chapter in this volume.
14 David Granick, *Enterprise Guidance in Eastern Europe* (Princeton: Princeton University Press, 1975), p. 241.
15 Janusz Zielinski, 'On System Remodelling in Poland: A Pragmatic Approach', *Soviet Studies*, Vol. 30, No. 1 (January 1978), pp. 27–8.
16 Granick, op. cit., p. 241.
17 Kenneth Jowitt, 'Inclusion and Mobilization in European Leninist Regimes', in Jan Triska and Paul Cocks (eds), *Political Development in Eastern Europe* (New York: Praeger, 1977), p. 101.
18 Walter Connor, 'Social Change and Stability in Eastern Europe', *Problems of Communism*, Vol. 26, No. 6 (November–December 1976), p. 28.
19 Stanislaw Widerszpil, 'Tendencje zmian w składzie klasy robotniczej w uprzemyslow-ionych społeczeństwach kapitalistycznych i w Polsce Ludowej' [Tendencies of changes in the composition of the working class in industrialized capitalist societies and in the Polish People's Republic], *Studia Socjologiczne*, 1964, No. 1, p. 47.
20 Connor, op. cit., p. 27.
21 Jerzy Wiatr, 'Kierunki przemian struktury społecznej i ich polityczne konsekwencje' [Directions of changes in the social structure and their political consequences], in Jerzy Kowalski (ed.), *Społeczeństwo a państwo socjalistyczne* [Society and the Socialist State] (Warsaw: Książka i Wiedza, 1972), p. 41.
22 Bozena Brunerova, 'Zrcadlo hospodářskych vysledků' [A reflection of economic results], *Tribuna*, No. 48 (November 1977), p. 4. For a Western discussion, see Robert W. Dean, 'Moscow and Eastern Europe: A New Look', *Problems of Communism*, Vol. 26, No. 4 (July–August 1977).
23 Ronald Inglehart, 'Policy Problems of Advanced Industrial Society: Introduction', *Comparative Political Studies*, Vol. 10, No. 3 (October 1977), p. 298.
24 Bogdan Mieczkowski, 'The Relationship between Changes in Consumption and Politics in Poland', *Soviet Studies*, Vol. 30, No. 2 (April 1978), pp. 262–3.
25 Zbigniew Fallenbuchl, 'The Polish Economy in the 1970's', in *East European Economies Post-Helsinki* (a compendium of papers submitted to the Joint Economic Committee, 95th Congress, 1st Session) (Washington, D.C.: US Government Printing Office, 1977), pp. 835 and 846.
26 Mieczkowski, op. cit., p. 265.
27 For details, see Zvi Gitelman, 'The Politics of Socialist Restoration in Hungary and Czechoslovakia', *Comparative Politics*, Vol. 13, No. 2 (January 1981).
28 Interview with Giuseppe Boffa, reprinted in Janos Kádár, *For a Socialist Hungary* (Budapest: Corvina, 1974), p. 144.
29 The statements quoted here are from Kádár's speech at the Ikarus factory (1968) and his press conference in Prague (1969), as published in Kádár, op. cit., pp. 17–18 and 161–2.
30 See *Pravada* (Bratislava), 2 June 1969, and *Rudé právo*, 17 April 1975, for Husák's statements.
31 *Nova mysl*, 1976, No. 9.

32 V. Vaculik in *Rudé právo*, 31 January 1970.
33 Report to the Fifteenth Congress of the Communist Party of Czechoslovakia (KSČ), *Rudé právo*, 12 April 1976.
34 Vladimir Trivala (a departmental head of the Slovak Party Central Committee), *Pravda* (Bratislava), 19 August 1975.
35 Editorial in *Rudé právo*, 11 December 1975.
36 Remarks by Kádár on his sixtieth birthday, in Kádár, op. cit., p. 399.
37 Ibid., pp. 399–400.
38 Dr Otto Pirityi, in *Társadalmi Szemle*, 1973, No.2, translated in US Joint Publications Research Service, *Translations on Eastern Europe: Political, Sociological, and Military Affairs* (hereafter *JPRS*), No. 672 (21 February 1973), p. 25.
39 See Radio Free Europe (RFE), *Czechoslovak Situation Report*, 1971, No. 19. Students are channeled away from the humanities and social sciences to technical and agricultural subjects. Even when admitting students to high schools, the political and social commitment of parents, as well as of students, must be taken into account. There is a 'point system' for university admissions where applicants of peasant or worker origin automatically receive a significant number of points. In 1970, 554 of those admitted at Comenius University were of worker or peasant origin. A pedagogical publication, *Učitelské noviny*, stated in April 1971: 'We make no secret of the fact that we want . . . to select students for these schools in a way that guarantees that . . . they will stand up loyally for socialism and will place their knowledge fully at the service of socialist society. When the preconditions for this do not exist, there is no reason to admit an applicant.' The factors to be taken into account were class background, civic–moral–political record, and the political commitment of parents. See RFE, *Czechoslovak Press Survey*, No. 2376 (7 May 1971), and RFE, *Czechoslovak Situation Report*, 1971, No. 12 and No. 17.
40 See also Stanisław Gebethner's chapter in this volume on the need for such reform.
41 For a detailed argument along these lines, see Zvi Gitelman, 'Development, Institutionalization, and Elite–Mass Relations in Poland', in Jan Triska and Paul Cocks (eds), op. cit.
42 Vincent C. Chrypinski, 'Political Change under Gierek', in Adam Bromke and John Strong (eds), *Gierek's Poland* (New York: Praeger, 1973), p. 51.
43 Alex Pravda, 'Gierek's Poland: Five Years On', *The World Today*, Vol. 32, No. 7 (July 1976), p. 275.
44 Terry, op. cit., pp. 8–9.
45 See, for example, Jerzy Lukaszewicz in *Nowe Drogi*, 1976, No. 4.
46 Jozef Korčak, speech to the Central Committee of the KSČ, broadcast on Radio Prague, 20 March 1978, as translated in US Foreign Broadcast Information Service (Department of Commerce), *Daily Report: Eastern Europe* (hereafter *FBIS*), 21 March 1978.
47 Alojzy Melich, 'System plac i zachęt materialnych' [The wage system and material needs], *Nowe Drogi*, 1977, No. 1, and his *Problemy plac w Polsce* [Wage problems in Poland] (Warsaw: Instytut wydawniczy CRZZ, 1978). See also the well documented discussion by Jan Danecki, 'Egalitaryzm społeczny a modele konsumpcji (artykul diskusijny)' [Social equality and models of consumption – discussion article], *Zycie Gospodarcze*, 10 December 1972. For some Hungarian data, see Zsuzsa Horváth, 'Vélemények a társadalmi különmbségkröl' [Opinions on social differentiations], *Valóság*, 1978, No. 12.
48 Pravada, 'Gierek's Poland', p. 278.
49 Terry, op. cit., p. 48.
50 Michael Kaser, 'Eastern Europe's Economies in 1976–80', *The World Today*, Vol. 32, No. 9 (September 1976), p. 338.
51 *Népszabadság*, 20 December 1973, summarized in *ABSEES*, Vol. 5, No. 2 (April 1974), p. 189.
52 Terry and Korbonski, op. cit., p. 388.
53 The immediate impact of world economic change on the political position of the current Hungarian leadership should, however, be distinguished from the less tangible impact on the credibility of the socialist system. For example, one party secretary has complained that world economic changes have made the task of propagandists harder, for people see that socialist countries are affected by crises in capitalism and begin to feel that socialism is not a genuine alternative to capitalism (Imre Gyori, Radio Budapest, 13 May 1977,

reported in *FBIS*, 17 May 1977). This is no doubt a minor problem and does not portend a crisis of faith in the population.

54 The statements quoted are from Gustav Husák's New Year Addresses given over Radio Prague on 1 January 1975 and 1 January 1977, as reported in *FBIS*, 2 January 1975 and 3 January 1977.

55 Husák's report to the KSČ Presidium, 17 March 1978, Radio Prague, reported in *FBIS*, 20 March 1978. A Czechoslovak minister said in October 1978 that 'many contracts are lost because the producer cannot provide reliable servicing and short delivery deadlines, essential demands of the contemporary world market' (*Rudé právo*, 25 October 1978).

56 See, for example, Prime Minister Štrougal's speech to the Federal Assembly, *Rudé právo*, 15 December 1976.

57 'Priklad a inspiracia' [Example and inspiration], *Pravda* (Bratislava), 28 November 1977.

58 *Lidova demokracie*, 1 September 1978, reported in *FBIS*, 7 September 1978.

59 See Štrougal's address to the Federal Assembly, *Rudé právo*, 29 March 1979.

60 B. Korda, 'A Decade of Economic Growth in Czechoslovakia, 1962–73', *Soviet Studies*, Vol. 28, No. 4 (October 1976), p. 520. A similar judgment is made by Vaclav Holesovsky, 'Czechoslovak Economy in the Seventies', in *East European Economies Post-Helsinki*, op. cit.

61 See Terry, op. cit., pp. 11–24; Terry and Korbonski, op. cit., pp. 379–88; and Zbigniew Fallenbuchl, 'The Impact of External Economic Disturbances on Poland since 1971', also in Neuberger and Tyson (eds), op. cit., pp. 280–304.

62 Terry and Korbonski, op. cit., pp. 381–2.

63 See, for example, Wladyslaw Baka, 'Doskonalenie systemu planowania i zarządzanie w Polsce' [Perfection of the system of planning and administration in Poland], *Nowe Drogi*, 1977, No. 6 (337).

64 Tadeusz Pyka, Radio Warsaw, 10 April 1978, reported in *FBIS*, 12 April 1978.

65 Former Politburo member Babiuch claimed as late as 1977 that the 'great achievement' of the last few years is the practice and improvement of consultation with society. 'Partia klasy robotniczej – partia całego narodu' [The party of the workers is the party of the whole people], *Nowe Drogi*, 1977, No. 6 (337). See also Waldemar Stelmach, 'Kilka refleksji o robotnikach wielkoprzemysłowych' [Some reflections on workers in large industrial firms], *Nowe Drogi*, 1977, No. 5 (336). The latter lauds the system of contact with the 164 large industrial firms.

66 RFE, *Background Report (Poland)*, 1978, No. 177.

67 An 'excellent discussion of the options for creditors and debtors in the East–West relationship is Richard Portes' article, 'East Europe's Debt to the West: Interdependence is a Two-Way Street', *Foreign Affairs*, Vol. 55, No. 4 (April 1977).

68 See, for example, Jacek Maziarski, 'Najbardziej aktualne' [What is most pressing], *Polityka*, 26 February 1977. Maziarski's article on the impact of world economic trends on the Hungarian NEM (*Polityka*, 1 July 1978, p. 12) specifically states that Poles are interested in the Hungarian experience because they might learn from it. The same idea is to be found in Aleksander Paszynski, 'Klocki do ukladanki' [Building blocks to arrange], *Polityka*, 28 January 1978. It is interesting that, in turn, Hungarians have commented favorably on Poland's use of Polish emigrants to promote trade with the West, implying that Hungary might do the same among the millions of Magyars outside Hungary. See 'The Role of the Polish Emigrants in the Polish-American Trade', *Világgazdaság*, 1976, No. 8 (118), translated in *Abstracts of Hungarian Economic Literature*, Vol. 6, No. 3 (1976), pp. 243–4. According to this article, 28 percent of Polish exports to the United States in 1975 were to Polish-American firms. Polish-Americans have been encouraged to invest in private enterprises in Poland, especially in the tourist sector.

69 Janusz Zielinski, *Economic Reforms in Polish Industry* (London: Oxford University Press, 1973), pp. 20–1. See also his article, 'On System Remodelling', op. cit.

70 See 'Changes in Consumer Prices Considering the Main Strata of the Population in 1976 and in the First Quarter of 1977', *Abstracts of Hungarian Economic Literature*, Vol. 7, No. 5 (1977), pp. 188–90, condensed and translated from *Statisztikai Időszaki Közlemények*, Vol. 408 (1977).

71 O. Gadó, 'The Expected Standard of Living in the 1976–80 Plan Period', *Gazdaság*, 1976, No. 1, summarized and translated in *Abstracts of Hungarian Economic Literature*, Vol. 6, No. 2 (1976), pp. 86–7.

72 See Istvan Folds, 'Public Thinking, National Economy,' *Népszabadság*, 18 June 1976, translated in *JPRS*, No. 1270 (22 July 1976): Dr Otto Pirityi, 'Meditation on a General Evaluation of Our Standard of Living', Radio Kossuth, 29 April 1973, in RFE, *Hungarian Press Survey*, No. 2283 (18 May 1973); RFE, *Hungarian Situation Report*, 1975, No. 41; and Prime Minister Gyorgy Lazar in *Népszabadság*, 26 September 1975, as summarized in *ABSEES*, Vol. 7, No. 1 (January 1976), p. 186.
73 One Hungarian commentator suggests that the 1968 NEM made later price rises easier to accept because it placed economic questions in the forefront of public consciousness, accustomed the public to flexible prices, established public trust in the economic and political systems, and taught state administrators to work with a system of flexible prices and incentives. See Mihaly Simai, 'Gazdasági reformunk es egy Amerikai megítélés' [Economic reforms and an American opinion], *Valóság*, 1978, No. 7.
74 Jan Zervan, 'Greater Efficiency in the Economy – The Foundation of Stable Prices', *Pravda* (Bratislava), 23 September 1974, reported in *FBIS*, 1 October 1974.
75 Speech at Nitra harvest festival, 28 August 1976, reported in *FBIS*, 1 September 1976.
76 *Hospodářské noviny*, 7 February 1977, reported in *FBIS*, 8 February 1977.
77 J. Redlich, in *Trybuna Ludu*, 23 June 1976, as summarized in *ABSEES*, Vol. 7, No. 4 (October 1976), p. 188.
78 Tadeusz Wraszczyk, 'Kierunki dalszego rozwoju gospodarki' [Directions of further economic development], *Nowe Drogi*, 1977, No. 1 (332).
79 An excellent analysis of this point is provided by Thomas Heneghan, 'The Summer Storm in Poland', in RFE, *Background Report (Poland)*, 1976, No. 176.
80 Mieczyslaw Rakowski, 'A Time to Think Things Over and a Time to Act', *Polityka*, 3 July 1976, translated in *JPRS*, No. 1267, p. 56.
81 The articles by Szeliga cited here were published in *Polityka*, 10 July 1976 and 17 July 1976, and translated in *JPRS*, No. 1276 (4 August 1976) and No. 1274 (30 July 1976), respectively.
82 The instructions to the censors discussed here are cited in *Czarna Książka Cenzury PRL* [The Black Book of Censorship in the Polish People's Republic] (London: Aneks, 1977), pp. 37, 38, 47.
83 See Eugeniusz Guz, 'Normalizacja z przeszkodami' [Normalization with interferences], *Nowe Drogi*, 1977, No. 4 (335), for data on indebtedness to West Germany. See, more generally, Roman Stefanowski, 'Poland's Growing Indebtedness: A Progress Report', in RFE, *Background Report (Poland)*, 1977, No. 245.
84 Quoted in RFE, *Background Report (Poland)*, 1977, No. 192, p. 2.
85 On this issue, see also Alex Pravda, Chapter 8 of this volume.
86 On this issue, see the Radio Free Europe research reports by Robert W. Dean, 'Dilemmas of Consolidation: The Czechoslovak Trade Unions before Their Eighth Congress', *Background Report (Czechoslovakia)*, 1972, No. 16, and H. G. Trend, 'Industrial Wages and Labor Productivity in Eastern Europe', *Background Report (Eastern Europe)*, 1978, No. 194. See also Korda, 'A Decade of Economic Growth', pp. 519–20; and Alex Pravda, this volume.
87 František Řiha, *Rúde právo*, 17 October 1974. The Slovak data are from Bratislava and Košice, as reported in V. Fabry (ed.), *Kulturny a spolecensky profil obyvatelov Bratislavy a Košič: Zbornik studii* [Cultural and social profile of residents of Bratislava and Košice: A collection of studies] (Bratislava, 1974), pp. 2–13, 38–53.
88 Alois Indra, *Tvorba*, 24 March 1976.
89 A survey of workers involved in party education showed that more than half of those under 25 took only an occasional interest. See the study by Mihaly Tamasi, cited by George Schöpflin, 'Hungary: An Uneasy Stability', in Archie Brown and Jack Gray (eds), *Political Culture and Political Change in Communist States* (New York: Holmes and Meier, 1977), p. 147.
90 Mihaly Orosz, 'Political Profile of University Students Analyzed', *Felsooktutasi Szemle*, Vol. 25, No. 2 (February 1976), as translated in *JPRS*, No. 1226 (7 April 1976).
91 David Andelman, 'Quiz Show: How Hungary Lures Its Youth to Participation', *New York Times*, 1 August 1978.
92 *Népszabadság*, 14 March 1976, summarized in *ABSEES*, Vol. 7, No. 3 (July 1976), p. 184; and *Népszabadság*, 25–26 June 1976, summarized in *ABSEES*, Vol. 7, No. 4 (October 1976), p. 171.
93 See Table 16 in Richard Portes, 'Hungary: Economic Performance, Policy and

Prospects', in *East European Economies Post-Helsinki*, op. cit., p. 803.

94 Ibid., p. 787.

95 Ibid., p. 795.

96 'Zadanie partii, państwa, i związków zawodowych w kształtowania warunkow pełnego zaangazowania twórczych sił narodu dla rozwoju kraju' [The tasks of the party, state, and trade unions in shaping conditions for a full participation of creative forces of the people for the development of the country], *Nowe Drogi*, 1973, No. 7 (290).

97 Piotr Karpiuk in *Ideologia i Polityka*, 1975, No. 10, translated in *JPRS*, No. 1186 (19 January 1976), p. 55.

98 The Polish data are cited in D. Zagródzka, 'Porzucają, dlaczego?' [Why are they abandoning it?], *Życie Gospodarcze*, 7 March 1976, summarized in *ABSEES*, Vol. 7, No. 3 (July 1976), p. 204. The Hungarian figure is from RFE, *Hungarian Situation Report*, 1970, No. 42.

99 Romuald Napiorkowski, 'From a Manager's Position', *Życie Literackie*, 8 April 1973, translated in *JPRS*, No. 730 (20 June 1973), p. 34.

100 See Karel Kovanda, 'Czechoslovak Workers' Councils', *Telos*, No. 28 (Summer 1976).

101 Marton Buza, 'Socialism and Democracy at Factory Level', *World Marxist Review*, Vol. 16, No. 12 (December 1973), p. 71. Buza is the director of the Trade Union Research Institute.

102 Ibid., pp. 69–71.

103 'The Right to Work – The Right to Manage', *World Marxist Review*, Vol. 20, No. 10 (October 1977), pp. 115–16. See also Sandor Gaspar's press conference on enterprise democracy, reported in RFE, *Hungarian Situation Report*, 1976, No. 36, and *Hungarian Situation Report*, 1977, No. 17.

104 Gyorgy Terek, in *Szakszervezeti Szemle*, 1972, No. 4, translated in *JPRS*, No. 649 (3 January 1973), p. 15.

105 Otto Pirityi, in *Társadalmi Szemle*, 1973, No. 2, translated in *JPRS*, No. 672 (21 February 1973), pp. 24–5. See also the discussion in RFE, *Hungarian Situation Report*, 1978, No. 14, of an article by Sandor Zsarnoczai on democratic centralism and economic life in the May 1978 issue of *Közgazdasági Szemle*.

106 For an example, see Gebethner's chapter in this volume.

107 Edward Gierek, quoted in RFE, *Polish Situation Report*, 1978, No. 16.

108 For details, see *Studium*, Vol. 2, No. 3 (July 1978), pp. 5–6; and RFE, *Polish Situation Report*, 1978, No. 6, pp. 8–9.

109 RFE, 'Review of Uncensored Polish Publications, October 1977–January 1978', *Background Report (Poland)*, 1978, No. 51. Kuroń's remarks were made in *Glos*, No. 1 (October 1977).

110 For details, see Zvi Gitelman, 'Public Opinion in Czechoslovakia', in Walter Connor and Zvi Gitelman (eds), *Public Opinion in European Socialist Systems* (New York: Praeger, 1977).

111 Jan F. Triska, 'Messages from Czechoslovakia', *Problems of Communism*, Vol. 24, No. 6 (November–December 1975), p. 38.

112 See Zygmunt Oleniak, 'Listy – ważne zródlo wiedzy i instrument społecznej kontroli' [Letters – an important source of information and an instrument of social control], *Nowe Drogi*, 1977, No. 6 (337); M. Kowalewski, '"Oni" to także "my"' ['They' are also 'We'], *Trybuna Ludu*, 26 November 1974, summarized in *ABSEES*, Vol. 6, No. 2 (April 1975), p. 211.

113 Jan Szydlak, in *Nowe Drogi*, 1973, No. 2 (285).

114 Many of the opinion surveys are reported in Adaline Huszczo, 'Public Opinion in Poland', in Connor and Gitelman (eds), op. cit.; and in Maurice Simon, 'Polish Student Attitudes and Ideological Policy', in Maurice Simon and Roger Kanet (eds), *Policy and Politics in Gierek's Poland* (Boulder, Colo.: Westview Press, forthcoming).

115 Statement of the Polish League for Independence, in *Dissent in Poland* (London: Association of Polish Students and Graduates in Exile, 1978), p. 169.

116 Ibid., p. 178.

117 The first view is expressed in Rezsö Nyers and Márton Tardos, 'Milyen gazdaságpolitikai stratégiát válasszunk?' [What economic strategy should be chosen?], *Gazdaság*, 1979, No. 1, pp. 5–25, English translation to appear in *Acta Oeconomica* (Budapest). The second view is argued by Ference Havasi, 'Gazdasági épitömunkánk sóron levo feladatai' [Contemporary problems of our economic construction], *Társadalmi Szemle*, 1979, No. 1.

Chapter 8

East–West Interdependence and the Social Compact in Eastern Europe

ALEX PRAVDA

John Hardt, the editor of a valuable and weighty compendium on the East European economies, recently noted that 'the industrial West still appears to be the major source of good news' for Eastern Europe. 'Western imports, technology, and supplies bear promise for necessary Eastern economic modernization and consumer improvement. Small as Western trade may be it often appears to represent the critical margin for economic success.'[1] Can Hardt's optimistic verdict be applied to the wider political aspects of the East–West linkage?

To examine the linkages between greater involvement with the West and the East European political scene, from without, is fraught with problems. To quantify the impact of world inflationary pressures on the East European economies seems difficult enough. Our task is complicated by at least two problems. First, we do not have enough information about policy making or public opinion to gauge the precise links between external factors, the domestic environment, and regime policy. We have to deduce these by comparing known external changes with policy outputs and developments in public attitudes and behavior. Second, as Sarah Terry and Andrzej Korbonski point out, those looking for political linkages must try to trace the metamorphosis of economic factors into social and political forms.[2] The exercise can be compared with trying to trace the passage of a quantity of fluid injected into the body. The introduced substance quickly interacts with and affects the makeup of endogenous elements; its contribution to changes in the body's metabolism and behavior can only be established in approximate terms. It follows from this that we must go through two stages.

First we have to establish the linkages between external and domestic economic developments; then we proceed to trace the connections between these and developments in the body politic. The linkages with which we are concerned are mediated, indirect ones. Either by penetration or by engendering reactions, external factors tend to hamper, reinforce, exacerbate, or catalyze ongoing domestic developments. Our task is made somewhat easier by the high degree of politicization of Eastern European systems where boundaries between the economic, social, and political spheres are very low or nonexistent. Nonetheless, to assess the political salience of the various external–domestic linkages we need a framework that would help pinpoint those areas of the body politic that are most susceptible to heightened East–West interchange. Our chosen framework is the relationship between the regimes and the populations of the East European states, most notably the industrial working class.

This relationship is based on the fulfillment of mutual expectations. As the East European Communist states have moved through de-Stalinization to a post-totalitarian stage of development, political stability and the power and authority of the regime have become increasingly dependent on performance-based legitimacy. People's relationship to the regime is conditioned by the authorities' satisfaction of what are largely economic welfare expectations. These expectations constitute what may be called a social compact between rulers and ruled, between those who run the workers' state and the workers themselves, which falls into three sections. The first consists of expectations in the production sphere. As producers, East Europeans have come to regard full employment and job security as socialist rights rather than earned privileges. This attitude is coupled with expectations of fairly slack labor discipline. Moreover, wages are seen as welfare payments rather than as rewards dependent on performance, and are generally expected to be distributed along rather egalitarian lines. The second section of the social compact relates to East Europeans as consumers. Popular expectations here are very modest by Western standards: availability of basic commodities and a slow improvement in the range of goods. But this is coupled with an expectation of stable and even unchanging price levels. Finally, there are the expectations of East Europeans as citizens. They generally accept the authoritarian and paternalistic state as requiring a high level of formal compliance but minimal commitment of any real significance.

To understand how the social compact can serve as a useful framework for analyzing the linkage between greater East–West interaction and East European political developments, these expectations have to be set against the background of systemic change.

The social compact as outlined above is the product of the stage in Communist East European development that was characterized by social upheaval, political mobilization, and extensive economic growth. It bears the marks of the goals and conditions of the command system of the 1950s and early 1960s: plentiful cheap labor, low consumption levels, quantitative economic targets, and a preoccupation with overcompliance. Under such circumstances the economic and civic costs of the social compact were outweighed by the benefits of mobilized change and political control. As Eastern Europe entered the intensive stage of political development, so the balance of the costs and benefits of what will be called the 'traditional social compact' altered. Higher levels of education and consumer production combined to raise expectations in the consumption sphere. These placed an additional burden on production capacities already strained by declining sources of extensive growth. General demands for the intensification of production increased the costs of abiding by the production norms of the traditional social compact. The authorities found themselves in a difficult situation. In order to maintain the economic development necessary to sustain the growth of both producer and consumer sectors, they had to exact higher performance from the work force and this meant changing social compact producer expectations.

One way out of these problems was economic reform. The thinking behind structural economic reform was to replace the traditional social compact with a more dynamic one. The producer would be offered higher material rewards for harder work and lower security; the consumer would benefit from more rapidly improving, if less stable, living standards; greater citizen and producer participation would go hand-in-hand with more responsibility and commitment. Essentially this meant changing the social compact from one based on security and a low level of economic performance, serving political and ideological goals, to a revised compact resting far more on economic rationality. But although economic reform seemed to offer the population a great deal, widespread wariness of sacrificing security and stability for uncertain higher rewards made the majority skeptical about its advantages. The political opponents of reform, who saw the traditional social compact as part of the old centralized system, capitalized on such natural conservatism.

At this juncture the foreign trade option came fully into play. Although an expansion of trade with the West was initially advocated by many economic reformers as a useful catalyst of domestic change, the rapid expansion of East–West trade in the early 1970s coincided with the emasculation or defeat of structural reform. Some observers have identified the policy of large-scale trade with the West with groups supporting administrative rationalization and increased reliance on technology as the solutions to problems of intensive growth. Import-led growth plus rationalization appeared to offer a viable substitute for wholesale reform, one that could accelerate growth without the attendant political risks of decentralization and social compact revision.[3] In the short term the injection of Western technology and other imports did help to relieve the strain on the economy. But the course of the 1970s has shown that this was only a temporary respite and that the foreign trade option in fact intensified many of the pressures stemming from the exigencies of intensive growth. Imports stimulate consumer demands, while the need to increase exports in a highly competitive world market imposes an additional burden on the production norms of the social compact. This does not mean that greater involvement with the West has brought the situation full circle, back to structural reform. The economic problems created by external factors have contributed to the general retrenchment and recentralization of recent years.[4] All the same, externally generated pressures are also partly responsible for recent efforts to tackle the waste connected with observance of traditional social compact production norms. Originally envisaged as a substitute for reform, greater East–West interdependence has thus underlined with new force the inefficiencies reformers sought to eliminate. To sum up, the social compact provides a useful framework for our purposes. It is not an all-embracing framework; the area of administrative and managerial structures and techniques largely falls outside our coverage. But it does highlight the critical links between the economy and the polity that constitute the main points of contact between greater involvement with the West and the East European domestic political scene.

Any attempt to examine these linkages for all of the countries of Eastern Europe is clearly beyond the possibilities of a chapter-length study. Our analysis of these links is confined to the German Democratic Republic (GDR), Czechoslovakia, Poland, and Hungary. We have chosen the northern tier states because they are most involved with the West and are also the most developed countries in Eastern Europe. As such they provide the most fruitful setting for an analysis of the interaction between external factors and political development in Eastern Europe. Furthermore, these four countries differ sufficiently from one another to permit an examination of some of the variables affecting the linkages between East–West interchange and the domestic political situation. The GDR and Czechoslovakia are clearly the most economically and socially developed; their per capita gross national product places them between Italy and the United Kingdom. In addition to being the most industrialized countries in the region, they have the most educated and mature working class enjoying the highest living standards in the Soviet bloc. Hungary and Poland can be described as at a medium level of development. In per capita GNP they are on a par with Greece. A far larger proportion of their populations are still on the land or are first-generation workers. Consumption levels are lower and tastes less sophisticated than in the GDR and Czechoslovakia.

Economic involvement with the West also varies considerably. Ranked by per capita value of trade with the West in 1977, Hungary heads the list, closely followed by the GDR, with Czechoslovakia and Poland quite a long way behind. In terms of the proportion of foreign trade conducted with the West, Poland leads the way – 40 percent in the mid-1970s – with the others' Western trade composing between 22 percent and 26 percent of their total foreign trade involvement. Hungary and the GDR are the most foreign-trade-dependent of the northern tier states.

If we try to assess the relative economic burden of trade with the West at the beginning of the 1980s, Hungary seems to be the most weighed down in terms of trade deficit, while Poland carries the heaviest hard-currency debt and by far the highest debt-service ratio. Although the GDR has a healthy track record, along with Hungary it has suffered the worst deterioration in terms of trade, has a large trade deficit, and a growing debt. Of all four countries, Czechoslovakia is by far the least involved or encumbered.[5] Perhaps a more important factor determining the impact of external involvement on the domestic scene is the dynamics of the 'Western connection'. The more rapid the development of involvement with the West, the greater the likelihood of its straining the social compact and destabilizing the domestic status quo. Gierek's import-led growth strategy meant that between 1970 and 1976 Polish imports from the West grew sixfold, that is, at twice the Hungarian, East German, or Czechoslovak rate.[6]

The capacity of a country to absorb the effects of greater interchange with the West without such interchange impinging on the domestic political scene via the social compact also depends on a variety of noneconomic factors. To levels of popular expectations one has to add the regime's 'reserves' of legitimacy, which might give it some room for maneuver on the social compact. While Hungary has a fairly demanding population, the widespread support for Kádár gives him greater leeway on the social compact than is available to the East German or Czechoslovak leaderships. Even if Honecker and Husák have somewhat more sober populations enjoying relatively high standards of living, the almost total dependence of popular legitimacy on the satisfaction of social compact expectations compels them to insulate their consumers from external pressures. Gierek enjoys neither the legitimacy reserves possessed by the Hungarian regime nor the GDR's and Czechoslovakia's economic stability. The combination of volatile popular expectations, a hurriedly developed and burdensome Western trade involvement, and low reserves of popular legitimacy makes the Polish polity particularly vulnerable to the pressures of increased East–West interdependence.

I   The Production Connection

There is a two-way linkage between East–West trade and the production dimension of the social compact. Imports of Western technology have made traditionally tolerated wastage and slackness more glaring and costly. These sources of production inefficiency have in turn acted as constraints on export performance and have thus contributed to burgeoning deficits and debts. Increased trade with the West has not in itself made such features of East European labor productivity into a problem. The growing labor shortage and steady exhaustion of sources of extensive growth, which affect the GDR, Hungary, and Czechoslovakia in particular, would have placed disappointing labor productivity high on any agenda of economic 'rationalization'. Typically, here, as elsewhere, external pressures have made it more urgent to modify social compact norms. The overall impact of pressures stemming from imports of Western technology has probably been greatest in Poland, while Hungary and the GDR have felt export-generated demands more strongly, contending as they do with unfavorable terms of trade and stiff international competition.

Three sets of problems affecting labor productivity are connected with the social compact production norms: absenteeism, full employment and job security, and the pace and quality of work. At a conservative estimate something between one-fifth and one-quarter of all working time in the northern tier countries seems to be wasted.[7] In the GDR and Czechoslovakia considerable additional losses are suffered through the gross underutilization of machinery caused by unwillingness to do shift work.[8]

Poor supplies and work organization are responsible for much of the time wasted, yet up to half the losses can be put down to absenteeism. While official figures tend to underestimate the problem, the evidence suggests that between 8 percent and 10 percent of the labor force absent themselves from work on an average day, and this number seems to be on the increase. This figure is higher than rates of absenteeism in the United

States (6 percent in 1974) and the gap widens if we add the far higher East European incidence of sickness absence, part of which seems to be thinly disguised malingering.[9] The authorities have been prompted to take a tougher line on absenteeism by the rising cost of unused production time – Western imports helped double the value of equipment per worker in Poland between 1970 and 1978.[10] Sustained attempts have been made to curb the consumption of alchohol since this is closely linked with absenteeism, as it is with time wasted on the job. However, many argue that what is really needed is a tightening up of the lax management enforcement of discipline, which workers have come to regard as an established norm. Managers have been urged to make much fuller use of their sanctions against absenteeism and lack of labor discipline in general. Suggestions have even been made, only to be categorically rejected,[11] to create a small pool of unemployed in order to dispel the widespread complacency among workers that breeds cavalier attitudes toward discipline.[12] Full employment is not merely a propaganda slogan but one of the cardinal components of the social compact. East Europeans may not fully appreciate this 'socialist achievement' but they do regard it as an inviolable right.

Previously relatively cheap to provide in the period of extensive growth, full employment and job security have now become major policy constraints whose effects are magnified by the pressures of external involvement. Not only do East Europeans, manual workers in particular, take it for granted that one can keep a job regardless of performance, but they also assume that one can change that job at will. Job changing can be seen as another cost stemming from the social compact. Labor turnover ran at between 18 percent and 25 percent of the work force through the 1970s.[13] Low as this may be by international standards (turnover in the US topped 40 percent in 1977) the time lost between jobs and the uncontrolled nature of the phenomenon make it a cause of concern to the East European regimes. That workers move quickly to exploit a seller's labor market was shown in Hungary in the first years of the New Economic Mechanism when turnover rates doubled. Only a series of administrative measures has managed to reduce job changing to pre-1968 levels.[14]

A far more serious aspect of the job security constraint is the problem of overmanning and the inefficient distribution of labor resources. Disguised unemployment amounts to an estimated 15–20 percent of their work force. The losses involved can be ill afforded by labor-short countries like Czechoslovakia, the GDR, and Hungary, which are also under heavy pressure to improve export performance. Nevertheless, East European regimes have moved gingerly in reducing manning levels and closing inefficient plants. Their reasons are twofold. First, slimming work forces and shutting unprofitable and overmanned plants raises protests from those who object on principle to the elevation of economic criteria above social or political considerations. Second, such objections are strengthened by the general reluctance of workers to accept the idea of directed redeployment. Accustomed to absolute job security, East Europeans tend to regard a few hundred temporarily unemployed with quite dispro-portionate apprehension.[15] Progress on this front has therefore been very slow. In Czechoslovakia and Poland only a tiny proportion of the labor force has been moved. In Hungary, where the pressures for action have been greatest, closure plans have affected between 200 and 400 smaller plants. Indeed, Hungarian experience has shown that as long as all is done gradually, and public fears of long-term unemployment are allayed, reducing disguised unemployment is a difficult but not impossible task.[16]

Even with labor efficiently deployed, the problem still remains of achieving higher standards of work. Long years of exposure to undemanding domestic and bloc markets have nurtured levels of work intensity and quality whose inadequacy has been revealed by greater East–West interdependence. The increased use of Western machinery has tended to highlight the gap between capitalist and socialist labor performance, while joint ventures have sharpened managers' and workers' awareness of the discrepancies. Anxiety about the effects of low-quality workmanship on export performance has prompted widespread calls for improvement. Faced with mounting trade deficits, the Hungarians and East Germans have been particularly emphatic about the need to raise quality and economize on the use of imported materials. One obvious way to tackle these problems is to tighten quality controls and increase penalties for shoddy workmanship. But the work rates and standards have deeper roots in poor worker commitment and inadequate incentives.[17] Conscientiousness and pride in one's work seem to be relatively low in Poland and Hungary where many blue-collar workers are still relatively new to the production line. Widespread cynicism about working hard is nurtured by a factory climate that tends to benefit those who overtly exploit the system. Most workers, and even more technicians and engineers, conserve their energies for moonlighting jobs where they can earn several times their normal rates of pay.[18] The administrative measures taken against moonlighting can never be more than partially successful and are unlikely to foster conscientiousness. Reducing workers' outside earnings is more likely to make them even more critical of their full-time conditions and pay. Nor have renewed attempts to instill a sense of social responsibility and thereby mobilize them to greater efforts enjoyed much success.

As most workers (and staff) put material rewards first, the most promising approach seems to lie in linking remuneration more effectively to performance. Despite a long-standing general commitment to tying pay to performance, in practice the connection between them still appears to be quite imperfect. Growth of trade with the West is related to this whole area in two senses. The rapid expansion in East–West trade of the early 1970s coincided with a sharp rise in wages; in Poland and Hungary pay grew faster than labor productivity. Concern about the inflationary effects of these wage increases was compounded by mounting trade deficits, which intensified the pressure on exports and thereby the need to stimulate higher labor productivity. All this helps to account for the pains taken by leaders in all four states since 1975–76 to spell out the simple message that all pay has to be earned.[19]

Quite apart from the considerable technical problems of tying rewards to performance and thus stimulating higher productivity, efforts in this direction run up against three problems. The first problem is that incentive schemes can only operate effectively in indirect wage regulation systems, which are incompatible with current centralizing 'rationalization' policies.[20] Second, talk of trying to reward strictly according to performance conflicts with the social compact welfare concept of wages. Workers have a traditional wariness of anything to do with more rational norms since in the past this was a euphemism for exacting more work for the same pay. The last and most politically signficant problem is that any attempt to distinguish between workers on the basis of performance encounters the obstacles of egalitarianism.

Income is more equally distributed in Eastern Europe than in the West. Within the northern tier, the GDR and Czechoslovakia are the most egalitarian and Poland the least. Differences in earnings between manual workers and technical staff are small, ranging from 40–50 percent in Poland and Hungary to a mere 20 percent in Czechoslovakia. Despite the attention drawn by economists and politicians since the 1960s to the economically counterproductive effects of such 'leveling' tendencies, recent years have seen a further narrowing of differentials, particularly in Poland and Hungary.[21] Survey evidence indicates that a majority of Polish and Hungarian managers see the widening of differentials as essential for an improvement in productivity.[22] Recent Hungarian steps to make enterprises stand on their own feet will increase differentials between workers in different factories and sectors. The promotion of export production also tends to widen differentials as the export sector usually pays better. The privileged treatment being accorded the export sector may well turn it into a powerful anti-leveling force within the economy.

Be that as it may, East European leaders have generally been slow to act to widen differentials. As in the case of overemployment, their caution stems from the political opposition and considerable popular antipathy to the policy. Opponents of the extension of economic criteria argue that increasing differentials violates the principle of socialist equality. The real strength of their case lies in its use of popular support for egalitarianism.[23] Popular egalitarianism is usually cited as a major constraint on widening differentials, yet the exact nature of that constraint only emerges upon closer examination of the nature of egalitarian sentiments in Eastern Europe. Polish and Hungarian survey evidence indicates that the great majority think existing differentials too great, and some fraction between one-third and one-half want to see these reduced to a maximum of 1:3 or even 1:2. In Czechoslovakia, where differentials are considerably lower, public opinion is not as critical of the status quo.[24] There is little doubt that strong popular egalitarianism will continue to be widespread, particularly among manual workers. Yet East European regimes tend to be somewhat paranoid about the blanket nature of the constraint imposed by blue-collar egalitarianism. By no means all attempts to reward good performance more fully would meet with workers' opposition. The survey evidence suggests that a reduction of the gap between the extreme poles of the income range would facilitate adjustments elsewhere to give greater recognition to skill and performance.[25]

In this light, recent Hungarian moves to dispel egalitarian myths and widen industrial differentials seem sensible and necessary, particularly given the unremitting external pressures on productivity. Here, as elsewhere in the production sphere, the linkage between East–West interdependence and the domestic scene is an indirect and 'reactive' one. Externally generated pressures exacerbate the strain on the maintenance of traditional social compact norms and thereby on the relationship between the regime as employer and the population as producers.

II   The Consumption Connection

Workers are not just producers. They are also consumers and, increasingly, the largest component of the consuming population. The consumption linkage between greater external involvement and domestic political developments is 'penetrative' and more direct than its production equivalent.[26] Not only is the impact of economic factors more tangible, but consumer expectations are more critical to regime legitimacy. Whereas in the production sphere the thrust of external pressures is to change the state's expectations of working populations, in that of consumption such pressures affect the regime's capacity to satisfy popular expectations. Problems on the consumption front are therefore more likely to occasion widespread popular protest than are the more gradual efforts to tighten the production screw.

Before proceeding to examine the nature of the consumption linkage, something should be said about the general development and significance of consumption in Eastern Europe. The rise in consumption levels and its central position in economic strategy can be traced back to ideological and secular trends stretching back to the mid-1950s. Since the New Course, living standards have increasingly become the major domestic and international yardstick for measuring progress towards communism. The current concept of developed socialism accords unprecedented prominence to the improvement of the material well-being of the population. These changes in ideological emphasis reflect two secular trends. A basic requisite of intensive economic growth has been the need to provide sufficient material stimulus to raise productivity. But paying out higher wages has little incentive effect if workers cannot buy the goods they want. Arguably the more important secular trend has been the growing role played by economic performance in regime legitimacy and political stability. Increasingly, Communist party leaders have found it both desirable and necessary to build up popular support by raising consumption levels. If the 1970s saw a clampdown on political dissent, they also witnessed higher-than-ever priority accorded to raising living standards.

The concurrent rise in consumption levels and in trade with the West is more than coincidental. Pro-consumption policies have generated a powerful force for the expansion of East–West commercial relations. Inevitably, higher living standards have fueled rising consumer expectations. Traditional expectations of an adequate supply of basic commodities have been extended to a wider range of consumer durables. Increased imports on credit from the West can be seen as the product of the need to satisfy such higher consumer demands without disrupting the prospects for economic growth.

The exact effect of Western imports on consumption patterns is difficult to estimate. Consumer goods have made up a small, albeit a slowly increasing, proportion of total imports from the West. All the same, marginal quantities can make the critical difference between consumer satisfaction and shortages where certain commodities are in heavy demand. This is the case not only with luxuries like cars but also applies to agricultural products. With domestic demand growing apace and Soviet deliveries affected by fluctuating performance, Poland has had to import increasing quantities of agricultural produce from the West. To keep abreast with domestic demand, Poland has also been forced to reduce traditional hard-currency-earning exports such as meat and coal.

Greater availability of Western goods tends to heighten awareness of the shortcomings of domestic products. This not only affects the saleability of goods but also intensifies pressure to increase imports of Western manufactured goods. An alternative solution to demands of this kind is industrial cooperation agreements. While this seems the best way to satisfy the demands for American jeans or West European cars, joint ventures can lay the regime open to charges of conceding the superiority of Western production methods and exposing the economy and society to capitalist influences.[27]

Over and above such relatively direct economic links, the growth of East–West contact has increased the permeability of the economic, social, ideological, and political boundaries dividing Eastern Europe from the capitalist world.[28] In the climate of détente East–West tourism has burgeoned. Such visits are not only expensive; they do damage to Communist party propaganda images of life under capitalism. We know of no evidence showing the precise effect firsthand experience of the West has on attitudes to socialism and capitalism; the likely tendency is to reinforce what appears to be widespread disillusion – strongest in Czechoslovakia and least marked in Hungary – not so much with socialist principles as with the way they have been put into practice. The short duration of East Europeans' visits to the West increases the chances of their taking away favorable superficial impressions, but also lessens the likelihood of any lasting impact on basic values.[29]

As the majority of East Europeans are more immediately concerned with material issues than with abstract values, increased information about Western living standards probably has a considerable impact on their evaluation of domestic conditions. In objective terms, Poland comes off worst in comparison with the West. But while the ease of making international comparisons may have aggravated the situation in the Baltic ports in the late 1960s, in general Poles are more likely to use the East Germans rather than Westerners as reference groups. Historical links and geographical proximity encourage Czechs, Slovaks, and Hungarians to compare their lot with that of the Austrians. Such comparisons tend to highlight the inferiority of East European standards, particularly in the case of Czechoslovakia, which, in contrast to Hungary, has slipped further behind Austria over the last twenty years.

The unique relationship between the two Germanies makes East–West contact and comparisons a far more powerful force in the GDR than elsewhere in the region. Since most of the tourists are visiting relatives, East–West traffic has a far greater capacity to break down the information barriers that East German propaganda tries to erect. These are also continually undermined by West German radio and television to which nearly all East Germans have access. West German television makes citizens of the GDR aware not merely of the situation in the Federal Republic, but also broadcasts revealing reports on East German life. It was largely reporting of East German consumers' dissatisfaction that prompted the imposition of stringent restrictions on Western journalists in early 1979.[30] Given the almost universal awareness in the GDR of the widening gap between East and West German living standards, the GDR is under unrelenting pressure to respond as best it can to domestic consumer demand. East–West contact and comparisons are a powerful motor generating rising expectations and keeping the improvement of living standards at the center of the Communist Party's policy. However economically successful the GDR has been by East European standards, enforced competition with one of the world's strongest economies is bound to continue to fuel domestic discontent and increase the very large number of those wishing to emigrate to the West.

The GDR also provides us with the clearest instance of the impact that hard currency can have on the domestic scene. East European states have long provided Western tourists with special hard-currency shops in which they can purchase domestically produced goods that are in short supply and a large range of imported goods unobtainable elsewhere in the country. Such special shops are also usually open to the considerable numbers of locals who receive hard-currency gifts from relatives living abroad and the few who have hard-currency incomes. The system provides a useful source of badly needed hard currency – in Poland the turnover of the Pewex shops in 1975 was $180 million while the recently expanded East German Intershops grossed $250 million in 1978.[31]

Against such benefits one has to offset serious negative repercussions and side effects. The existence of special shops in most major towns must heighten public awareness of the superior purchasing power of Western currency. This is particularly true of the GDR where direct comparisons can be made between the DM prices of goods in the Intershops and their cost in the second rank special shops, the Exquisit and Delikat chain, which trade in local currency. The four- to five-fold disparity in price further undermines confidence in East German marks and encourages an already flourishing black market. More significantly, the West German mark began to develop into a second currency as many recipients of gifts from the Federal Republic used them to pay for a whole range of services. This practice became so widespread by 1977 that workers in one East Berlin factory threatened to strike if they were not paid part of their wages in West German marks. This and other protests against the expansion of the Intershop network prompted the introduction of a voucher system designed to eliminate the general circulation of West German currency.[32]

Honecker's encouragement of the inflow of hard currency has provoked criticism on two counts. To start with, the policy is counterproductive in terms of stimulating productivity, because it promotes the distribution of valuable resources on a basis totally unrelated to performance. As Wolfgang Harich, the East German Marxist-dissident, has put it, the principle of distribution applied in the GDR is 'to each according to where his aunt lives'.[33] As well as annoying all those without generous relatives in the Federal Republic, Honecker's policy is particularly resented by middle-level bureaucrats who cannot afford contact with Westerners and whose high pay is undermined by the circulation of hard currency. This group has been the most vocal in attacking the policy as providing yet another channel for the infiltration of bourgeois-consumerist values.[34]

While East German bureaucrats undoubtedly exaggerate the dangers of 'capitalist infection', increased contact with the West has aroused wider apprehension about the dangers of consumerism for socialist societies. There are several senses in which a linkage of this kind could be perceived. Inasmuch as greater East–West interdependence has accelerated the rise in East European consumption levels, this could be seen as bringing the region nearer consumerism *qua* the widespread consumption of non-essential goods. Yet the thrust of Communist party policy has been to raise consumption levels; however worrying the implications of expenditure on nonessentials, this development has not been caused but only catalyzed by contact with the West. What really seems to divide legitimate socialist consumption from undesirable consumerism is not so much the level as the social role of consumption. Where consumption becomes conspicuous and takes on status-giving functions, it also becomes unacceptable in a socialist society.[35] East–West interchange may have contributed to expanding the scope for conspicuous elite consumption in Eastern Europe, particularly in Poland and Hungary, yet it can hardly be saddled with the responsibility for what are homegrown social elites, however ideologically and politically convenient this would be.

The greatest long-term problem of East European consumerism lies in its implications for the exercise of power and control. A glance at developments in the region over the last twenty-five years seems to show that stagnating living standards tend to precede periods of political instability, which in turn coincide with, or are followed by, rapid growth in consumption.[36] Higher living standards inevitably bring rising expectations – an inflation of the consumption section of the social compact. Once embarked upon, the policy of improving living standards is far more difficult to control than policy departures on the production front. Consumer pressures have increased the economic burden of greater East–West interdependence, and together these constraints have narrowed the regime's economic policy options. As control over economic resources constitutes the major source of power in Communist Party states, this reduction in the regime's room for maneuver qualifies its exercise of power. Indeed, the growing influence of consumer demand is seen as an increase in 'spontaneous' activity, that is, activity largely independent of control from above.

As we have noted, consumer demands swell import bills and in some cases limit traditional exports. To some extent they have also imposed higher standards. Not only are poor quality goods increasingly left unsold as consumers become more selective, but the pressure of rising levels of consumption imposes considerable strains on supply and retail networks. Where in the past deficient supplies were taken for granted, governments anxious to maintain their commitment to higher living standards now take steps to improve the situation. In Poland and Hungary such efforts have involved encouragement of the private retail sector.

Fears of consumption growth fueling consumerist 'spontaneity' have alerted academics and politicians in Eastern Europe to the need to regulate and shape consumer preferences. Ideally, a socialist consumption model would make possible the reconciliation of individual consumer demands and preferences with national interests and needs.[37] But apart from general references to the need to educate and guide and not to command, no real solution has been offered as to how such a model might be put into practice. And there still remains the problem of formulating socialist standards of consumption. All these are fundamental problems posed by the development of consumer societies in Eastern Europe. They have not been created by increased involvement with the West, yet by catalyzing consumption growth East–West trade and contact have intensified the pressures and constraints on the power and control of the central political authorities. Nowhere has this emerged more clearly than in the area of consumer prices.

III   Prices and Politics

Of all the repercussions of Eastern Europe's involvement with the West the most readily apparent has been the region's increased exposure to world inflationary pressures. In varying degrees all northern tier states have been affected by world inflation on two fronts. First, rocketing Western prices have multiplied import costs, which, except in Poland, have risen faster than export prices. More seriously still, world inflationary pressures have been reflected in steep rises in the price of Soviet raw material and fuel exports to Eastern Europe. While these rises have been phased and somewhat softened by Soviet credits, the days of cheap raw materials and fuel, particularly oil, are over.[38]

It is impossible to gauge the precise impact of world inflation on the East European economies. In a careful study of Poland, Fallenbuchl concludes that while higher fuel and raw material prices have contributed to inflation, domestic inflationary pressures have been 'much stronger'.[39] External inflationary pressures have probably made a greater impact on the other northern tier states where investment has been kept under tighter control and dependence on imported raw materials and fuels is greater.

Whereas capitalist companies and governments can pass increased import costs on to the consumer, East European regimes are constrained from doing so by at least two factors. First, there is the loss of face involved in allowing capitalist crisis to disrupt socialist stability. The stronger a regime's record of contrasting Western instability with domestic security, the more effective the 'loss of face' constraint. Czechoslovakia and the

GDR are more restricted in this respect than Poland or Hungary; Kádár has been the most open in admitting that world inflation took his country by surprise and checked domestic living standards.[40]

The 'loss of face' constraint stems from a more powerful and deeply rooted one: the popular expectation that government is both able and obliged to keep prices steady. Along with job security this ranks as a key component of the traditional social compact. East Europeans' preoccupation with price stability is not difficult to explain. After the fall in living standards associated with inflation in the early 1950s, price stability, particularly in foodstuffs, became a minimal demand. With wage growth low or stagnant it seemed the only way to maintain living standards. Furthermore, the command system militated against wage claims and favored administrative price controls. Subsidies became a vital part of the structure sustaining the regimes' performance-based legitimacy. Through the 1960s subsidies helped to keep price growth down to an overall 7–10 percent.[41] Although economic reformers' efforts to relate prices more to cost and demand resulted in some rises, the political authorities remained cautious about tampering with subsidies. With the Polish events of 1970–71 as a constant reminder, all East European leaders maintained their commitment to price stability up to the mid-1970s. In some cases, notably that of Poland, the policy of expanding trade with the West was itself prompted by the need to raise living standards without increasing prices. Through the early 1970s, East Europeans were heavily insulated from world inflation through budgetary subsidies.[42]

Cushioning the population from the effects of capitalist dislocation certainly helps to strengthen popular legitimacy and political stability, but it also has serious disadvantages. First, the very high subsidies on the price of basic foodstuffs, ranging from 25 percent in Czechoslovakia to between 70 percent and 75 percent in Poland and Hungary, increase consumer demand for what are already hard-pressed supplies. In Poland, for instance, continually rising demand has been partly responsible for the recurrent meat shortages. Second, because they are protected from the effects of inflation, the East European public tends to give little credence to government warnings about the need for the country to work harder to pay its way. A poll conducted in Hungary in 1975 found that only 21 percent thought that the country was in any serious economic difficulties.[43] Third, insulating foreign trade from domestic prices and maintaining separate user and consumer prices makes it extremely difficult to assess, let alone reward, efficient performance. Neutralization of world inflationary pressures only tends to obscure and aggravate the real problems, making their solution all the more difficult.

Last, but certainly not least, there is the sheer financial cost of the subsidy system. Hungary and Poland lead the way with one-third and one-quarter of their respective budgets taken up by subsidies of various kinds, approximately half this amount being spent on keeping food prices low. Exactly what proportion of the subsidy bill is devoted to insulating the consumer from external inflationary pressures is difficult to calculate. Fallenbuchl estimates that two-thirds of Polish price subsidies in 1974–75 were used for this purpose, and there is a strong correlation between the steep rise in import prices in 1973–75 and the growth of subsidies in Hungary, Poland, and Czechoslovakia.[44]

Faced with mounting subsidy bills, trade deficits, and hard-currency debts, East European leaders have since 1975–76 taken a tougher line on the need to relate prices more closely to costs. Those in particularly difficult political situations have moved very cautiously. Honecker remains fully committed to the subsidy system and has kept consumer prices insulated from external pressures.[45] The Czechoslovak regime has been somewhat less conservative; the July 1979 increases in the price of fuel, telephone calls, and clothing seem to be part of a general move to bring prices more in line with costs. After the abortive attempt to raise food prices in June 1976, Gierek moved more cautiously to cut a subsidy bill that grew by 60 percent between 1975 and 1978. Nevertheless, prices rose much faster than they did in the early 1970s, and the government's declared policy was gradually to bring them more closely into line with costs.

Characteristically, the Hungarians have gone furthest in their criticism of the subsidy system. Istvan Huszar, the chairman of the National Planning Office, has stated that the restoration of a balance between foreign trade and domestic prices must become the underlying principle of Hungarian price policy. Working with the most flexible price system in the region, the Hungarians have sought to use prices to regulate consumer demand and thus release commodities for export. To help stem a burgeoning subsidy bill, prices were increased by 24 percent between 1976 and mid-1979. Not only was this the most rapid rise in prices since the early 1950s but it embraced basic foodstuffs as well as fuel and durables.[46] However, apart from the usual grumbling there has been no sign of popular discontent and nothing resembling protest action.

An examination of how Hungary has managed to begin to adjust consumer prices might shed some light on the nature of the popular constraint on price increases that has inhibited the GDR and Czechoslovakia from taking similar action and has severely restricted Polish adjustments to external pressures. Indeed, a comparison of recent price rises successfully introduced in Hungary with the abortive Polish increase of 1976 may help to pinpoint some of the factors governing East European regimes' capacity to absorb domestic international inflationary pressures.

To what extent can the differences be attributed to varying public expectations? One of the most obvious factors shaping popular expectations and conditioning tolerance of price increases is the standard of living. Although personal consumption levels in 1975 were slightly higher in Poland than in Hungary, Poles had to work longer for and spend proportionately more on basic foodstuffs that were often in short supply. This situation would tend to make Poles more sensitive than Hungarians to changes in the price of food. By the same token, East Germans' high expenditure on nonessential goods might be held to account for their sensitivity to increases in this sector, as displayed by the 1977 strike in Karl-Marx-Stadt in protest against a rise in the price of coffee.[47]

Since expectations reflect past experience rather than any absolute norms, the development of living standards is a vital factor determining popular reaction. One might have thought that the spectacular rise in real income in Poland between 1971 and 1975 would have built up a large reserve of popular tolerance of price increases. Presumably this was part of the Polish leadership's calculations in 1976. However, there are two important flaws in this line of reasoning. The first is the assumption that real income growth is sufficient in itself to lower the threshold of popular expectations of price stability. Polish developments show that unless rises in real incomes are accompanied by real improvements in housing, services, and supplies, they have little effect on popular tolerance of price increases.[48]

The other and more significant point confirmed by Polish experience is that rapidly changing economic conditions make people uneasy and put them on the defensive. Following hard on the heels of the near-stagnant living standards of the later 1960s, Gierek's 'boom' strategy made Poles more rather than less sensitive to any attempt to cut back, to undermine the traditional bedrock of living standards: stable food prices. The key importance of consistency and steadiness is borne out by the far slower pace of change in Hungary, where real wages grew at half the Polish rate in the first half of the 1970s. The greater equilibrium of Hungarian development seems to have increased the population's capacity to absorb price increases. It also means that the recent general fall in real wage growth comes as less of a shock. In Poland there is a sharper contrast between the boom of 1971–75 and the slowdown in real wages since 1976, so Poles will probably continue to be extremely sensitive to price rises.

Important as the economic context in which price increases are introduced may be, the way in which they and all adjustments to social compact norms are handled has a crucial effect on public response. Once again the differences between Poland and Hungary are instructive. In Poland the 1976 price hike was sprung on an unprepared public. Rather than shocking workers and others into silent acceptance, the suddenness and size of the increase exacerbated resentment and tensions. By contrast the Hungarian authorities have taken great care to give considerable notice of impending price increases and to phase these over a longer period. Moreover, they have made some real effort to educate the public in the rudiments of economic life. Until very recently Polish officials tended to discuss economic difficulties in general terms and failed to explain the links between external pressures and domestic prices. The Hungarian leadership, on the other hand, turned the problems of externally generated pressures to some advantage. By admitting that Hungary is vulnerable to international factors largely beyond their control, Kádár, Csikos-Nagy, and others have helped to weaken the traditional social compact conviction that the party and government are wholly responsible for all that happens on the economic front.

The combination of relatively steady economic improvement, adroit handling of price increases, and public discussion of the reasons for such moves seems to increase the threshold of popular tolerance. It minimizes the likelihood that price rises will produce protest action – the ultimate constraint on East European regimes' adaptation to domestically and externally generated inflationary pressures. Yet, whether price increases trigger open protest also depends on the population's propensity to translate their discontent into direct action. This in turn is conditioned by a complex of political cultural factors as well as by the prevailing relationship between rulers and ruled. As far as orientations to authority and civil disobedience are concerned, the Czechs, and to a lesser extent the Slovaks, can be categorized as the most deferent and cautious people in the region. The East Germans can be seen as more disciplined and respectful of state power than the Hungarians, while the Poles emerge as the least deferent and the most volatile.[49]

Such basic tendencies are in turn shaped by different recent political experiences. Many East Germans may no longer be influenced by memories of the 1953 workers' revolt, but all are fully aware of the particular constraints imposed by the German Democratic Republic's key position in Soviet strategy. Memories of the 1956 Revolution keep Hungarians alive to the advantages of pragmatism, while the fate of the Prague Spring has reinforced traditional Czech skepticism about the possibilities of popular action. By contrast, the climacterics of recent Polish development – 1956, 1970–71, 1976 and 1980 – have served to strengthen public confidence in the power of popular protest. Past success has made Poles, particularly Polish industrial workers, more prone to take action against unpopular policies than their counterparts elsewhere in Eastern Europe.

In the final instance, the public's, and specifically the proletariat's, actual response to government measures depends on that regime's record and credibility. And because personalities figure more importantly in Communist than in liberal–democratic politics, this credibility often comes down to the credibility and political style of the country's political leaders. This in turn depends largely on the ways in which policy makers communicate and consult with the population.

IV   Communication, Institutions, and Participation

While the need to improve communication and increase the amount of consultation comes to the fore at critical junctures, it also emerges as an important factor affecting the general ability of East European regimes to adjust to the pressures of more complex and more open economies. Many of the problems on the production front that we noted earlier could be solved more effectively by consultation and participation than by the present mixture of mobilization, sanctions, and inadequate incentives. The long-term solution to the problems of consumption and consumerism lies in responding to and educating public preferences. To say this is not to resurrect the well-worn thesis that complexity and openness lead inexorably to liberal democracy. Our point is simply that the problems associated with greater East–West interdependence have intensified the need for improvement in the flow of communications between decision makers and the populace and in grassroots participation in the making as well as in the implementation of policy. What is really required in the long run is a radical change in the traditional social compact passivity of the population as citizens.

Recent years have seen a growing awareness in official East European circles of the importance of such improvements. Regime attitudes and action differ considerably from country to country. In Czechoslovakia and East Germany much lip service is paid to the general need to 'perfect' socialist democracy. However, the practical focus of this policy is on the improvement of mobilization and agitprop work. The more acute economic and political problems facing Poland have propelled the issues of consultation and participation toward the top of the political agenda. In the early 1970s Gierek made a great show of keeping in touch with popular feeling by touring factories, farms, and offices. By 1976, however, such visits had degenerated into a bureaucratized public relations exercise. Consultations on the June price increases were purely formal, and this was one of the main grievances aired by protesting workers.

Since the debacle of June 1976, public discussion of these problems has been sustained by the external and domestic pressures on the relationship between rulers and ruled. Calls for institutional reforms to increase feedback and participation have come from a wide spectrum of political opinion.[50] Gierek reiterated his commitment to consultation, but nothing he said or did indicated a basic change of line. The thrust still remains on increasing the facilities for general discussion so as to ensure more effective implementation of government policies, rather than to further the cause of meaningful rank-and-file participation in policy making. Precisely because he was faced with dangers of political fragmentation, Gierek was unwilling or unable (one must not forget the Soviet constraint) to embark upon any large-scale institutional reforms.

Instead of responding reluctantly to pressures along Polish lines, Kádár has generally taken the initiative on consultation. Since the mid-1960s the Hungarian regime has effectively recognized the legitimacy of different interests under socialism. To a greater extent than elsewhere in the region, conflicts of interest in Hungary have been reconciled by way of what may be called guided-consensus politics.[51] The Hungarians' political adroitness and their system of political communication will probably continue to enable them to adjust to external pressures, in the near future. In the longer term, however, more fundamental institutional changes are needed in Hungary (and in the region as a whole), not just to make possible the absorption of unpopular measures, but to generate an overall commitment to the common weal, a commitment that is essential to stable and prosperous development.

Over the last ten years institutional strain and adaptation related to these issues have appeared in four areas. In the first place, the importance of Parliament and local councils as mediators between mass and elite has been stressed a good deal. To improve their performance in this role, efforts have been made to raise the quality of candidates for office, to widen somewhat the choice available to electors, and to increase the scope and quality of parliamentary debate.[52]

Second, external and domestic economic pressures have placed an increasing burden on the Communist Party and have spotlighted two general weaknesses in its performance, which emerge most clearly from Polish developments. The first is poor communication within the party. In the lead-up to the 1970 crisis, local reports on workers' attitudes were filtered out at higher levels and grass roots activists were not given the chance to explain the need for the price increases. To avoid recurrence, Gierek established direct channels between the Central Committee and the party organizations of the largest enterprises, but the crisis of 1976 showed that streamlining is no real remedy. And even if one could remove all communications blockages within the party, this would still leave unresolved the frequent disparity between grass roots party opinion and central policies. The local party activist who is in touch with popular feeling and commands his members' confidence is often caught between sympathy with the rank and file and duty to his superiors. Unless the Communist Party's traditional role in the polity is radically altered, and that is highly improbable, it is difficult to see how this organization can effectively represent the whole range of societal interests. After all, the party's first duty is to see that the national interest overrides sectional ones. Even the Hungarian party, with its more flexible approach to interest accommodation, cannot be all things to all men. Consequently, throughout the region greater attention has been paid in this context to the possibilities of improving the performance of two major representative institutions: the trade unions and bodies promoting workers' participation.

In many ways the official trade unions are the key institutions for successful adjustment to pressures in both the consumption and production spheres. Their importance in this respect is best illustrated by comparing Polish and Hungarian experience. Polish developments show that workers' propensity to resort to direct action is increased by poor trade union performance. The need to make trade unions more effective defenders of workers' interests rather than management acolytes was one of the lessons drawn from the post-mortem of the 1970 crisis. Yet the measures taken to improve trade union performance were marginal, and whatever credibility they gained was lost in 1976, when the unions were unwilling or unable (or both) to prevent the government from breaking its pledge on price stability.

Just as weak official trade unions increase the destabilizing effects of unpopular economic policies and impede governmental adjustments to external economic pressures, so stronger unions can facilitate such adaptation. By voicing their members' interests at the national level, trade unions can moderate unpopular policies and soften their impact. If they can gain workers' confidence at the shop floor level, unions can help divert conflicts into more controllable institutional channels. Since the late 1960s, when they were given greater powers to balance the enlarged role of enterprise management, Hungarian trade unions have made some headway on both these fronts. At the national level they have acted as an effective pressure group. This has not always facilitated governmental adjustments to external pressures since the unions have generally been a conservative force. All the same, by moderating some of the more unpopular effects of external pressure, the official unions have helped to mitigate destabilizing repercussions. Because they have been frequently consulted on social and economic policy and have restrained the government on some issues, the unions have managed to build up credibility to help implement other unpopular measures.

Official local unions have proved less useful. Bonds between union and management at enterprise level remain strong, and unions generally refrain from using their considerable powers. The result is that workers look to foremen and supervisors rather than to official union officials to solve their problems.[53] As far as facilitating adjustment to economic pressures is concerned, local unions tend to be conservative and to support enterprise rather than national interests. (In Poland, depending on the final issue of the events of August–September 1980, the workers may now be able to turn to their own independent trade union leaders. The outcome is not yet clear.)

Hungarian experience underlines the more general point that strengthening unions has mixed benefits from the government's standpoint. Their involvement in policy making can ease the passage of unpopular economic measures, but can also narrow the government's room for maneuver. Transforming trade unions into the effective counterweights to management desired by most workers would increase their popular support and thereby their influence over the work force. Yet logically such transformation would lead to the unions playing a contesting role that would bring them into increasing conflict with the national employer – the state. Given the stable political situation in Hungary, Kádár can afford to go on allowing the unions to play a limited interest group role, under close Communist Party control. Despite Poland's urgent need for better trade union performance, that country's greater instability and the calls for independent unions probably make party leaders feel, quite mistakenly, that greater union autonomy is too perilous a venture.[54]

Expansion of workers' participation in management must appear as a safer complement or even alternative to thoroughgoing trade union reform. Throughout the region a great deal has been said about the need to upgrade workers' participation. The emphasis, however, remains largely on the instrumental concept of participation, as a means of raising labor productivity, rather than first and foremost giving workers and staff a larger say in enterprise policy. To date, the various bodies that supposedly give workers a voice in decisions have had an unimpressive record. The workers' councils, production committees, and conferences, which are frequently dominated by supervisory staff, support rather than monitor or challenge management policy and are therefore regarded by workers with skepticism and scant respect.[55]

Yet workers' participation is potentially capable of helping to tackle some of the problems generated by domestic and external economic pressures, especially on the production side. Survey evidence suggests that workers want a greater say in decisions affecting the shop or section in which they work, even if the majority are relatively indifferent to participation at enterprise level.[56] Equipped with co-decision making rather than their present consultative powers, workers' councils and production committees could help to diffuse tensions over conditions and pay, articulate employee interests, and raise the low level of commitment to improving economic performance. All this would undoubtedly ease adaptation to domestic and external pressures. At the same time, such stronger workers' councils would tend to be parochial in outlook and resist any 'rationalization' that might damage local interests.

On present evidence there is little prospect that either these benefits or drawbacks will materialize.[57] Czechoslovak and East German promises to improve participation have not been followed up with effective action. Despite the pledges made by the Polish leadership after 1970, little has been done thus far to revamp the workers' councils and the larger conference of workers' self-management of which they form a part. Workers' councils remain by far the weakest component of the self-management conference, which is dominated by party, union, and management officials. Concern over workers' participation in Hungary resulted in the establishment in 1978 of conferences of trade union stewards endowed with co-decision-making rights on a whole range of issues, including the distribution of incentives and the use of enterprise social funds. It is too soon to assess these new bodies, though by their very makeup they overlap excessively with the trade union committee, and one wonders how they can offer rank-and-file workers greater direct involvement in enterprise affairs.

Until real decision-making powers are given to bodies that are regarded by the rank and file as their own, the full potential benefits of workers' participation will not be realized. The likelihood of this happening is extremely small; participation of this kind would really amount to self-management. The short-lived Polish and Hungarian workers' councils of 1956–58 and those in Czechoslovakia a decade later, as well as their Yugoslav prototypes, show that self-management involves a degree of economic and political devolution that is incompatible with existing East European systems and is unacceptable to their leaders and to Moscow alike.[58]

In each of the institutional sectors we have briefly examined, a distinction should be drawn between two levels of adaptation. The first and most urgently needed is adaptation to improve the two-way flow of communication between decision makers and the mass of the working population. Something can be achieved by streamlining major institutions and by improving the quality of complaint procedures, agitprop work, and general public relations. Such minor adjustments, if made with greater skill than has been shown by the Polish authorities, help avoid popular protests. Yet, as we have noted, better communication is of little use without real consultation. And consultation brings us to the second and more fundamental level of institutional adaptation. If the East European regimes are to cope successfully with the problems of intensive economic development and greater involvement with the West, they will have to devise more effective mechanisms for the articulation and mediation of the interests of institutional and social groups whose cooperation is vital for stable economic and political progress. Kádár has shown in Hungary that a start can be made in this direction within the constraints of the Communist Party's leading role and Moscow's notions of permissible reform.

V   Conclusions

Have increased links with the West been 'the major source of good news' that John Hardt considers greater economic interdependence to have been? To a great extent the answer depends on whose cost–benefit account is being assessed. Looking at the issue from the vantage point of the East European consumer, involvement with the West has been generally positive. Imports have helped make possible higher growth rates and living standards. Greater East–West interdependence has been accompanied by an easing of travel and currency restrictions. Whatever unfavorable light such increased familiarity with Western goods and values may have shed on domestic conditions, imports and greater contact must surely appear as a gain to most of the East European populations. What is more, probably only a small proportion of East Europeans would hold involvement with the West responsible for the rise in prices or for the more frequent calls for higher productivity; both would be popularly attributed to the party and government.

Precisely this kind of attitude has made greater East–West exchange a problem from the standpoint of the political authorities. To be sure, trade with the West has brought some tangible material pluses. Especially in the early 1970s it enabled East European regimes to raise living standards and thereby increase their popular support, without having to sacrifice investment growth. In Hungary, and particularly in Poland, Western imports were the *deus ex machina* that allowed the simultaneous development of consumption and production. To use Khrushchev's terminology, import-led growth at least temporarily facilitated the satisfaction of both 'metal' and 'meat eaters'.

But the 'Western option' has turned out to be far from a panacea for all East European ills. Whatever the early hopes for it as a substitute for structural reform, the whole Western connection has tended to exacerbate the problems it was meant to alleviate. The exigencies of international competition have made economic inefficiencies more costly and less bearable. In this way greater East–West interdependence has placed additional strains on already economically outdated traditional social compact production norms for factory workers and thereby on the relationship between rulers and ruled. More directly, imports of Western goods and values, as a consequence of greater contact, have fueled the development of consumer appetites and accelerated embryonic consumerist trends. Quite apart from the ideological implications involved, the combination of rising consumer expectations and anachronistic production norms has exacerbated the underlying problems created by the demands of intensive economic development. Perhaps the most tangible and penetrative linkage of all has been the pressures and constraints generated by world inflation. Rising import prices have been an important factor contributing to the revision of subsidy policies. With the exception of the GDR, all the northern tier states have been compelled recently to increase prices at a faster rate even at the risk of incurring public annoyance.

The ease or difficulty with which the various East European states have been able to handle and absorb external pressures has depended on a variety of factors of which the size and scope of involvement with the West has not necessarily been the most important. The speed, handling, and wider economic and political context of involvement have probably been more crucial. The relationship between regime and population and the leadership's reserves of credibility emerge as particularly important variables. Thus, although Hungary has been the most economically burdened by its Western connections, it has proved the most successful in adapting to the pressures of greater openness. By dint of its economic strength and tight political controls, the GDR has managed to withstand the considerable pressures generated by its greater contact with the West, though in the process domestic economic and political tensions have increased. As the least involved with capitalist countries, Czechoslovakia has not faced the same order of pressure; but one should not forget that the regime's wariness of involvement stems largely from its basic political insecurity. Poland's high-risk strategy of import-led boom has made what has long been an unstable polity particularly vulnerable. Neither in the case of Poland nor in that of the other northern tier states have external pressures per se created wholly new problems. What they have done is catalyze ongoing domestic developments and aggravate existing problems. In this indirect sense East–West interchange can be seen as exerting pressure on the relationship between rulers and ruled and thereby on the institutional network that has to sustain that relationship.

Rather than categorize the effects of East–West interdependence as either 'beneficial' or 'harmful', perhaps it is more useful to note that they have served to stretch the system at its most sensitive points – critical points already weakened by the strains of intensive growth. No doubt this general effect of involvement with the West has presented politicians with what must appear to be a wholly undesirable problem. Yet from the vantage point of the long-term development of these regimes, such pressures might be considered as positive. What is certain is that, while trade with the West may be reduced and redirected to Comecon and Third World countries, the domestic repercussions of the growth of East–West interdependence of the 1970s will be far more difficult to erase.

Notes: Chapter 8

1 John P. Hardt, 'Summary', in *East European Economies Post-Helsinki* (a compendium of papers submitted to the Joint Economic Committee, 95th Congress, 1st Session) (Washington, D.C.: US Government Printing Office, 1977), p. x.

2 See Sarah Meiklejohn Terry and Andrzej Korbonski, 'The Impact of External Economic Disturbances on the Internal Politics of Eastern Europe: The Polish and Hungarian Cases', in Egon Neuberger and Laura D'Andrea Tyson (eds), *The Impact of International Economic Disturbances on the Soviet Union and Eastern Europe: Transmission and Response* (New York: Pergamon Press, 1980), p. 377.

3 For this view see Connie M. Friesen, *The Political Economy of East–West Trade* (New York: Praeger, 1976), pp. 50–1: and Zbigniew M. Fallenbuchl, Egon Neuberger, and Laura D'Andrea Tyson, 'East European Reactions to International Commodity Inflation', in *East European Economies Post-Helsinki*, op. cit., p. 57.

4 Morris Bornstein, 'Economic Reform in Eastern Europe', in *East European Economies Post-Helsinki*, op. cit., pp. 129–30.

5 For data on deficits and debts, see Paul Marer, 'Economic Performance, Strategy, and Prospects in Eastern Europe', in *East European Economies Post-Helsinki*, op. cit., pp. 550–2; and Morris Bornstein, this volume, Chapter 3.

6 Joan Parpart Zoeter, 'Eastern Europe: The Growing Hard Currency Debt', in *East*

European Economies Post-Helsinki, op. cit., p. 1353; and Benedykt Askanas, Halina Askanas, Friedrich Levcik, 'East-West Payment Problems', in Friedrich Levcik (ed.), *International Economics – Comparisons and Interdependences: Festschrift for Franz Nemschak* (Vienna and London: Springer-Verlag, 1978), p. 326.

7 *Magyar Nemzet*, 25 January 1976, translated in US Joint Publications Research Service, *Translations on Eastern Europe: Political, Sociological, and Military Affairs* (hereafter *JPRS*), No. 1218 (23 March 1976), p. 6; Vladimir V. Kusin, *From Dubček to Charter 77: A Study of 'Normalization' in Czechoslovakia, 1968–1978* (Edinburgh: Q Press and New York: St. Martin's Press, 1978), p. 228; *Svět práce*, 18 February 1976, p. 2; and P. Harrison in *The Guardian*, 3 July 1979.

8 *Statistická ročenka ČSSR 1977* (Prague: SNTL, 1978), p. 344; and Hartmut Zimmermann, 'The GDR in the 1970's', *Problems of Communism*, Vol. 27, No. 2 (March–April 1978), p. 27.

9 On the problem of absenteeism, see Radio Free Europe (RFE), *Background Report (Hungary)*, 1979, No. 23, p. 17; David A. Andelman, *New York Times*, 4 February 1979; *Rocznik Statystyczny 1978* (Warsaw: Główny Urząd Statystyczny, 1978), pp. 48, 130; *Biuletyn Statystyczny*, 1979, No. 5, p. 13; *Statistická ročenka ČSSR 1977*, p. 343; and G. Fekete, *Népszabadság*, 14 March 1976, abstracted in *ABSEES*, Vol. 7, No. 3 (July 1976), p. 184. For figures on absenteeism in the US, see Janice Neipert Hedges, 'Unscheduled Absence from Work – An Update', *Monthly Labor Review*, Vol. 98, No. 8 (August 1975), pp. 37–8.

10 A. Melich, *Życie Warszawy*, 6 December 1978, p. 3.

11 Janos Kádár, *Társadalmi Szemle*, 1976, No. 3, cited in RFE, *Background Report (Hungary)*, 1976, No. 77, p. 3; and Wroblewski, *Polityka*, 30 September 1978, p. 5.

12 *Polityka*, 30 September 1978, p. 5, and 21 October 1978, p. 4; and K. Bossanyi, *Magyar Hirlap*, 9 March 1979, cited in RFE, *Hungarian Situation Report*, 1979, No. 6, p. 14.

13 *Rocznik Statystyczny 1978*, p. 49; *Statistická ročenka ČSSR 1977*, p. 343; A. Schnorbus, *Frankfurter Allgemeine Zeitung*, 28 September 1976, p. 10; and Richard Portes, 'Hungary: Economic Performance, Policy and Prospects', in *East European Economies Post-Helsinki*, op. cit., pp. 872, 793.

14 Julius Rezler, 'Recent Developments in the Hungarian Labor Market', *East European Quarterly*, Vol. 10, No. 2 (June 1976); I. Kemény, 'La classe ouvrière en Hongrie', in G. Mink and J. Rupnik (eds), *Structures Sociales en Europe de l'Est*, No. 2: *Transformations de la classe ouvrière*, Documentation française: Notes et Etudes Documentaires, 4511–12, 1979, p. 67; *Statistical Abstract of the United States* (Washington, D.C.: US Government Printing Office, 1978), p. 406.

15 See, for instance, Portes, op. cit., p. 782; and Alex Pravda, 'Some Aspects of the Czechoslovak Economic Reform and the Working Class in 1968', *Soviet Studies*, Vol. 25, No. 1 (July 1973), pp. 109–11.

16 See *Magyar Hirlap*, 10 October 1976, cited in Portes, op. cit., p. 794; RFE, *Hungarian Situation Report*, 1979, No. 11, pp. 4–5; *Tribuna*, 13 December 1972; and J. Urban, *Polityka*, 3 February 1979, p. 1.

17 E. W. Hayden, *Technology Transfer to Eastern Europe: US Corporate Experience* (New York: Praeger, 1976), pp. 48–9; and *Trybuna Ludu*, 7 June 1977.

18 *International Herald Tribune*, 7 June 1979. Official Hungarian figures for multiple job holding (5 percent of the working population) compare closely with American levels. See *Elet es Irodálom*, 20 June 1970; and S. C. Brown, 'Moonlighting Increased Sharply in 1977', *Monthly Labor Review*, Vol. 101, No. 1 (January 1978), pp. 27–8. For Poland, see G. Mink, 'Salaries et niveau de vie des ouvriers', in M. de Felice and G. Mink (eds), *Egalité et inegalités en Europe de l'Est*, Documentation française: Problèmes politiques et sociaux, No. 364, 1978, p. 27.

19 For instance, see L. Štrougal, *Rudé právo*, 14 April 1976; and P. Jaroszewicz, *Trybuna Ludu*, 20 January 1979, p. 3.

20 Jan Adam, 'Systems of Wage Regulation in the Soviet Bloc', *Soviet Studies*, Vol. 28, No. 1 (January 1976), pp. 93ff.; and Gert Leptin and Manfred Melzer, *Economic Reform in East German Industry* (Oxford: Oxford University Press, 1976), pp. 128–9.

21 On the problem of wage differentials and leveling tendencies, see Walter D. Connor, *Socialism, Politics and Equality* (New York: Columbia University Press, 1979), p. 231; J. Večerník, 'Problémy příjmu a životní úrovně v sociální diferenciaci' [Problems of income and living standards in social differentiation], in P. Machonin *et al.*,

Československá společnost (Bratislava: Epocha, 1969), pp. 298, 301; Portes, op. cit., p. 806; Mink, op. cit., p. 28; and *Práce a mzda*, 7 April 1974.

22 B. Blachnicki, 'Równość ekonomiczna w świadomośći pracowników przemysłu' [Economic equality in the consciousness of industrial workers], *Studia Socjologoczne*, 1977, No. 4, pp. 50–1; T. Kolosi, *Társadalmi Szemle*, 1979, No. 4, translated in *JPRS*, No. 1685 (25 May 1979), pp. 68–9.

23 David Granick, *Enterprise Guidance in Eastern Europe* (Princeton, N.J.: Princeton University Press, 1976), p. 246. For discussion of the wider significance of this issue, see András Nagy, this volume, Chapter 9.

24 Blachnicki, op. cit., pp. 141, 143–4; Horvath, *Valóság*, 1978, No. 12, translated in *JPRS*, No. 1643 (2 February 1979), p. 7; and *Hospodářské noviny*, 1972, No. 12, p. 6.

25 See Kolosi, op. cit., pp. 71–3; Blachnicki, op. cit., p. 148; and Horvath, op. cit., pp. 5, 10–11.

26 On 'penetrative' and 'reactive' linkages, see James N. Rosenau, 'Toward the Study of National–International Linkages', in James N. Rosenau (ed.), *Linkage Politics* (New York: Free Press, 1969), pp. 44, 63, cited by Sarah Meiklejohn Terry, 'External Influences on Political Change in Eastern Europe: A Framework for Analysis', in Jan F. Triska and Paul M. Cocks (eds), *Political Development in Eastern Europe* (New York: Praeger, 1977), p. 309.

27 See also R. V. Burks, 'The Political Hazards of Economic Reform', in *Reorientation and Commercial Relations of the Economies of Eastern Europe* (a compendium of papers submitted to the Joint Economic Committee, 93rd Congress, 2nd Session) (Washington, D.C.: US Government Printing Office, 1974), pp. 73–8.

28 For further discussion of the issue of increased permeability of boundaries, see William Zimmerman, this volume, Chapter 5.

29 William Zimmerman's study of Yugoslav migrant workers showed that basic value changes became marked only after two or three years abroad ('National-International Linkages in Yugoslavia: The Political Consequences of Openness', in Triska and Cocks (eds), op. cit., pp. 354–5.

30 *The Guardian*, 30 April 1979; *The Financial Times*, 18 April 1979.

31 Zimmermann, 'The GDR in the 1970's', op. cit., p. 38; *New York Times*, 6 April 1979; and J. L. Kerr, 'Hard-Currency Shops in Eastern Europe', in RFE, *Background Report (Eastern Europe)*, 1977, No. 211.

32 S. Terry, *The Sunday Times*, 29 January 1978; *The Guardian*, 6 April 1979; and W. Volkmer, 'East Germany: Dissenting Views during the Last Decade', in R. L. Tokes (ed.), *Opposition in Eastern Europe* (London: Macmillan, 1979), p. 119.

33 Cited by L. Colitt, *The Financial Times*, 1 December 1978.

34 *The Financial Times*, 25 April 1979; Zimmermann, 'The GDR in the 1970's', op. cit., pp. 38–9; and P. Gerold and G. Wippold, 'Aspects of Moral Development in the Process of Industrial Consumption', *Deutsche Zeitschrift für Philosophie*, Vol. 26, No. 11 (November 1978), translated in *JPRS*, No. 1659 (20 March 1979), pp. 23–4.

35 Jan Szczepański, 'Consumption under Socialism', *World Marxist Review*, Vol. 19, No. 11 (November 1976), p. 39, and 'Economics and Politics under Developed Socialism', *World Marxist Review*, Vol. 20, No. 3 (March 1977), p. 64.

36 For further discussion of the relationship between consumption and political stability, see Zvi Gitelman, this volume, Chapter 7; Bogdan Mieczkowski, 'The Relationship between Changes in Consumption and Politics in Poland', *Soviet Studies*, Vol. 30, No. 2 (April 1978), pp. 262–9; and Philip Hanson, 'Mieczkowski on Changes in Consumption and Politics in Poland: A Comment', *Soviet Studies*, Vol. 30, No. 4 (October 1978), pp. 553–6.

37 Bogdan Mieczkowski, *Personal and Social Consumption in Eastern Europe* (New York: Praeger, 1975), pp. 53–70; Szczepanski, op. cit., pp. 39–40.

38 Martin J. Kohn and Nicholas R. Lang, 'The Intra-CMEA Foreign Trade System: Major Price Changes, Little Reform', in *East European Economies Post-Helsinki*, op. cit., p. 141; and *Világgazadaság*, 22 December 1978, quoted in RFE, *Hungarian Situation Report*, 1979, No. 1, p. 2.

39 Fallenbuchl, Neuberger, Tyson, op. cit., p. 98.

40 Kádár, *Társadalmi Szemle*, 1976, No. 3, cited in RFE, *Background Report (Hungary)*, 1976, No. 77, p. 2. See also Csikos-Nagy, *Közgazdasági Szemle*, 1978, No. 1, quoted in RFE, *Hungarian Situation Report*, 1978, No. 3, p. 3. Compare Honecker, 'The Tasks of the Party during the Continued Implementation of the IX SED Congress Resolution',

Neues Deutschland, 18–19 February 1978, pp. 3–8, translated in *JPRS*, No. 1512 (14 March 1978), pp. 38–42.
41 *Statistical Yearbook 1965* (Budapest: Statistical Publishing House, 1965), p. 259, *Statistical Yearbook 1975* (Budapest: Statistical Publishing House, 1975), p. 361; *Rocznik Statystyczny 1976* (Warsaw: Główny Urząd Statystyczny, 1976), p. 390; Michael Keren, 'The Return of the Ancient Regime: the GDR in the 1970's', *East European Economies Post-Helsinki*, op. cit., p. 758. For a discussion of the roots of popular attitudes in Hungary, see Richard Portes, 'The Strategy and Tactics of Economic Decentralisation', *Soviet Studies*, Vol. 28, No. 4 (April 1972), p. 642.
42 Fallenbuchl, Neuberger, Tyson, op. cit., p. 75; Portes, op. cit., p. 782.
43 R. Angelusz, G. L. Nagy, R. Tardos, in *Szociologia*, 1978, No. 1, translated in *JPRS*, No. 1640 (26 January 1979), p. 63.
44 Fallenbuchl, Neuberger, Tyson, op. cit., pp. 80–1.
45 Honecker, op. cit., pp. 50–1; and Leptin and Melzer, *Economic Reform*, p. 140.
46 *Statistical Pocketbook of Hungary 1979* (Budapest: Statistical Publishing House, 1979), p. 169.
47 *Le Monde*, 15 November 1977.
48 For Polish workers' dissatisfaction with housing in 1975, see A. Wajda, 'Jedność społecznych i ekonomicznych celow polityki partii w wielkich zakładów pracy' [Unity of social and economic aims in party policy in large enterprises], in A. Łopatka, J. Błuszkowski, K. Konstański (eds), *Organizacje partyjne wielkich zakładów pracy* [Party organization in large enterprises] (Warsaw: Ksiażka i Wiedza, 1976), p. 69.
49 Wide-ranging discussion of these issues is to be found in Archie Brown and Jack Gray (eds), *Political Culture and Political Change in Communist States* (London: Macmillan, 1969). For East Germany, see John M. Starrels and Anita M. Mallinckrodt, *Politics in the German Democratic Republic* (New York: Praeger, 1975), Ch. 2.
50 Calls for improvement here have come from members of the Central Committee, such as M. Rakowski (see *Polityka*, 25 December 1976), ex-leaders of the party like Ochab (see *Labour Focus on Eastern Europe*, Vol. 2, No. 1 [March–April 1978], pp. 15–16), and leading dissidents (see J. Kuroń in *Le Monde*, 29 January 1977).
51 See William F. Robinson, *The Pattern of Reform in Hungary* (New York: Praeger, 1973), pp. 257–8; and Peter Toma and Ivan Volgyes, *Politics in Hungary* (San Francisco: W. H. Freeman, 1977), p. 63.
52 Robinson, op. cit., p. 268; Eberhard Schneider, *The German Democratic Republic* (London: Hurst, 1978), p. 44.
53 L. Héthy and C. Máko, 'Workers' Participation and the Socialist Enterprise: A Hungarian Case Study' (Budapest: Institute of Sociology, 1978; mimeo), p. 30.
54 For calls for independent unions, see *Labour Focus on Eastern Europe*, Vol. 2, No. 3 (July–August 1978), pp. 21–3.
55 M. Hirszowicz and W. Morawski, *Z badań nad społecznym uczestnictwem w organizacji przemysłowej* [Research on social participation in industrial organizations] (Warsaw: Ksiażka i Wiedza, 1967), p. 241.
56 Héthy and Máko, op. cit., p. 18.
57 For a Polish argument advocating workers' councils, see Stanisław Gebethner's chapter in this volume.
58 For workers' councils in the 1956 and 1968 periods, see A. Babeau, *Les conseils ouvriers en Pologne* (Paris: Armand Colin, 1960); Bill Lomax, *Hungary 1956* (London: Allison and Busby, 1976); and Alex Pravda, 'Workers' Participation in Czechoslovakia, 1968–69', *Canadian Slavonic Papers*, Vol. 19, No. 3 (September 1977), pp. 312–34.

Part Four

East European Policy Responses

Chapter 9

Growth and Trade: The Hungarian Case

ANDRÁS NAGY

I Characteristics of Hungarian Economic Growth

The economic growth of Hungary has proceeded at a medium rate as compared to that of both the other centrally planned economies and the market economies of Europe. Table 9.1 demonstrates the increase in the production and use of national income in the period 1950–77.

Table 9.1 *Hungary: Average Annual Growth Rates of the Production and Use of the National Income, 1950–77*
(Percent)

	1951–60	1961–70	1971–77
National income	5.8	5.4	6.0
By sector of production:			
Industry	8.6	7.2	7.2
Agriculture	0.6	–0.1	2.1
By use:			
Household consumption	5.4	4.6	4.1
Accumulation of fixed assets	14.9	9.8	9.0^a

^{a}For the period 1971–75.
Source: *Népgazdasági mérlegek 1970–1977* [National account balances 1970–1977] (Budapest: KSH, 1978).

As the table shows, considerable efforts have been made to accelerate economic growth: the increase in the national income was substantially outstripped by the rate of accumulation of fixed assets, while the increase in the consumption of the population dropped markedly behind that rate. The growth of national income reached its peak value in the 1970s due to a rise in agricultural production, but the rate of increase of national income produced by industry has not changed from that of the preceding decade.

Regarding the growth rate of national income, development has been faster in Bulgaria, Romania, and Poland than in Hungary, while in the German Democratic Republic (GDR) and Czechoslovakia it has been slower. Until 1970 economic growth was faster in the Soviet Union than in Hungary, but since then the Hungarian growth rate has been more rapid.

Translated from the Hungarian by Pál Félix.

The growth rate of Hungary is relatively high compared to that of advanced market economies. Considering the relatively favorable market conditions of the period 1961–73 and disregarding the recession of 1974–75, the growth rates of the gross domestic product (GDP) may be ranked as in Table 9.2. Thus, in the thirteen years prior to the 1974 price explosion, of the countries in Table 9.2 only the growth indicators of Japan and two rapidly developing South European market economies had surpassed that of Hungary.

Table 9.2   *Average Annual Growth Rate of the Gross Domestic Product, Selected Countries, 1961–73*
(Percent)

Japan	10.0
Greece	7.5
Spain	7.1
Hungary	5.7
France	5.7
Netherlands	5.4
Finland	5.0
Belgium	5.0
Italy	4.9
Austria	4.9
Norway	4.7
Federal Republic of Germany	4.6
United States	4.4
Sweden	3.8
United Kingdom	2.9

Source: United Nations, *National Accounts Statistics,* and Organization for Economic Cooperation and Development (OECD), *Main Economic Indicators.*

Since the reform of economic management in 1968, the rate of growth of productivity has shown a marked improvement in Hungary. (See Table 9.3.) In spite of this, the increase in productivity approximates only the average international standard.

As demonstrated by the above data, the trend in the development of productivity in industry and agriculture is considerably different from the growth of national income produced in these sectors. Because of the migration of the labor force from agriculture to industry, productivity

Table 9.3   *Hungary: Average Annual Rate of Growth of Productivity, 1961–70 and 1968–75*
(Percent)

	1961–70	*1968–75*
Gross National Product	4.2	5.5
Industry	3.7	5.8
Agriculture	4.7	5.5

Source: Tibor Erdős, 'Gazdasági növekedésünk üteme és gazdasági fejlődésünk egyensulyi problémái' [The rate of economic growth and equilibrium problems of economic development in Hungary] (Budapest: MTA, Közgazdaságtudományi Intézet, 1978; manuscript).

increase in agriculture is considerably faster than the rise of agricultural production. The situation in industry is reversed, as the increase of productivity lags behind that of production. As a result, there is hardly any difference in productivity between the two main sectors of the economy, while the rate of growth of industrial production by far surpasses that of agriculture.

Regarding the problem of productivity, the ranking of the centrally planned economies is similar to that outlined in respect to the growth of national incomes. Comparison with market economies is rendered difficult because adequate employment data are available only on industry. Table 9.4 shows the ranking of industrial productivity.

Table 9.4   *Annual Growth Rate of Industrial Productivity, Selected Countries, Selected Periods*

Country	Period	Percent
Japan	1960–76	7.6
Netherlands	1960–76	7.6
Greece	1962–76	6.7
Hungary	1960–75	5.0
Federal Republic of Germany	1960–76	4.9
Sweden	1960–76	4.5
Italy	1961–76	4.2

Source: Same as Tables 9.2 and 9.3.

With respect to the growth of industrial productivity, Hungary's advantage is less than in increase of output. Industrial productivity growth in the Netherlands is strikingly faster, while at the same time her GDP rises only a little more slowly than that of Hungary. In the Federal Republic of Germany and Sweden industrial productivity develops almost at the same rate as that of Hungarian industry, whereas their increase in GDP is substantially slower. Furthermore, Hungarian productivity growth is less than might be expected in view of the fact that a country at a medium level of economic development should be able to raise productivity considerably by adopting more up-to-date technologies from more advanced countries.[1]

The rate of growth in productivity is becoming increasingly the determinant of growth in production since in Hungary, too, numerical increase of the work force as a source of economic growth has been by and large exhausted. Between 1950 and 1960 about 60 percent of the rise of industrial production originated from the increase of employment. Moreover, though the outflow of manpower from agriculture will be quite considerable in the ten or twenty years to come, a growing part of it will be absorbed by the services sector.

The medium rate of increase in production and productivity has not been due to the low level of, or the slow increase in, investments. Quite the contrary! As proved by Table 9.1, the growth of the part of national income used for accumulation of fixed assets has been rapid. As a result, the share of investments in the GNP has shown a markedly rising tendency (Table 9.5).

194   *East–West Relations and the Future of Eastern Europe*

Thus the rate of investment has reached a relatively high level. The share of industrial investments had been outstandingly high in the 1950s, while that of agricultural investments had been extremely low. This marked difference has gradually disappeared. In spite of the increase of the

Table 9.5 *Hungary: Average Annual Investment Rates, Incremental Capital/Output Ratios, and Incremental Capital/Productivity Ratios, 1951–60, 1961–70, and 1968–75*
(Percent)

	1951–60	*1961–70*	*1968–75*
Rate of investment[a]			
GNP	20.9	25.7	29.6
Industry	30.8	26.6	26.4
Agriculture	5.0	16.5	24.9
Incremental capital/output ratio			
GNP	3.67	4.76	4.77
Industry	3.58	3.91	3.88
Agriculture	8.33	18.33	15.66
Incremental capital/productivity ratio			
GNP	4.10	6.12	5.38
Industry	9.33	7.19	4.55
Agriculture	1.47	3.51	4.53

[a]Fixed investment in plant and equipment (including unfinished investment) as a percentage of value added.
Source: Data of the National Planning Board.

investment rate, the rate of growth of production had decreased in the 1960s, and this was reflected in the strong increase of the incremental capital/output ratio. After the introduction of the economic reform, both the investment rate and production increased. Thus the incremental capital/output ratio (the number of additional units of capital per one additional unit of output) leveled off, but it still did not decrease. A definite improvement was experienced, however, in the incremental capital/productivity ratio (the percentage increase in capital per 1 percent increase in productivity). This ratio started to decrease for the national economy as a whole and very significantly in industry. The difference between the incremental capital ratios in the development of industry and agriculture is conspicuous. Investment intensity of increasing agricultural *production* is almost four times that in industry (15.66 vs. 3.88), yet virtually the same capital investment is needed in agriculture to raise *productivity*. The capital intensity involved in raising productivity shows a reverse tendency: it has diminished rapidly in industry (from 9.33 to 4.55) and increased strongly in agriculture (from 1.47 to 4.53), until the great difference between the two has disappeared.

The rapid increase in the rate and share of investments has not brought about a substantial acceleration of economic growth. Therefore one must reject the theory that faster growth or technological progress was restricted by the low level or slow increase of investments. On the contrary, while all sectors are complaining of shortage of capital, the Hungarian economy shows signs of overinvestment tendencies, and in many fields of the economy the utilization of capacities is impeded by labor shortage. The deterioration of capital effectiveness is reflected by the fact that the capital/output ratio has risen significantly in the producing sectors and decreased in services.[2] The opposite tendencies would obviously have been more advantageous.

Economic journals have published many criticisms of the insufficient preparatory work preceding investment; high cost and delay in actual realization; a structure of investment not based on sound economic criteria; and ambitious attempts to invest beyond the available resources. Among such conditions, an even faster increase of investments and, consequently, a still slower increase in consumption would obviously have brought about socially inadmissible tensions. It may be stated on the strength of experiences gained so far that the increase of the investment ratio does not accelerate the rise of consumption. Moreover, further increase in the investment ratio would presumably trigger a reverse effect on consumption.

II The Role of Foreign Trade

Due to the limitations of her internal market, Hungary, a small country in both area and population, is highly dependent on international trade. The share of foreign trade in the gross national output is relatively large and shows a definite upward tendency (see Table 9.6).

Table 9.6 *Hungary: The Share of Foreign Trade and National Income in Gross National Output,[a] 1965, 1970, 1975, 1977*
(Percent)

Year	Exports	Imports	National Income
1965	14.2	14.6	40.2
1970	14.7	15.8	40.4
1975	18.9	22.3	37.5
1977	18.7	20.7	37.1

[a]Gross national ouptut is the total value of production, as shown in input–output tables, including all intermediate production.
Source: Népgazdasági mérlegek 1969–1972 and *Népgazdasági mérlegek 1970–1977* [National account balances 1969–1972 and National account balances 1970–1977] (Budapest: KSH, 1973 and 1978).

The share of imports in the gross national output has risen from 14.6 percent to 20.7 percent in the course of the past twelve years. At present it is more than half as much as the share of national income in gross national output (20.7 vs. 37.1 percent).[3]

The share of foreign trade in gross national output is often regarded as an index indicating the open character of an economy. To my mind this is an unfounded, or one-sided, oversimplified view. The openness of an economy has a qualitative character that cannot be measured simply by such quantities as aggregate shares. Although a relatively large part of goods consumed have been imported and of goods produced have been exported, an economy may remain quite isolated from the world market and the advantages of the international division of labor; and the dynamics and structure of economic development may be elaborated quite independently. It is true, however, that, despite this seclusion, the elimination of externally generated effects is the more difficult the higher the share of foreign trade in production and consumption. Part of Hungary's developmental difficulties occur because the economy is less open qualitatively than would seem justified by the quantitative share of foreign trade.

By means of the input–output balances prepared since 1959, the development of the import intensity of production, as well as of the different final uses, may be surveyed (Tables 9.7 and 9.8).

Table 9.7   *Hungary: Net Import Content of Domestic Use^a of Goods and Services, 1959, 1965, 1970, and 1975*
(Forints of Net Import Content per 100 Forints of Domestic Use)

	1959	1965	1970	1975
Total imports	14.9	17.2	24.3	32.2
Ruble imports[b]	9.0	11.2	12.5	15.9
Dollar imports[b]	5.9	6.0	11.8	16.3

^aImports – import content of exports / Domestic use.

^bHungarian statistics classify as ruble- and dollar-trade, trade conducted in transferable rubles and in convertible currencies, respectively, regardless of the countries with which the transaction was concluded.

Source: Calculation based on Hungarian input–output tables in *A magyar népgazdaság ágazati kapcsolati mérlegei 1959–1971* (Budapest: KSH, 1973).

Import intensity of domestic use has increased more than twofold in the period under review. Moreover, partly due to price rises, it increased by about one-third in the period 1970–75. Within total imports the share of dollar imports has increased from 40 to more than 50 percent. This change came about partly because world market prices rose faster than those applied within the CMEA. Moreover, the readiness of supply decreased in the centrally planned economies, particularly of certain raw materials, while at the same time the structure of Hungarian demand also did not fully conform to their offers and supplies.

Table 9.8 presents data on the direct import content and the total import content of Hungarian intermediate and final output in 1970 and 1975. The direct import content is considerably less than the direct content, because imports consist overwhelmingly of materials which reach final utilization in the Hungarian economy only after processing by Hungarian industry. This is especially true of imports paid for in convertible currency. For example, in 1975 in the case of final output for domestic use (row 2 of Table 9.8), the direct import content for ruble-area imports (6.8) was 42.8 percent of total import content (15.9), while the corresponding ratio for convertible-currency imports was 26.4 percent (4.3:16.3). Furthermore, in 1975 for total imports the direct import content of production was twice as

Table 9.8 *Hungary: Import Intensity of Intermediate and Final Uses of Output, 1970 and 1975* (Forints of Import Content per 100 Forints of Output, Current Prices)

	Direct Import Content						Total Import Content					
	Ruble Imports		Dollar Imports		Total Imports		Ruble Imports		Dollar Imports		Total Imports	
	1970	1975	1970	1975	1970	1975	1970	1975	1970	1975	1970	1975
Intermediate productive use	4.8	6.5	5.5	8.7	10.3	15.2	10.0	12.5	11.0	17.2	21.0	29.6
Final output												
Domestic use	5.5	6.8	3.4	4.3	8.9	11.1	12.5	15.9	11.8	16.3	24.3	32.2
Consumption	2.8	4.4	2.6	2.7	5.4	7.1	9.6	13.2	11.3	16.0	21.0	29.2
Investment	10.3	12.5	5.5	8.3	15.8	20.8	17.6	21.4	12.4	16.7	30.0	38.1
Exports							12.3	14.5	13.1	19.6	25.4	34.1
Ruble exports							12.4	15.1	13.3	19.3	25.7	34.4
Dollar exports							12.3	13.9	12.8	19.9	25.1	33.8

Source: Same as for Table 9.7.

high as that of consumption (15.2 vs. 7.1 in column 6), while that of investment was nearly three times as high (20.8 vs. 7.1).

Referring also to data for 1959, one finds that the total (ruble plus convertible currency) direct import content of Hungarian output rose 138 percent (from 6.5 percent to 15.2 percent) between 1959 and 1975, while there was an even more striking threefold increase in the case of imports for convertible currency.

Total import content incorporated in earlier stages of production amounts to almost double the direct import content. The 29.6 percent total import content of *productive use* (the last figure in row 1 of Table 9.8) should not be considered low. It indicates that the overwhelming part of imports is used not directly but through production for the aims of domestic and export utilization.

The cumulative import content of *consumption* (row 3 of the table) is rather high in comparison to its direct import content, adding up to quadruple the latter (29.2 vs. 7.1). Approximately 60 percent of *indirect* imports originate from hard-currency imports. But direct convertible-currency consumer goods imports were negligible (2.7) in 1975, as in 1970 (2.6). *Direct* and *total* import content of investments, too, is considerably higher than that of consumption whereas its *indirect* import content is only about three-fourths as great.[4]. Thus imports serve the aims of investments not only to a *greater extent*, but also much *more directly* than the objectives of consumption. Moreover, this difference is growing in the course of time.

Total import content of *exports* has risen rapidly and reached 34.1 percent by 1975. In 1959 the import content of 100 forints worth of exports was merely 20 forints, including 11.5 for ruble-area imports and 8.5 for dollar-area imports. Subsequently, mostly in the 1970s, the hard-currency import content rose 130 percent (from 8.5 to 19.6), while ruble import content increased by merely 26 percent (from 11.5 to 15.1). Within the indirect import content of exports, the share of convertible currency imports has been considerably higher than that of ruble imports each year since 1970. There is no substantial difference in the import content of the exports to different currency areas. As column 8 of Table 9.8 shows, it is unwarranted to assume that the share of ruble imports is higher in the total import content of exports to the countries of centrally planned economies than in exports to the market economies. For both kinds of exports, the share of dollar imports is higher and shows a tendency to increase.

The relatively high indirect import content of exports points to the importance of a uniform evaluation of foreign exchange receipts from exports and foreign exchange expenditures on imports. If this is not the case – and unfortunately it is not guaranteed in Hungary – there is a great risk that foreign exchange costs of imported materials are recovered insufficiently, or not at all, through foreign exchange receipts from exports and/or that the foreign exchange returns of value added domestically may be rather low.

Before tackling the problem of export structures and the significance of exports, one should examine the *intersectoral* specialization of the Hungarian economy. According to calculations by M. Tardos,[5] there are three net-importer sectors: mining, chemical industry, and electric energy industry. For these three, net imports are equal to a very substantial part of domestic production (22 and 38 percent, respectively, in the case of the first two). Though in all other sectors the value of exports has surpassed that of imports, the extent of specialization so measured is not considerable. For example, in agriculture and in the food industry it amounts to 7 and 9 percent, respectively, in engineering to 4 percent, and in light industry to a mere 1 percent. Imports originating from intersectoral commodity exchange make up 21 percent of total imports. This is a much lower ratio than the equivalent figure in the developed industrialized countries (58 percent in the US, 40 percent in Sweden, 36 percent in the Federal Republic of Germany and Britain).

As a result, *intrasectoral* exchange has reached relatively high proportions in Hungary but is limited mainly to the exchange of finished products. Exchange of semifinished products, spare parts, and component parts remains relatively small. Yet this would be the very field where, in the case of a small country, the benefits of the international division of labor should make themselves felt rather conspicuously. Moreover, this is the field that has undergone the most dynamic development in trade among the advanced industrial countries.

Tables 9.9 and 9.10 demonstrate the changes in the sectoral structure of foreign trade, broken down according to ruble- and dollar-trade. These data reflect both the structural changes over the past ten years and the structural differences between intra-CMEA trade and trade with market economies.

The bulk of imports in mining, metallurgy, and electric energy originates from the socialist countries, whereas the share of agricultural and food imports is extraordinarily low and is showing a definite downward trend. The share of machinery imports is markedly high and reflects a strong upward trend, amounting to 44 percent of Hungarian ruble imports in 1977. It is quite remarkable that the share of machinery imports from hard-currency markets has been much smaller, totaling only 28 percent in 1977. By contrast, chemical products compose a quarter of the imports from hard-currency areas, twice the size of the proportion of chemical products in Hungary's ruble imports. The overwhelming part of agricultural imports, too, comes from convertible-currency markets.

Hungarian exports to CMEA countries are dominated by machines, and their share has risen considerably, adding up to 55 percent in 1977. On the other hand, the share of machinery in exports to market economies is relatively low, only about one-third the size of the proportion exported to the CMEA countries. Agricultural goods, food, and metallurgical products, that is, mainly primary goods, represented about half of Hungarian exports to hard-currency markets in 1977, while the other half was shared by the commodities of the manufacturing industries. The respective shares in the ruble exports were 20 and 80 percent in 1977.

The last column of Table 9.10 displays a sectoral breakdown of total investments of the ten years under review in order to compare them with the changes in foreign trade structure. No close correlation could be found among them. Thus, in investment, among all branches of manufacturing

Table 9.9   Structure of Hungarian Imports and Cumulative Trade Balances by Branches, 1968, 1972, 1977

Branch	Ruble-Area Imports (Percent)			Dollar-Area Imports (Percent)			Cumulative Total of Balances 1968–77 (Million Forints)	
	1968	1972	1977	1968	1972	1977	Ruble Area	Dollar Area
Mining	12.0	10.8	15.3	1.4	1.6	3.9	−215	−633
Metallurgy	11.8	14.0	10.7	13.1	6.1	7.2	−1,389	+843
Chemical industry	12.2	10.9	12.3	25.3	24.6	25.1	−519	−3,049
Machinery	37.2	43.8	44.1	21.4	28.9	28.1	+1,427	−1,609
Light industry	13.4	10.8	9.2	17.9	14.6	13.9	+611	−280
Food and agriculture	9.0	4.6	3.7	18.9	21.7	19.8	+221	+1,972
Other	4.4	5.1	4.7	2.0	2.5	2.0	−558	−106
Total	100.0	100.0	100.0	100.0	100.0	100.0	−422	−2,862

Sources: Külkereskedelmi statisztikai évkönyv 1977 [Yearbook of foreign trade statistics 1977] (Budapest: KSH, 1978), pp. 62–3.

Table 9.10 Structure of Hungarian Exports and Cumulative Investments by Branches, 1968, 1972, 1977
(Percent)

Branch	Ruble-Area Exports			Dollar-Area Exports			Cumulative Investments,
	1968	1972	1977	1968	1972	1977	1968–77
Mining	1.8	1.5	1.5	0.4	0.5	0.2	7.7
Metallurgy	5.0	5.2	4.2	13.6	17.5	13.2	5.9
Chemical industry	9.8	10.0	8.7	10.8	7.8	14.1	13.1
Machinery	50.1	47.8	55.1	17.7	16.0	20.3	12.3
Light industry	15.3	14.8	12.2	19.6	17.2	13.7	7.9
Food and agriculture	16.2	17.5	15.0	34.8	38.9	34.4	37.5
Other	1.8	3.2	3.3	2.1	2.1	4.1	15.6
Total	100.0	100.0	100.0	100.0	100.0	100.0	100.0

Sources: Same as Table 9.9.

the highest share has been that of the chemical industry. Despite this fact, the share of chemical products has not decreased in imports and has not increased in exports either, so that actually such investments cannot be regarded either as of import-substituting or of export-oriented character. The last two columns of Table 9.9 list the ten-year cumulative balances of trade of the sectors. The trade deficit of the chemical industry has been higher than that of total trade. If calculated excluding the chemical industry, foreign trade shows a considerable export surplus. The trade deficit of the chemical industry has been considerably increased because the deterioration of the terms of trade has been the strongest in this commodity group.[6] Investment in Hungary has been oriented toward the production of lowest-value basic chemical goods, artificial fertilizers, and insecticides, whereas effective substances of higher value have to be imported to an ever-increasing extent.

Incidentally, such a high rate of development of the chemical industry is somewhat questionable in the case of Hungary because it is a very capital- and import-intensive venture, yet requires little highly qualified skilled work. According to international data, capital intensity per person in the petrochemical industry is twelve times, and in other fields of chemical production four times, as great as in engineering, for instance.[7] Owing to the high capital intensity of the chemical industry, the size of competitive output is beyond the absorptive capacity of the Hungarian market. Therefore import-substituting development that does not increase exports significantly is to be regarded as particularly uneconomical.

As illustrated by data of the cumulative trade balances in convertible currencies, 70 percent of the surplus originated from the exports of agricultural and food products and 30 percent from the export of metallurgical products. The import surplus of all the other branches was covered by these two branches as well as by indebtedness. The chemical industry was responsible for 54 percent of import surplus and engineering for 28 percent of it. Regarding ruble imports, the cumulative deficit of metallurgy was the highest, adding up to 52 percent of the total deficit. The most significant export surplus came from engineering products, while the surplus of light industry ranked second.

The Economic Commission for Europe has provided a significant analysis of the product structure of East–West trade.[8] In the analysis trade was grouped according to the intensity of production factors used, on the basis of a detailed breakdown of products (SITC 5 digits). Four degrees of factor intensity were distinguished: (A) natural resource-intensive products; (B_1) capital-intensive products; (B_2) labor-intensive products; (C) research-intensive and technologically advanced products.

As Table 9.11 shows, technologically advanced products prevail in eastward flows, adding up to nearly half of the imports of the East European countries, whereas natural resource-intensive products predominate in their exports. It is in this respect that balances show the greatest difference. The centrally planned economies dispose of an export surplus exclusively in natural resource-intensive products. In contrast, research-intensive products predominate in the export surplus of the industrially developed countries. While in the 1960s the balances of the two product groups were by and large in a state of equilibrium, by the mid-1970s the export surplus of Eastern natural resource-intensive products covered only about half of the import surplus of trade in research-intensive products. The great efforts of the centrally planned economies in industrialization, as well as in research and development, and particularly their efforts to develop engineering, have not achieved the expected results in East–West trade. The rise of the ratio of technologically advanced products in exports from 9 to 12 percent has not been proportionate to their shares in either the production structure or investments.

Table 9.11   *Commodity Composition by Factor-Intensity of East–West Trade*

Commodity Categories	1965–69	1973–77	Average Annual Growth Rate (Percent) 1965–69 to 1973–77
	Percentage of Total		
East European imports			
A	23	19	19
B_1	12	19	29
B_2	17	16	21
C	48	46	22
East European exports			
A	64	53	15
B_1	15	20	22
B_2	12	15	21
C	9	12	22
	Million Dollars[a]		
Trade balance			
A	–1,728	–4,374	
B_1	–93	+1,092	
B_2	+217	+1,023	
C	+1,643	+8,226	
Total	+39	+5,967	

[a]A negative sign indicates Western import surplus, and a positive sign indicates Western export surplus.

Source: United Nations, Economic Commission for Europe, *Economic Bulletin for Europe*, Vol. 30, No. 1 (New York, 1978), p. 100.

As compared to the trade structure expected on the basis of the distribution of productive factors, the share in imports of natural resource-intensive products seems high in the centrally planned economies, whereas the share in exports of labor-intensive products in westward flows is relatively small. The first is due presumably to the insufficient development of basic material extraction and agricultural production and/or to the fact that some Eastern countries buy industrial goods in the West in exchange for raw materials and food, while others have to import raw materials and food from Western countries. By various restrictions, some Western countries limit imports from the East of traditional labor-intensive products of the light industries. But this in itself does not explain why their share amounts merely to 12 to 15 percent. Undoubtedly the neglect of export-oriented development and deficiencies in competitiveness of products and marketing activities have an important part in this too.

On the other hand, a striking feature has been the high and steadily increasing share of capital-intensive industrial exports in westward flows. This reflects a characteristic of the industrialization of centrally planned economies, that is, highly capital-intensive investments in metallurgy, oil processing, and heavy chemical industry had top priority. Exports of such goods are hit by import restrictions in Western markets, as well as by quality and marketing problems, to a lesser extent than in the case of consumer goods or engineering products.

Despite the remarkable price rises in raw materials, the trade of natural resource-intensive products has shown the slowest increase in both directions, and the rise of raw material exports in westward flows seems to be especially slow. The fastest increase has been achieved in capital-intensive imports from the West: 29 percent annually on an average between the two periods. The strong increase of import surplus of the centrally planned economies has been due first and foremost to the growing import of research- and capital-intensive products.

III   Cyclical Growth and Trade

In Hungary, some of the indices related to economic growth reflect a high degree of stability. For instance, annual growth rates of the consumption of the population show little fluctuation. Other parts of the indices, however, reflect considerable fluctuation, such as annual growth rates of investments and foreign trade.

Figure 9.1 clearly demonstrates that the annual increase in accumulation and imports experiences much greater fluctuations than growth of exports, the development of the first two running almost entirely parallel. There has not been a single year when changes in the growth rate of investments went into another direction than that of imports. Two four-year cycles can be detected in the period under review, the trough years being in 1968, 1972, and 1976, and the peak years in 1970 and 1974.

The trade balance and the growth rates of imports in the overwhelming majority of cases moved in opposite directions until 1974. If growth rates of imports and accumulation have increased, the trade balance and the growth rate of exports have decreased, and vice versa. Scarcely was there a year when the changes in the trade balance and exports' growth rates were not of the same direction. However, since the peak year of 1974 this rule seems to have changed somewhat, and the changes of growth rates have assumed a one-way character. This is presumably only a transitory anomaly connected with the peculiarly low price rises of Hungarian exports, on the one hand, and, on the other, with difficulties of selling on the capitalist markets, which were in recession in the mid-1970s.

Recently research results of great interest have been published in Hungary concerning the cyclical development of centrally planned

Figure 9.1   *Growth Rates of Foreign Trade, Net Accumulation, and Trade Balance Changes, 1965–71.*

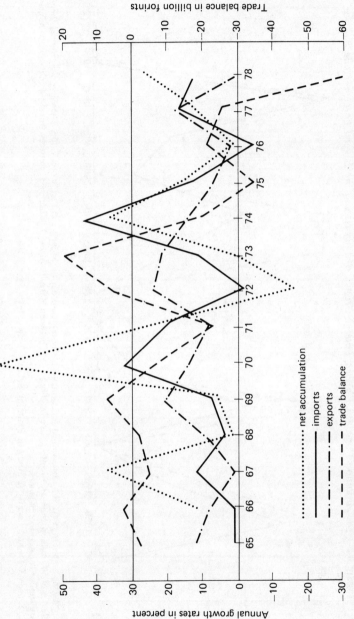

Sources: Külkereskedelmi statisztikai évkönyv, 1966–72 [Yearbook of foreign trade statistics, 1966–72] (Budapest: **KSH**, 1966–72); *Népgazdasági mérlegek 1970–1977* [National account balances 1970–1977] (Budapest: **KSH**, 1978), pp. 31 and 70–7; *Statisztikai havi közlemények* [Monthly bulletin of statistics], 1979, No. 1, p. 65.

Figure 9.2   *The Ambition Curve for Planned Rate of Growth of Imports and the Lagged Foreign Trade Balance*[a]

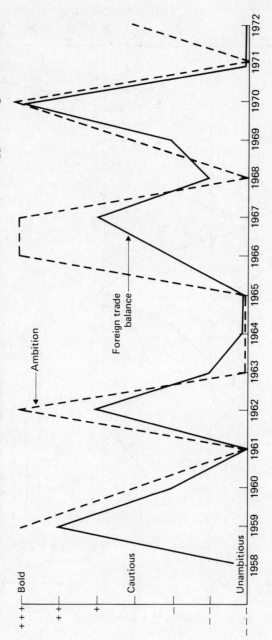

[a]As the ambition curve is a three-valued function, we could not consider the balances at their exact value. Therefore we grouped them by classes of 500 million domestic forints: above 1 billion: +++; between 500 million and 1 billion: ++; between 0 and 500 million: +. The classes are similar for negative balances.

Source: Gács and Lackó, 'A Study of Planning Behavior', op. cit. (n. 9), p. 110.

economies.[9] On the basis of a survey of the period 1958–72, Gács and Lackó pointed out convincingly that the trade balance has a considerable influence on the economic development and foreign trade plans of the subsequent year. If the balance improves, the plans become more ambitious (bolder); if it deteriorates, the ambitiousness of the plans decreases.[10] Naturally plans reflect the restrictive or more permissive character of all the other tools of economic policy, such as credit policy, income and fiscal policy, the licensing and subsidizing systems of foreign trade, the budget, etc. As an example, we are reproducing a diagram on the connection of change of trade balance to annual import plans. The import ambitions and the size of balance one year earlier are illustrated in a common set of coordinates in Figure 9.2, as published by the authors.

As the diagram shows, imports react directly to the change of the trade balance. If the balance deteriorates from one year to the other, import plans for the next year are set lower so that the balance can thus be regained. If this succeeds and the balance improves, import plans become more ambitious. A more liberal policy leads to the deterioration of the trade balance within a couple of years or so, and the cycle starts over again. A similar cycle with a contrary sign appears in the course of examining the export ambition curve, and there emerges the pattern of the planning cycle:

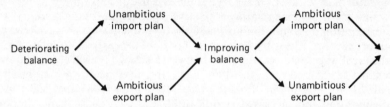

Gács and Lackó have emphasized that the changes in the trade balance affect not only the ambitiousness of foreign trade plans but the boldness of investments as well. However, this influence obviously manifests itself in the reverse way too. The trade balance is improved or worsened, respectively, under the influence of a more permissive or more restrictive investment policy. Thus, in addition to the changes of the import plan, the investment plan might also be plotted with an identical direction in the above pattern. These mutually reinforcing effects compel the authorities to make periodic changes in economic policy, introducing a cyclical rhythm into the economy.

It would be seriously mistaken to suppose that the simultaneous movement of investments and import growth originated from the fluctuations of imported capital goods. The fluctuation of investments here, too, naturally has a major effect. However, since capital goods compose only about one-fifth of imports, this in itself could not seriously influence the movement of total imports. Rather, the same expansionary factors that cause imports to soar are also at the root of the sudden rise in investment. Therefore, there is a common reason to curb the increases in imports and in investment.

In his work cited above, Tamás Bauer succeeded in demonstrating the regularity of investment cycles in all centrally planned European economies. Such cycles are initiated by a simultaneous launching of a great number of investment projects followed by a sharp increase in investment outlays, which may surpass the investment potentialities. The tension created by the shortage of investment capacities and delay in putting plants into operation results in disproportions in the utilization of national income, which then bring about a radical turn in economic policies. Planners have to put a brake on the increase of investments, and in some cases even approved investment projects have to be curtailed. When the tension caused by the overspending on investments and by the shortage of capacities slackens, the cycle starts again.

The buoyancy (or even overstraining) of investment activities naturally affects all spheres of economic life. Demands for materials, import requirements, overtime work, and wages paid all increase. Investment drains off some commodities destined for export or consumption. As a result the utilization of the national income undergoes a structural change: the more the ratio of investments is increased, the greater the drop in the ratio of consumption and/or the increase of the trade deficit (or the decrease of the surplus). Bauer distinguishes 'consumption-symmetrical' and 'foreign trade-symmetrical' cycles according to which component suffers as the share of accumulation grows. In the first case, the increase in the ratio of investments is realized at the expense of consumption while the foreign trade balance retains its relative equilibrium. In the second case, consumption does not diminish, and the investment surplus is covered by import surplus. Thus, the investment boom of the early 1950s in Hungary when real wages had decreased for two years was of a typical consumption-symmetric character. On the other hand, the investment wave in the first half of the 1970s in Poland was foreign trade-symmetrical since consumption too increased significantly, and as a consequence import deficits rose quickly.

It is often asked: What is the main or underlying cause of the cyclical movement of centrally planned economies?[11] And often the question is put in the following way: Is it the fluctuation of the investment cycle which brings about the cyclical changes of foreign trade? Or is it the greatly increased trade deficit which restricts the further growth of investment? Or could it be an unexpected export surplus resulting in complacency which triggers an investment boom? I tend to agree with those who do not want to choose among these alternatives, but instead search deeper for the motifs of cyclical movements and discover the basic cause in the underlying motifs constantly reproducing an economy of shortage.[12] Kornai traces shortage symptoms embracing almost all spheres of the economy back first of all to the phenomenon termed 'soft budget constraints'. This term refers to expenditures of enterprises that are not strictly constrained by their receipts because their investments or costs may transgress the limits covered by their receipts without serious risks, since they may rely on central support. This basically unrestricted nature of enterprise demand creates tensions in the field of material supply, in the market of investment goods as well as in foreign trade, which necessarily swing economic development away from a smooth trend and reproduce a cyclical rhythm of growth.

The role of foreign trade in cyclical changes may vary considerably, depending on expectations concerning the balance of trade. If equilibrium is maintained over the medium term, but an import surplus for investment purposes in a shorter period is allowed, economic policy may become an important factor of fluctuation. However, if a yearly equilibrium of the trade balance is sought, then the turning points of the cycle will be determined only by the constraints of investment capacities, labor force, and consumers' markets. On the other hand, a deterioration of the balance of trade may ensue not only because of the investment cycle but also as a result of the deterioration of the terms of trade. This happened in Hungary in the mid-1970s. Under such circumstances external resources not only further domestic accumulation but are also instrumental in avoiding a decrease in the rate of economic growth, or even a decline in the level of real output.

IV   Changes in Terms of Trade

Economic development has to grapple with a serious problem in Hungary. Because of the deterioration in the terms of trade, the economy has suffered extremely high losses, and retrieving these losses seems to be more difficult than in a number of other countries. Table 9.12 presents the series of indices of changes in Hungarian terms of trade and, for the purpose of comparison, data on the Soviet Union, Czechoslovakia, and Poland as well.

Apparently Hungarian terms of trade in 1975 were worse by 22.2 percent in hard-currency trade and 11.5 percent in ruble trade than in 1970. From 1975 to 1977 Hungary succeeded only in improving her position by 2.1 percentage points in her dollar trade whereas a further 4.5 percentage point deterioration took place in the ruble trade. At the same time, Soviet and Polish terms of trade improved since price changes proved favorable for both of them. From 1970 to 1977 Soviet terms of trade with the CMEA countries improved more than with market economies. From 1970 to 1975 Czechoslovakia's terms of trade declined 9.4 percent, but the deterioration in her trade with other centrally planned economies was stronger (14.5 percent) than with market economy countries (10.7 percent).

Only a few market economies (e.g., Japan, Australia, India) experienced a deterioration in terms of trade higher than 20 percent, and of the European countries only Spain suffered such a loss. Deterioration in the terms of trade of Greece and Italy was around 15 percent whereas that of all the other European market economies was lower than 10 percent.

Table 9.13 shows the changes in Hungary's terms of trade, broken down according to major commodity groups. Terms of trade with market economies of machines, raw materials, and food products deteriorated by 22–29 percent between 1970 and 1975. Since then terms have not improved or have only slightly improved, while price ratios of food products have continued to deteriorate considerably. Only terms of trade in industrial consumers' goods did not deteriorate in the trade with market economies in 1975, and since then this has been the only product group where

Table 9.12 Changes in Terms of Trade of Hungary, the Soviet Union, Czechoslovakia, and Poland, 1970–77
(1970 = 100)

Year	Hungary			Soviet Union			Czechoslovakia			Poland
	Total	Ruble Area	Dollar Area	Total	CMEA	Market Economies	Total	Centrally Planned Economies	Market Economies	Total
1971	98.6	97.8	99.2	104	101	109	99.7	99.0	100.0	105.1
1972	97.9	96.3	100.6	103	103	101	96.6	97.0	95.6	106.1
1973	96.6	96.6	98.1	109	103	118	95.1	100.2	89.4	104.7
1974	89.4	97.0	83.6	108	103	116	100.6	104.2	89.3	102.4
1975	83.1	88.5	77.8	102	109	93	90.6	85.5	89.3	102.8
1976	84.9	86.6	83.0	108	113	101	87.5	80.0	89.0	103.5
1977	82.0	84.0	79.9	115	117	110				

Sources: Hungary: Külkereskedelmi statisztikai évkönyv 1977 [Yearbook of foreign trade statistics 1977] (Budapest: KSH, 1978), p. 408.
Soviet Union: Calculated from data in issues of Vneshniaia torgovlia SSSR [Foreign trade of the USSR]. (Cuba is included in CMEA.)
Czechoslovakia: United Nations, Monthly Bulletin of Statistics, June 1978, and calculations based on K. Dyba, 'Pohyb československých směnných relací s kapitalistickými zeměmi a saldo československé obchodní bilance s těmito zeměmi v letech 1967–74' [Development of Czechoslovak exchange relations with capitalist countries and the Czechoslovak balance of payment in the period 1967–1974], Finance a úvěr, 1976, No. 10, pp. 667–76.
Poland: United Nations, Monthly Bulletin of Statistics, June 1978.

Table 9.13 Hungary: Changes in Terms of Trade, CMEA Commodity Groups, 1970–77
(1970 = 100)

Year	Machinery		Industrial Consumers' Goods		Raw Materials		Food	
	Planned Economies	Market Economies	Planned Economies	Market Economies	Planned Economies	Market Economies	Planned Economies	Market Economies
1971	101	97	97	106	99	93	99	100
1972	100	92	95	102	94	87	102	122
1973	101	88	92	100	94	83	105	121
1974	100	82	91	106	97	81	75	86
1975	103	71	96	98	77	78	64	78
1976	100	72	88	111	72	82	80	88
1977	98	75	88	117	69	78	76	69

Source: Calculated on the basis of data in Külkereskedelmi statisztikai évkönyv 1977 [Yearbook of foreign trade statistics 1977] (Budapest: KSH, 1978), p. 410.

Hungary has succeeded in achieving considerable improvement in relative prices.

In Hungary's trade with centrally planned economies only the terms of trade in machinery have not changed significantly. All other major commodity groups have experienced substantial deterioration. Greatest was the relative loss in the trade of raw materials (23 percent by 1975, 31 percent by 1977). It was higher than the loss resulting from the trade in raw materials with market economies. Food products, too, have suffered considerable losses in terms of trade, especially considering that CMEA export prices of these commodities were relatively low already as early as 1970. Industrial consumer goods have suffered a relative price loss of 12 percent, in contrast with an improvement of 17 percent in terms of trade with market economies.

Terms-of-trade deterioration therefore has encompassed, with few exceptions, almost all major commodity groups and both market regions, thus taking on very serious dimensions. Moreover, unlike many other countries that experienced similar heavy losses in relative prices, Hungary's situation has not improved substantially in the period following 1975. This undoubtedly is a consequence of the great differences in the economic policy reactions of the individual countries to the deterioration in terms of trade. Economic life in most of the countries was seriously affected by losses in terms of trade, and this touched off almost instantaneous reactions.

Following the 'explosion' in oil and raw material prices, the growth of demand has stopped and the volume of imports has not risen in many countries. At the same time considerable efforts were undertaken to increase exports, including the raising of export prices of finished products. The countries that succeeded were able to enhance the supply of products for which the demand remained high despite economic recession. Such goods were consumers' durables or investment goods required by oil-exporting countries. Relative price changes led to significant structural changes in production. Manufacture of goods rendered unprofitable by the new raw material prices was cut short and/or new technologies were sought to substitute for expensive inputs. In a number of countries structural changes have brought about serious difficulties resulting in economic stagnation or outright recession, considerable unemployment, and also in the bankruptcy of many less efficient small enterprises or their fusion with big companies.

Economic policy makers have succeeded in sparing Hungarian economic life all these difficulties. Deterioration in terms of trade did not lead to economic recession. On the contrary, the growth rate even increased, and import demand did not slacken since world market price rises were not allowed to have much direct effect upon domestic prices. Therefore, however, enterprises made few attempts to substitute inputs or introduce new technology. Nor was strong pressure exerted to increase exports and to raise export prices. The overwhelming majority of enterprises continued their traditional production, achieving profits and exporting goods even at a time when, owing to the deterioration of terms of trade, a considerable part of it was in the red. Deficits were covered by the budget through import price support, exemption from taxation or tax refunds, and various forms of subsidies.

Because imports were growing relatively more expensive while their volume was increasing, the trade deficit rose, as shown in Table 9.14. Since

Table 9.14 *Hungary: Foreign Trade Balances, Ruble Area, Dollar Area, and Total, 1971–77[a]*

Year	Ruble Area		Dollar Area		Total
	Million Rubles	Million Forints	Million Dollars	Million Forints	Million Forints
1971	−229	−9,148	−243	−14,588	−23,736
1972	+152	+6,083	−53	−3,019	+3,064
1973	+281	+11,255	+114	+5,194	+16,449
1974	+83	+3,320	−582	−28,005	−24,685
1975	−373	−14,930	−531	−23,617	−38,547
1976	−247	−8,872	−346	−14,652	−23,524
1977	−129	−4,776	−567	−23,599	−28,375
1978	−507	−17,056	−1,107	−42,788	−59,844

[a]At contract prices, with actual freight charges.
Source: 1970–77: Same as cited in Table 9.13, p. 11; 1978: Hungarian foreign trade statistics.

1974 trade with hard-currency markets has shown a considerable deficit, while trade with the CMEA region has been more nearly balanced. Yet the accumulated deficit in the trade balance should not be regarded as the result of a conscious policy of utilizing external resources to accelerate Hungarian economic growth. Rather, the deficit was caused chiefly by the combination of adverse changes in the terms of trade and the effort, despite them, to limit fluctuations around a path of smooth economic development.

Insulation from world market changes was achieved by central measures that put off structural changes, preferring instead uninterrupted production and supply of goods and materials. This not only resulted in a larger trade deficit but also permitted enterprises to be less able or inclined to adapt themselves to quickly changing world market conditions. Prices and profits became more remote from actual costs and net real returns, and the interest of enterprises in profits, too, decreased. Contrary to the objectives of the economic reform introduced in 1968, these administrative measures modified a considerable part of the economic policy tools and the system of enterprise interests, giving them a conservative slant.

V Development Alternatives of the Hungarian Economy

There were great expectations for the economic reform introduced in 1968. It was not an unfounded hope that more effective planned guidance of the economy could be attained by indirect means of control after the old system of overcentralized and compulsory plan instructions was eliminated and enterprises were given more independence. With more flexible domestic prices adapting themselves to actual costs and world market prices as well as profit-sharing, efficiency and the adaptability of production to demand would improve. A balanced and rapid development would begin, encouraging people's creativity and making them interested personally as well as collectively in efficient and quality-based economic progress.

Both friends and enemies of the reform have acknowledged after ten years the results and successes of the new system. In the course of the past decade considerable improvements have been achieved in almost every sphere of economic life. In spite of this, heated arguments are in full swing, many criticisms are voiced, and again the question is raised: 'How to proceed?' The actual system of economic management in force is vulnerable to sharp criticism because many a principle advocated has been realized inconsistently or not at all, and because it has not lived up to expectations nor has it explored sufficiently the unexploited sources of balanced and rapid development. It has not sufficiently encouraged people's creative energies, nor made enterprises interested enough in increasing efficiency of production, in acceleration of technological progress, and in the advantageous overhauling of production and foreign trade structures.

There are general agreement and dissatisfaction that efficiency of production and foreign trade have not improved as expected. Indeed, efficiency has stagnated or even deteriorated in certain fields. Most of the improvements were realized in the first half of the decade, when growth was faster and more balanced. Some economists try to explain this with changed world market conditions, the increasing difficulties of exporting to the developed countries, and deteriorating terms of trade. According to others, the effect of 'external' conditions, too, has been to a great extent due to internal economic policies: if enterprises had been motivated more strongly in the correct direction, Hungarian terms of trade would have deteriorated less and losses could have been eliminated sooner. According to them, with a better, more competitive supply of goods, sales problems would have been easier to solve. They note that a number of rapidly industrializing countries significantly increased their exports, despite the recession.

Though supply in the markets, particularly in the consumers' market, has improved considerably, the balance of other spheres of the economy could not be restored to the extent desired. The characteristics of the economy of shortage, even though decreased, have not been eliminated. In the field of investments there have been regularly recurring tensions, and in foreign trade chronic import surplus has been experienced since 1974.

There is a general agreement that major structural changes are needed in the Hungarian economy, but views diverge as to what directions these changes should take. Thus views have cropped up recently, for instance, according to which the solution is not to elaborate a strategy of transforming the economy into a more open, efficient, and competitive system, but rather to adopt an inward-looking economic policy of more isolation. If deterioration of terms of trade is really due to external factors independent of a country's economic decisions, against which this economy proves helpless, then the less open the economy, the smaller the inevitable loss. If, in the face of the rapid industrialization and increasingly keen competition of countries at a medium level of development, Hungary has even in the long run no possibility of extending her sales by means of competitive and profitable products, it may seem reasonable to orient the economy merely to the CMEA market, to purchase her growing raw material requirements there, and to develop her export capacities in accordance with the demands of that market.

In the light of these problems, heated argument has been going on in Hungarian economic periodicals regarding the choice between the alternatives of import-substituting or export-oriented economic strategies.[13] The debate was initiated by adherents of the strategy of import substitution, mainly representatives of mining and heavy industry who, on the basis of the relative price changes of the world raw material and fuel markets, demanded a revision of economic development strategy and an enhanced support and development of their respective branches.

The majority of participants in the debate, even those accepting the necessity of a revaluation of natural resources and their extraction, rejected the idea of greater isolation. They took a definite stand in favor of increased efficiency, competitiveness, and an export-oriented economic development strategy. They emphasized that the fundamental tasks of accelerating technological development and increasing efficiency cannot be solved by adopting either inward-looking isolation or one-sided, CMEA-orientation. In case of isolation the country's losses would be less when terms of trade underwent an unfavorable change, but, on the other hand, advantages too would diminish if terms of trade changed favorably (as they in fact did over a long period before 1973). And above all, Hungary would be deprived of the permanent advantages guaranteed by specialization: joining in the international division of labor renders it possible to decide what to produce, import, or export on the basis of long-term efficiency.

It is entirely mistaken to pose the question as *either* import substitution *or* export orientation. Plenty of examples are available proving that both strategies may be good or bad. It is solely on the basis of efficiency – the comparing of realistic prices and costs – that one can accurately decide when it would be worthwhile to substitute domestic production for imports, or vice versa, and when to develop export capacities surpassing domestic needs. A considerable part of Hungary's difficulties originated because the criterion of efficiency could not be, or has not been, taken sufficiently into account in regard to either investment or current production.

This explains why the question 'Is the Hungarian economy too closed or too open?' cannot be properly answered quantitatively. Only after the introduction of appropriate efficiency criteria can it be decided what to import, what to substitute, and what to export. Then we shall see how the total volume of trade is affected by structural transformation. But there can be little doubt that, qualitatively speaking, the Hungarian economy is not sufficiently open. We have seen that imports do not compete with domestic production in final stages of processing, and intrasectoral trade and specialization in semifinished products and component parts are very underdeveloped. The costs and profits of enterprises are still too isolated from world market prices, and their adaptability to changes in demand is far from sufficient.

This brings us to the debate on the economic mechanism – the problems of evaluating the reform and developing the system of economic management. The problem of objectives, that is, of future orientation, is inseparable from the means, that is, how the different alternatives can be realized. Discussions frequently have centered on whether we should try again to implement the initial reform ideas about economic management by eliminating the compromises, contradictions, and inconsistencies of realization. Should difficulties be overcome by enlarging independence of enterprises, profit-sharing, and indirect guidance? Or, on the contrary, should Hungary attempt to advance by strengthening central direction and by stricter discipline?[14]

One basic, though often unrecognized, dilemma in this respect is the antagonism between interests associated with income differentiation according to effectiveness and with egalitarianism, respectively.

Payment by results and profit formation at enterprises according to efficiency are founded on the socialist principle of distribution according to work. Its realization necessarily entails that significant differences emerge between incomes of workers in the same occupations or positions, and between the development possibilities of enterprises of similar size. This is regarded by many people as natural and just, since they are fully aware that high quality, disciplined work, genuine initiative, and reasonable utilization of local possibilities can be attained only if all these qualities are adequately rewarded, and/or if poor quality, unconscientious work, red tape, irresponsibility, waste, and negligence are penalized by society through lower incomes. By increasing efficiency, this method of income differentiation increases also the divisible total income. Thus it is in the interest of society as a whole, even of people doing shoddy work, to put this system into effect.

Yet, whenever there appears some kind of income differentiation within an enterprise or among several enterprises, immediately a contrary opinion is put forward declaring this differentiation to be unjust and gratuitous. Moreover, in practice this egalitarian view frequently gains the upper hand, and wages founded on outstanding performances are curtailed by various machinations, thus juggling away or restricting income differentiation.

A similar situation is that pertaining to interenterprise relations. Hungarian systems of taxation, price regulation, and foreign trade control are extremely complicated and change constantly because the egalitarian tendency makes itself felt very strongly at the level of central authorities. This tendency attempts, despite changing conditions, to narrow differences in enterprise profits around the average level.

As soon as significant differences in enterprise profits became evident after the reform of economic management, a veritable campaign was launched attempting to influence public opinion against 'gratuitously high' enterprise profits, profit shares, and development funds. Immediately, on the basis of egalitarian principles, certain measures (involving taxation, subsidies, preferences, and the like) were taken that hardly permitted any differences in profits – neither upward nor downward from the average. Consequently, despite extraordinarily lively world market price fluctuations and serious sales problems, almost no Hungarian enterprises at all went into the red, that is, were declared unable to pay profit shares to their employees. At the very most some slight differentiation has been permitted among enterprises in accumulating development funds.

Under such circumstances interest in profits has naturally diminished greatly. It is not worthwhile to attempt to achieve outstanding profits when these are skimmed off by taxation anyway, and at the same time enterprises need not fear deficits either, because subsidies can be obtained some way or other. The relationship between central authorities and enterprises is like that of a family where all children are equally dear to their parents; nevertheless, the less capable and lazier a child is, the more exceptions and help he gains, whereas the capable and diligent ones have to shoulder heavier burdens. The financial position of efficient, competitive, and truly profitable enterprises is often not better than the situation of those which have managed to conceal their losses only with the help of considerable public subsidies – real differences in effectiveness are reflected scarcely or not at all by differences in profits.

Price formation is an essential battlefield between differentiation and egalitarian endeavors. It is an inherent feature of the economic mechanism – based on the principle of the independence of enterprises, of profit-sharing, and of production adapting itself to changes in consumers' demands – that prices should be formed in the market under the influence of demand and supply, as a result of bargaining between buyers and sellers. Naturally this relates to foreign prices as well. Import users should pay the equivalent of foreign prices calculated on the basis of uniform and realistic exchange rates, while exporters should get as much as buyers are willing to pay. All this has been made unmistakably clear by the basic principles of the reform.

Actually, however, producer prices corresponding to the principle of egalitarianism have been widely adopted. They cover the costs of the producers and imply an average profit. They resemble what is termed 'cost-plus pricing' in market economies, which has become predominant in government contracts in those countries. At present, when a new producer price adjustment bringing about essential changes is in progress in Hungary, adherents of the opposite principles are waging an embittered fight. On the one hand there are the economists who wish to enforce world market price ratios as widely as possible and to extend the range of free pricing. On the other hand, their opponents would like to ensure by means of price formation, too, that not a single product or enterprise should be in the red but at the same time no 'excessive' profits should occur either. It is difficult to predict the results, but there is a danger that in practice once again egalitarianism and protection will gain the upper hand especially in manufacturing, even though the range of products (mainly raw materials) whose producer prices will be influenced by relative world market prices is extended.

The long-standing argument about how to establish the foreign exchange rate in Hungary also reflects the fight waged between adherents of differentiation and egalitarianism. One group of economists, whose views were accepted by the financial authorities, believes the exchange rate should be fixed at the *average* cost level of earning foreign exchange through exports. Another significant group condemns the overvaluation of the forint and advocates instead an exchange rate equivalent to the *marginal* cost of earning foreign exchange.

An exchange rate on the average cost level has a threefold effect on the income of enterprises. (1) It diminishes the incomes of enterprises exporting profitably. (2) It necessitates subsidizing about half of the exports constantly and with special regulations. (3) It renders imports relatively cheap for the users thereby encouraging inefficient exports and the deterioration of the trade balance. All three effects have an egalitarian character. (a) They do not allow 'excessive' profits to be created. (b) They help equalize enterprise profits by differentiated subsidies. (c) They help conceal actual losses.

A marginal exchange rate with no subsidy would obviously differentiate very strongly the profits of the exporting enterprises – not allowing inefficient export activities to continue. By helping to balance demand and supply for foreign currencies, it would allow a substantial reduction in the regulating instruments (high tariffs, import quotas on consumer goods) created as a consequence of disequilibrium.

The overvaluation of the forint may be reduced in two ways: by raising the forint price of the foreign currencies and by reducing the level of producer prices (or by a combination of the two). In the wake of the world market price rises of 1973–74 and the relative stability of domestic prices, the view has been spreading that the overvaluation should be eliminated not by raising the rates of exchange, but by reducing the net-income content of producer prices.[15] Through a cut in the profit content of producer prices and elimination of unjustified subsidies in consumer prices, the two price levels could be brought close to each other. Then the indicator showing the cost of earning foreign exchange would not differ from the consumer purchasing-power parity to such an extent as it does now.

Such a consistent reform of prices and exchange rates could be worked out with the objective of preparing the convertibility of the forint currency. The lack of convertibility is in contrast with the quantitative openness of the Hungarian economy, or it can be regarded as a sign of its insufficient qualitative openness. The debate over when and how the forint can be made convertible is obviously closely linked to the debates on inward-looking or export-oriented development and on differentiation versus egalitarianism.

As a matter of fact, also in the background of the debate between differentiation and egalitarianism, adherents of two opposing conceptions of the strategy of economic development are fighting against each other. The partisans of differentiation of individual and enterprise incomes take it for granted that the quality of work can be improved considerably. They believe that productivity and efficiency can be increased by enhancing personal and collective interest. This would involve a substantial change in both production and foreign trade structures. It is assumed that the only possible method of enhancing dynamic economic development and, concurrently, of restoring the balance of the national economy, is import substitution and export-oriented development based on increased efficiency.[16]

In contrast, the adherents of egalitarianism are more cautious and conservative. They think substantial structural transformation is neither feasible nor advisable, because these could lead to incalculable social disturbances. According to their view, more effective labor and raising living standards could be approached without unnecessary trouble through minor modifications of the economic management system, by filtering irrational elements out of the price system, and by a more thorough selection of development projects on the central level. It is admitted that such a development might be slower but would involve fewer risks.

The outcome of the debate and the course of progress would be difficult to predict. On the strength of the past ten years it seems probable that the direction of economic development will be set once again by the more cautious viewpoint. However, the reform initiated eleven years ago indicates that substantial changes can be carried into effect if the situation has become ripe for such transformations. The worst solution seems to be when two opposing views obstruct all structural change and improvement.

Notes: Chapter 9

1 If productivity of industry in the advanced industrial countries is twice as high as in Hungary, and if the increase in productivity is faster by one percentage point in Hungary, catching up with those countries would take 70 years. See Tibor Erdős, 'Gazdasági növekedésünk üteme és gazdasági fejlődésünk egyensulyi problémái' [The rate of economic growth and equilibrium problems of economic development in Hungary] (Budapest: MTA, Közgazdaságtudományi Intézet, 1978; manuscript), p. 12.
2 According to calculations by Magda Ács, the ratio of fixed capital and output in material production rose by approximately 30 percent in the period 1950–75, whereas in the national economy as a whole it was diminished by 40 percent, due to the rapid decrease of the capital/output ratio of services. See Magda Ács, 'A mult tükrében' [In the mirror of the past], in Mária Augusztinovics (ed.), *Népgazdasági modellek a távlati tervezésben* [Macroeconomic models in long-term planning] (Budapest: Közgazdasági és Jogi Könyvkiadó, 1979), p. 329.
3 Since foreign trade turnover is not calculated on the basis of value added, it cannot be directly compared to national income. The only aim of the comparison above has been the demonstration of orders of magnitude.
4 The indirect import content of investment, 17.3, equals the total import content, 38.1, minus the direct import content, 20.8, in row 4 of Table 9.8. The indirect import content of consumption, 22.1, equals the total import content, 29.2, minus the direct import content, 7.1, in row 3. Thus, the indirect import content of investment is about three-fourths (17.3 ÷ 22.1) as great as that of consumption.
5 M. Tardos, 'Külkereskedelmi forgalmunk áruszerkezete' [The commodity structure of Hungarian foreign trade], *Gazdaság*, 1973, No. 3, pp. 22–36.
6 The deterioration of the terms of trade of chemical products (SITC 5) was 47 percent between 1970 and 1977, as import prices increased by 46.4 percent and export prices decreased by 22.6 percent. See *Külkereskedelmi árstatisztikai adatok 1957–1977* [Foreign trade price statistical data 1957–1977] (Budapest: KSH, 1978).
7 Bela Balassa, 'The Changing Pattern of Comparative Advantage in Manufactured Goods', *Review of Economics and Statistics*, Vol. 61, No. 2 (May 1979), pp. 259–66.

8 United Nations, Economic Commission for Europe, *Economic Bulletin for Europe*, Vol. 30, No. 1 (New York, 1978), pp. 99–103.

9 János Gács and Mária Lackó, 'A Study of Planning Behaviour on the National-Economic Level', *Economics of Planning*, Vol. 13, Nos. 1–2 (January 1973), pp. 91–119; Károly Attila Soós, 'A beruházások ingadozásának okai a magyar gazdaságban' [Reasons for investment fluctuations in the Hungarian economy], *Közgazdasági Szemle*, 1975, No. 1, pp. 104–111; Tamás Bauer, 'A beruházási volumen a közvetlen tervgazdaságban' [The volume of investments in a directly planned economy] (Budapest: MTA, Közgazdaságtudományi Intézet, 1977); Tamás Bauer, 'Beruházási ciklusok a tervgazdaságban' [Investment cycles under central planning], *Gazdaság*, 1978, No. 4, pp.57–75; András Bródy, 'A ciklus egy linearizált modellje' [A linearized model of the cycle], *Szigma*, 1977, No. 4, pp. 241–8.

10 Let P represent plan targets; A, actual fulfillment results; t, the current period; and $t + 1$, the next period. Consider the following two cases: In Case I, $A_t > P_t$ and the plan is over-fulfilled, whereas in Case II, $P_t > A_t$ and the plan is underfulfilled. Then 'bold', 'cautious', and 'unambitious' behavior may be characterized – without value judgments and without reference to the realism of the plans – as follows:

	Case I $A_t > P_t$	Case II $P_t > A_t$
Behavior		
Bold	$P_{t+1} > A_t$	$P_{t+1} > P_t$
Cautious	$A_t > P_{t+1} > P_t$	$P_t > P_{t+1} > A_t$
Unambitious	$P_{t+1} < P_t$	$P_{t+1} < A_t$

11 It seems not to be worthwhile anymore to discuss the opinion denying cyclical movements, deriving these from the defective realization of infallible central decisions, or explaining them with some kinds of incidental phenomena. See, for example, Andor Berei (ed.), *A szocializmus politikai gazdaságtana* [Political economy of socialism] (Budapest: Kossuth Könyvkiadó, 1973); and S. Khavina, 'Vymysly o "krizisakh" i "tsiklakh" v sotsialisticheskom khoziaistve' [Fabrications on 'crises' and 'cycles' in the socialist economy], *Ekonomicheskie nauki*, 1967, No. 2, pp. 58–69.

12 János Kornai comprehensively describes the economy of shortage in his forthcoming new book, *A hiány* [Economics of shortage], parts of which were published as 'A hiány ujratermelése' [The reproduction of shortage], *Közgazdasági Szemle*, 1978, No. 9, pp. 1034–50, and 'Resource-Constrained versus Demand-Constrained Systems', *Econometrica*, Vol. 47, No. 4 (July 1979), pp. 801–19.

13 For a summary of the debate see R. Becsky, 'Economic Development Orientation in Hungary – a Press Debate', *Acta Oeconomica*, 1977, Nos. 3–4, pp. 395–408.

14 See, for example, Rezsö Nyers and Márton Tardos, 'Milyen gazdaságfejlesztési stratégiát válasszunk?' [What kind of economic strategy should be chosen?], *Gazdaság*, 1979, No. 1, pp. 5–25; English translation in *Acta Oeconomica* (Budapest), Vol. 22 (1979), No. 1–2, pp. 11–31.

15 See, for example, György Szakolczai, 'A termelöi árszint leszállitása' [Reduction of the producer price level], *Külgazdaság*, 1973, No. 9, pp. 681–9; György Szakolczai, 'Az árbázis és a külkereskedelmi elszámolások' [Price basis and foreign trade accounts], *Közgazdasági Szemle*, 1974, No. 1, pp. 36–54, and No. 2, pp. 174–88.

16 András Köves, 'A világgazdasági integrálódás és a gazdaságfejlesztés iránya' [Integration of the world economy and the direction of economic development], *Gazdaság*, 1977, No. 4, pp. 50–68.

Chapter 10

Importing Western Technology into Hungary

MÁRTON M. TARDOS

In less developed countries the exploitation of additional resources is very often expected to ease internal economic and social tensions. Technical transfer from developed countries in the surrounding area might be considered as one of these additional development resources.[1] East–West trade should be able to contribute greatly to the wide-scale utilization of advanced technology and to the relatively rapid diffusion of technical and economic experience necessary for adoption of new production methods.

This chapter surveys and explains the experiences gained in Hungary from taking advantage of the diffusion of new technology. Three principal questions are considered:

(1) What kind of economic–political strategies attach great importance to technology transfer, and how extensively will the efficiency of technology transfer be affected by the strategic objectives themselves?
(2) What kind of social, political, and economic factors hinder the exploitation of possibilities provided by technical transfer?
(3) To what extent does the present system of world trade foster the development of technology transfer based on mutual advantages?

No detailed discussion of possible definitions of technical transfer is to be expected here. As a whole, this definition comprises the imports of machinery and equipment (of greater or lesser technological superiority) and production expertise (know-how). We are fully aware of the corresponding literature distinguishing between vertical and horizontal technical transfer. The first is defined as the transfer of expertise across *different* stages of the entire product cycle, beginning with applied research through development to the setting up of production. The second covers the simple transfer of expertise between institutions concerning a *given* stage of the product cycle; for example, when a company possessing a certain technology establishes a factory or plant for another company. International technology transfer is regarded as a special form of the two types of technical transfer.[2]

The international transfer of technology will not always take place in the framework of some legal or economic action. Transfer also occurs through the utilization of scientific and technological publications as well as the exploitation of general scientific and technical knowledge during the elaboration of independent production processes. Several means of technology transfer executed in the framework of some legal or economic action are known as well, such as the purchase of machinery, licenses, the transfer of technological processes, the establishment of turnkey plants, etc. However, the examination of differences in the efficiency of the various forms is beyond the framework of this chapter.

This chapter is based partly on statistical analysis of the development of the Hungarian economy and partly on case studies of the development experience of Hungarian enterprises compiled in the Institute of Economic Sciences of the Hungarian Academy of Sciences and in the Institute for Economic and Market Research.

Three periods are distinguished: (1) the period of isolation from the West; (2) the first steps toward an opening for technology transfer from the West; and (3) the period following introduction of the new system of economic management (the New Economic Mechanism, or NEM). Finally, the remaining problems still to be solved are summarized, as well as the strategic objectives – often conflicting with each other – related to them, and the probable consequences of their implementation are examined.

I   Development of Hungarian Machinery Imports before 1960

During the Cold War years after the Second World War, Hungary followed an economic policy of autarky (to use the Hungarian term). This policy did not mean completely giving up foreign economic relations, but entailed a considerable curb on Western relations and an almost complete isolation of the economy from the influences of the world market. The implementation of this policy was rendered possible through the Soviet Union's substantial raw material supply to Hungary. In return, Hungary developed its domestic raw material base and delivered machinery, consumer goods, and food.

As a consequence, during this period Hungary's economic and technical development was highly influenced by the expansion of trade with CMEA countries, especially with the Soviet Union. At the same time its relations with the advanced industrial countries declined, due both to Western embargo and discrimination emanating from the atmosphere of the Cold War and to a policy of isolation by the Hungarian government.

The policy, which was characterized by efforts to develop intensive relations with the CMEA countries, on the one hand, and by an isolation from the advanced industrial countries, on the other, led to contradictory economic consequences. The large Soviet orders facilitated not only a fairly rapid postwar reconstruction for the small Hungarian economy, but also a considerable economic growth, which brought about a large-scale and rapid restructuring of the Hungarian economy. The mode and pace of the structural changes would have satisfied the desire of any developing country. Within one-and-a-half decades Hungary had developed from an agrarian country into an industrial nation, in the foreign economic relations of which the export of machinery played a decisive role (see Table 10.1).

However, the reconstruction and the development of manufacturing could not be coupled with a sufficiently rapid change in the design and technology of new production processes. The country managed to enter a quasi-advanced stage.[3] A specific feature of this stage was that those developments in production requiring considerable technical knowledge could not be achieved because the close relations of the most important Hungarian companies with major international corporations ceased to exist.[4] Purchases of licenses and know-how became very rare. At the same time the growth of machinery imports, the most important source of technological and design development, lagged behind that of machinery exports.

Table 10.1   *Main Characteristics of the Hungarian Economy, 1938, 1950, and 1960*

	1938	1950	1960
National income (volume index, 1950 = 100)	10.0	100.0	177.0
Share in the national income (%)			
Industry	22.0	26.0	42.0
Agriculture	64.0	48.0	29.0
Investment (volume index, 1950 = 100)	34.0	100.0	196.9
Exports (volume index, 1950 = 100)	35.0	100.0	292.0
Share in exports (%)			
Machinery	9.3	23.0	38.6
Other industrial goods	33.7	37.8	40.3
Agricultural products	57.0	39.2	21.1

Sources: Statistical Yearbook on Foreign Trade 1960 (Budapest: Hungarian Central Statistical Office, 1962); *Statistical Yearbook 1960* (Budapest: Hungarian Central Statistical Office, 1962); *A nemzeti jövedelem hosszúsoros indexeinek felülvizsgálata 1938 és 1950–65 évekre* [The revision of indexes of national income for the years 1938 and 1950–65] (Budapest: Központi Statisztikai Hivatal, 1967).

The most prominent feature of these structural changes was that Hungary had become, like other East European countries with close foreign relations with the Soviet Union, a member of the small group of net machinery exporters (the United States, Japan, West Germany, France, Switzerland, and two CMEA countries, Czechoslovakia and the GDR), and belonged to it as late as 1974.

The export structure of the small CMEA countries with significant machinery exports showed a certain disproportion. The share of machinery was actually only significant within exports to the Soviet Union. Much less important were machinery deliveries within the mutual trade relations of the small CMEA countries, while the share of machinery exports within the total exports of the small CMEA countries to the nonsocialist world showed no increase at all. Taking Hungary as an example, the share of machines within total exports rose from 9 percent in 1938 to 38 percent in 1960, while the share of machinery within exports to nonsocialist countries hardly exceeded 10 percent. This situation, which became characteristic not only of Poland and Bulgaria but of countries possessing a more advanced engineering industry than Hungary, like Czechoslovakia or the GDR, as well, showed that there was a contradiction between the level of technical development achieved by the country and the role played by engineering in foreign trade.

On what kind of technical expertise could the development of exports of manufactured goods, including machines, rely? The rapid and CMEA-oriented development of manufacturing, including the engineering industry, in the CMEA countries was greatly fostered by the system of intra-CMEA trade based on intergovernmental foreign trade agreements for one- and five-year periods. The efforts to establish an international specialization of production were based mainly on bilateral relations between the small CMEA countries and the Soviet Union. Multilateral forms of production specialization had no particular significance at that time, though the necessity of establishing such specialization was clearly recognized.

Another characteristic of these changes was that, despite growing manufacturing capacities in the majority of the small CMEA countries, the technical isolation from advanced nonsocialist countries increased. The growth pattern of manufacturing and engineering industries in the Soviet Union and other CMEA countries was not in line with world market requirements.

This increase in output not only relied on a concentrated allocation of investment resources but also required considerable intellectual efforts as well. The technical and scientific expertise needed for an expansion of output came mainly from internal (technical) resources, with some additional technical knowledge gained from publications on foreign scientific achievements and implemented in the production processes. In addition, despite the embargo imposed by the advanced Western countries, quite a number of technically advanced machines were purchased with the aim of building up large-scale production based on the technical knowledge vested in them.

The rapid increase in machinery exports of the small CMEA countries, including Hungary, was fostered primarily, not by the learning of new advanced technical expertise, but rather by knowledge accumulated earlier. Among the first factories nationalized in these countries after the Second World War were those operating with foreign capital and technologies, at a time when economic relations with organizations of advanced nonsocialist countries flourished and a part of these relations also took on legal forms, such as licenses and direct investment.

This technological knowledge provided a satisfactory base for rapid industrial development in Hungary as well, animated by a growing domestic investment demand in the 1950s and by demand from the other CMEA countries.

By listing the products and product groups playing an outstanding role in the expansion of production, one can outline the main features of the changes. In Hungary a decisive part was played by the production of rolling stock, which had a long history. The MAVAG and the Ganz Wagon and Machine Works had already produced engines and freight cars in large quantities during the Austro–Hungarian Monarchy. Therefore the retooling of these plants for the production of engines and freight cars meeting Soviet demand had not proved to be a difficult task. However, it did not bring about technical progress in Hungary by comparison with the goods produced earlier.

Shipbuilding developed in line with Soviet orders as well. The plants that previously produced river–sea and deep-sea vessels received orders from the Soviet Union for the production of ships suitable for coastal trade, in quantities permitting large-scale production unprecedented in this branch.

The bus industry took a remarkable upswing. The Ikarus Machine Works managed to introduce large-scale production of bus types that could have been produced only on a small scale in the prewar period.

An export-oriented development was accomplished in the machine tool industry as well. Through a modification of the product types elaborated before and during the Second World War, a rapid expansion of exports to the CMEA countries could be achieved.

Some attention must be paid, finally, to an important achievement of Hungarian industry – the development of energy engineering in Hungary. The Láng Machine Works, the Ganz Electric Energy Works, and other enterprises took advantage of their technical expertise, gained chiefly through the buying of licenses, when they produced furnaces, turbines, and generators for the rapid extension of the domestic power grid system. Besides substituting for imports in this field, they even devoted part of their output to exports.

However, the internal reserves of economic and technical progress had been exhausted by the mid-1950s. The Soviet Union, hitherto a secure market for an increasing output of products representing traditional technical know-how, successively curbed purchases of steam engines, locomotives, and railway cars. Moreover, it sought from its partners major innovative improvements in various fields.

II The Period of Centralized Development Programs

The gap in Soviet orders had to be filled by the development of new products. New efforts for technical innovation were needed for the Hungarian economy in the late 1950s and early 1960s to cope with these new requirements.

Among development objectives the diesel program, including the development of the production of diesel engines to replace steam engines, as well as the production of associated locomotives and freight cars, deserves prominent attention. However, other objectives were shaped as well. Emphasis was shifted from raw material production and heavy engineering increasingly toward less material- and energy-intensive branches like precision engineering and telecommunication equipment.

The scope of development continued to be greatly limited by the traditional technical expertise accumulated before and during the Second World War in Hungary and by the requirements of the Soviet market. Although the exploitation of technical expertise accumulated in Hungary itself and in the other CMEA countries remained the principal emphasis of Hungarian industrial development, the easing of Cold War tensions was followed by gradual abandonment of isolation from Western scientific and technical achievements.

In the highly centralized system of economic management decision making about economic development was influenced by three economic considerations neglected during the first period:[5]

(1) It was recognized that the raw material supply of the country could not be built on Soviet raw material resources previously thought inexhaustible. From the mid-1950s onward, leading Soviet bodies continually expressed their intention to curb the growth of raw material deliveries.

(2) On the other hand, it had become clear that the precondition of internal economic growth was the production of more sophisticated goods requiring more intellectual input. The popular political slogan of the early 1950s – 'Hungary, the country of iron and steel' – was replaced in the Hungarian press by new ones which drew attention to the achievements of Swiss industrial development and emphasized the importance of efficient participation in the international division of labor.[6]

(3) Finally, it was recognized that a small country like Hungary could not possess all the technical knowledge needed for the development of a modern industry. Therefore the Hungarian government strove for a more intensive international division of labor within the CMEA.

The development of Hungarian industry between 1958 and 1968 was characterized by the growth of preferred industrial branches, based on CMEA specialization programs and requiring rapid technical progress. As a result of the contradiction between the ambitious plans and insufficient development resources, economic growth was not accompanied by a corresponding rise in supplies. Development was accompanied by deviations, in many ways systematic, from the plan: the rise in production, though constantly lower than demanded by other member countries, very often not even meeting the commitments on the Hungarian side either, frequently still resulted in unsalable stocks of goods and unutilized capacities.

The imports of know-how and machinery needed from the hard-currency area, as well as the imports of semimanufactures and parts needed for current production, placed a heavier burden on the trade balance with the West than the planners might have foreseen. In turn, efforts to expand exports to Western countries along with the increased imports did not meet expectations.

Finally, rapid development was achieved by narrowing the product pattern of domestic industry, and output of branches of industry not enjoying preferential treatment became obsolete. In Hungary, the growing gap between a narrowing product pattern and a widening demand pattern should have been filled by expanding deliveries from CMEA countries. However, such a growth of CMEA deliveries did not take place. The insufficient increase in socialist imports, below plan targets, and a rapid widening of the demand structure, beyond expectation, led to grave conflicts. Difficulties could not be fully resolved even by stepping up Western imports and postponing planned shutdowns of obsolete plants. Thus procurement bottlenecks constantly disturbed both the supply of consumer goods and services to the population and the smooth operation of production.

Besides diagnosing the adverse consequences of a planning system based on preferred development projects conflicting with reality, it has to be underlined that, as had happened before, the simplest way of easing tensions was to increase Western imports. The question remains to be answered: what made an accelerated increase in hard-currency imports possible? The answer lies in the increase of revenues from the export of raw materials and foods. In the 1960s, both the demand for the most significant item in Hungarian exports at that time, slaughter cattle, *and* its price increased. In addition, considerable quantities of raw materials from CMEA countries could be exported, after some processing, to Western countries.

The results of the development strategy oriented toward the CMEA market while utilizing achievements of Western technological development did not meet expectations. Waste of resources emanating from the planners' forecasting difficulties were first of all manifested in a wide demand, but a narrow supply, pattern as well as in the adverse development of the hard-currency trade balance.

This development strategy, however, did not lead to greater difficulties than domestic supply shortages, because exports of processed and unprocessed food products and raw materials to the Western market increased.

III Innovation Policy under the New System of Economic Management

Hungary's economic administration elaborated new methods of economic management and a new strategy of technical development, for two reasons. First, the shortage of goods caused popular dissatisfaction, hampered production, and restrained economic development. Second, Western market possibilities, with the exception of manufactured goods, seemed to have been exhausted.

One of the principal objectives of the new system of economic management was to do away with the monopoly of the sellers' market in order to use accumulated manufacturing capacities for an efficient expansion of exports to the West.

The Hungarian authorities concluded that important inadequacies of the previous technical development were largely responsible for the two problems mentioned.

1 The sophisticated and continuously changing conditions in a number of fields of economic activity, such as manufacturing, agriculture, certain branches of services, and domestic and foreign trade in industrial and agricultural goods, made an efficient centralized control of production and marketing actually impossible. However, decentralizing the rights

of decision making did not mean giving up the planned state control of development projects, which was to be carried out through credit allocation and subsidies granted out of the state budget.

2 If enterprises were not given general criteria for the evaluation of their various costs and revenues, they would not be able to decide marketing or development issues. This problem was to be solved by giving unified criteria for the calculation of costs and the evaluation of various resources on the basis of the price system, by the introduction of operational rates of exchange, etc.

3 It was recognized that the utilization of internal technological expertise and designs must not be given preference by administrative means as well. The import of machines and equipment, licenses, and know-how from the West should be encouraged. Those enterprises with enough funds to purchase spare parts, licenses, or machinery were given the free right to decide whether to buy them for forints in the domestic market or for hard currency in the foreign market.

These new decisions seemed to give free rein at last to the efficient acquisition and use of Western technology. It was thought that the operational rates of exchange, together with centrally decided prices, taxes, and subsidies, would provide profit-oriented enterprises with satisfactory instructions on how to allocate their assets, considering the expected returns, when launching development projects. The same mechanisms might instruct enterprise management how to mix technology purchases on the domestic market with purchases from the CMEA or from the West.[7]

Based on these considerations, contacts were established with companies in advanced industrial countries. Administrative restrictions concerning the buying of licenses were diminished and new measures were taken to foster cooperation. The following figures reflect the new trends: while before 1960 Hungary bought practically no licenses at all, and during 1960–65 four or five licenses were acquired per year, by contrast in the year 1975 alone forty licenses were purchased.[8] In 1975 the costs of licenses made up 7.5 percent of total research and development (R & D) costs. This proportion was, however, still well below the level justified on the basis of international comparison. The corresponding figure varies between 15 and 45 percent in the advanced Western countries of Hungary's size, while in countries undergoing rapid economic development, like Spain or Greece, it is even twice as large as the cost of R & D itself.[9]

In the field of cooperation an even more rapid development has taken place. Through the end of 1977, altogether 550 agreements were registered in Hungary. Of those, 345 were actually operating at the end of 1977. The majority of these agreements were concluded by engineering companies, but this form of economic cooperation was introduced in other branches as well. (See Table 10.2.) Since 1972, in addition to the purchase of licenses and the conclusion of cooperation agreements, joint ventures may be founded in Hungary if the Hungarian partner's share of the capital funds exceeds 51 percent. However, no remarkable development has taken place in this respect since the passage of the law on the establishment of joint ventures. Only three agreements of the sort which might foster technical transfer have been concluded, but even these have not been able to show any considerable achievements as yet.

Table 10.2 *Distribution by Branch of Hungarian Cooperation Agreements in Actual Operation, 31 December 1977*

Branch	Number of Agreements	Percentage of Total Value of All Agreements
Engineering	250	67.4
Agriculture	21	20.4
Light industry	47	8.2
Chemicals	21	3.9
Building materials	6	0.1
	345	100.0

Source: A közös vállalat alakitás lehetösegei [The possibilities of joint ventures] (Budapest: Konjunktura és Piackutató Intézet, 1979; mimeo).

The acquisition of licenses, industrial cooperation agreements, and the possibility of establishing joint ventures in Hungary, together with the mechanism of planned economy, have all contributed to a rapid expansion of East–West relations, including the expansion of technical transfer. As a result, domestic supply could be improved, exports to the socialist countries have grown considerably, and the rate of increase in exports of manufactured goods to nonsocialist countries has accelerated as well. Despite harder market conditions, the share of Hungarian machinery and chemical sales in Western imports of these products has grown. Their share would have increased even faster had the Hungarian government been more willing to finance successful firms and less willing to subsidize weak firms, and had the government's efforts to restrict domestic demand and sales to socialist countries been more effective.

All this, however, could not save the country from the impact of international economic disturbances which hit Hungary in 1973 and subsequent years.[10] It must be emphasized that technical transfer was not the cause of the tensions arising in Hungary's foreign trade, but, on the contrary, even softened them.[11] Hungarian foreign trade with the West developed unsatisfactorily not only because of 'stagflation' in the West but also because of shortcomings in the control of the Hungarian economy. The composition of Hungarian imports was not entirely appropriate, on the one hand, and the imports obtained were not always used efficiently, on the other. Both shortcomings occurred also in regard to licenses bought from the West. Unfortunately, these licenses have not increased the competitiveness of Hungarian exports to the extent expected. According to opinions in both the East and the West, actual results of the NEM (see Table 10.3) still fall short of expectations.

Western firms complain that their sales to East European countries do not meet their expectations and that the expansion of their exports is connected with requirements for countertrade. At present Western companies are confronted with difficulties which they are unable to overcome and would rather not face. Western companies usually find that they can manage to build up relations with their Hungarian partners successfully only if they give them a hand – in the framework of cooperation or in any other form – in bringing the Hungarian industrial articles to market. If a Western company finally tries its best in this rather unusual field of selling Eastern goods as well as its own, it may face further difficulties because Hungarian companies often do not react quickly and reliably enough to market possibilities.

Table 10.3   *Main Characteristics of the Hungarian Economy, Selected Periods, 1950–77*
(Percent)

	1950–60	1960–67	1970–77
Average annual increase in real national income	5.9	5.1	5.0
Composition of national income at end of period			
Share in production of national income			
Industry	36.0	42.0	45.0
Agriculture	29.0	22.0	16.0
Share in use of national income			
Net accumulation	25.6	25.2	31.2
Average annual increase in volume of investment	7.0	8.4	7.6
Average annual increase in volume of exports			
Total exports	11.3	10.4	9.5
Exports to socialist countries	11.9	10.1	10.3
Exports to nonsocialist countries	11.3	11.6	6.5
Average annual increase in volume of imports			
Total imports	11.1	10.2	8.2
Imports from socialist countries	13.3	9.5	8.0
Imports from nonsocialist countries	9.6	11.8	8.0
Ratio of value of exports to value of imports at end of period			
Total trade	89.6	95.9	89.3
Trade with socialist countries	90.7	101.4	105.0
Trade with nonsocialist countries	86.8	90.2	70.5
Share of machinery in exports at end of period			
Total exports	38.5	31.6	33.6
Exports to socialist countries	49.9	42.8	53.8
Exports to nonsocialist countries	10.4	7.3	41.5
Share of machinery in imports at end of period			
Total imports	28.0	32.5	32.1
Imports from socialist countries	33.0	37.9	36.3
Imports from nonsocialist countries	15.2	21.7	27.5

Sources: Statistical Yearbooks, 1960–77 (Budapest: Hungarian Central Statistical Office, 1962–79).

In the framework of this chapter only the causes of dissatisfaction concerning technical transfer in Hungary will be summarized. Nevertheless, when evaluating reasons on the Western side for a loss of interest in

East–West trade, one should remember that, in the late 1950s and early 1960s (i.e. the period of rapid development of the West European economies), Western companies were ready to face these difficulties, not chiefly to find new markets, but because they hoped to find the solution to their labor shortages. At present, at a time of slower economic growth, the building up of cooperation is motivated only by efforts to improve utilization of Western production capacity. And cooperation with CMEA countries does not serve this purpose entirely, if it is coupled with a pressure for buying and selling. The presence of Western companies in the small CMEA countries is limited by the bilateral commitments undertaken within the CMEA, which restrict the presence of a company to one single market and do not foster the introduction of the goods in the total CMEA turnover.

Now let me sum up the basic difficulties of technical transfer experienced in Hungary on the basis of some case studies.[12] Three groups of difficulties can be outlined.

To the first one belong all those difficulties stemming from the specific features of the *institutional and management system* of the Hungarian economy. As already noted, a superficial observer might have thought that the introduction of the New Economic Mechanism in Hungary was accompanied by the establishment of an institutional and management system capable of decentralized decisions on development projects. However, the past ten years have proved that, while the new system managed to improve considerably the adaptability of current activities, no real changes could be achieved in investment efficiency.

One of the principal and still unsolved economic management problems is the rather slow reaction of the whole system to new requirements and cutbacks in demand. For example, no ways have yet been found to meet the demand for a new product by establishing a new company.

And in the opposite situation, if there is no effective demand for a company's product, the system will not suspend production and wind up the company. Instead production will be maintained by state subsidies until some government decision is taken.

Another important inadequacy is that in the field of enterprise investments the decision making of the company management is influenced by three sets of criteria that contradict each other. First, when deciding on investments, any company should consider the impact on its employees' incomes. The companies apply for credits to the National Bank, which has its own criteria for returns on investment when granting the credit. And, finally, the various branch ministries – the supervisors of companies – link investment decisions to the fulfillment of the non-obligatory plan targets. The conflict of the three sets of criteria leads finally to a compromise, after which no party will take direct responsibility for the success of the chosen investment project.

On the whole, companies were not able to act according to the intention of the reform even immediately after its initiation. The prevailing tax system does not allow enterprises to allocate their net profits to investment purposes in the hope that out of the revenue of the project they will manage to raise the average wage level of their employees. However, according to general experience, the companies, disregarding the normative rules of the NEM, not only invest their own funds but even apply to the National Bank for new credits. The development objectives of the companies are formed usually in conjunction with the conceptions of central planning bodies and supervising ministries. These can be carried out since economic units may well expect central bodies to supplement their funds as necessary to continue production, through tax relief and subsidies.

Because of this easing of financial restrictions on investment decision making, there is not a suitable mechanism to enforce efficiency requirements when Hungarian enterprises import machines from the advanced Western countries, buy licenses and know-how, or make industrial cooperation agreements with foreign firms. The decreasing influence of financial constraints on investment activity necessitated the introduction of administrative regulations, which, however, reduced the efficiency of technical transfer.

As a consequence of these administrative methods, not only have developments of minor importance been postponed but, for example, the bus development project based on Western technology has been affected as well. The Csepel Motor Works needed a new technology for the production of bus chassis. Ultimately, because the competent branch ministry insisted upon large-scale production, a technology offered by the Swedish Oerlikon Company was chosen, which proved to be profitable only in large-scale production. Consequently, the Hungarian company faces many difficulties in producing chassis for Western export where smaller series are required.[13]

One of the most prominent economic actions of the 1970s showed a lack of development criteria in buying Western know-how. Production systems were introduced in plant cultivation on cooperatives and state farms. Implementing the idea necessitated imports of American agricultural equipment and herbicides and pesticides, the foreign exchange costs of which were to be covered by corn exports. Only after the whole action had been carried out did it become clear that the companies would not have been able to cover their costs without being granted special state subsidies. After 1975, this led in the field of agriculture to an administrative curb of machinery imports from the nonsocialist countries.

The prominent action of 'the expansion of the production of goods salable on all markets' planned for the period 1976–80 involved a decision to favor imports from the West for investment projects to expand exports to the West. As a result, the demand for imports of Western machinery showed an extremely rapid increase in 1977–78. For this purpose an investment credit line of 45 billion forints was earmarked to finance some 13 percent of the total volume of industrial investments foreseen for the five-year period. The funds for machinery imports from the West for projects financed out of this credit line were readily available, especially for large firms. However, when some credits were extended, not only were the general requirements of rate of return enforced, but a repayment of the credit out of the net proceeds of additional exports was demanded as well. But companies often obtained these credits to use them for other kinds of investments (for production for the domestic market or the CMEA), so long as they could meet the special repayment condition by increasing exports to the West from existing capacity.

All this means that the development program involving the 45-billion-forint credit line would not have brought about the anticipated increase in Western exports even if companies benefiting from the credit line had met their commitments. But delays in fulfilling the commitments or even partial nonperformance are quite frequent.

Not only this inadequate monetary and administrative regulation of investment actions hindered technical transfer based on efficiency criteria. The problem was deepend by the special situation of Hungary in the international division of labor. *It is very difficult to exploit simultaneously both the advantages stemming from planned cooperation with CMEA countries and those arising from the division of labor prevailing on the Western world market.* The system of Hungarian economic management aimed at enforcing profitability on both markets by using the commercial rate of exchange. Those centrally decided rates of exchange were based on the average costs of exports calculated according to accepted principles.[14] However, the rates of exchange introduced did not come up even to this cost level either. Two problems arose in this connection.

One of them led to difficulties in finding a rational way to accomplish both technical transfer to Hungary and Hungarian exports to the West. In order to maintain a balance in foreign trade and because the rates of exchange failed to reflect the average production costs of exports, the state was forced to subsidize exports and to curb the import demand of public and private users by administrative measures from time to time. A balanced foreign trade with nonsocialist countries could not be achieved by these methods even before 1972. This was followed by the price explosion of the years 1973–75, leading to a deterioration of the terms of trade as a consequence of which exports covered import costs even to a smaller extent than before. With the exception of the years 1974–75, government bodies continued to define commercial rates of exchange at a lower level than the average costs of exports and therefore did not provide satisfactory orientation for the producers in their decisions.

The other problem is related to successful implementation of imported Western technology, which is regarded as really efficient if its impact is shown not only in the improvement of domestic supply and increase of exports to the West but also in the development of economic relations between CMEA countries as well. The latter possibility cannot be exploited because of specific features of relations between CMEA countries that differ greatly from those between Western countries.

The difficulties stem from the bilateral system of CMEA commercial relations and ways of fixing contractual prices within the CMEA. Because of the lack of convertible currency accounting and price negotiations considering supply and demand, the sale of goods – developed with Western licenses or produced with the help of Western know-how and machines – in CMEA markets quite often is simply not profitable, and therefore cannot contribute to meeting the costs of licenses, know-how, and machines.[15] Another obstacle arises when any other CMEA country develops the production and export of a certain product already produced in Hungary on the basis of some imported licenses and brought to market successfully both at home and in the West.

Characteristic examples showing the obstacles to expansion of CMEA exports are the cases of the Rába Works at Győr, where West German expertise helped launch the production of truck- and bus-axle housing, and of the Csepel Motor Works, where the production of hydraulic gears was started. Western technology and design have been implemented successfully in both products. However, these products, which otherwise met all requirements, could not have been marketed profitably in the CMEA because of the present CMEA price system, which involves artificial exchange rates between   convertible currencies and the transferable ruble (TR).[16]

A number of examples may be cited where machine-producing companies would be able to export up-to-date products only with the help of units imported from the West, due to the lack of modern domestic component and semifinished goods production and insufficient supply available from our CMEA partners. But such exports will not be developed, since the sale of the product in the CMEA markets would not be profitable.[17] If the company in question drops the idea of importing the semifinished product, either the quality of the good will be jeopardized through the incorporation of the inadequate domestic semifinished good, or the possibilities of development will be left unexploited.

Machines serving technological development imported from CMEA countries, mainly the Soviet Union, make up only a modest part of total Hungarian machinery imports.[18] Yet even these relatively small machinery imports often jeopardize a successful technical transfer from the West. This actually is what happened in the case of the Láng Machine Works, where the production of turbines was started with the help of a Swiss Brown-Bovery Company license.[19] This proved to be a very successful development, efficiently substituting high-quality products for Western imports for a couple of years. The production of the 200 MW turbine was continuously jeopardized by increasing competition from a Soviet product. The competing Soviet machine differed in three respects from the Hungarian one. Its technical parameters were less advantageous: the costs of starting and stopping the machine were much higher than those of the Hungarian counterpart, because its greater weight made it very difficult to heat up. The Soviet producer undertook fewer obligations than the Láng Machine Works for services and for the supply of spare parts. Finally, the Soviet machine was less expensive than the Hungarian one, when the two prices were compared, albeit not very precisely, by relating them to comparable services.[20]

The observed phenomena in the export and import turnover between the CMEA countries have the same explanation. Namely, the prevailing practice of price fixing in intra-CMEA trade and the national evaluation of the common currency – the transferable ruble (TR) used in bilateral accounting – are inconsistent with each other. As is well known, the contractual prices applied in intra-CMEA trade are supposed to be set on the basis of the average world market price of the past five years, considering the prevailing official rates of exchange.

This would not cause difficulties if the prevailing official rates of exchange between the convertible currencies and the TR considered at the fixing of the contractual prices in fact corresponded with the commercial rates of exchange applied by the management system of each national economy. But this is not the case. The official rate of exchange between a convertible currency and the TR (in which CMEA contract prices are expressed) overvalues the TR. Thus, on the average, for a Hungarian firm the forint equivalent of one TR is less than the forint equivalent of the number of units of the convertible currency to which a TR corresponds at the official rate.

This difference is rooted in the fact that the TR is not convertible. Countries with claims in TRs cannot convert them freely as they could in the case of the convertible currencies but have to use them for the purchase of goods offered by their CMEA trading partners. The field of utilization of the TR is more limited than that of convertible currencies. This is reflected in the difference between the commercial rates of exchange (or foreign exchange coefficients as they are called in many countries), on the one hand, and the official rates of exchange, on the other (see Table 10.4).[21]

Table 10.4   *Comparison of Ratios of Forint / Dollar Rate to Forint / Ruble Rate at Official Rates and at Commercial Rates, 1970–77*

	Forint / Dollar Rate ÷ *Forint / Ruble Rate*	
	Official Rates	*Commercial Rates*
1970	0.90	1.50
1971	0.90	1.50
1972	0.73	1.58
1973	0.72	1.20
1974	0.70	1.20
1975	0.66	1.10
1976	0.74	1.20
1977	0.70	1.18

Source: Külkereskedelmi árstatisztikai adatok 1957–1977 [Foreign trade price statistics 1957–1977] (Budapest: Központi Statisztikai Hivatal, 1978), p. 83.

It is clear without any closer examination of the causes that bilateralism itself and the inflexible pricing applied in bilateral trade agreements have led to a special contradiction. That is to say, under prevailing conditions, if a CMEA country manages by technical transfer or any other means to develop a new product meeting the requirements of advanced Western industrial countries, the sale of this product on the CMEA market will be less profitable than sale on the home market or export to the West, or will not be profitable at all. As a result, CMEA countries often refuse to deliver these kinds of products to each other.

For example, when one CMEA country (A) chooses to export to another CMEA country (B) a good salable on the Western market, this may cause problems somewhat analogous to 'dumping' if country B produces a similar item using imported Western technology. The reason, again, is the difference between official exchange rates (relating convertible currencies to the TR) and commercial exchange rates (as they are called in Hungary, though similar operational exchange rates are used in other CMEA nations). When these two different exchange rates are used, it may turn out that the domestic price that would be charged in country B for the good from country A will be less than the domestic selling price of the item produced in country B.

The third group of difficulties hampering technical transfer is actually to some extent a consequence of the uncertain position of enterprises, of the related and still unresolved problems of the domestic investment system, and of the close dependence of the Hungarian economy on the inflexible bilateral system of intra-CMEA trade. The large number of varied obstacles has hindered wide-scale development of entrepreneurial behavior in Hungary even after the economic reform was launched in 1968.

The most important consequence of this is that decisions of firms are mainly based on static considerations. Hence problems are considered only in relation to each five-year plan or reconstruction plan, and company management is just not able to make continuous adjustments to constantly changing conditions.

There are several explanations for this phenomenon. Because of the wide use of subsidies, it has remained unclear what interrelations connect long-run profit and planned technical indicators such as quantity of output and productivity per manhour. The pursuit of profit has been weakened because supervisory organs are interested in technical indicators, and the common experience is that the funds necessary for technical development can be obtained through state budget subsidies.

In turn, the separation of design and development units from production units remained common even after 1968. Consequently, research and design experts are not adequately aware of company objectives. The administrative separation of R & D and producing units often has resulted in bureaucratic, rather than economic, relations between them. Hence the development strategies elaborated for firms by planning and research institutes cannot cope with changing conditions, possibilities, and requirements.

For example, the lack of internal research staff has caused some difficulties in regard to refrigerators successfully developed by the Refrigerator Machine Works at Jászberény in cooperation with the Bosch Gmbh (Ltd). After achieving a rapid expansion of market share in Western Europe, the firm's sale prospects declined because design changes in the model were not made fast enough.[22]

Similar difficulties arose in connection with the West German MAN-Motors in the field of bus production. The producers recognized the design problems too late, due to the lack of an internal research staff. The production of new engines and gear-levers was needed, but it would have been much more advantageous if their production could have been launched gradually.[23]

Hungarian companies in need of semifinished inputs do not wish to contract for them with other Hungarian firms, since they cannot rely on their deliveries. Instead they make efforts to merge the potential partner, with the help of some government support, into their own enterprise. And in most cases companies succeed in realizing such ideas. This practice was followed – in a sense, successfully – by the already mentioned Rába Machine Works at Győr. The company managed to absorb almost all the casting and spare-part producing companies and those which could be transformed for these purposes, in the northwestern part of the country.[24] Although total production increased, the output of some products was curtailed, causing shortages, while for some other items production cost rose.

The Machine Tool Works did not act in such an aggressive way to integrate suppliers. However, because of this and its own inability to produce a new output, the company did not fully utilize the possibility of cooperation with the German firm Gildemeister in the production of microprocessor-controlled lathes. The large effective Western demand could not be met, because of a shortage of capacities, especially in the supply of castings.[25]

IV The Future of Technical Transfer from the Leading Western Industrial Countries

On the basis of the explanation given above, attention has to be focused on two, as yet unresolved, problems. First, the adoption of Western techniques is an expensive business operation. The anticipated rising costs of license and know-how acquisitions and the purchase of technically outstanding machinery and equipment cannot be covered in the future with the revenues of mining and agricultural production. There are no uncommitted mineral reserves in Hungary or in the CMEA with which to increase production of material-intensive exports. The increase in agricultural production offers little chance for a rapid increase in exports since the world market's demand for Hungarian agricultural products is not rising. The credit boom on the money markets of the leading industrial countries is also over. Thus the money market cannot be relied upon for securing suitable credits to cover the increasing costs involved in the importation of technical expertise. It follows that the prerequisite for the growth of technical transfer is the degree to which the development it generates enhances Hungary's export potential to capitalist countries.

The other important issue is that, in its effort to effectively adopt the leading industrial countries' technical expertise, even the changing Hungarian economic system has failed to create appropriate conditions. The difficulties in meeting the cost of technical transfer and the dissatisfaction with the results create doubts, in the first instance, about the expediency of East–West trade and, within that, about the usefulness of developing technical transfer. It is not difficult, however, to argue against the feasibility of isolationism. The acquisition opportunities offered by the world markets for mineral resources as well as in the technical field are not only valuable, but their exploitation is a prerequisite for development of the Hungarian economy as well as the advance of the other CMEA countries.[26]

To ask whether one or another CMEA country could make itself independent of the outside world, or whether the CMEA as a unit could achieve autarky, is not relevant. The questions to be solved are, by what means and to what extent should the CMEA countries become involved with the capitalist world market, and how should they shape this relationship?[27]

One of the possible options is supported by the recognition that the CMEA countries' manufacturing industry has not been able to score a real success on the capitalist world market and that, in the case of Hungary and some of the small CMEA countries, the difficulty was increased by the deterioration of the country's terms of trade during the 1973–75 price explosion.[28] Some authors conclude not that the economy must be better adapted to the processes of the world market in order to improve its performance, but that the world market does not appreciate the accumulated knowledge and generally undervalues the work of the CMEA countries. Pursuing this chain of thought would lead to the conclusion that the CMEA countries should import needed raw materials from capitalist markets in the process of their development and should also import some equipment necessary for their technical development, but should limit the likelihood that the relations between the two market systems become organic.[29]

Such an economic policy means a deliberate concentration of resources in order to develop priority branches as closed systems. This policy builds principally on the market-creating effect of the CMEA division of labor. The aim of this policy is growth of total output, not efforts to meet the more and more diversified domestic demand and the requirement of the capitalist markets. This development strategy does not require important changes in the regulatory and institutional system, and it does not hinder formal cooperation with the other CMEA countries.

However, this strategy faces social conflicts of considerable strength in three respects.

(1) Its success necessitates a sudden and profound change in CMEA cooperation. But such a change has been repeatedly programmed by the relevant authorities without suitable results.

(2) This development would be accompanied by a narrowing of the range of goods available for general consumption and for industrial raw material supply, which would produce significant discontent on the home market. The probability that investment projects for exports to the world market could also be carried out in the framework of CMEA-oriented development is not very high.

(3) Finally, the biggest obstacle in the way of this concept is that its success would require a vigorous restriction of domestic consumption and imports. The forceful curtailment of consumption and investment would, however, be the source of strong social stresses and could result only in a temporary abatement of the balance-of-trade deficit.

The other policy option focuses on the evolutionary development of the economy. It considers that the country's pattern of production cannot be successfully transformed with revolutionary methods. This policy places more emphasis on the efficient exploitation of available resources. In the process of its development, this economic policy acknowledges the fluctuations of prices and terms of trade even if these are in many ways detrimental to the country's interests, and endeavors to mobilize the country for utilization of the advantages provided by the international division of labor under the new conditions.

It envisages planned control over the money supply both for investment and consumption purposes, instead of quantitative restrictions on specific commodities. It places the emphasis not on quantitative increase, but on developing a range of goods that correspond to the demand.

This option does actively build on the development of the relations with the CMEA countries, but acknowledges that the development of CMEA integration can only be a slow process. Its starting point is the recognition that the bottleneck in the country's development is the availability of imports from the world market, which in turn depends on the ability to export to pay for them. This policy aims at using technical transfer from the leading industrial countries by encouraging the entrepreneurial spirit of firms, rather than in the framework of centralized development programs. Achieving this aim necessitates a further development of the 1968 economic reform, promoting autonomous, target-oriented enterprises. Its successful implementation is handicapped, however, because its aims do not agree with the ambitious development ideas of certain circles who resist social and institutional changes.

Finally, what are the prospects for the growth of technical transfer? Clearly, it will always be limited by the development of the CMEA countries' export potential on the world market. There is little chance for rapid improvement, because of internal factors such as insufficient changes in the economic control system, on the one hand, and external conditions such as the slow growth of world trade and the increasing competition of developing countries, on the other.

Notes: Chapter 10

1 Alexander Gerschenkron, *Economic Backwardness in Historical Perspective* (Cambridge, Mass.: Harvard University Press, 1962), esp. Ch. 1.
2 Edwin Mansfield, 'International Technology Transfer: Forms, Resource Requirements, and Policies', *American Economic Review*, Vol. 65, No. 2 (May 1975), pp. 372–6.
3 See F. Jánossy, 'Gazdaságunk mai ellentmondásainak eredete' [Origin of the present contradictions of the Hungarian economy], *Közgazdasági Szemle*, 1969, Nos. 7–8, pp. 806–29.
4 The nationalization of foreign capital had taken place already in 1946–48.
5 On the achievements of the centralized programs see my article, 'Relationship between the International Division of Labour and Hungarian Economic Policy', in I. Friss (ed.), *Economic Policy and Planning in Hungary* (Budapest: Corvina, 1978), pp. 224–79.
6 T. Liska-Másias, 'Hatékonyság és a nemzetközi munkamegosztás' [Efficiency and international division of labor], *Közgazdasági Szemle*, 1954, No. 10, pp. 75–94.
7 These statements concern so-called 'enterprise' investments which represent more than half of the total investment volume. Similar criteria are considered when allocating assets to 'state' investments (decided centrally) though profit considerations will not play any significant role in this case.

8 After 1968 it became a basic principle of Hungarian economic management that all enterprises with sufficient forints could decide themselves to what extent they used funds for the purchase of materials, semifinished goods, components, or investment goods in the domestic, the socialist, or the Western markets.

9 See P. Kardos, 'Licenc vásárlás vagy hazai fejlesztés?' [Import of licenses or domestic design?], *Külgazdaság*, 1978, No. 8, pp. 9–17.

10 On causes and consequences of external effects, see Alan A. Brown and Márton Tardos, 'Transmission and Responses to External Economic Distibrances', in Egon Neuberger and Laura D. Tyson (eds.), *Impact of International Economic Disturbances on the Soviet Union and Eastern Europe: Transmission and Response* (Elmsford, N.Y.: Pergamon Press, 1980), pp. 250–76.

11 My efforts at econometric measurement of the impact of technical transfer on the national income and foreign trade performance were not successful. Because of the numerous changing and interacting factors in domestic economic activity as well as foreign markets, the data available did not allow me to determine the relative significance of the different effects.

12 The following case studies will appear in a volume edited by M. Tardos and to be published in Budapest by Közgazdasági és Jogi Könyvkiadó in 1980:

   Tamás Bauer and K. Attila Soós, 'Kényszerpályák hálójában – jármüipar' [Compulsory paths – bus production].

   Károly Farkas, 'Intenziv termékváltás és terjeszkedés Győri Vagon és Gépgyár (Rába)' [Rapid change and development of the Rába Machine Works' product mix].

   Mihály Laki, 'Növekedés és rugalmasság Transzformátor Szövetkezet (TRAKISZ)' [Development and elasticity in TRAKISZ].

   Iván Major, 'A termékeszerkezet átalakulása a változó gazdasági környzetben – Beloiannisz Hiradástechnikai Vállalat (BHG)' [The change of the pattern of production in the BHG].

   K. Attila Soós, 'Müszaki szinvonal, irányitás-gazdálkodás, gazdaságosság a Csepel Autógyárban' [Technical level, regulation, and efficiency at the Csepel Motor Works].

   Éva Tárnok, 'A technikai fejlődés határai a Láng Gépgyárban' [Limits of technical development in the Láng Machine Works].

   Éva Tárnok and Péter Vince, 'A sebességváltó gyártás' [Case study of gear-lever production].

   Pál Valentyni, 'Vállalatfejlödés és állami beavatkozás Ganz Villamossági Müvek (GVM)' [Enterprise development and state intervention in the Ganz Electrical Equipment Works].

13 See the case study by Soós cited above.

14 Costs of earning a unit of foreign currency through export, expressed in forints.

15 As already noted, the problems connected with the exploitation of the results of technical transfer from the West within the framework of CMEA trade limit greatly the readiness of Western companies to develop relations with the small CMEA countries.

16 More details are provided in the studies of Bauer and Soós, and of Tárnok and Vince cited in n. 12.

17 For example, suppose the official rate is 0.69 TR = $1 and the Hungarian commercial exchange rates are 40 ft = $1 and 35 ft = 1 TR. If a Hungarian firm buys a Western component at a world market price of $0.90, the firm pays 36 ft (40 ft/$1 × $0.90) for it. Suppose further that the firm sells the finished product to a CMEA customer at a (moving five-year average) world market price of $1.10. At 0.69 TR = $1, the CMEA price is 0.76 TR ($1.10 × 0.69). The firm receives 27 ft (0.76 TR × 35 ft/1 TR) for its export sale. The difference between the cost of the Western component, 36 ft, and the revenue from the CMEA sale, 27 ft, is a loss of 9 ft. (In addition, of course, the firm has labor and other costs, and the total loss would be greater.)

18 I. Schweitzer, 'A Szovjetnióból származó gépbehozatal néhány sajátossága' [Certain peculiarities of Hungarian machinery imports from the Soviet Union], *Gazdaság*, 1977, No. 2, pp. 80–96.

19 For details, see the study by Tárnok cited in n. 12.

20 In this case we even ignored the fact that the Soviet firm asked a price for its equipment still lower than would have been justified if calculated on the basis of the CMEA price system.

21 On this question, see Franklyn D. Holzman, *Foreign Trade under Central Planning* (Cambridge, Mass.: Harvard University Press, 1974), esp. Ch. 11, 'Soviet Foreign Trade

Pricing and the Question of Discrimination', and Ch. 12, 'More on Soviet Bloc Trade Discrimination'.

22 *A közös vállalat alakitás lehetösegei* [The possibilities of joint ventures] (Budapest: Konjunktura és Piackutató Intézet, 1979; mimeo).
23 Ibid.
24 For details, see the study of Farkas cited in n. 12.
25 Ibid.
26 Andras Köves, 'A világgazdaság integrálódása eś a gazdaság fejlesztési iránya' [The integration of the world economy and the direction of economic development], *Gazdaság*, 1977, No. 4, pp. 50–68.
27 This subject is discussed in Rezső Nyers and Márton Tardos, 'Milyen gazdaságpolitikai stratégiát válasszunk?' [What economic strategy should be chosen?], *Gazdaság*, 1979, No. 1, pp. 5–25; English translation in *Acta Oeconomica* (Budapest), Vol. 22 (1979) No. 1–2, pp. 11–31.
28 See the study of Brown and Tardos, cited in n. 10.
29 Ferenc Kozma, *Mire képes a magyar gazdaság?* [Of what is the Hungarian economy capable?] (Budapest: Kossuth, 1978).

Chapter 11

Solving Poland's
Foreign Trade Problems

WITOLD TRZECIAKOWSKI

This chapter examines Poland's current foreign trade problems and how they might be resolved. Section I discusses the development strategy Poland adopted in the 1970s and some of its consequences. Section II analyzes weaknesses in the system of regulating foreign trade and recommends a number of specific improvements in it. Section III explains the reasons for my restrained optimism about the future prospects for Poland's international economic relations.

I The 'Outward-Looking' Development Strategy

The first half of the 1970s was directed toward acceleration of comprehensive development. Poland became an industrial country by implementing a policy of rapid modernization, massive imports of new technology, and a high rate of investment – financed both from internal resources (domestic investment reaching 38 percent of GNP in the peak year) and from foreign credits. At the same time the years 1971–75 witnessed a high rate of wage increases and a sharp rise in consumption. It was a strategy of rapid opening of the Polish economy to Western imports, but not an export-oriented strategy.

In the course of a too-rapid growth (see Tables 11.1 and 11.2) sharp constraints in further development were encountered:

(1) Foreign trade constraints were created by the growing surpluses of imports from Western countries over exports to these countries, which resulted in accumulated indebtedness. Imports of new technology brought a remarkable modernization of the equipment installed in Poland, yet they did not result in investment 'harvests' in new convertible-currency exports. The initial assumptions of such a 'self-repayment' policy proved to be mistaken. Instead, traditional raw-material exports were burdened with foreign debt repayments and interest charges. The overall import intensity of development increased rapidly. The conditions of a 'producer's market' did not favor high-quality standards of production and export expansion. The ratio of the rate of export growth to the rate of industrial production growth fell from 1966 to 1978 by more than 17 percent, and the ratio of

the rate of export growth to the rate of fixed assets growth fell in the same period by 50 percent. These results prove either that investment decisions were not really export-oriented or that the export effects are delayed and still hidden. If the second assumption is correct, potential reserves for export expansion still exist, provided that the system of foreign trade planning and management is improved.

Table 11.1 *Indicators of Polish Economic Development, Annual Average 1971–75, 1977, and 1978*
(Percentage rates of growth at constant prices)

Indicator	Annual Average 1971–75	1977	1978
National income created	9.8	5.6	2.8
National income distributed	12.0	4.5	0.5
Investment in the socialized economy	21.9	2.5	-0.2
Production by socialized industry (at seller's prices)	13.2	8.6	5.8
Total agricultural production	4.9	-0.8	4.4
Labor productivity in socialized industry	8.8	8.3	5.8
Employment in socialized economy	3.5	0.9	0.6
Cost-of-living index	2.4	4.9	8.7
Real wages in socialized economy per employee	7.1	3.8	-2.7
Exports	10.7	8.8	6.1
Imports	15.3	0.4	1.7

Source: Main Indicators of Polish Foreign Trade Development (Warsaw: Foreign Trade Research Institute, 1979).

Table 11.2 *Polish Foreign Trade: Value, 1970, 1975, and 1978, and Rate of Growth, Annual Average 1971–75, 1977, and 1978*
(At current prices)

	Value (Billion Foreign-Exchange Zlotys[a])			Rate of Growth (%)		
	1970	1975	1978	Annual Average 1971–75	1977	1978
Exports	14.2	34.2	44.7	19.1	11.3	9.7
Socialist countries	9.1	20.5	27.3	17.7	12.3	11.2
Capitalist countries	5.1	13.7	17.4	21.7	9.8	7.3
Imports	14.4	41.7	50.9	23.7	5.4	4.9
Socialist countries	9.9	19.1	27.6	14.0	16.8	9.4
Capitalist countries	4.5	22.6	23.3	37.8	-4.6	0.0

[a]US $1 = approximately 3 foreign-exchange zlotys.
Source: Main Indicators of Polish Foreign Trade Development (Warsaw: Foreign Trade Research Institute, 1979).

(2) Labor force constraints have resulted from demographic trends and the exhaustion of hidden reserves in the agricultural sector. These recent developments should favor the choice of intensive methods of production and the development of a suitable system of control.[1]

(3) Energy and raw material constraints exist because the demand for energy and materials has grown much more rapidly than the increase actually achieved in productive capacities. These constraints limit both the rate of growth and the commodity structure of export expansion and preclude activities that are highly energy- and material-intensive.

(4) Constraints in agricultural production, especially of corn and fodder, have resulted from lagging mechanization on private farms and the exodus of young people from rural areas to urban centers. These constraints preclude traditional agricultural exports as a source of export expansion. On the contrary, they result in hard-currency import expenditures.

(5) Constraints in transportation exist because of the insufficiency of existing transport facilities in relation to growing requirements. Hence transport-intensive activities cannot be included in the list of export expansion projects.

(6) Constraints have resulted from the very high capital intensity of recent investments connected with the development of extractive and heavy industries and characterized by lengthy construction periods. These constraints limit exports of additional raw materials to the possibilities from existing productive capacities.

(7) The rapid growth of nominal wages by comparison with the growth of consumer goods available on the domestic market has created tensions in the consumers' market. These scarcities limit the possibility of introducing major changes in money incentive systems on a broad scale in the course of the next few years.

Hence it is evident that in the second half of the 1970s there occurred cumulative tensions, scarcities, and disequilibria that forced the government to arrest the growth of investment and to restrict imports from Western countries. This situation led not only to the freezing of economic reforms but also to recentralization processes.

Given these constraints, what potential sources of export expansion remain for the 1980s? Exports of coal cannot be treated as a source of additional earnings, because the domestic requirements for energy preclude any substantial increase in the volume of coal exports. Since oil prices are rising faster than coal prices, receipts from coal exports can at best be expected only to cover the expenditures for oil imports. Nor can agricultural exports serve as a source of export expansion, because long-term domestic demand for agricultural products surpasses domestic supply. Similarly, capital-intensive and material-intensive exports cannot be treated as sources of further export expansion. Hence the continuation of existing patterns in the commodity structure of exports does not seem feasible. It will be necessary to develop highly processed exports based on appropriate labor-intensive technologies, as highly qualified labor represents Poland's relatively abundant factor of production. This, however, requires essential changes in the system of regulating foreign trade. Basic raw-material exports can be effectively managed within the framework of a highly centralized system of control. However, highly processed and diversified exports need decentralization within the framework of an indirect system of planning and management.

Export expansion calls for specialization. We know from experience that it is a difficult task. It assumes accurate prediction of long-term trends in foreign demand. It entails specific risks, because specialization increases dependence on foreign partners and therefore increases vulnerability to protectionist tendencies. Specialized development also requires a selective investment policy in exports and a selective structural policy in domestic production. A selective investment policy in exports is not compatible with the notorious practice of investment allocation based either on proportionality rules or on bargaining power. Moreover, a selective structural policy in domestic production means that inefficient domestic activities should be eliminated or, at least, should not be expanded. This requires strong central preferences. However, the domination of overall central preferences over partial branch preferences must at present be regarded more as a wish than as reality.

Poland's main trade partners are CMEA countries. These countries will face the exhaustion of labor force reserves and increasing costs in new raw-material resources. The years 1981–85 will persist, at least for smaller socialist countries, as a period of relatively considerable indebtedness to the West, although the current balance of trade will probably improve. Rising protectionist tendencies in the West and Eastern debt-service requirements may constrain, respectively, the rates of growth of Eastern exports to the West and Eastern imports from the West, and thus encourage intra-CMEA trade. Poland's main concern in her trade with the East is securing basic raw-material supplies to increase production. These include oil, gas, iron ore, cellulose, zinc ore, bauxite, and chemicals. The increment in supplies can be assured mainly by joint investments in the CMEA country endowed with the required resources, with the investments repaid by supplies of the resources thereby developed. The satisfaction of these needs is guaranteed by long-term agreements.

The main macroeconomic problem consists in compensating for the huge recent oil price rises. Problems of this kind are settled within the general framework of intergovernmental agreements, price-setting rules, and mutual credits. Probably trade among CMEA countries in the 1980s will still be based on a centralized, directive control system. However, the rising diversification of the commodity structure of trade will encourage a more flexible approach toward decentralized decision making, especially in the domain of specialization and coproduction agreements. These should be based on economic considerations and decided upon at the operative decision-making levels.

Much more difficult problems will arise in trade with developing countries and developed market economies. Poland's trade policy toward developing countries must consider the necessity of structural adjustments of Polish imports in the light of their economic development and diversification of production. At the same time our trade policy must take into account the emergence of newly created productive capacities competing with our exports. New forms of bilateral and tripartite coproduction arrangements, joint ventures of various types, and consulting activities must be envisaged. All these require more flexibility in foreign trade planning and management.

The greatest difficulties can be expected in foreign trade with developed market economies. Their economic prospects for the 1980s, according to the opinions of Western analysts, are not too bright: low rates of growth, high rates of inflation, and persisting unemployment reinforcing protectionist tendencies. All these prospects create a rather unfavorable context for the expansion of Poland's convertible-currency exports. If Eastern exports are determined by the income elasticity of Western imports, the forecast for Polish exports is rather pessimistic. (See Chapter 4.) However, the new capabilities created by our huge imports of new technology in recent years may increase the coefficient of elasticity, improving our prospects. At any rate, 'sensitive' exports should be avoided, and the expectation of abrupt increases of our share in the supply of a given market would be unrealistic. The question of how to expand exports vigorously and at the same time remain invisible on Western markets cannot be easily answered.

Any realistic variants of balance-of-payments equilibrium must rely on the continuation of heavy external borrowing. However, 'creditworthiness' of the borrower is assessed in accordance with the debt-service ratio, that is, by comparing annual interest charges and repayments of principal to annual export earnings. Experience shows that no country can sustain for more than a few years a debt-service ratio exceeding 50 percent. The indicator can be lowered by rescheduling debt, by restricting imports, and/or by expanding exports. Rescheduling is not feasible if the debtor has to deal with many creditors. Import cuts, if prolonged, are painful and lead to deterioration in the growth of GNP, domestic production, and exports. Hence the best solution is that of export expansion. Given the structure of the Polish economy, to maintain the annual rate of growth of GNP at 3 percent, imports must grow at 3.5–4 percent per year. For Poland to reach a trade surplus in the middle of the 1980s, exports must grow by at least 8 percent per year in constant prices. If the annual rate of world inflation is 6–10 percent, our exports should grow by at least 14–18 percent yearly in current prices. Analysis of the external demand for Polish exports by specific commodities and geographical markets shows that this strategic target is feasible. Hence revising the foreign trade control system is vital.

II   Improving the Foreign Trade Control System

In my opinion, the current foreign trade control system does not meet the needs of the Polish economy; specifically, it does not ensure the rapid growth of efficient exports. Such an aim does not truly have top priority in practice. In investment decisions, import substitution predominates over export expansion. In regard to foreign credits, overoptimistic expectations about 'self-repayment' led to borrowing for imports that cannot be repaid by resulting exports. Also, assuring the supply of inputs to domestically oriented branches has had higher priority than meeting the requirements of export-oriented branches. Domestic disequilibria and scarcities were considered more acute than balance-of-payments problems because foreign credits were, in the past, abundant.

The 'leading' role of medium-term planning has been reduced by active central intervention in current decision making. The latter shortened the effective time horizon of planning, especially in regard to debt service and the regulation of imports.

Directive planning in terms of foreign currency, with calculations in the 'devisa' or 'foreign-currency' zloty instead of the domestic zloty, eliminated the role intended for the foreign trade conversion coefficient that was supposed to link foreign and domestic prices and thereby relate domestic use of imports and production of exports to conditions on the world market. Instead, price comparisons in the 'devisa' zloty actually resulted in irrational decisions to maximize exports sales in 'weak' currencies and import purchases in 'hard' currencies!

In the mid-1970s in the large economic organizations (LEO) managerial incentives were supposed to be linked to profits, with special rewards for profits earned in foreign trade. But then these separate incentives for foreign trade profits were eliminated, and foreign trade profits were lumped with profits from domestic sales. The incentives for efficient exports disappeared when the performance indicators of exporting firms became dependent upon domestic prices, which firms could successfully manipulate, rather than upon 'parametric' (i.e. independent) foreign trade prices.

Also, a uniform standard of efficiency for exporters was not applied to at least half of Polish exports, because the foreign price conversion coefficients were differentiated for individual firms, which naturally bargained for the most favorable arrangements. The outcome was higher domestic prices that facilitated fulfillment of enterprise plans, but at the expense of efficiency in foreign trade. Thus fundamental deficiencies in the method of economic calculation adversely affected the choice, production, and growth of exports.

In Poland's economic relations with CMEA countries, the main emphasis is on the improvement of planned forms of cooperation through coordination of national plans. Obligatory plan directives will remain the main tool to accomplish agreed activities. In countries relying on an indirect system of foreign trade control, involving adjustment of operational exchange rates, special corrective subsidies or taxes must compensate for losses or profits due to specific bilateral pricing rules or barter agreements.

In relation to trade with capitalist countries, a strategy of rapid expansion of efficient exports to convertible-currency countries should guide the allocation of central investments. Along with the general efficiency criterion, the impact of a given investment on the balance of payments should become one of the decisive indicators for investment choice. Branch preferences should be subordinated to overall preferences. Investments for branches requiring continued irrational protection should be eliminated. The investment strategy should be adapted to the long-term needs of specific foreign markets.

The present division of the central foreign trade plan into two parts could be maintained.

Part A encompasses:

(1) deliveries of basic commodities fixed by central balances for the domestic market and for exports, including deliveries in kind resulting from international agreements;
(2) the minimum amount of exports to the CMEA and world market;
(3) foreign exchange limits on imports for investment.

This part is administered centrally by the Foreign Trade Ministry.

The remaining items forming Part B of the foreign trade plan have been decentralized. Here the structure of exports and imports is determined by LEOs and is controlled by industrial branch ministries only in the form of a target balance for convertible currencies. If a LEO increases its exports, imports may be increased accordingly. For the rational allocation of resources by a LEO within these flexible limits, an appropriate indirect 'parametric' management system is indispensable. It includes transaction prices based on foreign trade conversion coefficients, tariffs, and selective taxes and subsidies. In the past, in case of disturbances of external or internal equilibrium, *ad hoc* administrative interventions occurred, but such interventions should be exceptions. If the exception became a rule, the parametric system would become a fiction rather than reality. The LEO, and not the branch ministry, should become an independent agent of the plan. The branch ministry should serve as an executive organ of the central planner, not as the representative of the branch's vested interests. As long as it is evaluated by the plan fulfillment of the LEOs it supervises, the branch ministry will behave as a supercorporation rather than as an agent of the central planner. Without a change in the actual rules of the game, there will always be a danger that partial vested interests will dominate overall preferences.

Strategic long-term plan directives within the framework of a centralized control system cannot alone suffice to release all reserves of initiative at operative decision-making levels. Poland needs the reform of the system of management. Two possible solutions can be envisaged: a comprehensive economic reform, or a reform only of the system of foreign trade management. The first solution can solve the problems of expanding efficient exports, the rationalization of imports, and the optimization of the domestic allocation of resources. However, such a reform requires the elimination of the most acute structural disequilibria in the economy, and it requires time in order to prepare a price reform. Although I believe a comprehensive reform is necessary, because of its complexity and the delay involved we should not wait for it. It is possible to start the systemic changes in the foreign trade sector at once, so as to promote efficient exports. All conditions necessary for the introduction of such changes have now been fulfilled: the theoretical foundations have been worked out. Rules to implement changes have been tested in practice in various experimental management systems.[2] And central parameters of the financial system, such as taxes and subsidies, could easily be modified to suit the requirements of rational allocation of resources.

The system of control is now, and will be in the future, a mixed system – partly centralized, partly decentralized. With the increasing diversification of production and exports, the importance of the decentralized system is growing. To avoid inconsistencies between the two coexisting decision-making systems, that is, between administrative directives and the indirect control mechanism, the following conditions must be met:

(1) The criterion of choice in foreign trade should be the maximization of profit measured in parametric prices of a balanced plan, namely,

$$\sum_r M^r D^r - C = \text{maximum},$$

where M^r = the foreign trade conversion coefficient for currency area r,
D^r = earnings in foreign currency from area r,
C = costs in domestic currency.

(2) Parametric foreign trade price conversion coefficients must express the marginal cost, in domestic currency, of earning an additional unit of foreign currency in conditions determined by the plan. In practice, the coefficients should be set at a level encompassing at least 85 percent of profitable exports. These coefficients should be uniform for all commodities and the same in exports and in imports.
(3) Domestic prices for producers of imported and of exportable commodities should be fixed at the level of 'transaction prices', that is, foreign trade prices multiplied by the foreign trade conversion coefficients. If domestic prices of imported or of exportable materials are set at another level, it is necessary to introduce taxes or subsidies to correct the calculation of efficiency. Domestic prices for goods not entering foreign trade should be based on costs.
(4) If the allocative function of prices for producers is supposed to coexist with the distributive function of prices for consumers, corrective taxes or subsidies for consumers must be applied.
(5) The financial system in foreign trade must incorporate strong incentives for enterprise personnel, including both management and employees. If the assumption that there are large potential hidden reserves for improvements in productivity is correct, then the motivational system in foreign trade should be strong.
(6) Special investment funds should be given to the Foreign Trade Bank to finance investments aimed at improving the trade balance. These funds should be allocated solely on the basis of efficiency criteria and should be reserved for fast pay-off investments in exports or in import-substituting activities. The selection criterion for these investments should take the following form of profit maximization:

$$P = \sum \ M'D' - (C + \alpha I) = \text{maximum},$$

where P = profit,
      α = marginal rate of interest fixed by the central planner,
      I = investment outlays.

When both domestic and foreign trade effects are measured in suitable parametric (i.e., independent of the producer) prices, profits from domestic activities and profits from foreign trade activities can be integrated and incentives then related to combined profits.

But this should not be done when the links between domestic and foreign trade pricing are weak or nonexistent, or where central price control is ineffective, because domestic prices can be manipulated by producers. Then profit maximization linked with strong incentives may lead to distortions: bonuses are paid for manipulated price increments, not for real results. Thus, where domestic activities are measured in non-parametric prices while exports are measured in foreign trade prices, it is indispensable to separate profits, as only profits from foreign trade activities can safely be linked with incentives. Two variants of the financial system are necessary: (1) a variant with integrated profits, mainly for branches specializing in exports, where the bulk of production can be priced in parametric prices and where strong incentives can be linked with these integrated profits; and (2) a variant for the remaining activities, where strong incentives should be linked only with profits from foreign trade activities.

It is possible to envisage systemic solutions different from those described here, such as schemes still aimed at export expansion but preserving the centralized system of directives. Just as in the case of a military complex, it is possible to separate organizationally some of the LEOs and treat them as branches specializing in exports. They may be privileged in the allocation of investment, get better treatment regarding supply, and receive higher wages and bonuses. However, the efficiency of such centralized systemic solutions cannot surpass the limits of a traditional directive centralized system and cannot avoid all its weaknesses: bargaining for an easy plan, manipulating prices and subsidies, earning profits from inefficient solutions, etc. It is extremely difficult to delineate organizationally the sphere of export production, since usually the final product is the result of cooperation and coproduction of various branches. For these branches, production for the final exporter may be a negligible part of total production. In such a case the use of directives may not be effective. On the other hand, production for exports (excluding raw materials) must constantly respond to changes in external demand. Central directives are not well suited to follow these changes. Therefore it seems doubtful whether the creation of an 'export complex' within the economy can in itself improve sufficiently the export performance of the country. An 'export complex' can operate successfully in the areas where centralized decision-making works effectively, but these areas are limited.

III   Conclusion

To sum up, what are the prospects for the future? Let me list the arguments for my restrained optimism:

(1) In my opinion the main reasons for Poland's difficulties are rooted chiefly in the internal constraints, not the external ones. The abolition of the former constraints is within the power of the country's decision makers.

(2) The causes of recent difficulties are now generally understood.

(3) The return to a policy of broader participation of specialists in decision making is within the range of feasible solutions. This may lead to the abolition of bottlenecks of various types at no cost.

(4) There exist substantial 'reserves': lack of investment 'harvests', underutilization of productive capacities, low productivity of labor, etc. When various barriers creating them are abolished, exploitation of these 'reserves' can give spectacular results.

(5) The strengthening of overall preferences at the expense of branch preferences or regional vested interests seems fully compatible with the basic foundations of a socialist society.

(6) The reinforcement of complex planning, but with less detailed administrative intervention in investment policy, seems consistent with rational decision making in a centrally planned economy.

(7) The reorientation of investment policy toward export specialization seems to be an urgent necessity.

(8) The strategic necessity to expand efficient exports requires indirect methods of management. One may have serious doubts whether the current situation is ripe for a comprehensive economic reform. However, the introduction of a system of indirect management in foreign trade seems feasible and can be implemented right now.

(9) The share of Poland's exports to the West in total Western imports is a negligible 0.4 percent. The doubling of this share would solve the problems of Poland's balance of payments, without encountering much resistance in protected markets in the West.

(10) Common sense should prevail on both sides. Western protectionist measures constrain the repayment of our debts. Hence they should be abolished in the interests of the creditors. If one wants to trade, one has to determine which Polish exports are admissible, that is, not blocked by trade barriers, in the long run, so as to allow for export specialization and expansion.

Notes: Chapter 11

1 By the 'system of control' I mean the system of organization, planning, and management.
2 See Witold Trzeciakowski, *Indirect Management in a Centrally Planned Economy: System Constructions in Foreign Trade* (Amsterdam: North-Holland Publishing Company, 1978), Part III.

Chapter 12

Political and Institutional Changes in the Management of the Socialist Economy: The Polish Case

STANISŁAW GEBETHNER

This chapter deals with the contemporary political systems of the East European socialist countries, focusing mainly on the role of the political system in socioeconomic development and in the direction of the national economy. The essential aim is to investigate how the political system responds to the needs of an advanced socialist economy, how the basic political institutions have been changed, and how they ought to be adjusted to new circumstances. Such investigation necessitates tracing the factors that predictably must, or should, force the evolution of political institutions and the transformation of methods for directing the national economy. This study concentrates mainly on the Polish experience, but is not simply a national case study. Rather the focus on Poland is augmented by comparisons, primarily to other East European socialist countries and to the Soviet Union.

Political systems in all countries are changing. The issue is how rapidly they change and how able they are to adjust to conditions of socioeconomic development, that is, to the changing social and economic, as well as political, environments. Thus the political systems of socialist countries in Eastern Europe have changed significantly in the past two decades, and that process of transformation is still continuing.

Granted, these changes are neither rapid nor spectacular, especially in the institutional aspects of their political systems. Indeed the fundamental structure of the political institutions has remained unchanged even in Yugoslavia and Romania, as well as Czechoslovakia.[1] Moreover, it is true that in all European (but not only European) socialist countries the constitutions have been amended considerably or replaced completely. However, the essential feature of the constitutional changes in socialist countries is the enunciation of goals of social and economic development and the policy guidelines for reaching them. The newly adopted socialist constitutions deal in a more detailed manner than previously with political institutional aspects, such as the leading and guiding role of the Communist Party, the functioning and prospects for social self-management, the place of the national front in the political system, the objectives of the trade unions in socialist society, safeguarding the rule of law, and ways of making the decision-making process more democratic.[2]

The socialist system of values is clearly revealed in the new socialist constitutions. Of course, the wording of constitutional rules is to some extent a rather formal safeguard of human behavior. The implementation of constitutional guidelines depends on various extralegal factors. But constitutional rules express the desired pattern of behavior. In this sense they are an indication of the direction, or at least the desired direction, in which the political system will evolve.

Even if there are no major changes in the shape of governmental institutions – their structure and distribution of powers, in particular in the allocation of decision-making centers at top, regional, and local levels – in practice, however, there are many significant transformations in the functioning of the political systems in the socialist countries.

At the same time, it must be stressed, there are some constant and stable political institutions and unchanging fundamental principles of the functioning of these systems. Therefore, if one wishes to predict the probable future evolution of political systems of socialist countries, one has to distinguish between stable, unchanging elements of these systems and those which are variable. One way to locate these unchangeable and changeable elements of political systems is to analyze their past evolution. Consequently some references to history are inevitable.[3]

One must take into account also international relations, which have increasing influence on the working of political systems. When the given country enters into closer cooperation – economic, technological, scientific, cultural – with the outside world, its political system has to be more open and more flexible toward requirements of international interdependence even in the field of ideology. It is hard to evade the implications of such interdependence. The only way to prevent the influence of foreign inputs on the political system is to maintain it in isolation and to carry on more or less autarkical policies of self-reliance. Comparative studies of the evolution of the socialist constitutions and political systems prove obvious associations between such a policy of self-reliance and a rigid and highly centralized political system.[4] Albania and North Korea are cases in point.

One of the main aims of this chapter is to review the changes in the political systems of European socialist countries that will result because their ever more advanced and sophisticated national economies come increasingly under the pressures of the changing world economy and domestic pressures of the people, who demand satisfaction of their rising aspirations for higher standards of living.

In Western mass media as well as among scholars one sometimes encounters the opinion that the socialist political systems have become rigid and that they are too immobile, inefficient, and overcentralized to meet the new requirements of détente and the era of closer economic cooperation between East and West.[5] Such opinions are based on an oversimplified image of these systems and are therefore ill-founded. The main error is in ignoring the evolution of the socialist political systems. The second fallacy arises from a confused interpretation of what are the stable and unchangeable elements, presenting them as signs of the stagnation of the political systems. That is, for example, the case with the leading role of the Communist Party in the political systems of the Soviet Union and East European socialist countries. But in fact the stability of the crucial political institutions does not mean the stagnation or the decline of the political system. Hence it is very important to distinguish between invariable and variable elements of the contemporary political systems of the East European socialist countries.

I   The Political Meaning of the Socialist Constitutions

The concept of constitution and its meaning in socialist countries are slightly different from those of West European democracies. These differences are even more evident in comparing the socialist concept of fundamental law with the American concept of the constitution.

First, the socialist constitution is not only a legal instrument of government dealing chiefly with the structure of government and the relations between citizens and the state powers. It covers wider aspects of the political system, dealing with such matters as the role of the Communist Party (and allied non-Communist parties where they exist[6]), trade unions, national fronts, forms of social self-management, and so on. All these institutions are important for the functioning of the modern political system of the socialist countries. The Communist Party, however, plays the most important role as one of the pillars of the political system in socialist society.[7]

The new socialist constitutions create a fresh stimulus to development of social self-management and the direct participation of the population in public matters (both economic and political). The constitutional recognition of social self-management and of the direct participation of the people in government as fundamental political institutions is in fact a very important indication for the probable evolution of the political system. Of course, the constitution by itself does not yet create self-management as a social reality, but it opens the way for public activities by the people.

Second, socialist constitutions in recent decades have become in a broader sense a kind of political (and also ideological) charter for the nation. They are increasingly labeled the constitutions of the state and the society. This implies too that the general principles of domestic and international policies are proclaimed in the constitution. Domestically the constitution sets guidelines of economic, social, educational, and cultural policies,[8] and outlines the main strategic goals of socioeconomic development.

What is the value of such constitutional guidelines? Are they binding directives for the governmental bodies (the parliament, the administration, the local authorities, and so on), or are they only an expression of the wishful thinking of the 'founding fathers' of the constitution? Are they purely programmatic declarations without any legal significance, or are they obligatory political norms safeguarded by special social and political sanctions?

In my opinion – both as a constitutional lawyer and a political scientist –

such constitutional guidelines have the character both of legal and political norms. Their legal value will be real only if the political sanctions are effective. And this brings us to the third distinctive feature of a socialist constitution.

The socialist constitution in its substance is more programmatic than is the traditional constitution, which is primarily an instrument of government. The aims of the traditional constitution in Western democracies are to limit the use of power, to protect individuals, and to establish a check and balance mechanism among different bodies of government. Broadly speaking, in the Marxist interpretation the chief task of the bourgeois constitution is to protect the status quo of the capitalist social and economic system.

Of course, the protection of the social and economic system and of the ruling position of the working people are also aims of the socialist constitution. But this is not the only task – and that is an important point of differentiation – of the fundamental law in socialist society. Rather, the constitution is one of the means of vitalizing socioeconomic and political development toward the classless society and social justice. And in this sense constitutions in the socialist countries have not only binding legal force but also outline programmatically the directions of political evolution.

The socialist constitution assumes some functions of the political party program. The main difference between a constitution and a party program is that the former is a political act widely accepted by the nation at large. Such acceptance has been reached through (1) universal, open, public debates on the draft constitution, (2) the approval of the constitution by the parliament as elected supreme representatives of the people, and (3) (usually) a national referendum.[9] The constitution is binding on the whole nation. A party program is accepted by party members and has mandatory force only for them. Consequently the shape of the constitution in some vital matters is very often a kind of social and political compromise. A good example is provided by the debates – and their outcomes – on the draft amendments to the Polish Constitution, which were offered for public discussion in 1976. Ultimately the role of allied non-Communist parties was recognized in the Constitution as revised. Moreover, the Front of National Unity was described as the broadest patriotic platform of cooperation between believers and nonbelievers to safeguard the supreme national interests. In other words, the actual Constitution of the Polish People's Republic recognizes a plurality of world views. The Marxist Communist Party, on the other hand, proclaims in its program a materialist world view in which the final goal of the party's activity is the rebuilding of society in a socialist direction.

An analysis of debates on the draft constitution is sometimes very useful and important. That is why, for instance, the recognition of workers' collectives as an element of the political system in the new Soviet Constitution is not meaningless.[10] Nor are the functions of socialist constitutions limited to the field of management of basic units of the national economy in the Soviet Union. They are accepted – let us say authoritatively – as a political factor changing the shape of socialist democracy. The same significance can be attached to Article 17 of the new Soviet Constitution, concerning the limits of individual private ownership. Given the public debates (which exposed some controversies in this regard), its final wording must be interpreted in political terms.

Accurate interpretation of the socialist constitution can therefore serve as a valuable indicator in the analysis of the political and socioeconomic evolution of socialist society, although of course this indicator cannot be considered as sufficient by itself.

Consequently, the new socialist constitutions should be interpreted in terms of their legal functions and their political and ideological ones. These should be taken into consideration in analyzing the political dimension of directing and managing the economy. The traditional constitutional institutions of the government, such as parliament, local councils, central and local administration, formally remained unchanged. But there are also some interesting and significant innovations in socialist constitutions adopted in the 1970s, expressing trends toward strengthening the position of elected representative bodies (the parliament and local people's councils) *vis-à-vis* executive bodies, especially in the field of control over the administration. Some new constitutions, like the Soviet one of 1977, impose permanent, direct accountability and answerability to the local community on administrative bodies of the state apparatus and its officials.[11]

II Politicizing the Direction and Management of the National Economy

The directing and managing of the national economy in socialist countries is even more a political phenomenon than in any modern Western capitalist country. In socialist societies the same chief decision-making bodies command, broadly speaking, both economic and political power. Consequently the process of economic management is obviously influenced by political factors.[12] Not only is the process closely linked with the functioning of the political system, but also politicization of this process is increasingly institutionalized. This is best exemplified by the problems discussed and resolved at the sessions of the Central Committees of the Communist Parties and by the agendas of Politburo meetings. The predominance of economic issues is evident. The same holds for the activities of administrative bodies, including those of the Councils of Ministers and their inner steering cabinets. This is an additional reason for the difficulty of divorcing the political and socioeconomic aspects of the day-to-day management of the national economy, not to mention the overall direction of socioeconomic development.

The main problem of the socialist economy concerns the question of transformation from the extensive phase of development to the intensive one. This is not purely a technical problem that ought to be considered merely in economic terms. Such transformation implies the necessity of deep changes in the manner of directing the national economy and the management of all the sectors and branches of the economy. For this reason alone it is a political problem. It is, additionally, a problem because, faced with a thoroughly new situation, there is a need for a shift in people's behavior – both by the populaion at large and by the governing political elite. But most people are used to old forms of direction of the national economy and out-of-date management methods. How to resolve the conflicts between long-established habits and necessary modern attitudes is also a political problem. New methods of direction and new forms of management demand ever more highly qualified personnel at all levels of the system, from the bottom to the top. This requires a modern-minded group of politicians and managers well suited to handle new, far more complicated, social and economic conditions. These also present important political questions to be solved by the political system.

All the problems mentioned above are of internal politics. However, with the exception of the Soviet Union, the East European countries are not able to convert successfully from an extensive to a more advanced, intensive economy without intensifying the bonds of international economic relations. The East European countries are of course interested both in promoting closer cooperation within the commonwealth of socialist states and well-balanced interchange with Western capitalist countries in the fields of economy, technology, science, and culture. These two aspects of external relations must be resolutely counterbalanced. Limiting them only to cooperation within the commonwealth of socialist states would by and large lead to a slowdown in the dynamics of economic development. On the other hand, one-sided promotion of external relations primarily with the Western countries would result in economic and political dependence on capitalist countries, which may suffer from economic instability.

In Poland, especially because of the experience of the 1920s and 1930s, the fears of such dependence are still intense. Poles still remember that before the Second World War Poland was economically a semicolony of the Western powers (Germany, France, Great Britain, and others) and politically was manipulated in the Western powers' interest. The scars of Poland's betrayal by her Western allies in 1939 are still in the flesh of the Polish nation.

Broadly speaking, that is a deep-seated reason for the very cautious attitude in the 1960s toward Western offers to expand economic relations with the socialist countries. It is no accident that the development of Polish–West German economic relations flourished in the 1970s only after the political treaty between Poland and the German Federal Republic had been concluded in December 1970. The progress of détente and of developing European security will continue to determine the development of the socialist countries' economic relations with the Western countries.

The restraint of the socialist countries regarding economic cooperation with the West so evident in the 1960s (and earlier) was likewise caused by the fear that imported foreign capital might overthrow the socialist economic system from within. However, in the 1970s this suspiciousness has gradually been disappearing. The current economic foundation of the socialist system is far stronger and at the same time resolutely supported by the transformed consciousness of the general population, which has internalized the socialist system of values. The extent of openness of the economic system in socialist countries toward the West is conditioned by political and social premises. It is difficult to agree with the opinion that relaxation of the socialist economic system (marked, among other things, by permitting foreign capital and/or internal, private small business activities) is a kind of present-day NEP. The flexibility of the economic system is not caused this time by the fragility of a newly created socialist economic system. On the contrary, a mature economy exists now in all the East European socialist countries. The economic difficulties that emerged at the end of the 1970s are by-products of both rapid economic growth and large structural changes in world markets. These factors produced the new needs for a rational approach to further economic expansion.

Probably in the 1980s, after inevitable transformations in the political systems that will enhance the legitimacy of political institutions in socialist countries, the economic systems will become even more open. Restraints inherited from the revolutionary period as well as from the Cold War era will probably disappear for good.

Of course, we ought to consider another possible future course of events in the West and in the East: that is, building up a feeling of external danger as a political solution to overcome actual troubles and to mobilize domestic reserves. That would mean a retreat from détente and the return to Cold War. For the East, such a solution seems ill-suited to the present stage of socioeconomic development and level of national political consciousness. Briefly speaking, this solution is out of date. What is more, there are no social forces interested in such a political solution. Even if somewhere in the political elite in the socialist countries are people supporting this option, they are by and large isolated, becoming ever more weak and characterized by decreasing support. A more likely possibility is that Cold War could be aggravated by the Western military–industrial complex.

Although the course of events in Afghanistan at the end of 1979 and at the beginning of 1980 – and its impact on East–West relations – can be interpreted in different ways, one thing seems evident. Détente is so deeply rooted now, after the decade of the 1970s, that neither side unilaterally, nor one political faction within the leadership of one superpower, is able to destroy immediately the complex net of relations of peaceful coexistence. The process of détente produced greater independence in the political sense for the smaller and medium size states of Europe, which are vitally interested in détente and which try to influence the superpowers to avoid a return to the Cold War. And that is an optimistic lesson from this apparently pessimistic situation at the beginning of the 1980s.

Whichever way we look at the interactions between politics and economics in the 1980s, we must expect greater predominance of politics over economics, in particular because a technocratic concept of steering economic development has failed in the 1970s, both in the East and in the West. There are stronger signs of revival of the political economy. The system of direction and management of the economy in the socialist countries, especially on the national level, will be even more politicized, that is, involve more political aspects that will provoke many-sided changes in the working of the whole political system. In other words, when the economic reserves have already been drained, one must replenish these reserves through reform of the political system.

III   Stability and Transformation of the Political System

Theoretically it is sometimes difficult to discern what are stable elements and what are changeable elements of the system. But in fact the political systems have been transformed and are still developing. Therefore to understand what are the stable elements and what are not is a valuable aid to discussion of probable changes in the political systems of the socialist countries in the 1980s, especially in the field of direction of the national economy. The most difficult problem here is that the very criteria themselves are subject to a dialectical process of reevaluation.

In the early 1950s, for instance, the possibility of coexistence of private ownership with public socialist ownership in agriculture (not to mention other fields of the economy) was treated as a deviation from basic principles of the socialist system. Today the compatibility of private ownership with a socialist economy is accepted. Mixed ventures with foreign capital manifest the same pattern.

The criteria of what is stable and what is changeable change in themselves. Nevertheless, it still makes sense to discuss the problem of unchangeable and changeable elements of the political and socioeconomic systems in socialist countries: The reevaluation of criteria is produced by a transformation in the environment, an evolution of the systems themselves, and also by developments of political and constitutional doctrine. One important factor determining changes in the environment of the social and political system is the evolution of the social consciousness of the working class (and its politicization) – and of the population at large – in the socialist countries. But the supreme criterion of evaluation remains the same and unchanged: the interests of the ruling classes, that is, the workers and their allies. Briefly put, changes cannot touch the essence of the class structure of power.

Changes in the model of implementing the leading and guiding role of the Communist Party in the political system *can* be discussed. But one cannot predict a disappearance of the principle of the leading role of the Marxist workers' party. One can discuss transformations in planning procedure, but not consider an abandonment of planning as such. It is possible to foretell long-term existence of a different kind of private and state–private sector economy within the socialist system, but it would be completely false to predict that the dominant position of public socialist ownership will be reduced. The interpretation of the principle of social equality would probably present more controversy in ardent ideological disputes, but this principle as such cannot be undermined. We can consider to what extent personal and political freedoms as well as social and economic rights of individuals are limited, or how the existing limitations are to be eliminated; however, essential freedoms and rights can never be challenged, because personal liberties and human rights are inseparable from socialism. It is also impossible to speak about a socialist system at least in Europe where a democratic form of government does not exist. The changeable elements of the political system include the ways in which the people exercise the power vested in them by the socialist constitutions and the forms of democratic participation.

More closely related to the focus of this study are the stable and unchangeable elements of the political system in socialist countries that in crucial ways influence the system of directing the national economy and of steering the socioeconomic development of the nation. The most significant of these are:

(1) the dominance of socialist public ownership of the fundamental means of production in essential spheres of the national economy;
(2) planning of socioeconomic development as the basis for directing the national economy and the foundation of its operational management;
(3) the homogeneity of economic and political power and the leading position of the Communist Party; and
(4) the establishment of a classless society and the achievement of full economic and social justice as the general and eventual long-range target of socioeconomic development.

By contrast, the main changeable elements of the political systems in socialist countries along the dimension here are:

(1) the possibility of existence of some types of private ownership, limited to an extent authorized by the socialist state;
(2) various alternative methods of socialist planning;
(3) different models of the operational, day-to-day management of the nationalized economy;
(4) the existence of various forms of workers' and/or social self-management acting within the national economy;
(5) different models of the distribution of powers between the political bodies (mainly the Communist Party) and the executive bodies of the state administration, as well as between the central and local authorities; and
(6) alterations in short-term and medium-term purposes and priorities of socioeconomic development.

IV Socialist Public Ownership and the Limits of Private Ownership

Public ownership of the essential means of production is the fundamental factor in the socialist economic system and the socialist political system. The national economy is based on socialist public ownership, which plays a dominant role in all branches of industry and commerce. Cooperative ownership as one type of socialist ownership also predominates in agriculture. In some socialist countries public ownership is merged with cooperative ownership in agriculture. In the Soviet Union in particular differences between these types of socialist economy are continually diminishing concerning the method of management.[13] It is, however, far too early to predict that this trend toward merging the types of socialist ownership – the public (state-operated) one and the cooperative one – is of universal relevance for the future of the economic system in socialist countries.

In my opinion an opposite trend would appear likely: the development not only of cooperative ownership, but also of the other types of socialist ownership like the collective ownership by the workers of a given enterprise, operated by self-management bodies. The Yugoslav experiments performed with this aim for thirty years provide good examples of the latter. But, especially in the case of Poland, the long-term process of modernization, and, as a consequence, socialization, of agriculture underlies the general strategy of socioeconomic restructuring of farming. The essence of this restructuring is a slow and gradual, but voluntary and consistent, evolution from individual farms to cooperative or state-operated farms. We cannot exclude also different forms of semiprivate or semistate (or collective) forms of farming. Now the main problem is to develop highly productive individual farms closely linked with the state-controlled national economy.

The form of land ownership, however, is not so important in this case. Even now, when in Poland individual farming based on the private ownership of the land outweighs the socialist forms of farming, the whole agricultural sector is tightly merged through the sophisticated system of economic, legal, and financial incentives into the national planned socialist economy. In fact, in Poland doctrinal disputes over the problem of the form of land ownership or over the production methods in agriculture are rare. The real issue is how to increase the productivity of Polish agriculture and to safeguard the nutrition of the whole nation – a problem that is particularly acute now, because of the increasingly bothersome lack of manpower in agriculture, owing to constant migration of the population from rural to urban areas.[14] The problem is how and when these important questions will be solved in Poland. While the detailed scenario is difficult to predict, the problem must be solved in the 1980s. Otherwise there will be great trouble for the Polish economy as a whole, and the political system will also be seriously challenged.

There is, however, a broader reason for discussing the Polish experience in agriculture, and this concerns the question of the existence of private ownership in a socialist economic system. The most controversial point here is whether the very existence of private ownership, and/or permitting this kind of ownership in industrial or commercial activities, is an indication of a return to capitalist forms of production. Is it a kind of retreat from socialist economic philosophy and fundamental principles of the socialist system? The problem became more acute when the scope of permission for private ownership was extended in the past decade. This was done in two directions, the first being the establishment of mixed companies operating in some sectors of industry and external commerce. Foreign capitalist companies participate in these ventures. The second field is individual craftsmanship, small-scale commerce, and other forms of services (cafeterias, snackbars, and so on).

This last kind of private ownership is generally accepted in East European socialist countries and in the Soviet Union.[15] (See, for instance, the wording of Article 17 of the 1977 Soviet Constitution.) In any case, all of these Polish, Yugoslav, Hungarian, Bulgarian, East German, and also Soviet (i.e., the kolkhoz market) practical experiences with private ownership, as well as its acceptance in the most recently adopted East European constitutions, prove that the private sector of the economy is compatible with the socialist socioeconomic system. But at the same time, it has to be strongly stressed, there is no ground to predict reprivatization of socialist ownership. The private sector of the economy allowed in socialist countries is still, and in the future will be, auxiliary to the socialist sector of the economy and is permitted only within deliberately settled limits. These limits are determined by the necessities of relieving the pressures on the socialist sector of the economy, especially in satisfying pressing needs of the population.

Nor is the presence of foreign private capital, as manifested in mixed companies established jointly with agencies operated by the socialist state, a sign of the reprivatization of the socialist economy. These ventures modify, of course, the old-fashioned image of the socialist economic system. Moreover it is not just the image which is changed, since these obviously influence management methods in public branches of industry and external commerce. These mixed companies must be relatively autonomous in managing their own affairs. As in the case of agriculture or in some domains of small-scale domestic commerce and services, however, the real issue does not inhere in the form of ownership. Such mixed companies, or other similar ventures, are after all authorized by the socialist state, and limits of their activities are always under the control of this state. The essential point is in what manner that ownership is exploited and to what extent socialist principles are respected in the distribution of the profits of those joint ventures in which the socialist state is a partner. Such mixed ownership does not undermine the socialist foundations of the socioeconomic and political system.

There are, however, some ideological problems that arise in connection with these joint ventures. They threaten some widely accepted moral values of the socialist system. As a result, acceptance of foreign private capital is limited in at least two ways. First, it is limited by the very basic foundations of the socialist economy, which cannot be infringed. This refers in particular to the principle of fair and equitable distribution of wealth and profits gained from people's work. No system of economic exploitation can be restored. The role of external private capital, even if it is presently involved in investment policy in East European socialist countries to a far greater extent than in previous decades, will still be a somewhat marginal one in the future. The overriding predominance of socialist public ownership in the economic system of these countries will be preserved.

Second, there could emerge in certain circumstances more or less strong opposition on ideological grounds to the extension of external private capital. Such opposition may arise irrespective of the real role played by foreign private ownership in the socialist economy. Implications in the ideological sphere could be far greater than the real impact of private capital on the economy. This prediction is not based on sectarian doctrinal dogmas but on the assumption that the people's acceptance of the socialist system of values is now wider and deeper than it was decades or even a decade ago. Moreover, the emergence of difficulties that caused a slowdown in carrying out the strategy of accelerated national socio-economic development is to a great extent caused by inflation and recession in the Western world economy, with which the national socialist economies of countries like Poland and some other socialist countries have become more tightly linked, particularly in the 1970s.[16]

Ideological controversies (or even deeper contradictions) are virtually certain. According to some economists, further integration of the socialist economies with the world economy is imperative at their current stage of development, a view that we share.[17] Hence we foresee an occurrence of some contradictions between economic reality and ideology in the 1980s. They will probably disappear in the 1990s following the establishment of the new world economic order and an adjustment of some ideological aspects of the socialist system of values to the transformed world environment at the end of the 1980s. The establishment of the new world economic order discussed here implies that the domination of the traditional capitalist system will be reduced and balanced by the just partnership and equal participation of the socialist countries and developed countries as well in the world economy. The 'export' of recession and inflation to the socialist countries, which is still possible, sometimes causes serious troubles in their domestic economies. As long as this situation is maintained, it will aggravate these contradictions. At the same time, inasmuch as the active participation of the socialist countries in the world economy is increasing, an evolution of the consciousness of the people (and of the governing elite in particular) will be accelerated, and consequently the contradictions between ideology and economy will be tempered. Such are the dialectical interactions between economics, ideology, and politics.

Given the realities of the present period, the coincidence of these above-mentioned factors – domestic economic troubles and the challenge to the accepted socialist system of values – could influence the political systems of particular socialist countries in diverse ways. In some these factors could produce negative political consequences. Economic tensions and ideological controversies could halt the steps toward further democratization of the political system (such as stimulation of new forms of participation, extension of the political and economic rights of individuals, and so on). They could also impede the implementation of reforms in the mechanism of direction and management of the national economy. And such reforms are intimately connected with the functioning of the political system. In turn delay in further democratization of the political system could well sharpen existing social and economic tensions.

Conversely, in other countries a controlled process of deliberate, consistently implemented democratization of the political system will ease tensions and facilitate a gentler transition from the extensive phase of economic development to the intensive one. Achieving such transformation is the main problem now faced by the socialist countries in Eastern Europe.

This transformation is already urgently needed in some countries (such as Hungary, Czechoslovakia, Poland, and the German Democratic Republic). Also in other socialist countries (like Romania) this necessity will be more evident in the 1980s.

The course of events predicted depends, in a given country, on many variables. But among the most important are: (1) how and to what extent the political system is prepared to adjust to the changing social and economic environment, (2) the stage of maturity of the working class, which is the main social force vitally interested in progressive changes, and (3) the flexibility of people currently in power.

Realities at the end of the 1970s are such that the domestic economic setbacks encountered after a couple of successful years in implementing an attractive program of rapid improvement in the standard of living must produce general disillusion in public opinion. The Polish case illustrates this. Disillusion with the state of the economy could in turn provoke an adverse reaction against further close economic ties with Western economies and strong social pressure for more consistent and rigid socialist policies in various fields of the economy. In an extreme case a failure of the economic program, combined or coincident with ideological and social pressures for implementing stricter social equality in the distribution of goods and wealth, could eventually produce new political factors halting the introduction of further foreign capital investment. These social and ideological drifts should not be ignored in an analysis of future political development.

In such a course of events another factor that could also be involved is the issue of national sovereignty, particularly but not solely in the case of Poland. The Polish people especially are very sensitive on this point, being hostile to any foreign interference. If foreign creditors should try to intervene in matters of day-to-day management carried out by debtor partners, that kind of interference could have considerable political repercussions.[18]

To summarize, it is necessary to stress that fundamentals of the economic system, as well as political factors, are taken into account in limiting the infusion of external capital into the socialist economic system. Even if closer cooperation with the Western capitalist countries indicated some signs of weakening the socialist foundations of the socioeconomic system, there are several important social and political safeguards preventing a reprivatization of socialist ownership. Moreover, it is unrealistic to predict that in the 1980s a model of mixed economy would develop in the socialist countries as a new type of socialist system. The socialist type of ownership will be dominant and will shape the way of directing the national economy as well as the methods of management of industry, agriculture, and commerce in the socialist countries.

V   Problems of Changing Forms and Institutions of Direction and Management of the National Economy

Some general points must be made before discussing the particular issues of possible institutional changes in directing the socialist national economy and altering methods of managing the state-operated industry. Most important, it is necessary to differentiate between two terms often used in this study: (1) *directing* the national economy and (2) the *management* of the economy. The first of these terms means general guidance, control, and supervision of conduct of the national economy and the activities of subordinated, more or less autonomous, bodies responsible for carrying out general guidelines of economic policies in particular fields. Management, on the other hand, refers to the way of handling operational activities of detailed day-to-day conduct of affairs in a given shop, plant, enterprise, amalgamated industrial–agricultural– commercial unit, industrial branch, local community or region. The directing of the economy is more linked with *policy-making functions*, while management is more connected with *policy implementation* and is rather narrowly limited to a specified field of the economy. Directing the economy ought to be focused chiefly on outlining long-term targets, while management should concentrate on achieving short-term aims.

These distinctions are theoretical ones. In reality the boundaries are not so sharp. In the practical functioning of political institutions, governmental bodies, and economic boards in socialist countries, the working of these two distinctive activities are often, indeed too often, confused. This is an imperfection of the mechanism of directing the national economy in most socialist countries. In practice the top policy-making bodies, instead of concentrating on outlining the general directions of the economic policies and reviewing the main trends in performance of the national plans of socioeconomic development, become involved in the operational, day-to-day, managerial decision-making process. Consequently, the top-level political and executive bodies are sometimes enormously overloaded with many details of day-to-day management rather than leaving them to be dealt with at the much lower level of management of industry or commerce or at lower levels of public administration. These tendencies to overload the top-level policy-making bodies with details of current management and administration were criticized by Lenin nearly sixty years ago.[19]

The fact that Lenin's critical remarks are still valid in regard to present-day structures and functioning of socialist political and economic systems could be interpreted as evidence of systemic rigidity. This is, however, not so. The apparent similarity between the present situation and that of sixty years ago is misleading. At that time a natural trend to overload the top-level body, that is, the Council of People's Commissars, was chiefly caused by the inexperience of those responsible for managing economic affairs and public relations. Today this trend derives from the great complexity of problems linked with the general direction of the national economy and the management of its particular branches. Now, many issues that seem to be of no great significance for the macro-scale economy eventually produce unpredicted side effects in unexpected fields of the national economy and social life, necessitating the coordination of the various stages of the decision-making process, which is formally decentralized. The coordinating functions are placed in the top-level policy-making body. The increasing volume, complexity, and interdependence of the issues make this coordination of current decisions necessary. But at the same time that factor leads to the increasing tendency toward the concentration of decisions of a managerial nature in the hands of the policy-making bodies.

This trend is stimulated by two mutually reinforcing subjective elements of human behavior. On the one hand, the people sitting in policy-making bodies in pursuit of more power assume the responsibilities of the lower and/or subordinated decision-making bodies, while on the other hand, the people nominated to the latter tend to abdicate the duty to make decisions, for they can pass their responsibilities to a higher level or to politicians. What is more, when the general economic situation is good, and the performance of the plan for socioeconomic development is going well, some drift toward devolution of the decision-making process is revealed, and more autonomy is allotted to the lower level of decision-making centers, because people at these lower levels then feel less strained in taking on the burden of responsibility for decisions they have made. Conversely, when the general economic situation is deteriorating, and social tensions are building up, and the main objectives of the national plan of socioeconomic development are not fully achieved, then the process of concentration and centralization returns. Usually the process is justified as a remedy for overcoming economic difficulties and social tensions.

Then, in turn, the continuing process of overconcentration and overcentralization of the decision-making procedure brings about situations in which the policy-making bodies, in particular at the top level, are overloaded with day-to-day issues to such an extent that they lose real control over the state of affairs, and their capacity for directing and managing becomes less efficient. This, consequently, produces more spontaneous activities of the departmental and local decision-making bodies, over which superior bodies have lost control. The managers at lower levels take into account departmental or local interests (or sometimes their own personal interests, though not so often as seems apparent) more than the general interests elaborated in the national plan of socioeconomic development. This, in effect, aggravates economic and social difficulties and tensions, and deepens the imbalance in the national economy. Eventually devolution and decentralization of the decision-making process become necessary and the allocation of more autonomy to lower decision-making bodies inevitable. And in that way the process of decentralization starts again.

The Polish experiences of the last three decades are a prime example of this generalization. With some variation it applies to the experience of other socialist countries, such as the Soviet Union, Czechoslovakia, the German Democratic Republic, Yugoslavia, and Hungary, although in this last case it seems to be less evident. Devolution and decentralization are followed by concentration and centralization. Then again comes devolution and decentralization, and the cycle starts again from the beginning.

In practice, though, the new cycle of concentration and centralization never begins at the same point as the previous one. Every time such a swing of the reform pendulum is a bit narrower. One of the best examples of this phenomenon was the reform of the late 1950s in the Soviet Union, which was then followed by another reform in the mid-1960s. Khrushchev's reform of the management of industry and the direction of the national economy left significant traces after the 1964 reorganization of the governmental system, in particular in the wider autonomy left to republics in the domain of directing the national economy on their territories. Parallel findings could be established from the examination of the several Polish consecutive reforms of the direction of the national economy and management of its particular branches, carried out in the late 1950s, the late 1960s, as well as in the early and late 1970s. This is even more evident in regard to the cycles of centralization and decentralization in Poland in relations between the administration of central and local government.

Before discussing the Polish experiences in more detail, two important points concerning centralization and decentralization must be made, for without them most of what follows will be baffling to political scientists and economists who are not so familiar with the realities of socialist countries. The first is the necessity to distinguish among the national interests, the interests of various social groups (the workers' collectives or local communities), and the personal interests of individuals. In fact, the present crucial issue of politics in the East European socialist countries is how to combine these different (and sometimes contradictory) interests in order to stimulate further economic and social development and at the same time in what way to satisfy the demands and needs deriving from these differentiated interests. The second is that centralization must be examined at least in three dimensions: political, economic, and administrative.

In considering centralization or decentralization in the political dimension, one must analyze the extent to which decisions concerning general strategic direction of the development of national and regional policy – and personnel policy – are concentrated in the hands of top-level political leadership. In the case of personnel policy the criteria and mechanism of selection and nominations of economic managers and local leaders (and administrators) are of great significance. In an evaluation of political centralization and decentralization, a model of the implementation of the leading role of the Communist Party in the political system and degree of inner-party democracy are the important factors.

In the economic dimension the crucial point is the extent of discretion given to managers of the lower economic organizations and administrators in the local government system in directing their enterprises or local communities' affairs so that they can really give priority to the economic interests of these units and social needs of these communities. Of course, the relative autonomy of their position is influenced by other factors in addition to the scope of centralization in the other two dimensions. Among these is the size of economic organizations and administrative units of the territorial divisions of the country. Measurement of centralization in this aspect and evaluation of the optimal size of such organizations and/or units cannot always be unequivocal. In the 1970s in Poland, for instance, large economic organizations (LEOs) were created in manufacturing, domestic commerce, in many service branches, and in the building industry. They achieved a strong position against central governmental agencies and even became more autonomous in relation to top-level policy-making bodies. They were especially influential in shaping investment policy, including the import of foreign technology. On the other hand, such concentration in industry and in internal commerce limited the autonomy of the subordinated enterprises that were amalgamated into these large economic organizations. At the same time in most cases such subordinated enterprises were forced to change their specializations and often to sever their previous links with other enterprises and with the market. Consequently this concentration got the domestic market into trouble and led to deterioration of consumer goods supplies in this market, which was extremely vexing for the general population. The overheating of the Polish economy in the first half of the 1970s and difficulties in the capitalist world market had also plunged the national economy into growing debt. All these factors led to far-reaching restrictions on the LEOs' autonomy. Their rights were taken over by central governmental agencies and ministries.

At the same time parallel results were produced by the reverse process in the reorganization of the local government and territorial administration of the country. The bigger territorial units, that is, seventeen voivodships, were scattered into forty-nine smaller voivodships. The new local communities became economically weaker. With the passage of time many local enterprises, previously subordinated to local authorities, were taken over by the newly created large industrial and commercial economic organizations or even liquidated completely. The idea of the previously initiated reform, aimed chiefly at the creation of bigger and economically stronger communes situated at the lowest levels of territorial division, gradually evaporated.[20] And consequently such decentralization was counterproductive. Ultimately this also aggravated the deteriorating situation in the domestic economy. The most important issue for economic centralization (or decentralization) is to find an optimal size of the industrial, commercial, or regional organizations. In one case the better solution will be in larger economic organizations, while in another case smaller units will be more suitable. What we lack are scientifically elaborated, sophisticated criteria of centralization in one domain combined with accurately balanced decentralization in other fields – criteria that take into account specificities of different branches of the economy and the character of various territorial units. The simplistic opinion that there is a single optimal size, big or small, of economic organization or territorial unit that will achieve economic effectiveness is completely unacceptable with reference to the advanced economy of the country at its present stage of development.

Therefore, if one compares the degree of centralization in the economic dimension of the early 1950s in Poland with that of the 1970s, the present decade appears as the decade of a great decentralization. But if the present situation is analyzed with reference to the actual stage of economic development of the country, it is easily discovered that the management in particular fields of the national economy is now overcentralized.

Administrative centralization (or decentralization) is to a great extent determined by the model of relations established by legislation, and also by historical traditions between agencies of the central administration and administrators of territorial units, as well as by the scope of their autonomy. When the local administrators are nominated and discharged by central administrative bodies, and consequently responsible chiefly to the central government, then we can clearly speak about the existence of administrative centralization.[21] This is the case in the Polish reforms of local administration of the 1970s.

But the Polish experiments in this field are unique and isolated in comparison with the other European socialist countries and the Soviet Union. In these countries, by contrast, efforts of varying effectiveness are being made to further tighten the liability of local administrators before both local communities and their elected representative assemblies.

The degree of centralization or decentralization of political and economic systems in the socialist countries must be examined in all three of these dimensions. What is more, it seems obvious that only decentralization that is simultaneously well balanced and synchronized can be fully successful. Economic decentralization unaccompanied by administrative decentralization, and vice versa, will be fruitless or only partially successful. And both of them eventually come to nothing if not supported by reasonable and resolute political decentralization. Interactions among these three dimensions of centralization and/or decentralization are sometimes sophisticated, as witnessed by another example from Polish experiences in this field. The administrative decentralization carried out at the end of the 1950s produced decentralization primarily in the economic dimension (by strengthening the economic power of regional and local authorities) and then in the political dimension. The latter reached its peak at the Fifth Congress of the Polish United Workers' Party in 1968, accelerating the crisis of political leadership (among other things) at the end of 1970. In the 1970s the economic centralization achieved at the expense of regional autonomy strengthened administrative centralization, and both these factors caused further political centralization.

Repeating and alternating cycles of centralization and decentralization of the decision-making process may be shorter or longer in individual socialist countries, and the frequency of these cycles may differ. They are obviously inextricably linked with cycles of socioeconomic growth, but these linkages are not simple. The two types of cycles do not cover the same periods of time.

In the case of Poland, in particular, the past thirty years could be divided into several distinctive alternating periods of economic development. Initially a cycle began with a period of extremely accelerated development carried on at the highest economic growth rate. These phases of an economic strategy were inspired by ideological, political, or social objectives. In 1949–56 ideological objectives prevailed. These included a profound revolutionary reconstruction of the national economy and society according to socialist principles. These socialist ideological objectives were correlated with political ones, namely, a quick recovery from the war's damages and escape from the underdevelopment inherited from the prewar semicapitalist, semifeudal economy. The social aims of improving the people's standard of living were postponed to the distant future with the rationale that people should mobilize their efforts for the happiness of coming generations.

In the second phase, 1957–70, political objectives dominated, but this period saw the completion of moderated ideological aims. In this phase the fundamental political goal, based predominantly on patriotic national interests, was to join as quickly as possible the group of relatively well developed countries in the world. This goal had to be achieved mainly through rapid, extensive, and comprehensive industrialization, chiefly at the expense of the peasantry (and with a low growth rate of agriculture as a whole). At the same time, the principal social and economic gains of the new socialist socioeconomic order were cautiously and consciously preserved and the socialist way of life deliberately promoted. The aims of improving the people's standard of living were also taken into account to a greater extent than in the previous phase. They were, however, largely ignored, in spite of a growing public pressure, in the last years of this period, culminating in 1970, when a program of extremely accelerated economic growth, also at the expense of the current standard of living, was proposed. That program was dramatically rejected by the working class in December 1970.

After 1970 a new phase began. At the beginning prompt improvement of the standard of living was put forth as the predominant aim. For the first time the priorities of socioeconomic policies were reversed. This changed philosophy of the new economic strategy was also reflected in the amended text of the Polish Constitution.[22] The theoretical background and reasoning of this new strategy (of general validity for other socialist countries) is best explained in the excellent and exhaustive study by the prominent economist Professor K. Secomski.[23] These social priorities were closely combined with political and ideological objectives.

Those priorities include the creation of a comprehensive, modern, and advanced national economy, correctly adjusted to the world economy and well prepared to meet growing demands for speedier satisfaction of public pressure for an ever higher standard of living. At the same time this comprehensive, developed economic system must still be established according to the socialist principles of social justice. These are, broadly speaking, the main highlights of the current strategy of developing a well-balanced economy appropriate for an advanced socialist society, which has to be achieved in the 1980s.

In the mid-1970s, however, problems again appeared. They were caused equally by at least three main factors, especially in Poland. One was the negative influence of the recession in the Western capitalist economy. The second one arose from the overambitious expectations of the population for higher standards of living, which exceeded the capacity of the national economy. The third problem was an overheating of the national economy due to the policy of rapid investment. In Poland all three reasons appeared about the same time, causing cumulative effects. In the case of Hungary the most important was the influence of world recession. In Czechoslovakia the necessity of curbing the hopes and pressures for further growth of the standard of living appeared primary.

In Poland it was not only a question of the cumulative impact of all three reasons for economic problems. They were also revealed earlier than in Hungary and Czechoslovakia. In effect, in Poland at the end of the 1970s economic development had to slow down mainly through curbing investments and reducing the growth rate. Past Polish experiences were sometimes disturbed by tensions prompted by various reasons. Each time attempts were made to change the way of directing the national economy and to alter the methods of management. To what extent they were effective is another question. It could be said, without going into detailed analysis, that until now at least three cycles had been occurring in almost regularly repeating sequence at the top levels of the governmental machinery.

When the tendency to concentrate power in the policy-making process and to centralize the decision-making process reaches its peak, a hesitant, half-hearted step to decentralize is taken. Thus it was in 1954 and 1969, and the same seems to be the case in 1979. The example of 1969 is perhaps slightly different from the other two.

Especially in the case of 1954 the reshuffle of the Cabinet and the reorganization of its work were not as effective as had been expected.[24] The first step was not followed by further attempts to decentralize the decision-making process and devolve policy-making powers. Moreover, there was a lack of consistency in carrying out a program inspired by the debate and resolutions of the Second Congress of the Polish United Workers' Party (PUWP).

The inconsistency both in pursuing changes of top-level governmental executive machinery and in correcting the entire strategy of socioeconomic development of the phase resulted in the grave social and political crisis of 1956. The lack of an effective concept of directing the national economy and the management of particular branches of this economy then highly aggravated the political crisis, which in the end brought to power a new political leadership.

This event played a decisive role in propelling radical changes in the structure of governmental machinery and process of decentralization and devolution in directing and managing the national economy. In late 1956 and early 1957 the Presidium of the Council of Ministers (acting as a powerful inner Cabinet) was abolished; the number of deputy prime ministers was drastically reduced and they lost their position as overlords; the overfragmented governmental departments were amalgamated into larger offices, headed by ministers who were granted wider responsibilities and more autonomy in directing their departments; and the status of the Planning Commission was transformed from an operational managing body to a policy-making body in the field of planning. An inner body, an Economic Committee, was created inside the Council of Ministers. This committee was composed of those ministers who headed the main economic departments of the government, with the Prime Minister as its chairman.This body was intended to be the highest center of coordination for the operational management carried on by particular ministers. The Council of Ministers as a whole, freed of the day-to-day management of the national economy, was to be the chief policy-making body in the field of directing the national economy.

In a short time (by the end of the 1950s) it became apparent that the plan was not working perfectly. Probably it was premature and unsuited to the phase of socioeconomic development strategy of that time, since the program of industrialization was then still an extensive one. Perhaps also there were some political causes of that regeneration of the tendency to centralization and concentration.

In the 1960s the Economic Committee of the Council of Ministers grew more similar to the Presidium of the Council of Ministers of the previous decade. It took over both the responsibilities of particular ministers in the sphere of operational management and the powers of the whole Council of Ministers in the field of policy making. The number of nominated deputy ministers was expanded and their function became again more that of overlords: they were placed over the group of specialized departmental ministers whose autonomy, by the same token, was considerably reduced. The Economic Committee was enormously overburdened and therefore not able to control the national economy in both dimensions – of current operational management and that of policy making. The cycle was complete.

In 1969 a radical structural reform was made. The Economic Committee was replaced again by the Presidium of the Council of Ministers, which was this time initially constituted as a strictly internal steering body of the Council of Ministers, composed of the Prime Minister, his deputies, and the Chairman of the Planning Commission. Simultaneously the decision-making process in the domain of the management of the national economy was explicitly devolved. The ministers heading the economic department were empowered with broad responsibilities and granted various instruments for interdepartmental coordination in particular fields of the economy, such as transportation, energy, raw materials supply. The deputy prime ministers were to be super-coordinators and policy makers free of operational managerial responsibilities.[25]

This sophisticated but attractive plan did not work at all – or, strictly speaking, was put into effect without achieving the expected results. Presumably it was simultaneously both belated and premature. This paradox can be easily explained.

First, this reform was initiated and carried out too late to prevent the overloading of the top-level decision-making bodies with an endless stream of current operational issues. The restructuring of the top governmental executive machinery was in fact a belated response to the challenge of social and economic circumstances.

Second, it was premature and ill-suited to that new phase of the accelerated intensive and selective economic development of the country planned by the political leadership of that time. This abortive economic strategy was abandoned after December 1970.

Those were the main reasons for such inconsistency in the implementation of that reform of the mechanism for the direction of the national economy. This time also, as it had been previously, the reform initiated at the top was not followed by further steps of decentralization and devolution of economic and political power downward to lower levels of the economic and political systems. But to some extent extraneous political circumstances were involved at this crucial moment. Among several others there had been extremely unattractive experiences in Czechoslovakia after a spontaneous and uncontrolled process of decentralization and devolution simultaneously pursued in the economic and the political system. On the other hand, the Hungarian attempts to initiate a new system of directing the national economy and of management were rather cautiously and suspiciously observed.

The lack of a powerful and efficient center directing the national economy then resulted in multiple manifestations of the tensions in all three dimensions: economic, social, and political. The most fundamental cause of the collapse of the institutional reconstruction then initiated was the stage of economic development. The Polish economy had not yet matured at this time to the intensive stage of development.[26]

After the far-reaching political and social changes of December 1970, the framework of the governmental structure was adapted to demands of the new phase of the strategy of socioeconomic development. Continuing, rather pragmatic corrections were made subsequently. Several personnel reshuffles of varying importance in the Presidium of the Council of Ministers and at ministerial posts followed. But what was most relevant at this time was that the Presidium became again the highest decision-making body of operational management within a framework of an increasingly centralized system of directing the national economy. The role of the whole Council of Ministers was slowly downgraded; it became more a deliberating than a policy-making body. The latter function was taken over by the Politburo of the PUWP Central Committee. With the passage of time the Politburo also became the decision-making body for the economy. The distribution of roles to be played in the political system by the party's top executive body and the top-level state executive body – so strongly declared at the beginning of the 1970s – soon practically disappeared. Moreover, the Politburo's capacity to pursue effective control over the governmental administration of the national economy was to some degree relaxed because nearly half, if not more, of the Politburo members were at the same time members of the Council of Ministers, and of its Presidium in particular. That proportion was modified slightly after the reshuffle of governmental posts completed in February 1979.

In addition, the deputy prime ministers' positions as overlords were strengthened at the expense of the ministers' responsibilities. In turn, the ministers' powers were widened at the expense of local levels of public administration. The number of deputy prime ministers gradually increased and ultimately reached the highest level in postwar Poland. Their number at the beginning of 1979 was, however, reduced to seven, and their powers were transformed to those of interdepartmental coordination. Belated minor changes in 1979 did not go beyond a minimal response to the challenge of economic, social, and political realities.

That is why, during the nationwide debate that anticipated the Eighth Party Congress and during the discussions within the Congress (11–15 February 1980), inefficiency of the central administration in directing and managing of the national economy was strongly and publicly criticized.

The Eighth Congress of the Polish United Workers' Party was a clear recognition of the necessity for changes in the ways and style of directing the national economy so that it would be better fitted to the needs and demands of the internal and external situation, a stance reaffirmed by the new Prime Minister, Edward Babiuch, in his speech to the Parliament after being elected to this post. (Babiuch was subsequently replaced after the workers' strikes in Gdansk and elsewhere in August–September 1980.)

Undoubtedly the ultimate success of these efforts will depend on whether they are given consistent and concrete legal–administrative form. Success will also depend on whether the process of reorganization of the top-level decision-making machinery can be carried out in an appropriate manner. An initial harbinger of such changes seems to be a sharp reduction of the role of the Presidium of the Council of Ministers, which was a powerful inner cabinet during the 1970s. As a result, the constitutional powers of the Council of Ministers as a whole must be restored. At the same time the role of individual ministers in day-to-day management of particular branches of the national economy will be strengthened. This must entail enlargement of the powers of the lower levels (state-operated enterprises and local administration). Broadly speaking, a new cycle of decentralization has begun since the Eighth Congress of the PUWP. The crucial question is whether this will again be followed by a new cycle of centralization and how quickly, if at all, such recentralization will come about. Such recentralization could be prevented only if the devolution of power within the governmental administration is accompanied by authentic development of societal self-management. The Eighth Party Congress opened the way for such development. The previous Party Congress had initiated a process of political reforms, which created an opportunity for profound changes in directing and managing the national economy. But at the beginning of the 1980s this program still awaits implementation.

One would be hard put to find a strict analogy to the special Polish experience in the other European socialist countries. In Hungary the Politburo of the Hungarian Socialist Workers Party maintains a dominant position in general policy-making and programmatic decisions. In the direction of the national economy the policy-making functions are left to the Council of Ministers and general decisions to particular ministers. Managers of particular economic organizations and their amalgamations command considerable discretion in managing their units. The inner cabinet acting within the Council of Ministers does not exist in Hungary. In Czechoslovakia also there is little evidence that the existing inner cabinet substitutes for the whole Council of Ministers in policy-making functions in directing the national economy. In still a different way, within the Soviet Union, the German Democratic Republic, and Bulgaria, the inner cabinet became a policy-making body in the direction of the national economy and at the same time the supreme center of operational management. The political bodies, specifically the Politburo of the Communist Party, are not involved in the operational decisions of management. The present Romanian model is the closest to the current Polish one.

As the 1980s begin, one of the most important and fascinating questions is whether in Poland a new cycle will start again from the beginning with the same sequences repeated. The answer is presumably no, because the current situation is different than in the past. Previously, the schemes of decentralized and devolved top-level machinery of the direction and management of the national economy were in fact repudiated by hard economic and social realities of the necessities of extensive development of the national economy. Today, on the contrary, there exist entirely changed economic and social circumstances, which sooner or later should force the implementation of a consistent scheme of devolution in the policy-making process and decentralization of the decision-making process. These changed conditions in economics have come about because the national economy has reached such a stage that further development is not possible without radical improvement of the methods of directing and management of the national economy. Conversely, the present institutional framework of the directing of the national economy cannot remain untouched much longer without becoming an intolerable restraint on the future socioeconomic development of the country.

In the sphere of social life these changed circumstances, causing inevitable alterations of institutional frameworks, mean that the working class is now far more mature and conscious of its decisive role in society than it was in the 1950s and 1960s, as the events of August–September 1980 once again bear witness. The chief agent in future transformations of the political system will be the working class. Politicians and managers belonging to the political elite, some of them of technocratic inclinations, must understand this social fact. If they do not, they will be deposed – sooner or later and violently or peacefully – by the working class since this class is the biggest and the most genuine social force in the political system of socialist countries. This class is the true ruling class in society, not only in an ideological sense but in the political sense as well. 'Ruling class' does not automatically mean the governing class. The working class must now be admitted to genuine participation in the mechanism of governing the country. As in the ancient Greek tragedy, the working class is on the scene as a great, massive chorus, and the politicians play their parts at the front of the scene, but only with the consent of the chorus standing behind them. In the years ahead the chorus will step forward to the front of the stage as active players. One of the faults of Western political scientists is that they very often focus only on factional games within the political elite, ignoring the essential role, passive or active, of the working class and its rapid promotion in socialist countries, owing to the fundamental revolutionary social changes of the past forty or sixty years. The strikes of 1980 reaffirm this proposition.

Now a new generation of the working class has emerged from the extensive socialist industrialization of the past thirty-five years in Poland since the socialist revolution. This time reforms at top levels will have to be coordinated with the devolution of decision-making power to lower levels of economic administration (as well as to local public administration) and correlated with widening the powers of workers' self-management.

Such a coordinated scheme of devolution and decentralization of policy-making and decision-making processes will have to embody also transformations of planning procedures and will change the very nature of the plan of socioeconomic development. At the same time the ways of fulfilling the political leading role of the Communist Party will be reevaluated and rethought. But both these important issues should be discussed in a separate study.

VI   Probable and Necessary Institutional Changes for the 1980s

Although this study has focused mainly on the Polish experience, the general problems discussed here with regard to Poland are to a great extent applicable to other East European socialist countries. Sooner or later during the 1980s they will be faced with challenges similar to those to which the Polish political system is forced to respond now on the threshold of the 1980s. Hungary and Yugoslavia are in some sense exceptions, each for different reasons. The first was forced earlier than other East European countries to change over from a strategy of extensive economic development to an intensive one and – what is most significant in this case – has found fairly suitable institutional and political responses to these new circumstances.

In Yugoslavia thirty years ago a different path of socialist transformation and development was chosen, and was put into practice mainly through the promotion of producers' self-management. This variant of socialism was, however, corrected recently by inserting into the Yugoslav political system more elements of centralism, especially through the consolidation of the political leading role of the Communist Party. That trend marked the course of events in the 1970s.

There is a strong likelihood that the other socialist countries, including Poland, will profit from both the Yugoslav and Hungarian experiences in searching for a response to the challenges they face. Surely every country will invent its own contribution based on its own experiences of the past three decades. In Poland, for example, the experiences of short periods (of 1957–59 and of 1969–70) of anticipated but unsuccessful solutions (unsuitable to the circumstances of that time) will probably also be reevaluated.

The general priorities of socioeconomic development for the 1970s will be continued also for the 1980s. In other words, the social goals of a substantial improving of the standard of living will still be predominant. The strategy of extensive or intensive development of the national economy, applied in particular countries according to their stages of national economic development, will be subordinated to this fundamental social goal. The people's growing cognizance of these demands and their articulation in various – more or less mild or violent – forms will presumably be a pressure for accelerating the implementation of those priorities. At the same time, however, a complete retreat from détente and a return to the Cold War could reverse these priorities.

There are various other secondary priorities of which two are especially worth mentioning: the necessity for higher industrial productivity and improvement of managerial efficiency. The two issues are closely linked. The overwhelming need to fulfill these priorities is constrained by international as well as domestic factors. Internationally, there is the pressure to be competitive with industrial products on the world market. Domestically, there is the necessity of matching the growing demands of the internal market with the declining supply of manpower. For Poland the need to respond to these two pressures is the crucial concern facing the national economy in the coming decade. The solution of these crucial problems is to work out correct social and economic policies and to establish the appropriate optimal structure of the mechanism of direction and management of the national economy.

This in turn points us, in conclusion, to the predictable institutional and functional changes in the direction and management of the national economy in socialist countries likely in the 1980s.

1 The decentralization of decision-making processes as well as the devolution of the policy-making process may be expected, especially in those countries where these two processes are overcentralized and overconcentrated beyond the needs of the given stage of socioeconomic development. This decentralization must be well balanced in all three dimensions discussed in this study – political, economic, and administrative.

2 The decentralization of the decision-making process in the field of operational, day-to-day management will bring about more autonomy for the lower levels of both the management system of the main branches of the national economy (in manufacturing in particular) and local public administration. The lower levels of economic management and local administration will become more responsible for the realization of national policies commensurate with particular local needs and interests articulated at these lower levels of social communities. The need to aggregate global interests with interests of local communities or workers' collectives in manufacturing, combined with the personal interests of individuals, is evident now. The only way of finding a procedure for conciliating potential conflicts of interest at these three levels is to install an institutionalized game of interests in order to achieve reasonable and acceptable consensus. Otherwise both the political system and economic system will be blocked by immobilism and in the extreme case faced with another violent social clash like those of 1970 and 1976. It is also the only way to incorporate complex motivations, altruistic and selfish, in public and economic life. Without the exploration of such combined motivations, inspired by individual incentives and people's participation in management of industry and/or local communities, and supported by conscious acceptance of national goals of social and economic development, a new boost to economic life is impossible. Reserves for further extensive economic development have already been exploited. In the phase of intensive economic development a reasonable devolution of political power and active popular participation are necessary.

Development of various forms of societal self-management is highly probable. A return to classical parliamentary democracy with a pluralistic, conflictual party system is, however, unlikely, since it would be ill-suited to the socialist political and economic system.

3 Devolution of political power must also evoke the stimulants of various forms of civic participation in policy making and popular control over decision making. That implies a promotion of new forms of societal self-management, above all workers' self-management, and genuine activation of its existing forms.

In other words, the devolution of the policy-making process and decentralization of the decision-making process must and will be closely correlated with the development of self-management in industry and in local communities. All contemporary socialist constitutions in European countries (with the exception of Albania) are moving in this direction. Hence there are no doctrinal restraints to curb these trends in social evolution. Any remaining restraints are of a practical social or political nature. Therefore the issue is when and in what way social forces will be mature enough to propel the efficient, resolute achievement of the desired state of affairs. The restraints mentioned are not only bureaucratic inclinations of administrators or disinclinations of managers and politicians toward societal self-management. Of course, such restraints exist as practical realities, but they are not as decisive as they appear to be. More important is a lack of interest in self-management activities among workers, their unpreparedness for such activities, and their occasional apathy. Hence education for participation is vital.[27]

The development of the various forms of societal self-management is theoretically desirable and urgently needed. And that is why the development of societal self-management is predicted in this study with such strong conviction as an element of the institutional changes expected in the socialist countries in the foreseeable future.

An additional aspect has to be raised here: namely, the psychological. Obviously economic and social development depend also on human motivation. In the economic and social development of the human community the point is reached when such motivation is more important than previously dominant ones, a fact that is sometimes, perhaps too often, neglected by contemporary economists and politicians. The personal satisfaction of active participation in public life is an important motivation in doing a more effective and efficient job. This factor must be fully recognized and channeled in institutional forms of self-management – in genuinely authentic forms of participation and self-management.

4 The decentralization of the decision-making process will surely have an impact on the policy-making process. The devolution of policy-making power is inextricably linked with the decentralization of the decision-making process. At the same time, if top-level bodies of political and governmental machinery are liberated from the necessity of solving current problems of operational management, they will acquire greater capacity to shape long-range policies of socioeconomic development and to direct the process of economic and social equilibrium in the society. But, as mentioned earlier, it is extremely difficult both in theory

and in day-to-day practice to establish a strict and rigid boundary between the domains of general policy making and of executive decision making to carry out the policy once established.

Probably a key to the solution of this issue is again hidden in human nature, with human qualifications and experiences being decisive factors. People tend to be mixtures of virtues and imperfections, and politicians and managers are not immune from society nor free of these natural human entanglements.

The time is coming when the political systems in socialist countries, in order to respond to the social and economic challenges to be faced in the 1980s, must perfect their procedures of selection, as well as improve the mechanisms of responsibility, promotion, and succession of politicians and managers. This is the most urgently needed of the expected institutional changes. It is even more important than working out a rational division of labor in relations among the Communist Party's directing bodies (the Central Committee, the Politburo, the Secretariat) and governmental bodies (the Parliament and its permanent bodies like the Presidium or Council of State; the Council of Ministers and its Presidium and ministries).

The Communist Party's directing bodies ought to be freed of the pressure that involves them in the operational decision-making process. Such involvement, as past experience has proved, weakens the policy-making capacity of the party. The shaping of policy obviously is among the major functions of contemporary political parties. When the Communist Party loses initiative in this field, it is then losing its sense of vision and its capacity to shape attractive programs that would mobilize people and motivate their economic and other public activities.

Above all, the Communist Party in socialist countries is the most important pillar of their political systems, because the party possesses the ability to articulate and aggregate people's needs and interests and the capacity to shape long-range programs and formulate complex policies in all fields. When the policy-making ability of the Communist Party declines because it is overly engaged in day-to-day administrative activities, the political system's response to the demands and challenges of economic and social life becomes increasingly inappropriate, as the past experience of socialist countries in various periods of their history testifies. Consequently a rationally conceived and institutionally guaranteed division of labor between the Communist Party's policy-making functions and the policy-implementation activities of the socialist state's agencies is urgently needed.

There are many models – from the Yugloslav one of the 1960s to the Romanian one of the 1970s – of this division of labor.[28] In my opinion, none thus far has been satisfactory and adequate to meet current social demands and expectations.

By way of conclusion, it may be worthwhile to emphasize that the leading role of the Communist Party in the political system of the socialist countries is taken for granted and the historical, social, ideological, political, and constitutional arguments justifying this principle are beyond the scope of this study. It is likewise assumed that the principle of parliamentary democracy, linked closely with the pluralist concept of a party system, is the cornerstone of the political systems of Western developed capitalist countries. It would be interesting to compare the effectiveness of these two political systems, capitalist and socialist, in encountering and solving the social and economic problems of their countries and of the contemporary world as well. This issue is beyond the scope of this book.[29]

Indeed, the 1980s will be a decade of implicit competition of the political systems' comparative efficiency. But probably this will be a showdown more on the social and economic planes than on the ideological one. That does not mean, however, that in the coming decade the pragmatic approach of both sides will continue. Ideological controversies and disputes presumably will develop, and both the system of values and the concept of the way of life will be hotly debated, as will the moral aspects of human life and activities.

It is very likely that these ideological disputes and controversies – sometimes too spectacular and as such publicized, consciously or unconsciously, in a simplistic manner by mass media – will overshadow the real interactions and interdependencies evolving mainly in the economic, social, and political planes. In other words, in the 1980s détente on the economic, political, cultural, and even military, planes of international relations will presumably continue, while on an ideological plane we can expect no détente. Rather, ideological controversies will sharpen, and they could become the main contradiction during the decade, especially if we also take into account North–South relations.

Notes: Chapter 12

1 The federal structure of the government introduced in Czechoslovakia in 1968, the establishment of the Presidency of the Republic in Romania in 1974, and the changing concept of social self-management in Yugoslavia did not change in substance the general shape of the fundamental institutions of the socialist political systems in these countries.

2 The referendum has been introduced in some socialist constitutions, such as the Yugoslav and Bulgarian. In the Polish Constitution, after the amendments of 1976, the unique institution of public consultations was inscribed into the Fundamental Law (Article 86).

3 For the decades of the 1950s and 1960s, see István Kovács, *New Elements in the Evolution of the Socialist Constitution* (Budapest: Akadémiai Kiadó, 1968). See also B. Strashun, 'Constitutional Regulation of the Political System in the Socialist Countries', paper presented to the XI Congress of the International Political Science Association in Moscow (12–18 August 1979), and published in *Political Systems: Development Trends* (Moscow: 'Social Sciences Today' Editorial Board, USSR Academy of Sciences, 1979).

4 See my paper, 'Ogólne i specyficzne cechy nowej Konstytucji ZSRR 1977r. w świetle rozwoju konstytucji radzieckich i socjalistycznych' [General and particular features of the new Constitution of the USSR of 1977 and the development of the Soviet and other socialist constitutions]. This paper will be published soon in a book on the theoretical implications of the new Soviet Constitution of 1977.

5 See, for example, Sanford Gottlieb, 'Russia's Weakness', *Newsweek*, 9 April 1979.

6 Non-Communist allied parties exist now in Poland, the German Democratic Republic, Czechoslovakia, and Bulgaria.

7 Some of these political institutions are now regulated also by the newest Western constitutions, as in Italy, the German Federal Republic, France, Spain, or Portugal. In these countries the fundamental laws describe goals and conditions of political parties' activities. But the essential difference is that in the socialist constitutions the leading

and/or guiding role of the Communist Party is acknowledged not only as a sociopolitical fact, but also sanctioned as the legal principle of the government system. At the same time, however, Communist Party activity is subordinated to the rule of the fundamental law. This means, simply, that the Communist Party, although its dominant position in the political system is evident and constitutionally recognized, is not placed over the law, but on the contrary, the democratic rule of law established in the socialist constitution is superior to the Communist Party. That is why it is difficult to agree with the opinion that Communist Party dictatorship is a basic principle of the socialist system of government.

8 Concerning constitutional principles of foreign policy, see my article, 'Cele i zasady polityki zagranicznej w konstytucjach państw socjalistycznych' [Objectives and principles of foreign policy in the constitutions of socialist countries], *Państwo i Prawo*, 1970, No. 6.

9 Such referenda took place in the German Democratic Republic in 1968, Bulgaria in 1971, and Cuba in 1976.

10 Initially in the Draft Constitution presented for public discussion the article concerning the workers' collectives was placed in the chapter dealing with the institutions of the economic system.

11 See Article 94 of the Soviet Constitution of 1977.

12 For details see Artur Bodnar, *Ekonomika i polityka. Podstawowe zależności* [Politics and economics. Fundamental interactions] (Warszawa: P.W.N., 1978).

13 See L. Brezhnev, 'Historical Stage towards Communism', in *Problems of Peace and Socialism*, 1977, No. 12.

14 Now in Article 15 of the Polish Constitution, after the amendments of 1976, the basic principles of socioeconomic policy in the domain of agriculture are subordinated to the main purpose, which is the nutrition of the whole country.

15 See Article 17 of the Soviet Constitution of 1977, as well as Article 12 of the Hungarian Constitution of 1949/1972, Article 21 of the Bulgarian Constitution of 1971, Articles 64–68 of the Yugoslav Constitution of 1974, and Article 14 of the Constitution of the German Democratic Republic of 1968 (after the amendments of 1974).

16 For the case of Hungary, see an interview with the Hungarian Prime Minister György Lázár in *Társadalmi Szemle*, 1979, No. 1.

17 The Hungarian scholar and prominent economist József Bognár wrote recently: 'The events prove in an irrefutable way that the Hungarian economy and those of the other socialist countries are looking for a way out, not in retreat, but in extension of external economic relations.' See *L'Humanité*, 13 August 1979.

18 For example, see the *New York Times* of 11 January 1979, although the story seems rather exaggerated and playing for headlines.

19 See especially Lenin's letter to Stalin and other Politburo members as reproduced in the 1960 Russian edition of Lenin's *Complete Works*, Vol. 33, p. 364, and his letter to A. D. Ciurupa, in Vol. 35, p. 528.

20 The 1973 reform created 2,000 new, larger communes out of nearly 4,000 previously existing communes.

21 In these terms also the way in which the managers of economic organizations are nominated and dismissed is a crucial criterion of the degree of centralization in the mechanism of direction and management of the national economy.

22 That is the main difference between the previous wording of Article 7 of the Polish Constitution as adopted in 1952 and the present wording (now Article 17) after the 1976 amendments to the Constitution.

23 Kazimierz Secomski, *Polityka społeczno-ekonomiczna. Zarys teorii* [Socioeconomic policy. An outline of the theory], 2nd edn (Warszawa: P.W.E., 1978).

24 In March 1954 the responsibilities of the First Secretary of the PUWP and of the Prime Minister – until then combined by B. Bierut – were separated and the two First Deputy Prime Ministers were assigned the task of general coordination of activities carried on by other Deputy Prime Ministers with departmental responsibilities.

25 For details see my 'Nowe elementy w organizacji Rządu PRL' [New elements in the organization of work of the Council of Ministers of PPR], *Państwo i Prawo*, 1970, No. 6.

26 A particular incentive for continuing the extensive way of development was the necessity of creating nearly two million new jobs for the young generation just coming into the work force. Otherwise, Poland was faced with the threat of unemployment. That was a simple consequence of the demographic expansion of the 1950s.

27 The need for education for participation was very strongly emphasized in Romanian

papers presented to the XI World Congress of the International Political Science Association in Moscow (August 1979).

28 Without going below the surface of this problem, we can say that one model of performing the Communist Party's leading role can be reduced to general guidelines formulated by the party's policy-making bodies. This political solution is connected generally with separation of functions exercised by party members. That means in practice that members of the top-level policy-making body, that is, members of the Politburo (or of the party's Presidium of the Central Committee), are not nominated to the executive posts in government and in public administration. The holders of the latter offices are not instructed in detail by strictly binding directives of the top-level policy-making bodies (the Central Committee and/or its Politburo or Presidium). They are only politically responsible to these bodies according to the internal party rules and principles of inner-party democracy. At the same time members of the government and other party members in administration are closer to elected representative bodies of the people (the Parliament and local assemblies). Broadly speaking, this model existed in Yugoslavia in the 1960s.

The second model – let us call it one of detailed guidance – consists in punctilious steering of all political activities of party members nominated to government and other posts in administration. Most of the governmental decisions are discussed in detail by the highest party policy-making bodies. Consequently a personal union is introduced, which means in this case that holders of the top-level functions in the party hierarchy combine at the same time their party posts with important offices in the governmental machinery. Such personal union is applied from the top to the bottom of the party and state apparatus. This is the present Romanian model. This solution is theoretically justified as a result of the liquidation of so-called superfluous parallelism of the state and the party apparatus but is not widely accepted by other socialist countries. The arguments against it are, among others, that in this model the elements of responsibility and of control are weakened. Probably that is one of the reasons why, in the late 1970s, this initial model was corrected by promotion of new institutions of social control over administration and some kind of workers' self-management.

At present in most socialist countries an intermediate model of the leading role of the Communist Party is applied. In many variants the elements of general steering are combined with detailed guidance.

29 We know, however, that such political systems as the Italian, British, Finnish, or Danish, not to mention others, are not so efficient in solving the economic and social troubles of their own countries and the difficulties emerging from their involvement in the world economy's contradictions.

Chapter 13

Conclusion: East–West Relations and the Future of Eastern Europe

WILLIAM ZIMMERMAN

This volume has been concerned with the linkages between three sets of relationships. These are, first, significant global phenomena such as the American–Soviet strategic balance and the state of East–West political and economic relations; second, the evolving economic and political patterns among the states making up the Soviet–East European regional system; and third, the changing pattern of regime–society relations in Eastern Europe during the 1970s and their likely configuration in the 1980s. In particular, as Zvi Gitelman noted in the Introduction, the volume addresses three questions. How have world economic developments and changing East–West relations affected Eastern Europe in the 1970s, and what consequences will these developments have for the evolution of Eastern Europe in the 1980s? How have global economic changes and political developments in Eastern Europe affected the relations of the East European states with the Soviet Union? What are and will be the internal determinants and domestic consequences of East European links with other states? This chapter summarizes the major findings of the study with respect to these questions and also identifies those areas of divergent interpretations, especially as these divergencies have substantial implications for assessing the evolution of Eastern Europe in the 1980s.

I East–West Relations

There is little doubt that East–West relations intensified considerably along several significant dimensions during the early 1970s or that the momentum of East–West relations declined during the latter half of the 1970s. Of these dimensions, perhaps the one that most symbolized the increasingly complex interrelationship was East–West trade. The attentive public is doubtless more aware that there were substantial international political considerations behind the intensification of East–West relations in the early 1970s than it is cognizant of the economic factors that underlay the intensification. Thus there is widespread recognition that the emergence, for the first time really, of the Soviet Union as a world power, and the condition of virtual strategic parity in the early 1970s, together provided an important backdrop to the American–Soviet agreements of the early 1970s – especially SALT I and a list of agreements relating to American–

Soviet trade. In like fashion, the global strategic and political bind of the American leadership prompted largely by the Vietnam war is well known.

Consequently Coral Bell's chapter quite appropriately devotes little space to detailing why, at the outset of the 1970s, virtually any American president 'would have had a strong incentive towards détente, to relieve the pressures on American society created by the Vietnam war' (Chapter 2, p. 14). Similarly there is broad awareness of the political context in which the Soviet leadership was prompted to seek to augment East-West linkages. Lists specifying that context might vary, but I suspect most would include, as Sarah Terry's has, the following as among the most important elements underlying the Soviet calculus in creating 'the material bases of détente' at the beginning of the decade:

> . . . a sharp deterioration of Sino-Soviet relations (the Ussuri River clashes), which convinced the Kremlin of the need to ease tensions on their Western flank; the coincident fading of the German danger with the emergence of Brandt's Ostpolitik; on the domestic scene, the failure of the 1965 economic reform and Moscow's apparent retreat, in the wake of the Prague Spring, from systemic change in the direction of decentralization; finally, and related to the above, Soviet recognition, perhaps best symbolized by the American landing on the moon in the summer of 1969, that the inefficiencies endemic to their economic system continued to be an obstacle to closing the technological gap between East and West, indeed that the gap was growing wider rather than narrower. . . .[1]

Less well known are, on the one hand, the links between political developments within Eastern Europe and the intensification of East-West relations, and, on the other, the substantial extent to which economic factors per se drove the change in East-West economic relations (including credit, industrial cooperation, etc.) in the early 1970s. Each of these propositions emerges as central findings of this volume. With respect to the link between regime-society relations and the intensification of East-West relations, Zvi Gitelman and Alex Pravda both show that at the outset of the 1970s East European elites, in particular in Poland, conceived of greater East-West interdependence as a surrogate for an economic reform-based social compact (Pravda's term) between leaders and led. The latter compact would have been based on abundant consumer goods and greater citizen and producer participation in decision making along with a concomitant increase in citizen support for the political system. The alternative attempted by the Polish leadership was premised on an assumption that East-West trade would provide the means to obtain an abundance of consumer goods and a rapidly and consistently improving living standard. These personal consumer gains, it was evidently calculated, would defuse societal demands for authentic political participation and enhance the legitimacy of the political system and its leadership. Regime performance consequently would increasingly be defined in terms of the regime's ability to provide such consumer goods.

Similarly, economic factors provide a sizable fraction of the explanation for East-West trade developments. As Vladimir Pertot, the Yugoslav economist, asked rhetorically in commenting on views that stress the strategic and political motivations for the growth in East-West trade: given that 'until recently so few things took place in the policital arena, how was it possible for so many things in the field of [East-West trade] exchange to occur as they did if that political element weighed so crucially?'[2] Thus, global strategic considerations aside, the Soviet leadership became increasingly aware that Eastern Europe was becoming an economic liability to the USSR. The Soviet leadership concluded that it made good economic sense to sell fuels and raw materials for hard currency and world-class technology, rather than sell the same goods to the East European states in return for substandard machinery and manufactured goods – goods that the East European states could only sell on the socialist market.

There is, moreover, a direct analogue between the political calculus of the East European leaders and the economic rationale given the economic conditions that obtained in the East European states. In Chapter 3 Morris Bornstein has shown persuasively that in the 1960s most member states of the Council for Mutual Economic Assistance (CMEA) initially concluded that the new intensive phase of the development of their economies warranted either, or both, administrative or economic decentralization of what were then highly centralized economies. With the exception of Hungary, however, the leaders of East European states, fearful lest they lose control over the economy (and society), elected not to decentralize substantially and consequently rejected major systemic reform. Instead, Bornstein argues, several East European states, some more than others, saw the burgeoning of trade with the West as a way to enhance economic performance in three ways: by providing state-of-the-art machinery and equipment unavailable within CMEA, by providing access to relevant 'unembodied' technology through licenses, and by providing credits that would overcome the 'gap' in foreign exchange and domestic savings needed for additional investment projects. Thus both economic considerations for Soviet and East European regimes and the domestic political strategies of East European leaderships played crucial roles in the intensification of East-West ties in the early 1970s.

In like fashion, the studies in this volume indicate that not only political and strategic developments caused the loss of momentum in East-West relations. It is appropriate, as Professor Bell does, to identify perception of a shift in the East-West strategic balance and the efforts by Western states to alter the strategic balance as having exacerbated East-West relations, just as it is to depict the Carter administration's concern with human rights as having had deleterious effects on Soviet-American relations (though not on American relations with Romania, Hungary, and Poland). It was not merely appropriate, but percipient to the point of prescience, to write – as Professor Bell wrote in her original draft completed during summer 1979 – of the likely consequences for general East-West relations of crises in the Middle East and Southwest Asia (Chapter 2, pp. 26–8). From the perspective of 1980, Professor Bell's summer 1979 projections seem well nigh uncanny.

But this volume also explains the economic reasons for growing East–West trade in the early 1970s and why the dynamic of East–West relations attenuated as the decade progressed. More than anything else perhaps the momentum of East–West trade was slowed by the consequences for Western Europe and (both directly and indirectly) for Eastern Europe of the dramatic jump in energy prices initiated by the OPEC decisions in 1973. These decisions led to slower economic growth in the West and thus reduced the possibilities for expanding East European exports to the West. At the same time, OPEC's actions greatly increased the extent to which East European exports to, or even direct investment in, the USSR were essential to pay for oil and natural gas imports from the Soviet Union. Increased Western protectionism only added to an already difficult situation. The most salient (and novel) feature of the situation was East European indebtedness to the West, which obliged East European states to commit a substantial part of their hard-currency earnings to servicing debt obligations. Consequently, while Eastern Europe has become an important market for several Western states, the Federal Republic of Germany most notably, and while Western imports are immensely attractive to East European elites and plain citizens, real economic impediments to expanding East–West trade existed at the end of the 1970s.

Both the economic reasons for, and impediments to, the further intensification of East–West trade relations will continue in the 1980s. But a more satisfactory balance between Western exports to, and imports from, Eastern Europe will be essential to any substantial intensification in real terms in East–West trade during the 1980s, as Levcik's projections in Chapter 4 suggest.

At the outset of the 1980s, when American–Soviet political relations are clouded by the Soviet invasion of Afghanistan and by American decisions to alter the East–West weapons configuration in its favor, it is important to keep in mind the solid economic basis for East–West trade. Both the United States (whose grain sales strengthen the dollar) and the Soviet Union (whose need for Western technology is manifest) have an interest in East–West trade. For the West European and East European states the impetus is considerably greater.

At some junctures in the 1980s the prospects for overall East–West relations will quite probably seem brighter than they did at the very beginning of the 1980s. Stabilizing strategic arms control measures will enter into force at least during some parts of the 1980s. When they eventuate, they may produce yet another large oscillation in expectations about East–West relations. When that occurs, the politically based optimism will still be constrained by the economic realities limiting the rapid growth of East–West economic ties.

II Soviet–East European Relations

There is a sense in which Soviet–East European relations remained essentially unaltered throughout the 1970s and give every indication of persisting in that constancy during the 1980s, irrespective of fluctuations in East–West relations, shifts in the global strategic equation, and dramatic changes in the world economy. At the beginning and end of the 1970s, the USSR had the resources to effectuate its claim that Soviet–East European relations differed from other interstate relations. There was nothing to indicate that such would not be the case throughout the 1980s. Although the East European states, especially Poland and Hungary, increased their trade substantially with the West during the 1970s, the European socialist states (other than Romania) still traded primarily within CMEA as the 1980s began, just as they had (again with the exception of Romania) at the beginning of the 1970s. Again this too seems likely to continue in the 1980s. Overt commitment to increased CMEA integration was as pronounced at the beginning of the 1980s as at the onset of the 1970s. Increasing intra-CMEA integration still further will be a slogan throughout the 1980s as well. The Warsaw Treaty Organization (WTO) was restricted in domain to Europe and in membership to Eastern Europe when the 1970s began and when they ended. Both statements will likely hold for the 1980s.

Moreover, both Bornstein's and my chapters on Soviet–East European relations imply that structural features, which have characterized Soviet–East European relations for more than a decade, are not likely to change substantially in the 1980s. Integration throughout the 1970s turned out in practice largely to mean intensified coordination of national plans, especially in regard to fuels and raw materials. Bornstein finds this a probable scenario for the 1980s as well. He expects that integration will occur chiefly via joint investments in Soviet energy and raw material extraction (a phenomenon that dates largely from the jump in global oil prices beginning in 1973) and the further coordination of research and product standards. He regards as fairly weak the prospects for effective coordination of agricultural and industrial production, for much greater multilateral trade, or for much more interstate labor mobility. These aspects of integration he sees as running athwart obstacles that have persisted throughout the history of CMEA: conflicting national economic interests between the more developed and less developed countries, and between the raw materials-exporting and industrial goods-exporting states; the absence of economically sound internal price systems within the various nations; the correspondingly arbitrary official exchange rates; the consequent disputes over how to use world market prices as the basis for intra-CMEA trade; and, finally, given the prevailing pattern of foreign trade monopoly, the absence of direct contacts between domestic producer enterprises and foreign customers, and between domestic user enterprises and foreign suppliers.

Similarly, I contend that the structural features of interstate political relations in Eastern Europe will be similar to those of the 1970s. For the 1980s it will still be most appropriate to treat Soviet–East European relations as a hierarchical regional international system. They will be hierarchical in the sense that the degree of interstate inequality will not change substantially in the 1980s. They will be regional despite the Soviet Union's increasingly global role and activities. Soviet priorities will continue to reflect a very substantial commitment to Eastern Europe.

Soviet–East European relations will, moreover, remain those of an international system. While witnessing increased long-term plan coordination in particular areas, notably energy, on the part of the Soviet Union and the various East European states, the main actors will continue to be national states. The emergence of a single Soviet–East European economic 'complex' is not in the cards for the 1980s. Nor are changes that will fundamentally alter the number of units in the regional system in the offing for the 1980s. To these extents, in short, the theme of continuity predominates for Soviet–East European relations in the 1970s and 1980s.

There is, however, an equally strong sense that change and/or divergence ought to be the motifs of Soviet–East European relations in the 1970s and 1980s. These changes and divergences, moreover, are linked in significant ways to changing East–West relations.

The motif of change is manifest in shifts over time in the pattern of Soviet–East European relations that are directly traceable to changes in the international system. We cannot hypothesize a range of plausible East–West distributions of power in the 1980s that are such as to alter materially the present pattern of Soviet–East European relations. The climate of East–West relations, however, will affect the nature of Soviet–East European relations. A relatively benign East–West climate will likely exacerbate the *frequency* of overt Soviet–East European clashes over several issues. Disputes over the burden of defense within WTO are more likely in conditions of relative East–West tranquility. Similarly, East European states will be somewhat more reluctant to invest in Soviet energy extraction the greater the harmony in East–West relations, and thus the better the possibilities to earn hard currency to buy oil on the world market. The greater the tension between East and West, by contrast, the greater the *intensity* of disputes among member states of the Soviet–East European regional system. Soviet tolerance for ambiguity *vis-à-vis* East Europe diminishes directly as East–West relations deteriorate.

Changes in East–West economic relations will also have their impact on Soviet–East European relations. The West European stagflation initiated by the energy crisis had a significant impact in accelerating long-term plan coordination and East European investment in the USSR during the 1970s. That impact will continue and increase in the 1980s. There is little evidence that the energy crisis has produced or will produce significant changes in other realms of Soviet–East European relations.

Possibly, however, Soviet–East European relations may be aggravated in the 1980s because the East European states have to intensify trade with the West to earn hard currency with which to buy Western machinery and technology to make manufactured products good enough that the USSR will accept them in return for Soviet oil and gas. East European states in such circumstances would serve largely as 'pass through' vessels employing Western machinery, thus producing a rather involved linkage between East–West economic relations and Soviet–East European relations. To the extent that Eastern Europe incurs debts in the West to get the means to produce goods that go to the USSR, the linkage is one likely to result in charges by East Europeans that they are the victims of Soviet exploitation.

The theme of divergence makes itself prominent in two ways.

Divergence shows up clearly in the differential impact on the various East European states of changes in the international system and in the postures that East European states adopt toward links between the Soviet–East European regional system and the international system. Each has reverberations for Soviet–East European relations. To take one example: a reasonable hypothesis might be that there would be a causal relationship between East–West détente and military spending by East European states. Such a tie may indeed exist, but it is certainly not uniform in its consequences for all East European states. Rather the evidence of the 1970s suggests that a favorable East–West climate is associated with a decrease in the proportion of GNP allotted to defense by those states – Poland, Hungary, and Romania – most inclined to strategies that reduce the barriers separating the Soviet–East European regional system from the general international system. Bulgaria, Czechoslovakia, and East Germany, by contrast, either maintained or increased the proportion on defense spending during the same time.

A parallel inference emerges if we recall the impact during the 1970s of the global energy crisis on the trade orientation postures of the East European states. Once again there are striking differences. As this volume has shown, it is not merely that some East European states, Czechoslovakia and Bulgaria for instance, are more insulated from the extraregional environment than others. Rather some East European elites maintained policies throughout the 1970s that entailed an orientation toward the extraregional environment. Romania, whose citizens are every bit as insulated from the extraregional environment as those in Czechoslovakia and Bulgaria, persisted and gives every indication of persisting in a whole range of policies with respect to that milieu that bore on her relations with the USSR. Whether one examines Romania's UN voting behavior, its trade orientation, or defense spending, one is struck by how much Romania is bent on giving substance to its claim that it is both a socialist and an independent developing country.

Poland is considerably more vulnerable to changes in the general international environment. It is certainly the most politically fragile country in Eastern Europe. (The Soviet–East European specialists contributing to this volume would not share Coral Bell's depiction of Poland as one of the 'chilled-steel party autocracies'.) Its strategic location renders it quite susceptible to vicissitudes in East–West political relations. The chapters by Gebethner, Gitelman, and Pravda show that Poland was strongly committed in the 1970s to a Western trade expansion program as a way of enhancing consumer satisfaction and, thereby, regime legitimacy. That policy was severely hampered by Western stagflation. While Western stagflation had therefore significant consequences for regime–society relations, Poland has not turned inward. Instead, not only has its indebtedness to the West increased (a common pattern for the East European states) but it allowed a degree of Western economic penetration which has not hitherto been characteristic of East European socialist states.

Hungary is the most open economy of the East European states, and not as subject to changes in the East–West political climate as is Poland. But

Hungary has felt most acutely the direct economic effects of Western stagflation. Although András Nagy depicts the intense dialogue about the costs and desirability of the links to the world economy, the prevailing Hungarian posture has been to emphasize the importance of East-West trade and to continue quietly affirming that Hungary is both a socialist and Danubian state.

Thus the East European states had brought home to them throughout the 1970s that East-West political and economic relations limited their capacity to intensify ties with the extraregional environment and had consequences for their relations with the Soviet Union as well. At the same time the divergent responses were not to be explained solely by objective factors having to do with resource endowments, geographic location, and the like. Instead, elite preferences and the domestic political contexts in which elites engaged bore appreciably on the impact of exogenous political and economic developments in particular East European states. Similarly, much of the explanation for the future of Eastern Europe will depend as it did in the 1970s on regime–society relations and particular elite strategies and policy preferences.

III East-West Relations and Internal Developments in Eastern Europe

In the early 1970s, as we have seen, the East European states expanded ties with the West to a considerable extent as a surrogate for extensive economic reforms. Initially such a strategy seemed appropriate; East European masses would appreciate Western consumer goods and give the regime credit for having made them available. There seemed a real basis for expecting that East European states could have the best of both economic worlds. They could have the job security and egalitarianism which East European masses associate with a system that insulates workers and enterprises from market forces, on the one hand, and the quality and variety of consumer goods which these same East European publics associate with the West, on the other. Soviet power plus electrification may have meant socialism in Lenin's Russia, but in the Eastern Europe of Gierek and Kádár it was hoped that job security and consumerism would yield regime legitimacy.

The actual turn of events has proved somewhat more complicated. It does turn out, as Alex Pravda observes, that greater East-West interdependence has had beneficial consequences for consumers in the East European states that have increased their ties with the West. Travel and currency restrictions have been eased in Hungary, Poland, and the German Democratic Republic, and consumer goods have become more available.

A sense of the more complicated picture of reality begins to emerge when one reflects on the consequences of eased currency restrictions in East Germany. The West German mark has become a second currency. Moreover, its ready but asymmetric availability (pithily summarized in the slogan reported by Pravda, 'to each according to where his aunt lives') has had consequences for the distribution of income. The complexity of the picture becomes more obvious when one realizes the consequences for the East European consumer of the slowdowns in the Western economy. Having had his expectations lifted, he was doubtless disappointed to discover that the state of the Western economy had tangible effects on the capacity of the East European states to export goods in order to pay for the importation of Western products, including consumer goods, and on the willingness of the West to extend credits.

The bittersweet quality of the ties between intensified East–West relations and internal developments emerges tellingly when one examines what Pravda terms the 'production connection'. East–West interdependence, while providing state-of-the-art technology, at the same time contributes to nonegalitarian pressures in various East European states. This, as Pravda concludes, aggravates the already existing 'strain on the maintenance of traditional social compact norms and thereby on the relationship between the regime as employer and the population as producers' (Chapter 8, p. 170).

The nexus between East–West relations and prices in Eastern Europe reveals most clearly the complex nature of the ties between East–West relations and internal developments in Eastern Europe. East European citizens expect that governments will maintain stable prices. The Polish government in particular was prompted to a policy of trade expansion by the desire to raise the standard of living without price increases. But in reality external ties have generated quite considerable pressures on price stability for East European publics, especially as a result of the global jump in oil and raw material prices and the subsequent increase in the price of Western manufactured goods. In some instances, for Poland especially, the gap has widened between prices and real costs, a gap which in the case of food has reached virtually irrational proportions. In the case of Hungary, by contrast, the leadership has been much more candid about the impact of international economic changes on real costs and has succeeded in making widespread changes in retail prices. This, Pravda observes, has weakened the 'traditional social compact conviction that party and government are wholly responsible for all that happens on the economic front' (Chapter 8, p. 177). In either event the result has been a sharp awareness that changes in the global economy reverberate on East European societies. The 1980s will not witness a replay of the obtuse smugness with which some East European elites in 1973–74 greeted the global economic tremors that followed the OPEC-induced jump in energy prices. By the 1980s East European elites had become painfully aware that directly or indirectly (through changes in Soviet oil prices) internal economic policies were constrained by the world economic developments.

How the East European states have thus far reacted and are likely to react in the future to such developments would appear to be largely a function of the overall strategies for regime–society relations. These strategies, as Zvi Gitelman argues in Chapter 7, stem from particular historical patterns and the domestic political configurations that the various East European leaderships confront. In the case of Hungary and Czechoslovakia, the formulas invoked by their respective leaderships speak volumes. For Janos Kádár, 'he who is not against us, is with us' – a direct reversal of the Stalinist dictum. For Gustav Husák, 'he who is not against us is our potential ally'. In Kádár's view passivity is acceptable and perhaps desirable, whereas Husák regards passivity largely as 'muted hostility'. Given what we know about Czechoslovakia and Hungary, each is probably correct.

In the case of Poland no single slogan summarized the Gierek leadership's stance. Clearly, though, the regime's strategy was relatively straightforward. Aware of the gap between state and society and aware that there exists another institution, the church (headed now by a Polish pope), which claims to symbolize the nation, Gierek was more committed than any other leader to achieving the 'with us' through economic satisfaction while precluding the possibility that 'with us' entails widespread political participation at the national level. Indeed Gitelman is of the view that aside from a reform of government administrative structures below the national level, the present leaders have shown no intention of changing Poland's institutional structure.

The respective leaderships' dispositions toward their societies show up in their response to global economic developments. Hungary has been the most candid and has passed along price changes in the most open fashion. Czechoslovakia, which has felt the effects of the changes in the global economy largely in an indirect manner as a function of increased prices for Soviet fuels, finally recognized in 1978 what the Hungarians had stated openly in 1973, namely, that external economic developments had aggravated the internal situation. The Czechoslovak government has turned more toward intra-CMEA trade. But even in a relatively closed Czechoslovakia, global economic changes have had consequences for the social compact. Once again, in a fashion reminiscent of the 1960s, there are calls for greater productivity and more rapid adjustment to world conditions.

In Poland, the regime's effort to trade off high consumption and low participation met with considerable success in the early 1970s. Whether such a strategy would have ultimately proven effective we will never know. The Polish boom collapsed in the mid-1970s to a considerable extent because of international economic factors. When this occurred, the leadership (in an unusually maladroit manner) in 1976 sprang a series of price jumps on the citizenry, the social compact was severed, and the workers took to the streets. Poland illustrates most dramatically an important general proposition about the impact of East–West interdependence on regime–society relations in Eastern Europe. In Pravda's words, the 'whole Western connection has tended to exacerbate the problems it was meant to alleviate'. Poland reflects this process *in extremis*. But for all the developed East European states greater East–West interdependence has 'placed additional strains on already economically outdated traditional social compact production norms . . . and thereby on the relationship between rulers and ruled . . . [and] the combination of rising consumer expectations and anachronistic production norms has exacerbated the underlying problems created by the demands of intensive economic development' (Chapter 8, p. 183).

How the East European states will cope with these problems in the 1980s remains to be seen. There is a natural tendency for elites in all states to revert to that which is tried but not necessarily true when confronted by adverse circumstances. One of the most significant findings to emerge from our study, however, is that thus far elites in those East European states (Hungary, Poland, and Romania) committed for political and/or economic reasons in the early 1970s to policies of intensifying linkages with the West have continued to press for such ties. Even though greater East–West interdependence has strained traditional practices in Eastern Europe, elites in Poland, Hungary, and Romania have not reverted to the kind of autarkic thinking that characterized earlier attitudes about appropriate strategies for relations between socialist states and their external environment.

IV Coping with the 1980s: East European Perspectives

Indeed, the four chapters contributed by East European scholars suggest that, at least among technical and professional specialists, the commitment to intensified East–West ties is alive and well in Eastern Europe as the 1980s commence. Moreover, in differing ways each sees institutional adaptation as necessary in order for their respective countries to cope effectively with the challenges and opportunities proferred by increased East–West interdependence. András Nagy describes the debate in Hungary between those who seek greater links with the West, despite the uncertainties and risks, and those who prefer the more staid and drab predictability of a predominantly intra-CMEA orientation. While Nagy is not demonstratively assertive about his values, one does not need to read between the lines to detect his preferences, both as a citizen and as an economist, for a Hungary that carries out the further implementation of the 1968 reforms (the New Economic Mechanism, or NEM). In such a way, he contends, Hungary can become an effective competitor and benefit maximally from the world market both economically and politically.

Márton Tardos carries the argument developed by Nagy another step. He analyzes a key aspect of Hungary's links with the international market and CMEA, namely, the import of Western technology. He provides a detailed analysis of the ways that institutional arrangements within Hungary limit the benefits that Hungary can derive from technology importation. He is explicit in arguing that institutional change in the directions initiated by the NEM in 1968 are necessary for Hungary to benefit optimally from its ties with the West. In fact, he does not even consider it relevant to raise the issue 'whether one or another CMEA country could make itself independent of the outside world, or whether the CMEA as a unit could achieve autarky'. Rather, he asserts, 'the questions to be solved are, by what means and to what extent should the CMEA countries become involved with the capitalist world market, and how should they shape this relationship' (Chapter 10, p. 238). His analysis suggests strongly that his preferred strategy is one that 'aims at using technical transfer from the leading industrial countries by encouraging the entrepreneurial spirit of firms, rather than in the framework of centralized development programs' (Chapter 10, p. 239). He stresses that this is a political choice, however, and one opposed by powerful forces within Hungary.

Witold Trzeciakowski, a Polish economist, is equally forceful in analyzing Poland's foreign trade problems. He describes the consequences of what he regards as the excessively rapid growth in the Polish economy and the trade imbalances *vis-à-vis* the West, which were a part of Poland's growth in the early 1970s. In so doing he identifies a number of constraints, domestic and international, that limit export expansion in the 1980s. These constraints notwithstanding, Trzeciakowski strongly advocates a strategy of export expansion to the West based on product specialization. This, Trzeciakowski argues, will require improving the foreign trade control system either as part of a comprehensive economic reform or, he thinks more likely, with the introduction of a system of indirect management in foreign trade in which profit maximization is the guiding principle. Such a scheme, he emphasizes, 'should not be done when the links between domestic and foreign trade pricing are weak or nonexistent, or where central price control is ineffective, because . . . then profit maximization linked with strong incentives may lead to distortions . . ., not . . . real results' (Chapter 11, p. 250). Nevertheless, he clearly stands with those in Poland who advocate greater links with Western economies.

In a somewhat different fashion than the three economists, the Polish political scientist and lawyer Stanisław Gebethner also argues for greater ties, especially economic, between Poland and the West and for institutional reform domestically. In his analysis, he makes several points that are of particular interest to Western as well as East European social scientists. Gebethner argues, persuasively in my view, for the normative role of socialist constitutions. He also presents a nice inventory of those elements in Communist systems that are constant and those that are mutable. He candidly notes that 'changes cannot touch the essence of the class structure of power' (Chapter 12, p. 259), but still presents a view of the possible variety of Communist systems in the 1980s. He also is careful to emphasize that 'there could emerge . . . opposition on ideological grounds to the extension of external private capital' in Poland 'irrespective of the real role played by private ownership in the socialist economy' (Chapter 12, p. 262). At the same time, he explicitly associates himself with the view that 'further integration of the socialist economies with the world economy is imperative at their current stage of development' (Chapter 12, p. 263).

He does not view this integration as serving, as it did in the 1970s, as a surrogate for internal reform. In the early 1970s there was some slack in the economic system. That is now gone: 'Reserves for further extensive economic development have already been exploited. In the phase of intensive economic development a reasonable devolution of political power and active popular participation are necessary' (Chapter 12, p. 277). Thus his solutions to the problems that Poland confronts in the 1980s are those that many advocated in the 1970s and previously: links with the international system combined with forms of authentic workers' control.

Gebethner does not share Gitelman's pessimism that the leadership will shy from making adequate concessions to the working class; he believes it possible for participation to be both authentic and authorized by the regime. Should that not happen, though, he is not sanguine about the consequences: 'The chief agent in future transformations of the political system will be the working class. Politicians and managers . . . must understand this social fact. If they do not, they will be deposed – sooner or later and violently or peacefully – by the working class' (Chapter 12, p. 275).

Indeed, while Western readers will find the explicit policy advocacy of the East European contributors to this volume of interest, what is particularly noteworthy about, for instance, Gebethner's analysis is that, notwithstanding the explicit divergence noted in the previous paragraph, his analysis meshes rather well with those of Gitelman and Pravda. All three – in chapters drafted months before the August–September 1980 strikes in Poland – agree that Poland is a country where the working class really matters. Each stresses Polish political vulnerability. They generally assess similarly the consequences of the expansion of Polish trade when coupled with West European recession.

Analogously, one is struck by the economic analysis and its implications for policy of the East European economists, Nagy and Tardos, and Bornstein's assessment of East European economic developments. (Compare, for instance, Bornstein, Nagy, and Tardos on the incompleteness of economic reform and Bornstein and Tardos on problems of intra-CMEA trade.)

This leads to a more general point. However complex the linkages between East European developments and East–West relations, it is clear that professional economists describe what they regard as reality in relatively similar terms, and political scientists – Polish, British, and American – depict internal events in East European states, Poland most notably in this context, in ways each other would recognize. However little there is to say for East–West convergence, there does seem to be considerable parallelism in the perspective of the economists and political scientists, East and West, contributing to this volume.

As a result, one has a somewhat greater feeling of confidence in the reliability of the projections in this volume than one might from the product of only a single scholar or a small research team. There are persisting structures, power relations, and problems identified by all who have assessed the ties between East–West relations and the future of Eastern Europe, including Eastern Europe's relations with the Soviet Union. There is the important awareness that the future of East–West relations hinges not just on the strategic relation of the Soviet Union and United States or on the vicissitudes of Soviet–American relations. Rather, economic considerations, East and West, provide much of the impetus for the dynamic of East–West relations and will set limits to the growth of East–West interdependence in the 1980s regardless of political circumstances. The chapters in this volume moreover have emphasized the importance of leadership preferences, values, and strategies – conditioned in turn by mass–regime relations in the particular East European state – as mediating factors influencing the links between the external world, Soviet–East European relations, and the future evolution of Eastern Europe. This is scarcely to suggest that East European states are sufficient to themselves in any meaningful ways or that the East European elites control their own destiny. Rather, it is to suggest that the strategies East European elites elect to foster mass–regime ties and to relate to the general international system will bear considerably on the evolution of both these relationships throughout the decade of the 1980s.

Notes: Chapter 13

1 Sarah Meiklejohn Terry, 'Discussants' Remarks', Research Conference on East–West Relations in the Eighties (Rockefeller Foundation Study and Conference Center, Villa Serbelloni, Bellagio, Italy, 18–23 June 1979), pp. 1–2.
2 Vladimir Pertot, 'Discussants' Remarks', Research Conference on East–West Relations in the Eighties, op. cit., p. 10.

Index

traditionalist assumptions in international politics 13–14, 20

transferable rule (TR) 118–21, 234–6

translations of Russian books 94–5, 104 n. 15

'transmission belt' view of organizations 140

Triska, Jan F. 87, 151

Turkey 20

'turnkey' plants 46, 48

'umbrella theory' 40–1

unemployment, disguised 167–8

U.S. Congress: Angola resolutions (1975–6) 16, 20; arms control treaty 22; sanctions against Turkey 20

U.S. Export Administration Act (1979) 52

USSR: Communist Party (CPSU) and Twentieth Party Congress 88, 91–2; Constitution (1977) 255–6; energy production 101–2, 110–15; indebtedness to West 37–42, 80–1; international organizations 56–7; as regional hegemony 88, 96–7, relations with China 24, 26–8, 99; trade with West, value of 34–5, 65, and projected to 1990 74, 80–1; as world power 88, 96, 99

see also balance of payments, Soviet-East European relations, trade balances

Vaňous, Jan 35–6, 107

Vietnam 24, 90–1

Vietnam war, impact of 14–15, 25

Vladivostok guidelines (1974) 21–2

wage policies 155, 163, 168–70, 216–19, 259

Warsaw Treaty Organization 89, 91–2, 94, 99, 102

Western alliance 16, 24–6, 28–9, 30 n. 9 *see also* NATO

working class 132, 139–40, 148–52, 155–6, 180–2, 275

world economy, impact on Eastern Europe 34–6, 152–6, 174, 183; public discussion of impact 127, 141, 143, 146–7, 175–7 *see also* oil price increases

Wyszynski, Cardinal Stefan, 153

Yugoslavia, 88, 90, 104 n. 15, 150, 276, 282 n. 28

Zielinski, Janusz, 145